A DICTIONARY OF RELIGION AND RELIGIONS

A DICTIONARY OF RELIGION AND RELIGIONS

including

Theological and Ecclesiastical Terms

By

RICHARD INCE, M.A., Camb.

Author of

Calverley and Some Cambridge Wits, When Joan Was Pope, Shadow-Show: An Autobiography, England's High Chancellor

'Tis a whole population of gentlemen
and ladies out in search of religion.
EMERSON (*Worship*)

GYAN

Published by

GYAN

Gyan Publishing House
5, Ansari Road
Daryaganj, New Delhi-110002
Phone: 011-47034999, 9811692060
E-mail: books@gyanbooks.com

Distribution Network
gyanbooks.com
India, USA, Canada, UK, Australia, France

ISBN : 978-81-212-6358-0 (PB)
First Published, 1935

2nd Impression 2022

Printed at: Gyan Press, Delhi.

A DICTIONARY OF RELIGION AND RELIGIONS
Author: RICHARD INCE

A DICTIONARY OF RELIGION AND RELIGIONS

including

Theological and Ecclesiastical Terms

by

RICHARD INCE, M.A., Camb.

Author of

Calverley and Some Cambridge Wits, When Joan Was Pope, Shadow-Show: An Autobiography, England's High Chancellor

'Tis a whole population of gentlemen
and ladies out in search of religion.

EMERSON (*Worship*)

1935

INTRODUCTION

The aim of this book is to provide the student of religion as well as the general reader with a handy volume that is up to date, comprehensive and comparative in treatment. Where-ever it seemed necessary, reference has been given to useful books on the subjects treated.

I take this opportunity of thanking Mr. Eric Partridge, the general editor of this series, for his unfailing kindness, encouragement and assistance. His wide knowledge of authorities in the religious and philosophical fields, so untiringly put at my service, rendered the work far easier than it would otherwise have been. I have also to thank Mr. Meredith Starr for assisting me in the elucidation of certain psychological and occult terms that without his help would have been inadequately treated. Mr. Archibald Weir, author of *Light, Darkness* and other philosophical works, has kindly allowed me to use his definition of Timeless Being and has lent me books that have been of great assistance. Miss Evelyn Underhill of her generosity permitted me to use certain reviews of hers in the press.

To write a dictionary of religion is like climbing a high mountain and looking down upon all the kingdoms of the earth. The climber sees so much and so little; the view is everywhere changing and deceptive; mists twine and twist about the hills; the sunlight dazzles; great clouds roll up from distant valleys. Far upward soars the peak of Truth, a crest unscalable by man.

Those reviewers who diligently seek out faults in this volume as monkeys in the Zoo hunt fleas on one another's backs, will no doubt be rewarded, for who can escape the rod of the professional fault-finder?

INTRODUCTION

I have tried to secure accuracy, but even if every statement between these covers were true, every date correct, every exposition accurate, every estimate just, every definition beyond dispute, yet misleading statements would abound. For human knowledge can never be more than an approximation. And were everything correct, even to the smallest detail, yet visions of another—the Perfect Book—would still haunt the writer's dreams:

I take the Dictionary down
  But this is not the book I read;
Thought strays to a volume never writ
  By mortal man for mortal need.

In that great Book of which I dream,
  Lie hid the secrets never told:
The thoughts that dared not find relief
  In words men write for love or gold.

Dread Missal of the souls of men
  Who knew too much to break the spell
Of Silence that all mysteries shroud
  Of things on earth, in heaven and hell.

There should I learn how springs the seed
  Out of our dreaming Mother, earth:
And what death is, and why we fare
  Down the dark corridors of birth.

Surely in heaven this golden Book
  Lies closed to wandering eyes of men:
Lest dreaming, they should read, and wake
  And seize, with trembling hand, a pen.

RICHARD INCE.

FRIDAY'S,
MARLEY COMMON.

LIST OF ABBREVIATIONS

Ar.	Arabic
Aram.	Aramaic
art.	article
archit.	architecture
A.S.	Anglo-Saxon
b.	born
Cath.	Roman Catholic
C.	Century
c.	circa (about)
cf.	compare
Ch.	Church
C. of E.	Church of England
Class.	Classical
comp.	comparative
d.	died
eccles.	ecclesiastical term
e.g.	for example
Egypt.	Egyptian
Ency. Brit.	Encyclopaedia Britannica
Expos.	Expositor's
fig.	figurative
gen.	genitive
Ger.	German
Goth.	Gothic
Gr.	Greek
Heb.	Hebrew
Herod.	Herodotus
It.	Italian
L.	Latin
mus.	musical term
myth.	mythology
N.T.	New Testament
O.T.	Old Testament
philos.	philosophy
Prof.	Professor
q.v.	which see
Sans.	Sanscrit
schol. theol.	scholastic theology
Scand.	Scandinavian
S.P.C.K.	Society for the Propagation of Christian Knowledge
theos.	theosophy
Tib.	Tibetan
trans.	translated, translation
Ved.	Vedic

A DICTIONARY OF RELIGION AND RELIGIONS

A

AARON. Elder brother of Moses, whom he helped to lead the Israelites from Egypt to Canaan (Exod. vi. 20).

AB. Jewish month corresponding roughly to July and August.

ABADDON. (1) Jewish destroying angel. (2) Hell (Milton). (Heb. *abad* = to be lost.)

ABANA and **PHARPAR.** Rivers of Syria reputed for their excellent water (2 Kings v. 12).

ABARIS. Legendary Scythian priest of Apollo said to have visited Greece riding a golden arrow (Herod. iv. 36).

ABBA. (1) Chaldee form of the Hebrew *ab* = a father. The term *abba* was never used by slaves even to indulgent masters. Hence the force of the passage in Mark xiv. 36. (2) A bishop in Syriac and Coptic churches.

ABBACOMITES (also **ABBATES MILITES**). Laymen who were rewarded by abbacies as offices of profit.

ABBACY. Office of an abbot: an abbey.

ABBÉ. French for abbot; loosely used for a priest. Before the Revolution *abbés* were frequently absentee holders of benefices, either in minor orders, or laymen. They wore a short violet robe.

ABBESS. A lady superior of a nunnery.

ABDALLAH. Father of Mohammed; reputed so attractive that when he married, two hundred virgins broke their hearts. (See Washington Irving, *Life of Mohammed.*)

ABDALS. Persian fanatics whose highest ideal is to kill those of a different faith.

ABDIEL. The seraph who refused to revolt with Satan.

ABEDNEGO. A companion of Daniel in the furnace (Dan. i. 7, etc.).

ABEL. Adam's second son, murdered by his jealous elder brother Cain (Gen. iv. 1–16).

ABÉLARD, PETER (1079–1142). French theologian of philosophic tendency and persuasive eloquence. Abélard took a leading part in the controversy between Nominalism, which regarded concepts as mere abstractions, and Platonic Realism (q.v.), which held abstract concepts as more real than concrete objects. He stressed the imperative need for reason and logic, thereby antagonizing the Church. His romantic passion for the accomplished Héloïse, daughter of Fulbert, Canon of Paris (which led to his being brutally castrated by Fulbert), and his personal magnetism over his students, have rendered him world-famous. (See McCabe, *Life of Abélard*; also George Moore, *Héloïse and Abélard* (1921); R. H. Lloyd, *The Stricken Lute* (1934); Helen Waddell, *Peter Abélard* (1934).)

ABELIAN, ABELITE, ABELONIAN. Christian sect of N. Africa who lived in married continence as (they believed) Abel did (4th C.).

ABENDANA. (1) Jacob (1630–95), rabbi of the Spanish Jews in London. (2) Isaac (c. 1650–1710) (brother of above) taught Hebrew at Oxford and Cambridge. Both brothers promoted Jewish scholarship among Christian theologians.

ABENEZRA (IBN EZRA). Jewish savant, born at Toledo, an extensive traveller. He wrote wise and witty commentaries on the Bible which were widely read. 11th–12th C. (See M. Friedländer, *Essays on the Writings of Ibn Ezra*.)

ABERDEEN, UNIVERSITY OF. Founded by Bishop William Elphinstone in 1494, including King's College. Marischal College was founded in 1593. These colleges were united to the University in 1858.

ABGAR EPISTLES. See *Apocrypha* of N.T.

ABHISEKA. (1) Indian vedic ceremony to confer power on kings and rulers. (2) A Hindu term for ceremonial bathing. (3) The last ten stages of the Buddhist path to perfection.

ABIATHAR. The tenth in succession of Jewish high priests (1 Sam. xxii. 29).

ABIB. Jewish first month, corresponding roughly to March and April. (Heb. "green ear.") See *Jewish era*.

ABIGAIL. Wife of David, self-styled "handmaid" in 1 Samuel xxv. 25 f.; hence the word is used for a lady's-maid. (See Beaumont and Fletcher, *The Scornful Lady*.)

ABIHU. Priestly son of Aaron, consumed by fire (? lightning) for ceremonial disobedience (Lev. x. 1, 2).

ABIJAH, ABIJAM. Name of nine different persons in the O.T. (2 Chron. xii. 16–xiii.; 1 Sam. viii. 2; 1 Chron. vi. 28; 1 Kings xiv. 1–17; 1 Chron. xxiv. 10).

ABILENE. Syrian Province. Capital, Abila, north of Galilee.

ABIMELECH. (1) King of Gerar in Palestine, deceived by Isaac, who represented his wife, Sarah, as his sister. Warned in a dream, Abimelech narrowly avoided adultery. The story represents an advance in the Hebrew moral code (Gen. xxvi). (2) A son of Gideon (Judges ix. 18).

ABINGDON ABBEY. Benedictine abbey, 6 miles south of Oxford, now a picturesque ruin. Founded c. 675 by Cissa.

ABJURATION. A renunciation of heresy.

ABLEGATE. Papal envoy to newly appointed cardinal.

ABLUTION. Washing of priest's hands and sacred vessels before, during and after celebrating Mass.

ABNER. Saul's beloved general (2 Sam. iii. 38).

ABODE OF LOVE: Agapemone. A religious establishment founded by the Rev. Henry James Prince (Church of England clergyman), near Bridgwater, Somerset, in 1845. His followers held all things in common, including wives, with the result that gross scandals arose. On Prince's death the Rev. T. H. Smyth-Pigott became head of the sect and proclaimed himself the Messiah. (See Hepworth Dixon, *Spiritual Wives* (1868).)

ABRACADABRA. A gnostic magical formula to invoke good spirits.

ABRAHAM, or ABRAM (Heb. "father on high"). The first of the Biblical patriarchs (15th C. B.C.). Abraham was a Bedouin sheik who, with his wife and their household, migrated from Mesopotamia to Canaan. The Hebrews came to venerate him as their chief ancestor; an ideal father of his people, with his large family, flocks and herds and his staunch loyalty to the one God Jehovah. For the stories gathered about him, see Genesis xi. 27; xvii. 20; xxv. 16; xviii. 19; xxi. 10–13, 23–31; xxii. 14. (See Pinches, *O.T. in Light of Hist. Records* (pp. 208–36). For a good reconstruction of his life and times, see W. G. Hardy, *Father Abraham* (1935).)

ABRAHAM, TESTAMENT OF. An apocryphal Jewish book describing Abraham's last days.

ABRAHAMITES. A Bohemian sect of deists, followers of pre-circumcised Abraham, suppressed by the Emperor Joseph II in 1783.

ABRAHAM-MEN. Tudor beggars who professed to belong to the Abraham ward at Bedlam.

ABSALOM. Third son of David, king of Israel. He rebelled against his father, was defeated and slain. (See 2 Samuel xiii.–xix.)

ABSOLUTE. That which exists without relation to any other being (metaph.). (The Absolute = God.)

ABSOLUTION. The sentence the priest pronounces in the name of Jesus Christ to remit the penitent's sins. For certain serious offences a Catholic priest cannot grant absolution without authorization from the bishop or Pope, save in the hour of death.

ABSTEMII. Persons who, from aversion to wine, would not partake of the Eucharistic cup. Calvinists and Lutherans disagreed violently concerning the Abstemii.

ABU SIMBEL, or **IPSAMBUL.** A group of cliff temples (c. 13 B.C.) on the Nile discovered by Burckhardt in 1812, dedicated to the sun-gods. They are inscribed with *graffiti* of considerable literary value. (See J. H. Breasted, *Ancient Records*, vol. iii.)

ABYSSINIAN CHURCH. Christianity was introduced into Abyssinia in the 4th C. by Frumentius, who became first bishop of Ethiopia. The church came under the influence of Jesuit and Portuguese missions. Coptic ritual and practice prevails. Saints and angels are venerated, but images forbidden. The clergy may marry once.

ACCIDENT. A property not essential to an object (schol. theol.).

ACCOMMODATION. The adaptation of a word or phrase to the capacity of the reader. In the 18th C. theologians carried the principle too far, wresting Bible texts from their obvious meaning.

ACELDAMA. The name of the field outside Jerusalem bought with the blood-money given for the betrayal of Jesus (Matt. xxvii. 6–8). (Aram. " field of blood.")

ACHERON. A river over which departed souls were ferried by Charon (Gr. myth.).

ACOEMETI. An Eastern order of monks who celebrated divine service night and day by means of alternate choirs. (Gr. *akoimetoi* = sleepless.)

ACOLYTE. (1) Member of the highest of the minor orders (Cath.). (2) An attendant.

ACTA MARTYRUM. A collection of legends of the Christian martyrs from the 1st to the 4th C.

ACTA SANCTORUM. A collection of lives of the saints. See *Bollandists*.

ACT OF FAITH. See *auto da fé*.

ACT OF SETTLEMENT. An Act passed in 1689 secluding Roman Catholics from occupying the British Throne.

ACT OF SUPREMACY. The Act by which Henry VIII annulled papal control and appointed himself " supreme head of the Church of England."

ACT OF TOLERATION. An Act passed in 1689 relieving Dissenters from the penalties incurred by non-attendance at church and for holding conventicles provided they took the oath of allegiance and subscribed to the Thirty-Nine Articles.

ACTS OF THE APOSTLES. See *Bible : N.T.*

ACTS OF UNIFORMITY. Certain Acts to secure uniformity of worship in the Anglican Church : (1) In 1549 an Act ordered priests to use the Book of Common Prayer under severe penalties for refusal. (2) By an Act of 1552 laymen who failed to attend church on Sundays and holy days were rendered subject to excommunication. (3) In 1559 an Act was passed imposing a fine for non-attendance at church. These Acts were modified by the passing of the Act of Toleration (q.v.).

ADAM. The Hebrew "adam" in Genesis signifies "man," and with the article prefixed means "the first man" (Gen. ii. 7, 8, 16; iv. 1). The Adam legend of Genesis has parallels in many other early scriptures. In Christian theology Adam represents man before the Fall (q.v.) and so is regarded as the ancestor of the human race and transmitter of Original Sin (q.v.). Thus Milton:

> Of Man's first disobedience, and the fruit
> Of that forbidden Tree, whose mortal taste
> Brought death into the world, and all our woe . . .

But though in the system of Christian theology the Adam myth or legend has assumed this definite doctrinal form (which has given rise to much heresy and, in the 19th C., to fierce controversy between orthodox theologians and the Darwinians or Evolutionists), the story is capable of a much wider, and possibly deeper significance. The seemingly simple narrative of Adam and Eve and the Serpent reveals a variety of meanings according as it is considered by the psychologist, the evolutionist, the theologian, the occultist or the theosophist. For in its sublime simplicity it goes to the roots of being. Regarded from the modern anthropological angle, it represents the passing of the human race from the state of tribal or herd consciousness (a mental state analogous to that of the brutes) to the condition of self-consciousness (development of the ego). This led inevitably to the stress, warfare and sex-consciousness which characterize mankind in the present evolutionary stage. The seeking for private property breeds patricidal strife, and sex is regarded as the old Serpent ever in wait to betray and entangle in purely selfish gratification. (See Tennant, *The Sources of the Doctrine of the Fall and Original Sin* (1903); Arthur C. Headlam, *Christian Theology* (1935); Edward Carpenter, *Pagan and Christian Creeds* (1920).)

ADAMITES. (1) A Christian sect, founded by a North African, Prodicus, in the 2nd C. A.D. They went naked, rejected prayer and held it unnecessary to confess Christ. (2) A sect founded at Antwerp by Tandemus, whose followers were criminal rather than Christian (12th C.). This sect was revived by a Fleming, Picard, in 1415, but was suppressed in 1420.

ADAMNAN (also **ADOMNAN**). Irish saint, ninth abbot of Iona, who wrote a valuable Life of St. Columba.

ADAMS, THOMAS (d. c. 1655). English divine and brilliant preacher. "The prose Shakespeare of Puritan divines" (Robert Southey).

ADAR. Jewish month comparing roughly with February and

March, in which the feast of Purim occurred. See *Jewish era.*

ADEPT. One who has attained the great secret of alchemy; also used of one who is skilled in the secrets of any art, craft, or science. The word is used by occultists and theosophists to signify one who has attained illumination (see *Mystery Religions*) or a higher consciousness. For a deeply interesting imaginative picture of a Rosicrucian adept, see Bulwer Lytton, *Zanoni*. See also *Initiation.*

ADMONITION. The mildest of ecclesiastical censures (Fuller).

ADOMNAN. See *Adamnan.*

ADONAI. (1) Hebrew for Lord; substituted by the Jews for the name Jahweh, too sacred to be uttered. (2) The God of Light of the Rosicrucians.

ADONIS. A Roman god of vegetation, famed for beauty, born of a virgin (Nature). Venus and Proserpine typifying the Upper and Underworlds fell in love with him. Zeus calmed the strife by arranging that Adonis should spend half the year (summer) in the upper and half in the lower world (winter). He was killed by a boar in autumn. The festival of his resurrection was celebrated in the spring. His image was placed in a coffin and his rising again celebrated with eager rejoicing. (See Theocritus, Idyll XV, and Sir J. G. Frazer, *The Golden Bough*, vol. ii.)

ADOPTION. Pauline doctrine by which God's attitude to the believer is that of father to child.

ADORATION. Profound regard for the ideal seen in a concept or a person.

ADULTERY. Carnal intercourse of a married person with anyone of the opposite sex not his or her spouse. The term is used figuratively by Jewish prophets for unfaithfulness to God. It is also applied to the enjoyment of the profits of a benefice at the expense of the legal incumbent.

ADVAITA. Doctrine of non-dualism. Spirit and matter, self and not-self, are manifestations of the One Reality. (Vedanta philos.)

ADVENT. (1) The coming of Jesus Christ into the world. (2) The four Sundays preceding Christmas. (3) The coming of the Holy Spirit.

ADVENT, SECOND. The expected coming of Christ as Judge. See *Judgment, Day of.*

ADVENTISTS. A Christian sect founded by William Miller in 1816, who believe in the imminent return of Jesus Christ in the flesh. Many minor groups have separated from the parent sect.

ADVOWSON. The right of presentation to an Anglican benefice. (L. *advocatus* = patron.)

ÆLRED, ALRED, ETHELRED (1109–66). English theologian of extremely ascetic life. Became abbot of Rievaulx.

AESCULAPIUS. Legendary Greek god of medicine, son of Apollo. For a sympathetic account of the Roman worship of Aesculapius, see Walter Pater, *Marius the Epicurean* (chap. 3).

AESOP. A slave of Iadman of Samos, author of the famous *Fables*. (6th C. B.C. (See J. Jacobs, *The Fables of Aesop* (1889).)

AESTHETICS. Science of the perception of beauty and the principles of taste.

AFFECTION and **AFFECTIVE.** Psychological terms dealing with analysis of sensation. All sensation phenomena are primarily either pleasurable (affective) or the reverse.

AFFINITY. Kinship: relation by marriage. The table restricting marriage within certain degrees was set forth in the English prayer-book of 1563. Marriages within the forbidden degrees are declared void. For the Jewish laws of affinity, see Leviticus, xviii.

AFRICAN CHURCH. Little was done to Christianize Africa till 1875. Raymond Lull's attempts in Tunis (14th C.) proved ineffective. In the 17th C. the Dutch commenced missionary efforts in S. Africa. David Livingstone (q.v.) was the first to penetrate Central Africa, opening a way for commerce and Christianity. There is to-day (1935) no united African Church, but Christian activities are represented as follows:

(1) In Egypt and N. Africa the United Presbyterians have mission stations from Alexandria to the Nile cataracts. The Moslem population renders their work difficult.

(2) In S. Africa the Anglican Church commenced operations in the early 19th C. In 1847 the bishopric of Capetown was founded, Dr. Robert Gray being appointed first bishop. The work of the Church has been ably assisted by the American Board (Congregational), the London Missionary Society and other organizations, Scottish, German and Scandinavian.

(3) In E. and Central Africa the labours of Stanley in Uganda and Livingstone in Nyasaland opened the way for the Universities' Mission to East Central Africa in 1861. This enterprise was organized by Charles Mackenzie, bishop of Central Africa, and six clergymen. Four, and also the bishop, died from disease and privations. Two returned in 1864. Other missions followed; the United Free Church and Church of Scotland (1875–6): London Missionary Society (1877). Missionary enterprise in Uganda has made steady progress, establishing schools, hospitals and dispensaries.

(4) W. Africa is occupied by Britain, France, Belgium and Portugal. In this region missionary work was carried on in the 19th C. by the Church Missionary Society, the Wesleyan and other societies. All missions in this region are hampered by the unhealthy climate and the strong Moslem influence. Here Christianity and Mohammedanism meet in a more or less open conflict. The Great War introduced a new

problem owing to Germany's loss of her colonies and the retirement of her missionaries. The work of all African missions lies along the line of education. The innumerable African tribes are, for the most part, steeped in ignorance and superstition. (See James Stewart, *Dawn in the Dark Continent.*)

AGAPË. A love-feast of the early Christians out of which the eucharist seems to have grown. These feasts, friendly gatherings of like-minded persons, began and ended with prayer. A Christian agapë bore a strong resemblance to certain pre-Christian gatherings, notably the Charistia (see Valerius Maximus, ii. 1, 8), a religious feast at which those who had quarrelled were reconciled at the Sacrament of the Table (*apud sacra mensae*). (See J. F. Keating, *The Agapë of the Eucharist* (1901); A. Allen, *Christian Institutions* (1898).)

AGAPEMONE. See *Abode of Love.*

AGAPETAE. A sect of Christian "virgins" who lived with celibate monks in the early Middle Ages. The Lateran Council of 1139 suppressed the practice.

AGNES, SAINT. Virgin martyr (Cath.) said to have suffered martyrdom on 21 January 304, at the age of thirteen. St. Agnes is patron saint of young girls, who formerly practised country magic on St. Agnes's Eve (20–21 Jan.). The rustic rites of St. Agnes are very beautifully treated in Keats's "The Eve of St. Agnes."

AGNI. The Hindu god of fire, represented with two faces, symbolic of his benevolent and malevolent qualities. (See W. J. Wilkins, *Hindu Mythology* (1900).)

AGNOSTICISM. The philosophic attitude which affirms that nothing which transcends material phenomena can be known. The word was brought into prominence by T. H. Huxley, who maintained that an admission of ignorance is preferable to religious or materialistic dogmatism in the face of metaphysical problems. (See Leslie Stephen, *An Agnostic's Apology* (1893); A. W. Benn, *English Rationalism in the 19th C.* (1906).)

AGNUS CASTUS. Athenian ladies strewed their couches with the leaves of *Agnus castus* as a preservative of chastity. The monks mistaking *agnos* (chaste) for *agnus* (a lamb), added *castus* to denote its quality—*Vitex agnus castus.*

AGNUS DEI. See *Lamb of God.*

AGOBARD. Appointed archbishop of Lyons in 816, Agobard actively supported the Carolingian renaissance. Reforming zeal led him to denounce trial by ordeal; belief in witchcraft, and the ascription of tempests to magic. He even opposed the adoration of the saints. His saintly life won him the love and veneration of his people.

AGRAPHA. Uncanonical sayings attributed to Christ. Perhaps the most beautiful are "Pearls could not equal the whiteness of his teeth," spoken in rebuke to his followers when passing the carcass of a dog: and "The world is a bridge; ye are to pass over it but not build your dwellings thereon."

AGRIPPA, HEROD I. Appointed king of Judea by the emperor Claudius. Notorious in Scripture history for his execution of James, brother of John the Evangelist and the imprisonment of St. Peter. (1st C. A.D.)

AGRIPPA, HEROD II. Son of the preceding, and the last king of the family of Herod the Great. Chiefly remembered for St. Paul's eloquent speech before him (Acts xxvi.). ("Then Agrippa said unto Paul, Almost thou persuadest me to be a Christian.")

AGRIPPA VON NETTESHEIM, HENRY CORNELIUS (1486–1535). German writer, physician, soldier and (reputed) magician. Travelled and lectured on occult subjects (*De occulta philosophia*). A man of outstanding ability and supreme courage, Agrippa attacked the existing sciences and the pretensions of his more orthodox medical confrères. In religion he advocated a return to the simpler faith of the early church. (See H. Morley, *Life of H. C. Agrippa*.)

AHAB. Became king of Israel about 875 B.C. (1 Kings xvi. 29–34). He married Jezebel, the rich daughter of the king of Sidon. He was killed in warfare with Shalmaneser, king of Assyria, and was succeeded by his sons Ahaziah and Jehoram (1 Kings xxi. 19).

AHASUERUS. Name of several people in the Bible. (1) In Daniel ix. 1, Ahasuerus is son of Darius the Mede. (2) In Ezra iv. 6, Ahasuerus is a king of Persia, possibly Xerxes. (3) The legendary cobbler said to have insulted Jesus on his way to Calvary and doomed for his offence to wander earth until the return of Jesus in the flesh, is usually referred to as Ahasuerus.

AHAZIAH. (1) Son and successor of Ahab, king of Israel (1 Kings xxii. 40). (2) Son of Jehoram and Athaliah, also called Azariah (2 Chron. xxii. 6).

AHIMELECH. The high priest to whom David fled from Saul's anger (1 Sam. xxi. 1).

AHIMSA. The Hindu doctrine which forbids injury to sentient life in any form, from human to verminous.

AHITHOPHEL. A trusted adviser of King David who took a leading part in Absalom's revolt (2 Sam. xvi. and xvii.).

AHMADIYA. Moslem reform movement in India instituted in 1891 by Ghulam Ahmad, who claimed to be the expected Mahdi of Islam, a reincarnation of Khrisna and of Christ. Membership about 70,000.

AHRIMAN. The principle of evil in the dualistic system of Zoroaster (q.v.). Ahriman is the enemy of Ormazd (the good principle) and will eventually be overthrown by Ormazd. The myth is the subject of a magnificent poem by Sir William Watson, "Ormazd and Ahriman."

AIN SOPH. The Supreme Spirit of Judaism, akin to the Shakti of Brahmanism.

AKASA, AKASHA. Sanscrit term for the all-pervading ether.

AKBAR (1542–1605). Emperor of N. India and wisest of the Mogul emperors. Notorious for his wide religious tolerance and eclecticism. Himself a deist, he welcomed representatives of all religions to his court. Few rulers have shown so much enlightenment in their treatment of religious problems. (See G. B. Malleson, *Akbar* (1890); Laurence Binyon, *Akbar*.)

AKHNATON, IKHNATON. Pharaoh of Egypt who in 1375 B.C. attempted a religious reformation. See *Egypt, Religion of*, § 3.

AKIBA, BEN JOSEPH. One of the greatest of Jewish rabbis. He supported the Jewish messiah Bar Kokhbar (q.v.) (1st–2nd C.) in his revolt from Rome.

ALACOYNE, MARGUERITE MARIE. French nun and mystic. See *Sacred Heart*.

ALAIN DE LILLE (ALANUS DE INSULIS). French theologian and poet of strongly mystical tendency who taught in the schools of Paris and Chartres. (12th–13th C.) (See Steiner, ***True and False Paths in Spiritual Investigation***.)

ALB. White linen vestment worn by the priest celebrating Mass (Cath.).

ALBAN, SAINT. A legendary English monk, said to have been born at St. Albans and to have suffered death during the Diocletian persecutions. (3rd–4th C.)

ALBERTUS MAGNUS (c. 1193–1280). A Dominican schoolman of extensive learning in theology and philosophy. Though an Aristotelian, he favoured Platonic metaphysics. Placed by Dante in heaven among lovers of wisdom.

ALBIGENSES. Catharist antisacerdotal heretics of southern France. Their doctrines are obscure, but they appear to have rejected the O.T. and to have forbidden private ownership of property. The Inquisition practically exterminated them. (12th–13th C.)

ALCHEMY. The art of transmuting base metals into gold, traced to Arabia and Egypt. Its chief exponents were the mythical Hermes Trismegistus, Zosimus (5th C. B.C.), Roger Bacon (13th C.), Albertus Magnus (q.v.) and Paracelsus (q.v.). Dr. Price of Guildford claimed in 1782 to have "transmuted" gold but, challenged to repeat the experiment, committed suicide. The Rosicrucians (q.v.) applied alchemical terms to philosophy and claimed that man can be transmuted to perfection by a life of meditation, contemplation and increasing self-knowledge. In this sense alchemy becomes a system akin to the

Buddhist Eightfold Path. (See long article in *A Survey of the Occult.*)

ALCUIN, also **EALHWINE** (735–804). A Yorkshire scholar, persuaded by Charlemagne to reside at his court where his influence became wide and deep. He wrote charming Latin lyrics and was greatly beloved by his pupils. (See C. J. B. Gaskoin, *Alcuin*; also Jack Lindsay, *Medieval Latin Poets*; and Helen Waddell, *Medieval Latin Lyrics* (1929).)

ALDHELM (c. 640–709). Bishop of Sherborne and pioneer of Latin scholarship in England. Since his people refused to come to church he stood on a bridge singing songs in the vernacular, thus collecting a crowd. (See G. F. Browne, *St. Aldhelm* (1903).)

ALEXANDER OF HALES. Celebrated English scholastic theologian, trained in the monastery of Hales. (13th C.)

ALEXANDRIAN LIBRARY. The greatest library of antiquity, founded by Ptolemy Soter, said to have been partly burned in A.D. 389 by the Christian bishops, and again by the Arabs in A.D. 642, when the calif Omar ordered the books to be used as fuel to heat the city baths for six months. (" If agreeable to the Word of God they [the books] are unnecessary, if contrary to the Word, they are harmful.")

ALEXANDRIAN SCHOOL. A centre of scientific, literary and theological influence with its headquarters at the museum or academy founded by Ptolemy Soter. From the Alexandrian school sprang: (1) The eclectic spirit first impersonated in Philo (q.v.), 1st C. (2) Neo-Pythagoreanism and Neo-Platonism best exemplified in the work of Plotinus (q.v.). The great Christian thinkers of the 3rd C., Clement and the mystic Origen, were Alexandrians. (See Kingsley, *Alexandria and Her Schools.*

'ALEYAH. Jewish ritual of going up to the reading-desk in the synagogue to read the scriptures. (Heb. " going up.")

ALFORD, HENRY (1810–71). Dean of Canterbury. The author of about fifty volumes, including poetry, theology, criticism. Esteemed for his learning and beloved for his gentleness.

ALFRED, KING (c. 848–900). One of the noblest of England's kings. He conquered the Danes, divided England into shires and organized the administration of justice. " Never before King Alfred had the world seen a king who lived solely for the good of his people. . . . Alfred was the noblest as he was the most complete embodiment of all that is great, all that is lovable in the English temper " (J. R. Green). (See W. H. Stevenson, *Asser's Life of Alfred* (1904).)

AL-GHAZALI (1058–1111). Persian sufi philosopher and mystic who revealed his inner life in an autobiography of great interest. One of the keenest intellects of the Moslem Church. (See William James, *The Varieties* *of Religious Experience.*) See also *Arabian Philosophy.*

AL-KORAN. See *Koran.*

ALLAH. The Arabic name used by Moslems for God. (Ar. *al-ilah* = the worthy to be adored.)

ALLEGORY. A figurative use of speech to convey a further and deeper meaning than the literal. The parable or fable is a short allegory with a definite moral. Allegory is found in every literature. The Hebrew scriptures are encrusted with it (e.g. Psalm lxxx.). In classical literature Ovid used allegory freely; also Livy (Livy 2. 32, the stomach and its members). In English literature Edmund Spenser, Swift, Addison and Bunyan made a very free use of allegory.

ALLELUIAH. See *hallelujah.*

ALLEN, WILLIAM (1532–94). English ecclesiastic who refused the oath of supremacy, was deprived by Queen Elizabeth and escaped to Louvain. He settled at Douai, was made a cardinal and with Father Parsons (q.v.) rendered Douai a hot-bed of political and religious sedition. (See *Diaries of the English College, Douai* (1878).)

ALLEYN, EDWARD (1566–1626). English actor of high repute and founder of Dulwich College. Married (2nd wife) Constance, daughter of John Donne, the poet and divine (q.v.). Among Alleyn's papers was found the famous Diary of Philip Henslow, the actor manager. Shakespeare's name not appearing anywhere in the diary, John Payne Collier, an eminent Shakespearean critic, made spurious entries in the diary, but was detected and exposed.

ALL SAINTS' DAY, ALL-HALLOWS, HALLOWMAS. Festival observed on 1 November by the Catholic and Anglican Church in honour of all known and unknown saints and martyrs.

ALL SOULS' DAY. Catholic festival (2 Nov.) on which the souls of the faithful departed are commemorated. It had its roots in pagan antiquity and many of its ancient rites linger in Brittany and other Celtic countries. See also *Samhain.*

ALMERY, AUMERY, AUMBEY or **AMBRY.** Recess in wall of a church, in which the sacred vessels are kept.

ALMONER. An officer in religious houses responsible for the distribution of alms.

ALMONRY. The place in churches and monasteries where alms were distributed. Sometimes a separate building, as at Westminster Abbey.

ALMUCE. See *amice.*

ALOKA. Hindu goddess, a personification of light.

ALPHA AND OMEGA. God as the beginning, middle and end of all natural processes. From Greek Α and Ω. (See Revelation i. 8; xxi. 6; xxii. 13.)

ALPHEGE, SAINT (954–1012). Archbishop of Canterbury, murdered by the Danes at Greenwich.

ALRED. See *Ælred.*

ALSATIA. Name given to the precinct of Whitefriars, London, as a sanctuary for thieves. (See Walter Scott, *Fortunes of Nigel.*) (From Alsace, between France and Germany.)

ALTAR. A block or stone on which sacrifice is made to gods. Pagan altars have been found: (1) In Egypt where polished granite or basalt was employed. (2) In Mesopotamia of sun-dried bricks and (Herod., i. 183) of gold (the latter have disappeared). (3) In Palestine, where circular spaces marked by small stones were used.

§ 2. The O.T. references show differences due to development. Altars were usually set up where there appeared to have been a manifestation of deity. In Greece and Rome altars were of two kinds, (*a*) pedestals inside the temples, before the sacred images, so low that the worshipper could kneel on them, and (*b*) larger tables for burnt sacrifice, usually in front of the temples. The pagan altar gradually found its way into the Christian church. The early Christians were taunted by the pagans for having no altars. "The altars," replied Origen, "are the heart of every Christian." In the Catacombs the bench-like tombs (*arcosolia*) were probably used as altars, the earliest being made of wood, but more costly materials were used as persecution ceased.

§ 3. In the Catholic Church the altar consists of a stone slab, or table (*mensa*); the support, usually columns (*stipes*); and the sepulchrum, a cavity for relics of martyrs. The "high" altar is the principal cathedral altar. The Reformation caused altars to be regarded as symbols of the unreformed doctrine and in the English revised prayer-book of 1552 "God's board" or "the table" was substituted for "altar." See also *Sacrifice.*

ALTAR-CLOTH. The covering of silk, velvet, etc., over the altar.

ALTAR-LIGHTS. Symbolic candles placed on the altar.

ALTAR-PIECE. The decorative screen behind an altar.

ALTAR-RAILS. Railings separating the sacrarium from the chancel.

AMALEKITES. A tribe of southern Palestine hostile to the Israelites (1 Sam. xv. 6).

AMARANTH, AMARANT. Certain plants typifying immortality, used by the Greeks to decorate images of their gods. The flower is described by Milton in *Paradise Lost*, iii. 353.

AMBARVALIA. A Roman feast held on 29 May to bless the growing crops. The Arval Brothers (q.v.), acting as priests, led the sacrificial victims, ox, pig and sheep, round the *ager Romanus.* The Christian festival of the Rogation appears to have grown from it. (See W. W. Fowler, *Roman Festivals* (1899).)

AMBO, AMBON. A reading-desk which served also as pulpit in

early Christian churches. It was later superseded by the lectern and pulpit.

AMBROSE, ISAAC (1604–1663). English Puritan divine, vicar of Preston until 1662, when he was ejected as a nonconformer. His writings are distinguished by much beauty and pathos. His *Looking to Jesus* attained wide popularity.

AMBROSE, SAINT (c. 340–397). One of the four Latin doctors of the Church. An orator and ascetic who wielded great political power. See *Fathers, Church*, § 7.

AMBROSE THE CAMALDULIAN (1386–1439). A learned humanist monk at the court of Cosimo de' Medici.

AMBROSIAN CHANT. A chant attributed to St. Ambrose, very popular until the Gregorian chants of the 6th C. superseded it.

AMBROSIANS. (1) A Milanese sect of the 14th C. (2) An anabaptist sect of the 16th C., claiming direct revelation.

AMBRY. See *almery*.

AMEN. A liturgical word of ratification. For its first liturgical use, see 1 Corinthians xiv. 16. (Dr. Temple, archbishop of York, is reported to have said that the singing of Amen at the end of hymns is "always a bore.") (From Heb. *Amen* = truth.)

AMENTA. The Egyptian Hades.

AMERICAN CHURCH. See *United States Protestant Episcopal Church*.

AMES, WILLIAM (AMESIUS) (1576–1633). Puritan divine born at Ipswich, Suffolk, and educated at Cambridge. Owing to persecution, found refuge in the Netherlands. Ames was an accomplished scholar and a master of theological controversy. (See Winwood, *Memorials*, vol. iii, pp. 346–7.)

AMICE. A square of linen, diagonally folded, worn over the shoulders by celebrant priests (Cath.). Term sometimes confused with the earlier almuce, a clerical head-covering.

AMIEL, HENRI FREDERICK (1821–81). Swiss philosopher and man of letters. Famous for his *Journal Intime*, a work of great beauty and sympathetic insight. (See Mlle Bertha Vadier, *Life of Amiel* (Paris, 1885).)

AMMON. An Egyptian deity who became identified with the sun-god Ra. In Greek mythology Ammon was identified with Zeus and his consort Mut with Hera.

AMMONITES. A people of eastern Palestine hostile to the Israelites. They claimed descent from Lot (Deut. ii. 19). Their national deity was Moloch or Milcon.

AMORA. Title applied to the rabbis of the 2nd–6th C. who compiled the Talmud. (Heb. "speaker.")

Amorites. The original inhabitants of Palestine when the Israelites entered. Their five kings were defeated and hanged on five trees by Joshua (Josh. x. 16–27).

Amos. An Israelitish prophet, born at Tekoa, south of Bethlehem. A shepherd by profession, Amos refused to be called a prophet. There was no need for him, as in the case of other prophets and dervishes, to live on the profits of preaching. He had poetic gifts of a high order as appears in much of his vivid imagery, e.g. "As if a man fled from a lion, and a bear met him; or leaned upon the wall, and a serpent bit him." And, in his description of amazing fruitfulness: "The plougher shall overtake the reaper, and the treader of grapes, the sower of seed." (See Driver, *Joel and Amos* (1897).)

Amphictyony. An association of the tribes of ancient Greece for worship at a common shrine. The most famous was the Delphic Amphictyony. The primary function of the league was to conduct the affairs of the shrine. Its later activities dealt with wider problems, including the more humane conduct of warfare between league members. (See E. H. Freeman, *History of Federal Government in Greece and Italy* (1895).)

Ampulla. A flask containing the consecrated wine, water or oil (Cath.).

Amulet, Charm, Talisman. Gems, metalwork, herbs, etc., worn round the neck to protect from evil. They were popular with the Egyptians and Israelites. The fish was the favourite charm of the early Christians.

Anabaptists. The name given to various sects that arose in the age of Luther. In 1521 three "prophets" came to Wittenberg—Thomas Münster, Nicholas Storch and Mark Stübner—for whom Luther's reforms were not drastic enough. Luther had accepted the baptism of Rome which they held to be neither primitive nor scriptural. It did not insist upon repentance, faith, spiritual illumination or free surrender of self. It caught, they asserted, all the little fishes in its wide net, but the fishes were the same after baptism as before. The ferment grew and became involved in the Peasants' War in S. Germany (1525). Münster became the centre of this anabaptist activity. There John of Leiden (Johann Bockholdt) seized control, the bishop and magistrates having been expelled. He claimed absolute power in the new Zion. Inspired by visions "from heaven," he imagined he was beyond good and evil, sanctioned polygamy, took four wives himself, one of whom he beheaded with his own hands in the market-place. Münster for twelve months was given over to prophecy and profligacy. In 1535 the town was captured and Bockholdt executed. The sect spread to Switzerland, Holland, Italy and England. The English anabaptists of the 17th C. were the originators of the Baptists of to-day (q.v.). (Gr. *ana* = again; *baptizo* = I baptize.)

ANADYOMENE. Descriptive epithet of Venus (Aphrodite) who was born of the sea. (Gr. *anaduomai* = to come up, arise.) Cf. Rupert Brooke:

> Is dawn a secret, shy and cold
> Anadyomene, silver-gold ?

(The Old Vicarage, Grantchester.)

ANAGOGIC. Mystical or exalted interpretation of Scripture. (Gr. *anagein* = to lift up.)

ANAHITA. A Persian goddess of war and fertility.

ANAMNESIS. The Platonic doctrine that the soul remembers ideas experienced while in a purer state.

ANANDA. The beloved first cousin and disciple of Buddha.

ANANIAS. (1) Member of the first Christian community, miraculously punished by Peter with death for falsehood (Acts v. 1–10). (2) A disciple of Damascus (Acts ix. 10–17). (3) Son of Nedebaios, a high priest (Acts xxiii. 2; xxiv. 1–5).

ANAPHORA. The most venerated part of the eucharistic service in the Greek liturgy.

ANATHEMA. Originally a gift dedicated to a god by Greek worshippers. Hence, something set apart. Used by the early church of something set apart for evil purposes. In 1 Corinthians xvi. 22, anathema maranatha is merely intensive, maranatha being a formula of confirmation, like Amen.

ANCESTOR-WORSHIP. In all ancient patriarchal civilizations ancestor-worship had a prominent place. The Roman Manes were the friendly ghosts of deceased ancestors. Under the name of Lares offerings were made to them, and for them the sacred fire was kept alight on the hearth. The Manes were friendly spirits; whereas the Lemures, like our ghosts and spooks, were mischievous or hostile. (See Ovid, *Fasti*, v. 432.) One reason why the Romans were hostile to Christianity was their attachment to the family and family ties. Christ's saying, "If any cometh to me and hateth not his father and his mother and his wife and children . . . he cannot be my disciple," seemed impious to a devout Roman. The Christian cults of the saints and the dead are a link with the older rites of ancestor-worship still observed in China and Japan.

ANCHORITE, ANCHORET. A monk who isolates himself for ascetic purposes. See *asceticism*.

ANCREN RIWLE. A prose treatise of devotion written in the 12th or 13th C. for certain anchoresses of Dorset, and attributed to Richard Poor. (Pub. in The King's Classics.)

ANDREA, GIOVANNI (1275–1348). A learned Italian doctor of canon law. He was so short of stature that in an audience with Pope Boniface VIII, the Pope, thinking he was kneeling, three times begged Giovanni to rise. His daughter, Novella, was so accomplished that she read her father's lectures at

Bologna in his absence, and so beautiful that she had to read them behind a screen.

Andrew. An apostle of Jesus Christ and brother of Simon Peter (John i. 40).

Andrews, Lancelot (1555–1626). One of the most learned and saintly of English divines. Received preferment under Queen Elizabeth and James I. As dean of Westminster he took keen interest in the boys of Westminster School, where he rendered the teaching of Greek and Hebrew so fascinating that no "compulsion or correction was necessary." Andrews was an intimate friend of Francis Bacon (q.v.) and King James delighted in his wit and sturdy honesty. When the parliament of 1621 had refused the king supplies, Neil, bishop of Ely, and Andrews, bishop of Winchester, were in presence. King James asked Neil if he might not levy money without consent of parliament. "God forbid you might not," replied the prelate, "for you are the breath of our nostrils." The king put the same question to Andrews, who gave a non-committal reply. King James insisted on an answer: "I think then," replied Andrews, "it is lawful for you to take my brother Neil's money, for he offers it." Andrews' piety was that of an early saint and, combined with his enormous learning and ready wit, fascinated his contemporaries. (See A. T. Russell, *Lancelot Andrews* (1863).)

Angel. A superhuman being who figures chiefly in monotheistic religions, e.g. Islam, Judaism and Christianity. The ἄγγελος (messenger) corresponds to the Heb. *mal'akh.* The Mal'akh Yahweh of the O.T. is an appearance of Yahweh in human form (Exod. iii. 2, 4). Jacob beheld the angels of God at Bethel (Gen. xxviii. 12) and the "man" with whom Jacob wrestled at Peniel is the Mal'akh Yahweh (Gen. xxxii. 24, 30). In Isaiah vi., seraphim, six-winged angels, are described. In Daniel (2nd C. B.C.) the angels Gabriel and Michael appear as guardians of the nations. The Fall of the Angels is not scriptural, though supported by Genesis vi. 2. The pagan gods take new form as angels in Daniel, the source from which Milton took *Paradise Lost.* Jesus, in N.T., refers to angels as ministers of God who "neither marry nor are given in marriage." Angels in O.T. drink, walk and speak, exercise miraculous powers, appear, vanish, fly. In Revelation i.–iii., the angels of the churches appear to be guardian spirits. There is no doctrine of angels in the creeds and confessions and the modern rationalizing mind tends to deny their existence. Regarded, however, from the evidential and scientific points of view, such negative dogmatism is unwise. The N.T. pronouncement that each individual has a guardian angel (Matt. xviii. 10) is no doubt derived from the Roman belief in the genius, or higher self, which accompanies every man in life and beyond. See also *genius.*

Angelici. (1) Heretical sect advocating the worship of angels.

(2nd C.) (2) Monkish order instituted by the Emperor Angelus Comnenus. (12th C.)

ANGELICO, FRA (1387–1455). One of the greatest painter-monks of the Italian renaissance. His best works are to be seen at S. Marco, Florence. Angelico's pure and gentle life is everywhere reflected in his paintings. (See Vasari, *Lives of the Italian Painters*.)

ANGELUS. A Catholic devotion to commemorate the Annunciation, recited at dawn, noon and sunset, at which hours the angelus bell is sounded.

ANGELUS SILESIUS (1624–77). German mystic, influenced by Jakob Böhme. He composed some beautiful hymns.

ANGER. A negative, destructive emotion. Psychology teaches that, like all unworthy emotions, it can be overcome by the victim frankly admitting its presence and focusing his consciousness upon it.

ANGILBERT. Latin poet and minister of Charlemagne; became abbot of Riquier and married Charlemagne's daughter Bertha. (See Jack Lindsay, *Medieval Latin Poets* (1934).)

ANGLICAN CHURCH. See *Church of England.*

ANGLO-CATHOLIC. That section of the Church of England which claims catholicity; the "high-church" party.

ANGLO-ISRAELISM. That sect founded by Richard Brothers (18th C.) which believes that the British people are descendants of the "lost ten tribes" of Israel. The theory is fully dealt with in the book *Philo-Israel.* It is regarded by scholars as without foundation.

ANIMALS, CRUELTY TO. The Royal Society for the Prevention of Cruelty to Animals was instituted in 1824. It opposed vivisection in 1860. Headquarters: 105 Jermyn Street, London, S.W.1.

ANIMAL WORSHIP. See *totemism.*

ANIMA MUNDI. Platonic doctrine of the world soul or vital force of matter.

ANIMISM. The doctrine that the inanimate kingdom, in company with all animate beings, is possessed of reason, intelligence and volition. The belief is predominant amongst primitive tribes and modern scientific research tends to endorse it. Shelley has beautifully expressed the animistic faith:

> The moveless pillar of a mountain's weight
> Is active living spirit. Every grain
> Is sentient both in unity and part,
> And the minutest atom comprehends
> A world of loves and hatreds.

(See Tyler, *Primitive Culture*; Frazer, *Golden Bough*; Edward Carpenter, *Pagan and Christian Creeds.*)

ANNA. The daughter of Phanuel who prophesied concerning the infant Jesus when he was taken to the Temple (Luke ii. 36).

ANNATES (FIRST FRUITS). The custom which decreed that the Pope should receive the first year's income of every benefice. In 1534 the annates in England reverted to the Crown; in 1704 Queen Anne appropriated them to the poorer clergy, thus establishing "Queen Anne's Bounty."

ANNO DOMINI (A.D.). Signifies time computed from the birth of Christ. In 532 a Scythian monk, Dionysius Exiguus (q.v.), a learned Roman astronomer, was instructed to fix the day and year of Christ's birth. He assigned the year since adopted and for day and month selected 25 December on which the birth of Mithra (q.v.) had been celebrated.

ANNUNCIATION. (1) The tidings of the birth of Jesus which the angel Gabriel conveyed to the Virgin Mary (Luke i. 26). (2) The festival commemorating this event (25 March: Lady Day).

ANOINTING. See *unction, extreme.*

ANSELM, SAINT (1033–1109). Archbishop of Canterbury in the reigns of William Rufus and Henry I, with whom he had many differences of opinion concerning ecclesiastical privileges. Anselm was a scholastic theologian of high attainment. In his works, while he endeavoured to reconcile Christian dogma with reason, he insisted on the initial necessity for faith. (See R. W. Church, *St. Anselm* (1870).)

ANTECHAPEL. West end of a college chapel.

ANTEPENDIUM. Frontlet or covering for an altar.

ANTHEM. Sacred music sung in parts introduced in the 4th C., and into the Church of England about 1565.

ANTHESTERIA. A Greek vintage festival of Dionysus, also connected with the cult of All Souls (q.v.). (See E. Rohde, *Psyche* (1907).)

ANTHONY OF PADUA, SAINT (1195–1231). A follower of St. Francis of Assisi. Patron saint of Padua and Portugal; reputed to assist his devotees in finding lost objects. (See A. Lepître, *St. Antoine de Padoue* (Paris, 1902).)

ANTHONY, SAINT (THE GREAT). First Christian monk, born in Egypt about 250. He retired to the desert, where many ascetics gathered about him. (See Alban Butler, *Lives of the Saints.*)

ANTHROPOMORPHISM. The ascription of human attributes to gods.

ANTHROPOMORPHITES. (1) An Egyptian sect. (4th C.) (2) A Western Church party. (10th C.)

ANTHROPOSOPHY. A movement initiated by Rudolf Steiner (q.v.) in Germany for research along mystical and scientific lines. Its headquarters are at Dornach, Switzerland, and it has branches in England, France and Germany.

ANTICHRIST. The mighty ruler who will at the end of time, battle with the Christ forces. The idea derives, through Jewish eschatology, from the apocalypses of Iran, where the great conflict between Ormazd and Ahriman preludes the "end of the world," or Armageddon. The Jewish prophets seized on the idea and from the Jews it entered Christianity. From the earliest times unpopular rulers have been identified with Antichrist, Antiochus Epiphanes and Nero being amongst the earliest, and ex-Kaiser Wilhelm II of Germany the latest, to be so distinguished. The reformers saw the papacy as Antichrist and the papal party took a like view of the reformers. Such traditions and ascriptions are of little importance, but are of interest as indicating the continual change of the religious outlook. (See Bousset, *Antichrist* (1895).)

ANTILEGOMENA. Books of the N.T. not at first admitted to be genuine (2 Peter, James, Jude, Hebrews, 2 and 3 John, Apocalypse). (See Eusebius, *Eccles. Hist.*, iii. 25.) (Gr. "spoken against.")

ANTINOMIANS. A name applied by Luther to Johannes Agricola, a German reformer, and his followers. The Antinomians stressed the view of faith as against law. (Gr. *anti* = against; *nomos* = law.)

ANTIOCH. City in Asia Minor where Jesus' followers were first called Christians (Acts ii. 26). Important synods and councils were held there during 3rd and 4th C.

ANTIPHON, ANTIPHONY. Chant sung responsively between choir and congregation or precentor and choir; introduced by Ignatius (2nd C. A.D.) in response to a vision.

ANTIPOPES. Rival popes set up by factions between 1305 and 1439. See *Papacy, Pope.*

ANTI-SEMITISM. An anti-Jewish agitation found in many European countries based rather on commercial than racial or religious grounds. In medieval times, owing to persecution by church and state, the Jews were forced into their ghettos, with the result that they became strongly democratic and commercial. When the movement for political freedom came, they threw in their lot with the *bourgeoisie.* Especially was this the case in Germany (18th C.), where many distinguished Jews (Heinrich Heine, Ferdinand Lassalle, Karl Marx, Moses Hess) took an active part in affairs. After the establishment of the North German Union (1867) the Jews entered the national life of Germany and their business acumen, sharpened by the hardships of the ghetto, carried them to the front professional ranks. Inevitably their competitive success aroused forces of jealousy which culminated in a book by Wilhelm Marr—*The Victory of Judaism over Germanism* (c. 1870). The German people lost their heads and Jews were everywhere insulted and boycotted, the Crown Prince declaring the agitation to be

" a shame and disgrace to Germany." With the spread of education and more enlightened views anti-semitism declined. The present régime in Germany (1935) appears to have rekindled the flames, but as a better knowledge of psychology comes to prevail it will, no doubt, give place to wiser counsels. In Russia and France similar animosities have waxed and waned. The Dreyfus case (see Anatole France, *The Isle of Penguins*) served as a climax in France. In England, periodic attempts to introduce the violent doctrines of Marr have met with little response, the temper of the English people being opposed to petty persecution. (See Bernard Lazare, *L'Antisémitisme* (1894) ; James Parkes, *The Conflict of the Church and the Synagogue* (1934).)

ANU. The Babylonian king of the gods.

ANUBIS. In Egyptian mythology god of the dead, identified with the Greek Hermes. (See Budge, *Gods of the Egyptians.*)

APHRODITE. The Greek goddess of love and beauty. See *Venus.*

APIS. The sacred bull of Memphis. (See Budge, *Gods of the Egyptians.*)

APOCALYPTIC LITERATURE. A collection of Jewish and Christian writings covering a period from 200 B.C. to A.D. 350, of a generally prophetical nature, and deriving from early Semitic traditions. The chief extra-Biblical apocalyptic writings are : (Jewish) Assumption of Moses, Apocalypse of Baruch, Apocalypse of Abraham, 2 Enoch, Testament of Job ; and (Christian) Shepherd of Hermas, Apocalypse of Peter, Vision of Isaiah, Revelations of Bartholomew, Christian Sibyllines. (See M. R. James, *The Apocryphal New Testament* (1924).)

APOCRYPHA. Certain Jewish and Christian sacred writings not admitted into the canon (q.v.). The apocryphal books of the O.T. are : 1 and 2 Esdras, Tobit, Judith, Esther, Wisdom of Solomon, Ecclesiasticus, Baruch, Song of the Three Children, History of Susannah, Bel and the Dragon, Prayer of Manasses, 1 and 2 Maccabees. Chief N.T. Apocrypha : various fragmentary gospels (Peter, James, Thomas, etc.) ; the Acts of Paul and Thekla ; Epistles of Paul to the Laodiceans ; the Apocalypse of Peter ; the Teachings of Peter and Paul, the Abgar Epistles and various Infancy Gospels. (See M. R. James, *Lost Apocrypha of the O.T.* and *The Apocryphal New Testament.*)

APOLLINARIANISM. Followers of Apollinaris, bishop of Laodicea (310–90), who denied the complete humanity of Jesus. His belief was condemned by the Council of Constantinople in A.D. 381. Apollinaris is also remembered for his attempt to popularize the O.T. by translating it into a Homeric epic.

APOLLO. A sun-god and vegetation-god of Greek mythology, son of Zeus and Leto. Also a god of prophecy, see *Oracles.*

The chief festivals in honour of Apollo were the Carneia, Daphnephoria, Delia, Hyacinthia, Pyanepsia, Pythia and Thargelia. (See L. Dyer, *The Gods in Greece* (1891); W. W. Fowler, *Roman Festivals.*)

APOLLONIUS OF TYANA. A Greek mystical and Pythagorean philosopher of the 1st C., who travelled extensively in the East and was credited with miraculous powers. Early Christian apologists regarded him as a charlatan, but without evidence. (See F. W. G. Campbell, *Apollonius of Tyana* (1908).)

APOLLOS. An Alexandrian Jew, co-worker with St. Paul at Corinth and Ephesus (1 Cor. iii. 6; xvi. 12).

APOLLYON. The fiend in Bunyan's *Pilgrim's Progress*, derived from Revelation ix. 11.

APOLOGETICS. That branch of theology which defends Christianity as a historical supernatural revelation. Opposition drove the early Christians to defensive methods. The earliest Christian apologetics are the Gospels and the Epistles to the Hebrews. The matter and manner of apologetics continually vary with the changing spirit of the age. The early Christian apologists had to meet crude slanders of cannibalism, sex-promiscuity, etc., and retorted by attacking the "obscene myths" of their opponents. With the passing of persecution the onus of opposition shifted to Hellenism. Justin Martyr, Origen and Augustine dealt with anti-Christian arguments of Greek and Jewish opponents (2nd C.). The supremacy of Christianity during the Middle Ages rendered apologetics unnecessary except against Jews and Mohammedans. But with the growth of intellectual freedom after the Reformation, the need arose for apologetics to defend the Faith against Deism, Pantheism and Free Thought. The chief problem of modern apologetics is to reconcile theological dogma (the divinity of Christ, revealed religion, original sin, the Virgin birth, etc.) with science and philosophy. The result of this is that Christian apologists tend to turn from the dogmatic to the ethical sphere. Jesus Christ is regarded more as ethical teacher than revealer of an original divine cosmic plan. The necessity for apologetics would appear to arise from (1) too strongly stressing the need for rationalization of experience; (2) the belief that pure reason is the final arbiter in man's destiny, a theory which science and history alike disprove; and (3) a too strong clinging to tradition and disregarding of the phenomena of experience. The chief Christian apologists are: Tertullian (2nd C.); Augustine (*City of God*; 4th–5th C.); Blaise Pascal (17th C.); Joseph Butler (*Analogy of Religion*; 18th C.). (See H. Bushnell, *Nature and the Supernatural*; *Encyc. Bib.* (article "Jesus").)

APOSTASY. A classical Greek term for revolt applied by the Catholic Church to (1) renunciation of monastic vows; (2) abandonment of the clerical profession. Used loosely for abandonment or change of faith.

APOSTLE. The N.T. word for the immediate followers of Jesus Christ (Simon Peter; Andrew; James and John (sons of Zebedee); Philip; Bartholomew; Thomas; Matthew; James and Jude (sons of Alpheus); Simon; Judas Iscariot. It is doubtful whether the word was ever used by Jesus himself, " apostle " in the N.T. standing for " envoy," " representative."

APOSTLE SPOONS. Silver baptismal figured spoons (15th-16th C.). Complete original sets are very rare. A set of thirteen was sold at Christie's (1904) for £4,900.

APOSTOLIC CANONS. A collection of catechetical teaching (4th C.) of unknown authorship.

APOSTOLICAL CONSTITUTIONS. A collection of Church doctrine dating from about the 3rd C. Its value has been variously estimated and the authorship much debated. (See H. S. Maclean, *Recent Discoveries* (1904).)

APOSTOLIC DELEGATE. See *legate*.

APOSTOLIC FATHERS. The early Christian teachers who fill a gap between the age of the Apostles and the age of the Apologists (i.e. to c. A.D. 140). The chief of these are: Clement of Rome, Barnabas, Hermas, Ignatius, Polycarp and Papias. (See Lightfoot, *The Apostolic Fathers* (1891).)

APOSTOLICI. (1) A Christian sect (2nd C.) who renounced marriage, wine, flesh-eating, etc. (2) A sect founded by Gerard Segarelli (13th C.) who renounced baptism, the Mass, etc., and led a wandering life. Segarelli was burnt as a heretic at Parma in 1300.

APOSTOLIC SEE. The Church of Rome which claims apostolic authority. See *Papacy*.

APOSTOLIC SUCCESSION. Doctrine of the uninterrupted episcopal succession from the apostles to the present time. See *holy orders*.

APOTHEOSIS. Exaltation of rulers to divine rank. See *Emperor-worship*.

APPAREL. Borders on ecclesiastical vestments (Cath.).

APPARITION. An appearance not occasioned by any external object. The cause of an apparition may be: (1) pathological; (2) due to telepathy or clairvoyance; (3) occasioned by animistic influence or haunting; (4) induced by hypnotic suggestion. See *spiritualism*.

APPARITOR. An official attached to an ecclesiastical court.

APSE. A vaulted semicircular recess at the east end of a church.

AQIBA, BEN JOSEPH. Jewish rabbi and martyr. His school at Jaffa is said to have had 24,000 scholars. (1st–2nd C.)

AQUILA. (1) A Roman Jew with whom St. Paul stayed (Acts xviii. 2, 3). (2) A Jew of Pontus who translated the O.T. into Greek (2nd C. A.D.).

AQUINAS, SAINT THOMAS. "The Angelic Doctor" (1227–74). Son of Landulf, count of Aquino, near Naples, Aquinas was educated at Monte Cassino (q.v.), Naples and the Dominican school at Cologne. His profound theology rendered him a famous teacher in the chief European universities. Aquinas's influence in theological thought was extensive and lasting. His great work was the blending of Aristotelian philosophy with the doctrines of the Church. He taught that while reason and revelation are distinct sources of truth they are not antagonistic but derive from the one absolute truth of the Godhead. His abiding influence on Catholic thought is witnessed in the fact that Pope Leo XIII in his Encyclical of 1879 directed the clergy to regard the teaching of Aquinas as the foundation of their theological position. English editions of the *Summa Theologiae*, J. Rickaby (1872), and J. M. Ashley (1888). (See R. B. Vaughan, *St. Thomas of Aquin* (1872).)

ARABIAN PHILOSOPHY. A medieval system of Greek thought goes by this name chiefly because it arose among the Moslem people about the 9th C. A.D. Certain so-called "Arabian" philosophers (Al-Kindi, Al-Farabi, Avenpace, Al-Ghazali) kept alive, amongst their Moslem brethren, the teachings of Aristotle. These Arabian philosophers, and their Spanish brethren, made no claim to originality, though their influence upon European thought was considerable. Al-Ghazali, Avenpace and Averroës were outstanding figures of this school. Avenpace taught that the individual, by following a certain method of life, may rise from sense perceptions to the region of pure intelligence or intuition and divine thought. Averroës, though he was interpreter of Aristotle to the later schoolmen (q.v.), was much more. He was a man of deep religious experience and keen insight. Religion, he taught, is not a system of dogma but an inner life in nowise contradictory to scientific law. Theology he regarded with distaste because it fosters the disturbing belief that religion and science are antagonistic. The world and God are alike eternal. Change and growth induce a search for finality which in time and space cannot be attained. Finality is attained, now and for ever, but beyond the element of time. In the age of Roger Bacon, Averroës had become "an authority." Averroism worked like leaven until by the 14th C. it pervaded the philosophic atmosphere in England. John Baconthorpe (q.v.) was an outstanding Averroist. (See T. J. de Boer, *The History of Philosophy in Islam* (1903).)

ARAHAT. See *arhat.*

ARALU. Babylonian Hades.

ARAMAIC LANGUAGES. Ancient Semitic dialects current in Mesopotamia and N.E. Palestine.

ARANYAKAS. Indian sacred books of later date than the Vedas and Brahmanas. See *Scriptures*, § 5 (*a*).

ARARAT. A mountain of Armenia (17,000 ft.), reputed the resting-place of Noah's ark.

ARCHANGEL. An angel of highest rank. The four great archangels are (Koran): Gabriel (revelation and inspiration), Michael (war), Azraël (death), Azrafil (the awakener).

ARCHBISHOP. A Christian bishop of superior rank with jurisdiction over other bishops. The office is found in the Catholic, Anglican and certain of the Lutheran churches.

ARCHDEACON, ARCHPRIEST. A medieval ecclesiastical official. The power of the archdeacon has declined since the 16th C. In the Anglican Church the archdeacon's duty is to assist the bishop in his diocesan administration. In the Catholic Church the office is merely titular. See also *dean, rural.*

ARCHES, COURT OF. An Anglican court of appeal, formerly held at St. Mary-le-Bow, where the original steeple was supported on arches.

ARCHIMANDRITE. The superior of a monastery (Gr. Ch.).

ARCHITECTURE. The principal styles of architecture in England, with approximate dates, are as follows:

Early Saxon	700–950
Later Saxon	950–1050
Transition to Norman	1050–1080
Early Norman	1080–1110
Norman	1110–1150
Transitional	1150–1190
Early English	1190–1250
Geometrical	1250–1280
Decorated	1280–1360
Perpendicular	1360–1480
Tudor	1480–1600
Renaissance (Italian)	1510–1560
(Elizabethan)	1560–1600
(Jacobean)	1600–1650
(English)	1660–

ARCHITRAVE. The part of the entablature resting on the abacus of a column (archit.).

ARCHPOET, THE. A Latin poet, student of the medical school at Salerno, who held office in the household of Reginald von Dassel, chancellor to Frederick Barbarossa. (See Jack Lindsay, *Medieval Latin Poets.*)

ARCOSOLIUM. Tomb in arched recess as in the Roman catacombs.

AREOPAGUS, or MARS' HILL. The seat of a famous Athenian tribunal where St. Paul preached (Acts xvii.).

ARÊS. See *Mars.*

ARGEI. Name of the twenty-seven puppets which the Vestal Virgins threw into the Tiber on 14 May. The origin of the custom is unknown. (See W. W. Fowler, *Roman Festivals.*)

ARHAT, ARAHAT, ARHANT. In the Buddhist system one who has attained complete enlightenment, a perfected saint.

ARIANISM. See *Arius.*

ARISTOTLE (384–322 B.C.). Greek philosopher, born at Stagira (hence "the Stagirite"), was a pupil of Plato and travelled extensively till his fiftieth year, when he became a teacher of philosophy at Athens. He agreed with all the moral and metaphysical doctrines of Plato, but refused to accept Plato's teaching that reality is not here but only above. Aristotle differed from Plato in holding that all things are substances and not, as Plato taught, shadows and unsubstantial things, that the one and the many, universals and forms, are real and not separate entities. It was on these metaphysical grounds that Aristotelianism differed from Platonism. The importance of Aristotle in the development of religious thought is due to the fact that, following the Arabian philosophy (q.v.), Aquinas was powerfully influenced by Aristotle, finding him of inestimable service in building up a theological system. It was in fact due to this use (or misuse according to the point of view) of Aristotle by the schoolmen that Francis Bacon so vigorously opposed Aristotelianism in the schools. (See J. W. Blakesley, *Life of Aristotle*; R. W. Livingstone, *The Legacy of Greece.*)

ARIUS (256–336) and **ARIANISM.** Arius was presbyter of Alexandria in the age when Hellenic culture had given place to ecclesiastical disputations and Christianity had become mainly a matter for theological argument. He maintained that the Son was different in essence from the Father, thus stressing the *human* nature of Jesus. The Arian position was condemned at the Council of Nicaea over which Constantine presided in A.D. 325.

ARJUNA. The hero of the Mahabharata in Hindu mythology. The epic reveals him as a man of noblest qualities. See *Scriptures*, § 5 (*c*).

ARK. (1) The vessel built by Noah to escape the deluge (Gen. vi. 5–9). (2) The basket in which baby Moses was hidden (Exod. iii. 12). (3) The ark of the Covenant, a chest of acacia wood which symbolized Yahweh to the Israelites. (4) The ark of the law, a chest in synagogues containing the Torah (q.v.).

ARMAGEDDON. Symbolical battlefield on which the final conflict between good and evil will be fought (Rev. xvi. 16). Possibly derived from Yesemmigadon, Babylonian god of the underworld.

ARMARIOL. A church locker for keeping sacred vessels.

ARMENIA, CHURCH OF. A Church founded by Gregory the Illuminator (4th C.), resembling the Greek Church in ritual but independent of it. The Armenian Council of Tiben in 552 put the Greek Orthodox Church under a curse. The Armenian Christians have suffered grievous persecutions by the Turks.

ARMINIUS and **ARMINIANISM** (1560–1609). James Harmensen (Arminius), a Protestant theologian of Leiden, Holland, differed violently from the Calvinists, chiefly on the subject of

Predestination. The Arminian doctrines were condemned at the Synod of Dort in 1619. James I, who suffered from his Calvinistic upbringing, favoured Arminianism.

ARNOBIUS. (1) Christian apologist influenced by Lucretius and Plato. Author of *Adversus Gentes*. (4th C.) (2) A Gaulish priest who wrote a commentary on the Psalms. (5th C.)

ARNOLD, SIR EDWIN (1832–1904). English journalist, poet and man of letters. Remembered for his verse translations of Eastern scriptures: *The Light of Asia* (1879); *The Light of the World* (1891); etc.

ARNOLD, MATTHEW (1822–88). English poet and critic, son of Thomas Arnold (q.v.). He wrote extensively on religious themes (*Literature and Dogma; God and the Bible; Culture and Anarchy*). The questioning tendency of his mind offended the ultra-conservative spirit of his time and he provoked much controversy. His poetry is distinguished by an exquisite beauty of phrase and imagery.

ARNOLD OF BRESCIA. A reforming Italian monk, pupil of Abélard. He opposed corruption and spoke out boldly: ("Clerks who have estates; bishops who hold fiefs; monks who possess property cannot be saved"). His doctrine proved so distasteful that he was put to death by Pope Adrian IV in 1155.

ARNOLD, THOMAS (1795–1842). A famous head master of Rugby. Under his supervision Rugby became a leading centre of education with renewed religious and intellectual ideals. (See Stanley, *Life of Dr. Arnold* (1845); also Lytton Strachey, *Eminent Victorians* (1926).)

ARSENIUS and **ARSENIANS.** (1) An anchorite of the Thebaid. (4th–5th C.) (2) A patriarch of Constantinople who excommunicated the emperor Michael Palaeologus for blinding his colleague, John Lascaris, in 1261. He was deposed in 1264, but his followers ("Arsenians") continued the struggle.

ARS MORIENDI. A medieval work concerning death and the life after, of which there are many versions in Latin, English and French. (See F. M. M. Comper, *The Book of the Craft of Dying* (1917).)

ARTEMIS. See *Diana*.

ARTHUR, KING. The probably mythical hero of a cycle of romance. Some authorities incline to the view that he derives from Celtic vegetation deities. See also *Grail, Holy*.

ARTICLES, THIRTY-NINE. The final Confession of Faith drawn up by the Church of England in 1563, and ratified in 1571. See *Church of England*.

ARVAL BROTHERS. Priesthood of twelve in ancient Rome whose duty was to bless the crops. The Emperor Augustus secured his election to the Fratres Arvales. (See W. Warde Fowler, *The Roman Festivals*.)

ARYA SAMAJ. Indian religious reform movement established by

Dayanand Sarasvasti in 1875. Though the Samaj is opposed to Christianity, it advocates a high ethical standard founded on the Vedas.

ASA. A king of Judah, Rehoboam's son (1 Kings xv. 9–24).

ASANAS. Postures adopted by yogis during meditation. See *Yoga*.

ASCENSION, FEAST OF THE. An ecumenical festival of the Christian Church, commemorating the *ascensio*, the ascension of Christ by his own power in contradistinction to the *assumptio*, the taking of the Virgin Mary to heaven by the power of God. (See L. Duchesne, *Christian Worship* (1904).)

ASCETAE. An order of early Christians whose aim was to master the lower nature by discipline.

ASCETICISM. Severe self-discipline practised with the purpose of gaining control of the more animal qualities. The Christian Church of the earliest age tended towards an excessive asceticism. This was due, in part, to revulsion from the sex-worship which formed a recognized part of many pagan cults. St. Paul had to fight hard to secure for the baptized the right to marry, to own property, to engage in war or business or to hold public office. The early apocryphal gospels insisted that marriage was evil and that converts must remain celibate.

ASCHAM, ROGER (1515–68). Writer, scholar and educationist. Ascham was tutor to Princess (afterwards Queen) Elizabeth. His *Schoolmaster* (1570) had an immense vogue and occasioned the introduction of more intelligent methods of education.

ASGARD. The Norse abode of the gods.

ASHER. The tribe of Israel called after Asher, son of Jacob and Zilpah (Gen. xxx. 13).

ASHTAROTH. Phoenician moon-goddess, sometimes worshipped by the Israelites (Judges ii. 13).

ASHVAGHOSHA. A great 1st C. philosopher of Mayhayana Buddhism.

ASH WEDNESDAY. The first day of Lent in the Western Church. The custom of sprinkling ashes (derived from public penance in the early church) has been dropped by the Reformed Churches, but is observed in the Catholic Church. The ashes are placed in a vessel on the altar before High Mass.

ASINARII. Epithet applied to the first Christians by Tacitus because their opponents said they worshipped an ass.

ASIR. The hierarchy of twelve gods and twelve goddesses of Norse mythology. Gods: Odin, Thor, Baldur, Niord, Frey, Tyr, Bragi, Heimdall, Vidar, Vali, Ullur, Forseti. Goddesses (4 chief): Frigga, Freyya, Iduna, Saga.

ASKEW, ANNE. English Protestant martyr, tortured and burnt at Smithfield by the Catholic ministers of Henry VIII in 1546.

ASMODEUS. A demon sometimes identified with Beelzebub and Apollyon (Rev. ix. 11). He figures in the apocryphal book of Tobit.

ASOKA (273–231 B.C.). A famous Buddhist emperor of India. His vast empire was governed with a wise tolerance which has shamed many succeeding ages. He was the most powerful and enlightened sovereign of his time. (See Vincent Smith, *Asoka* (1901).)

ASPERGES. The Catholic rite of sprinkling with holy water.

ASPERGILL. A brush for sprinkling Catholic worshippers with holy water.

ASPERSORIUM. Holy-water vessel in Catholic churches.

ASS. This animal is frequently mentioned in the Bible. Christ's entry into Jerusalem on an ass (Matt. xxi. 1–11) appears to have symbolic meaning, his Kingdom being founded on humility and not on force, ecclesiastical pride or contentious argument.

ASSUMPTION. Ecclesiastical doctrine of the bodily transference of a person to heaven. See *Enoch* and *Elijah*. The Roman and Greek churches teach that the Virgin Mary was, after her death, taken bodily into heaven.

ASSYRIA. An ancient empire adjoining Babylon on the Euphrates, composed of Semites and Akkadians with a polytheistic worship.

ASTARTE. Phoenician moon-goddess.

ASTRAL BODY. The difference between a plant and an animal is due to the possession by the latter of an astral body. It is closely connected with the muscular system and the principles of feeling and movement. It is the embodiment of the desire nature and in man corresponds to the animal kingdom (theos.).

ASTROLOGY. The ancient art of reading the character or destiny of human beings by the position of the sun, moon and planets at the moment of birth. Astrology is first found in Babylonia about 3000 B.C., where it was used by the priests to forecast public events. In later times it was applied to the lives of individuals. Dr. Richard Garnett of the British Museum was the latest and best accredited believer in the claims of astrology to define character and foretell events.

ATAR. The Iranian god of fire.

ATARGATIS. Syrian mother-goddess. See *Cybele*.

ATHANASIAN CREED. See *Creed, Athanasian*.

ATHANASIUS, SAINT (293–373). Bishop of Alexandria at the time of the Arian controversy. He supported the divinity of Christ as against Arianism and was five times expelled from office and recalled owing to the Emperor Constantius's changes of opinion.

ATHEISM. Disbelief in the existence of a First Cause or controlling Creator. It was professed by Lucretius and other early philosophers. The term has often been used of the unorthodox by the orthodox in theology and of those whose opinions are disliked (e.g. Socrates, Voltaire and the poet Shelley). Francis Bacon summed up the atheistical position neatly: "Though a small draught of philosophy may lead a man into atheism, a *deep* draught will certainly bring him back again to the belief of a God . . . But the great atheists indeed are hypocrites which are ever handling holy things but without feeling; so as they must needs be cauterized in the end."

ATHENAGORAS. Christian apologist of Athens. (2nd C.)

ATHENE, PALLAS. One of the chief goddesses of Greek mythology, the wise mother and craftswoman of the Olympians. To her was attributed the invention of the plough and the implements for spinning, weaving and working in metal. Her symbols are the helmet, the shield, the spear, the olive branch, the owl, cock and snake. Her great festival was the Panathenaea represented on the frieze of the Parthenon. (See L. R. Farnell, *The Cults of the Greek States* (1896).)

ATHOS. A Greek mountain on the Aegean Sea famous for its establishment of twenty monasteries of Greek monks and their library of valuable manuscripts. (See A. Riley, *Athos* (1887).)

ATLANTIS. A legendary island in the Atlantic to which Plato refers (Timaeus, and Critias). According to tradition Atlantis attained a very high degree of civilization, but was suddenly destroyed by earthquake.

ATMAN, ATMA. The Hindu term corresponding to the Christian *soul*, the Moslem *ruh* and the Greek *psyche*. It is the death-surviving element.

ATONEMENT. In Christian theology the reconciliation of God to man through the death of Christ. The idea of such reconciliation probably derives from tribal life in the far past. A member of the tribe errs by cutting the sacred corn or killing the totem-bear or lamb. The wrong done could only be set right (atoned) by an offering or sacrifice to the ancestor-god. In this way reconciliation or at-one-ment was effected.

§ 2. The idea entered Christianity by way of the Jews (see Lev. xvii. 11). In the N.T. it does not appear that its writers were aware of any formal dogma of atonement, though they speak of "salvation" (σωτηρια) through Christ. St. Paul introduced the Jewish doctrine of vicarious suffering. The Divine Righteousness, outraged by men's sin, is appeased by Christ's suffering and death. Much has been written on the subject and varying views held. The belief in an objective atonement is still widely held by orthodox Christians, but the tendency is towards eclectic views, seeking to bring the doctrine more into line with the requirements of science and psychology. (See J. Denny, *Death of Christ*, *Atonement and The Modern Mind* (1903); Edward Carpenter, *Pagan and Christian Creeds*; H. Rashdall, *History of the Christian Doctrine of the Atonement* (1920).)

ATONEMENT, DAY OF. The most solemn observance of the Jewish calendar, marked by fasting and prayer. The purpose of the ritual is to cleanse the nation from sin and obtain Yahweh's forgiveness. It takes place in autumn (10th day of Tisri—Sept.–Oct.).

ATTIS. The Syrian saviour-god, born of the virgin Nana, and killed by a boar, symbol of winter. His worship was widespread in the Roman Empire. (1st C.) See also *mystery religions*. (See J. G. Frazer, *Adonis, Attis, Osiris*.)

ATTRITION. Imperfect repentance (Cath. theol.).

AUGMENTATION COURT. A court established by Henry VIII in 1535 to try cases affecting the suppression of monasteries. The court was abolished by Mary and restored by Elizabeth.

AUGSBURG, CONFESSION OF. A confession of faith drawn up by Luther, Melanchthon, Jonas and Bugenhagen with the object of making peace between the mutually opposed Protestant states of Germany. This Confession was the main source of the Thirty-Nine Articles of the Church of England.

AUGSBURG, DIET OF. A council convened by the Emperor Charles V in 1530 to resolve the religious and political troubles of Germany.

AUGUSTINE, SAINT (354–430). Greatest of the four fathers of the Church (Ambrose, Augustine, Jerome, and Gregory the Great). Augustine, born at Tagaste, Numidia, was the son of a pagan citizen and a Christian lady, Monica. His mother was devout and devoted and her Christian zeal lovingly pursued husband and son. Augustine, despite his mother's zeal (or in consequence of it), grew up without any profession of Christian Faith. By nature, keenly intellectual but of strong passions, the young Augustine sowed his wild oats. He fell in love, had an illegitimate son, the dearly loved Adeodatus ("by God given"), and caused his mother much suffering by his naughty life and daring views. The sect of the Manichaeans attracted him, with their wide intellectual outlook and teaching of the dualism between Good and Evil. His father trained him for a rhetorician (lawyer) and he became devoted to the Latin poets. He grew dissatisfied with Manichaeism and while travelling in Italy experienced a sudden conversion to Christianity. This occurred at Milan, whither his mistress and Adeodatus had accompanied him. After a short retreat, he was baptized and received into the Church. Augustine's keen intellectual endowments and many friends led to rapid promotion and he became bishop of Hippo. His episcopate was memorable for his long controversy with the

Pelagians (q.v.) on the doctrine of original sin—which Pelagius denied, Augustine insisting that babies who die unbaptized go to hell. Divine grace, he held, was all-important, men being doomed by Adam's sin. His nature, though enlightened and keenly intellectual, appears to have lacked that balance which alone leads to the highest enlightenment. (See Joseph McCabe, *St. Augustine and his Age* (1902); also Rebecca West, *Saint Augustine.*)

AUGUSTINE, SAINT. First archbishop of Canterbury (d. 613), was sent as missionary to the Anglo-Saxons by Gregory the Great in 596. He was given authority over the Celtic churches in Britain and over all bishops. The Catholic Church in England may be said to date from his time.

AUGUSTINIANS. The religious order of which the foundation is ascribed to St. Augustine of Hippo. The rule requires humility, poverty and chastity. Luther was an Augustinian monk. The order appeared in England soon after the Conquest. Their monastery at Austin Friars, London, was erected in 1354 and after the Reformation used by Dutch Protestants.

AUMBEY or **AUMERY.** See *almery.*

AURA. A light emanating from the body. (See Dr. Filmer, *The Human Aura.*) See also *clairvoyance.*

AUREOLA, AUREOLE. The gold disc surrounding the persons of Christ and the Virgin and Child in early Christian art; and distinct from the nimbus surrounding the head only.

AURICULAR CONFESSION. Confession of sin at the ear of a priest. (Lat. *auris.*) The practice of confession once a year was decreed by the Lateran Council of 1215. It was abolished in England at the Reformation, but its revival has been attempted by the Anglo-Catholics. See *Oxford Movement*; *Ritualists.*

AUSTRALIA, RELIGION IN. There is no Australian state church. The Church of England claims 39% of the population; the Roman Catholic Church 22%; the Wesleyan and other Methodists 12%; Presbyterians 11%; Congregationalists and Baptists each 2%. The religious views of the aborigines are vague. They believe in a god, Baiame, a gigantic old man who lies asleep in the sand. One day he is expected to awake and swallow the world. Totemism (q.v.) also prevails. There are initiatory rites (Bora) for boys and girls. Boys are circumcised, or a tooth is knocked out to the accompanying booming of the bull-roarer (q.v.).

AUTHORITY. In an ecclesiastical sense Authority is the right to declare what is binding upon followers of a cult. A bed-rock of such authority is sacred scripture. Mohammedanism, Christianity and Judaism all find authority in their inspired writings. The Catholic Church adds to the authority of the Scriptures, the dogma of the Church; the Pope, as St. Peter's successor, having the right to speak as the final authority. Protestantism refuses to acknowledge any authority save the Scriptures and the private conscience, though in practice the various Protestant beliefs have been influenced by the authority of previous confessions and creeds.

AUTHORIZED VERSION. The English Bible of 1611, which was *not* officially "authorized." See *Bible, the English.*

AUTO DA FÉ. The Spanish ceremony in which sentences against heretics were announced and the condemned handed over to the civil power for burning at the stake.

AVATAR, AVATARA. Hindu term to describe the incarnation of a Master of life, i.e. one who has overcome Sangsara (q.v.) and for whom birth and death are normally at an end. The conqueror returns, if at all, as a divine incarnation (*avatar*)—a Buddha, a Krishna or a Christ.

AVE MARIA (HAIL MARY). A Catholic prayer authorized by Pius V in 1568, founded on Luke i. 28.

AVERNUS. A sulphurous lake in Campania, Italy, anciently believed the entrance to Hades. Famous from Virgil's line:

> Facilis descensus Averni sed revocare . . .
> (Easy is the descent to Avernus, but to return . . .)

AVERROËS (1126–98). Last of the medieval Arabian philosophers. He studied mathematics, law, medicine, theology and philosophy. Through his influence, Aristotle became the outstanding authority of Scholasticism (q.v.). See also *Arabian Philosophy.*

AVESTA (ZEND-AVESTA). See *Scriptures,* § 9.

AVIDYA. In Brahmanism there are two paths: Vidya (knowledge) and avidya (ignorance). Vidya leads to Nirvana (full enlightenment) and avidya to recurring lives and deaths (Sangsara).

AYËSHAH. Mahomet's second wife, whom he married when she was nine.

AZARIAH. (1) Son of Zadoc the priest (1 Chron. vi.). (2) Son of Nathan (1 Kings iv. 5). (3) King of Judah (2 Kings xv. 1, 2). (4) Son of Ethan (1 Chron. ii. 8). (5) Son of Jehu (1 Chron. ii. 38). (6) A prophet of Judah (2 Chron. xv. 1). (7) Two sons of Jehoshaphat (2 Chron. xxi. 2). (8) King of Judah, son of Jehoram (2 Chron. xxi. 17). (9) Son of Jeroham and (10) son of Obed (2 Chron. xxiii. 1). (11) Son of Hilkiah (Ezra vii. 1). (12) Son of Maaseiah (Neh. iii. 23). (13) Son of Hoshaiah (Jer. xliii. 2). (14) Companion of Daniel (Dan. i. 6; iii. 8–30).

AZAZEL. The Israelitish scapegoat. The name rose from the casting of lots; one for the Lord, one for Azazel (Satan). The goat on whom the latter fell was the scapegoat. See also *scapegoat.*

AZRAËL. The Moslem angel of death. See *archangel.*

AZYMITES. The Catholics so called by the Greek Church because they use eucharistic unleavened bread. (Gr. *azumos* = unleavened.)

B

BA. The Egyptian bird-like figure symbolizing the soul.

BAAL, BEL, BEEL. A Semitic word signifying lord or possessor. The name was applied to a variety of gods (including Yahweh) by the Israelites, who incurred the anger of their prophets for departing from the worship of the one God. Baal-worship was connected with many practices that came to be regarded as licentious. (See J. G. Frazer, *Golden Bough,* vol. ii.)

BABA (FATHER). The Hindu title for the innumerable religious teachers of India.

BABEL. The tower built to reach heaven after the Deluge (Gen. xi. 1–9). The idea may have been suggested by the temple towers of Babylon, Babel being the native name for the city. Similar myths, to account for the diversity of languages, are found in many parts of the world, notably in Central America, Northern India and among the Africans of Lake Ngami.

BABIISM. A Persian sect, founded in 1843 by Mirza Ali Muhommad, at Shiraz. He termed himself the Gate (Bab) of Knowledge and claimed to be a master or messiah. His chief follower, Mullah Husayn, combined political and war-like principles with spiritual doctrines, with the result that trouble ensued and the Bab was executed in July 1849. Revelation, according to Babiism, is progressive and evolutionary, no revelation being final. (See E. J. Browne, *Materials for the Study of the Babi Religion* (1918).)

BABYLON. Chief city of ancient Babylonia on the left bank of the Euphrates, by tradition one of the most magnificent and luxurious cities of the ancient world. Its famous Hanging Gardens rose in terrace above terrace to the height of the city walls. These walls were forty-five miles in circumference and would include three cities as large as modern London. Babylon became a byword with the Israelitish prophets for luxury and debauchery. (See A. H. Sayce, *The Ancient Empires of the East* (1884).)

BABYLONISH CAPTIVITY. The seventy years during which the Jews were held captives in Babylon by Nebuchadnezzar. They were released by Cyrus in 538 B.C.

BACCHANALIA. The wild festivals of Bacchus (Dionysus, q.v.). At first they were celebrated only by women and in secret. In later times men were admitted. The senate, believing that political conspiracies were hatched at these festivals, prohibited them under severe penalties, in 186 B.C.

BACK-CHOIR, RETRO-CHOIR. The space in a church behind the high altar.

BACON, FRANCIS (BARON VERULAM, VISCOUNT ST. ALBAN) (1561–1626). One of the greatest European thinkers and man of letters. Called to the Bar in the reign of Queen Elizabeth, he became attorney-general under James I and finally lord chancellor. Owing to the fierce demand for a scapegoat by the parliament of 1621, he was falsely accused of corruption and deprived of the chancellorship, fined £40,000 and imprisoned, but his fine was remitted by the king, he was immediately released from the Tower and a full pardon given him. His wisdom, courage and broadness of mind were of signal value to King James in composing the heated religious controversies of the time. His *Advancement of Learning* and *Novum Organum*, by their insistence on the cardinal importance of induction, profoundly influenced the stream of human thought. His philosophy in its depth and range is equalled only by the profound philosophy of the Shakespeare plays. (See Spedding, *Life and Letters of Francis Bacon*; Charles Williams, *Bacon* (1933); and (for an identification of Bacon with Shakespeare) Richard Ince's romance, *England's High Chancellor* (1935).)

BACON, ROGER (1214–94). One of the most remarkable thinkers of his age. He studied at Oxford and Paris. His attacks on the ignorance and vices of the clergy and his daring speculations led to two terms of imprisonment. As a philosopher he ranks with Thomas Aquinas and Albertus Magnus. (See E. Charles, *Roger Bacon, Sa Vie, Ses Ouvrages*, etc. (1861); J. H. Bridges, *Roger Bacon* (1914).)

BACONTHORPE, JOHN (d. 1346). A Carmelite monk of Blakeney, near Walsingham. One of the most learned Averroists of his time.

BAIAME. See *Australia*.

BAIRAM. Two movable Moslem feasts.

BAKIS. Generic name for the inspired Greek prophets and oracles, from 8th to 6th C. B.C. (Gr. *Bakis* = speaker.)

BALAAM. Biblical magician and prophet, son of Beor. He was commanded by King Balak to curse the Israelites, but refused. The story tells how his ass spoke in man's voice. (See Numbers xxii., xxiii., xxiv. and xxxi.)

BALDUR. Son of Odin (Scand. myth.).

BALKIS. The queen of Sheba who visited Solomon (Koran).

BALM OF GILEAD. The resin of the balm-tree formerly esteemed as an antiseptic.

BALTHAZAR. One of the three Magi (q.v.) who visited the infant Jesus.

BAMBINO. A picture or figure of the infant Jesus in Catholic churches.

BAMPTON LECTURES. A series of lectures on the Christian faith instituted by John Bampton, at Oxford, in 1780. The endowment provides £120 for the lecturer. Famous Bampton lecturers have been: H. P. Liddon in 1866 ("The Divinity of Our Lord"); C. Gore in 1891 ("The Incarnation"); J. R. Illingworth in 1894 ("Personality, Human and Divine"); W. R. Inge in 1899 ("Christian Mysticism"). (For complete list, see *Oxford Historical Register.*)

BAN. See *demon.*

BANCROFT, RICHARD (1544–1610). Archbishop of Canterbury who succeeded Whitgift. A strict disciplinarian and "chief overseer" of the authorized version of the Bible. See *Bible, the English.*

BAND. Linen strips worn below the collar by some Protestant clergymen.

BANDHAS. Movements of the internal organs by means of voluntary muscles practised by yogis. See *Yoga.*

BANNS OF MARRIAGE. Public announcement of impending marriage. The Catholic Church still requires banns and they are customary in the Church of England but not required for a legal marriage.

BAPTISM. Ceremonial washing or sprinkling of a person on becoming member of a church. There is little doubt that Christian baptism derives from similar ceremonies in the older cults (e.g. Isis, Mithras, Dionysus, etc.) as Sir J. G. Frazer and other authorities have shown; initiation into the mystery religions of ancient Greece demanded a washing in water or (in the case of Mithras) the blood of the sacred bull. The Christian phraseology ("washed in the blood of the lamb") shows the intimate connection of the Christian with the older rites. The Christian fathers, in an uncultured age, were troubled by this similarity and ascribed it to the activity of devils. The study of comparative religion leads to a broader view since it appears unlikely that any one faith can justly claim a monopoly of the whole and ultimate truth.

§ 2. The doctrine of Christian baptism has varied in different ages. With St. Paul it assumed a mystical aspect (burial and resurrection with Christ). Tertullian attributed magical virtue to the baptismal water. Thomas Aquinas ascribed to baptism the washing away of original sin. The Church of England teaches that original sin is removed and a seed of eternal life implanted in the baptized which may grow or wither according to the use made of free will. It is extremely doubtful whether Christ himself instituted baptism, the only direct ascriptions (Mark xvi. 16 and Matt. xxviii. 18–20) being both suspect.

BAPTISM FOR THE DEAD. An early Christian custom by which a proxy was baptized in place of a candidate for baptism who had died.

BAPTISTERY. The church or portion of a church where baptism is administered.

BAPTIST, THE. See *John the Baptist.*

BAPTISTS. A Christian sect derived from the Anabaptists of Germany (q.v.). Little is known of the coming of Anabaptists to England, but there is reference in 1535 to "certain Dutchmen counted for Anabaptists" (Fox), of whom ten were put to death. These refugees appear to have been the fathers of the modern baptists, whose fundamental doctrines are: (1) that only those capable of a profession of faith should be baptized; (2) that true baptism consists in total immersion. A Baptist Church was founded by Roger Williams in America in 1638. English baptists number about 500,000.

BARBARA, SAINT. Virgin saint (probably mythical) of the Catholic and Eastern churches, regarded as a protectress against lightning and patron saint of armourers.

BARDO. Tibetan term for the intermediate state between death and re-birth. It signifies neither the heaven nor the hell state, but the Desire-World. (Tib. *Bar* = between; *do* = two.) (See Prof. W. Y. Evans-Wentz, *The Tibetan Book of the Dead.*)

BAR-COCHBA, BAR-KOKBA. A self-proclaimed messiah, acknowledged by many Jews, who led an unsuccessful revolt against Rome in Hadrian's time (A.D. 132–5).

BARHAM, RICHARD HARRIS (1788–1845). Author of the *Ingoldsby Legends* and better known by his nom de plume, Thomas Ingoldsby. The *Ingoldsby Legends,* contributed to *Bentley's Miscellany* in 1837, at once attained popularity. Barham's metrical power and facility of rhyming set him in the front rank of humorous verse-writers. He was appointed a minor canon of St. Paul's in 1821. (See *Life and Letters of Richard Barham,* by his son (1870).)

BAR-HEBRAEUS. A theologian of the Monophysite Church (3rd C.). Author of the *Storehouse of Secrets,* a critical commentary on the Scriptures.

BARING-GOULD, SABINE (1834–1924). An Anglican clergyman who wrote many popular novels (*Mehalah,* 1880) and works of history, theology and mythology.

BARLAAM AND JOSOPHAT. A Greek 7th-C. romance, very popular in medieval times, which presented a christianized version of the life of the Buddha.

BARNABAS. Name given by the apostles to Joseph, co-worker with Paul (Acts iv. 23).

BARNABAS, EPISTLE OF. A 2nd-C. epistle written by an Alexandrian and regarded as canonical by the Eastern Church.

BARNABITES. A Catholic order founded in Milan in 1530, taking its name from the monastery of St. Barnabas.

Barnardo, Thomas John (1845–1905). Irish doctor and philanthropist, founder of the Barnardo Homes for destitute children. Barnardo claimed to have proved that "if the children of the slums can be removed from their surroundings early enough, and can be kept sufficiently long under training, heredity counts for little, environment for almost everything."

Baronius, Caesar (1538–1607). Italian cardinal, author of a valuable ecclesiastical history.

barrel-vaulting. Vaulting with a semi-cylindrical roof (archit.).

Barrow, Isaac (1630–77). Learned divine and mathematician, appointed to the Greek Chair and also a professorship of mathematics at Cambridge. His sermons were greatly admired for their eloquence and forceful logic. His *Pope's Supremacy* is a controversial work of genius.

Barsom. The sacred ceremonial rods of the Parsee religion.

Bartholomew. One of the apostles of Jesus, usually identified with Nathanael (John i. 47).

Bartholomew's Day, Massacre of St. The massacre of Huguenots in France which began on 24 August 1572 (St. Bartholomew's Day) and continued for a week. It was instigated by Charles IX and his mother, Catherine de Medici. The slain were estimated at from 10,000 to 100,000.

Barton, Elizabeth (1506–34). A neurotic girl who became a nun and won notoriety as "The Maid of Kent." She went into trances lasting for days. For prophesying that if Henry VIII divorced Catherine he "should die a villain's death," she was condemned by a bill of attainder and executed at Tyburn.

Baruch. Secretary of the prophet Jeremiah. The apocryphal Book of Baruch was probably the work of several authors and dates from the 1st C.

Bashan. A rich pastoral region east of Jordan ruled over by King Og, of gigantic stature. He was slain by the Amorites (Num. xxi. 33; Ps. xxii. 12).

Basil the Great. A 4th-C. bishop of Caesarea, member of a distinguished family. His sister was the saintly Macrina; Gregory of Nyssa and Peter, bishop of Sebaste, were his brothers. Naucratius the jurist was his eldest brother. He was deeply influenced by Origen and after visiting the hermit saints of Syria and Arabia in pursuit of the ascetic ideal, founded a monastery in Pontus. Here his mother Emelia, his sister Macrina and other ladies, joined him in a life devoted to prayer and charitable works. (See Canon R. T. Smith, *Basil the Great* (Fathers for English Readers).)

Basilians. Followers of the Order of St. Basil which became the chief religious order of the Greek Church.

basilica. A large Roman hall with double colonnades and an apse at the end, used for judicial and commercial purposes. The Christian communities of the 3rd C., unwilling to copy the pagan temples, built their meeting-places in the form of the basilica which, with variations, has since remained the standard of ecclesiastical architecture.

BASILIDES (117–38). An Alexandrian gnostic teacher of Hadrian's reign. His doctrine appears to have inclined towards Persian dualism. See *Gnosticism*.

BATHSHEBA. Wife of Uriah the Hittite with whom David committed adultery (2 Sam. xxiii. 39).

BAUER, BRUNO (1809–82). German theologian of extremely critical tendency. He regarded Mark as the creator of the Gospel "myth" from whom all later writers borrowed. His work had value in stressing the need to consider the influence of environment on the growth of the Christian Scriptures.

BAUR, FERDINAND CHRISTIAN (1792–1860). German writer on theology and philosophy. His views were revolutionary and extreme, but he did good service in examining the rise of Christianity from the strictly historical point of view.

BAXTER, ANDREW. Scottish 18th-C. metaphysician. The property of matter he held to be inactivity. All movements in matter are caused by an immaterial force. Consciousness does not depend on the body but on the immaterial soul.

BAXTER, RICHARD (1615–91). English Puritan theologian. He was ejected from the Church of England and suffered continual persecution. Baxter's works were voluminous. His *Saints' Everlasting Rest*, a masterpiece of style, is the best known.

BEAD-HOUSE. An almshouse where the inmates were required to pray for the founder's soul.

BEADLE, BEDELL. Anglican ecclesiastical official who attends to the church, keeps order, etc.

BEAD-ROLL. A pre-Reformation term for the list of the dead to be prayed for.

BEADS. Little balls pierced to run on a string, to form a rosary.

BEADSMAN, BEDESMAN. One inhabiting a bead-house.

BEATIFICATION. A papal declaration that a deceased person is worthy of limited homage and the title of "Blessed." Frequently a step towards canonization (q.v.).

BEATIFIC VISION. A vision of God, or ecstasy. Many degrees of ecstasy, or extended consciousness, have been experienced by the mystics.

BEATITUDE. The blessings offered the faithful by Jesus (Matt. v. 3–11).

BEAUFORT, HENRY (1377–1447). English Cardinal and bishop of

Winchester; half-brother to King Henry IV. Under Henry V he became chancellor and took a leading part in government. (See L. B. Radford, *Henry Beaufort* (1908).)

Beck, Adams. Nom de plume of the American authoress, E. Barrington. Her novels, *The House of Fulfilment*, *The Way of Stars*, *The Garden of Vision*, etc., deal with Eastern philosophy and Buddhism in the light of modern scientific research and are of considerable value to students of these subjects. She died in 1933.

Becket, Thomas à (1118–70). Archbishop of Canterbury and chancellor under Henry II. He championed the ecclesiastical power against the king and the conflict resulted in the Constitutions of Clarendon (q.v.), to which Becket was forced to subscribe. He fled to France and with Pope Alexander III's assistance continued the struggle. Peace was made in 1170 and Becket returned to England but was murdered by an overzealous courtier. (See W. H. Hutton, *Thomas Becket*.)

Bede, The Venerable (673–735). A learned monk attached to the monastery at Jarrow. Author of the *Ecclesiastical History of the English Nation*, a valuable historical work of great beauty. The epithet "Venerable" is probably a courtesy title given to priests in his day.

bedell. See *beadle*.

bedesman. See *beadsman*.

Beecher, Henry Ward (1813–87). American Presbyterian minister and an active leader in the anti-slavery agitation. His powerful preaching had immense influence.

Beel. See *Baal*.

Befana. The good fairy of Italian children who fills their stockings on Twelfth Night. The name is a popular corruption of Epifania.

Beghards. Belgian lay brotherhoods similar to the Beguines. (13th C.)

Begtashi. An Ottoman religious Order founded by the Dervish Hadji Begtash. (14th C.)

Beguines. Lay sisterhoods in Germany and the Netherlands founded by Lambert de Bègue in 1187.

behaviourism. A method of psychology based on the observation of the responses of the organism in animals and man to stimuli. The aim of the behaviourists is to make psychology an objective science. Thus cerebration becomes a result of the movements of nerve-cells, and a crude materialism takes the place of metaphysics.

behemoth. The animal mentioned in Job (xl. 15), probably the hippopotamus.

Behesth. The Persian Elysium.

Bel. See *Baal*.

Bel and the Dragon. An apocryphal continuation of the

Book of Daniel in which Daniel (identified with Cyrus) is cast into the lions' den for destroying a sacred dragon.

BELFRY. The part of a steeple or tower where bells are hung. Cf. campanile (q.v.).

BELIAL. A wicked being identified with Antichrist and Satan in the N.T. (2 Cor. vi. 15). In Milton, one of the fallen angels.

BELL. There is no trustworthy evidence of the use of bells before the Christian era. The instruments which called the Romans to public baths and functions were probably metal plates, like the Egyptian timbrels (*sistrum*), struck together. Paulus, bishop of Nola, is reputed to have used bells in Campania (A.D. 400) ; and Pope Sabinianus (A.D. 604) is said to have instituted church bells. Bede (7th C.) mentions a bell brought from Italy for his abbey at Wearmouth. The passing-bell is a bell tolled immediately after a person's death, inviting prayers for the departing soul.

BELLAMY, EDWARD (1850–98). American author, journalist and social reformer. In 1888 he attracted public attention with his romance, *Looking Backward*, in which he described a Utopia where most of life's hardships and difficulties had been surmounted. His ideal state was run on co-operative lines, free from the stress and strain of party politics. As a thoughtful contribution to social science the book is of permanent value. He followed it by a sequel, *Equality* (1897).

BELLARMINE (BELLARMINO), ROBERTO FRANCESCO ROMOLO (1542–1620). Italian cardinal, archbishop of Capua and professor of theology at Louvain and Rome. He was a friend of Galileo and took a prominent part in the examination of Galileo's writings by the Sacred Office. While not proscribing Galileo's discoveries, Bellarmine urged that they should be presented as hypothetical until scientifically proved.

BELLOC, HILAIRE (b. 1870). Publicist and Catholic writer. Author of *The Path to Rome*, and much history and biography written from the Catholic standpoint.

BELPHEGOR. A licentious Moabitish deity.

BELSHAZZAR. Son of Nabonidos and not (as was supposed until the decipherings of the cuneiform inscriptions) the son of Nebuchadnezzar. The legends of Belshazzar's Feast have been shown to be apocryphal.

BELTANE. A May-day Celtic festival of bonfires believed to be derived from Druid sun-worship.

BEMA. The sanctuary in ancient churches. (Gr. *bema* = a step.)

BEMBO, PIETRO (1470–1547). Italian scholar and cardinal, secretary to Pope Leo X and a distinguished Italian stylist.

BENARES. One of the most ancient cities of the world venerated by the Hindus. Pilgrims gather there to bathe in the sacred Ganges, the banks of which are lined with shrines and temples. (See E. B. Havell, *Benares* (1906).)

BENCH-TABLE. A stone seat running round the walls and piers of churches.

BENEDICITE. Medieval form of blessing (*benedici te* = bless you).

BENEDICT OF NURSIA, SAINT (480–544). Founder of the Benedictine Order of Monks. Educated in Rome, he fled as a young man to the mountains of the Abruzzi. For three years he lived in a cave near Subiaco, spending the time in prayer and contemplation. The monks of a neighbouring monastery prevailed on him to become their abbot but soon found his ascetic discipline too hard for them. He returned to his cave at Subiaco and disciples flocked to him. A little later he journeyed south and established the monastery on Monte Cassino, which remained for centuries the chief religious centre for the west. The Benedictine rule was strict but not harsh. Time was divided between reading, study and devotion and work in the fields. The Benedictine Order was introduced into England in 596. (See Montalembert, *Monks of the West*; Hodgkin, *Italy and Her Invaders*.)

BENEDICTION. A brief afternoon Catholic service concluding with the priest giving the benediction of the sacrament. See *breviary*.

BENEFICE. The holding of an ecclesiastical office, with or without the cure of souls. In medieval times benefices were frequently held in plurality by laymen. Thus Sir Philip Sidney was inducted to a Welsh benefice in boyhood and Queen Elizabeth bestowed benefices on Francis Bacon. By the English Pluralities Act of 1838, no person was allowed to hold more than two benefices; other Acts followed to prevent prevailing abuses. The word derives from *beneficium*, the land granted to Roman soldiers on retirement from military service.

BENEFIT OF CLERGY. The privilege the English clergy enjoyed in the Middle Ages of being tried in the ecclesiastical instead of the secular courts. Later it was extended to all who could read. In England it was abolished in 1827 and in U.S.A. in 1790.

BENJAMIN. The youngest and favourite son of Jacob (Gen. xxxv. 18).

BENSON, EDWARD WHITE (1829–96). Appointed archbishop of Canterbury in 1883. A distinguished scholar of devout life and great social gifts. His chief literary work was his *Cyprian* (1897). He was the father of three distinguished writers, Arthur Christopher Benson, Edward Frederick Benson and Robert Hugh Benson. (See A. C. Benson, *Life of Archbishop Benson* (1899).)

BENTHAM, JEREMY (1748–1832). The founder of the Utilitarian philosophy ("the greatest happiness of the greatest number"). His writings had a deep and abiding influence on English religious and political thought.

BENTLEY, RICHARD (1662–1742). Regius Professor of Divinity and Master of Trinity, Cambridge. A scholar of immense learning but irascible temper, Bentley incurred the hostility of Alexander Pope and was given a little corner in the *Dunciad*. He was the first of England's great classical scholars in the modern sense and has been styled "the founder of historical philology" (Bunsen). (See R. C. Jebb, *Bentley* (1882).)

BERENGAR OF TOURS (1010–88). Scholar noted for his controversy with the Church on Transubstantiation, a doctrine he refused to accept.

BERENICE (PHERENICE). The name of five Egyptian and two Jewish princesses. The best remembered being Berenice, daughter of Magas, king of Cyrene and wife of Ptolemy III (Euergetes). When her husband went to war with Syria, she gave her hair as an offering to Venus for his safe return, placing it in the temple of Zephyrium. The hair was lost and Conon of Samos, a courtly astronomer, saved the situation by saying that it had been carried to heaven and placed among the stars as Coma Berenices. No further questions were asked. See Catullus: poem lxvi (" The Lock of Berenice ").

BERKELEY, GEORGE (1685–1753). Irish bishop of Cloyne and one of Britain's greatest philosophers. His views in physics and metaphysics caused him to relinquish scholasticism. The new principle he introduced was based on the proposition that no existence is conceivable which is not either conscious spirit or the ideas of which such spirit is conscious. No object exists apart from mind. His ability, courtesy and refreshing honesty rendered him a popular figure in London society. Such was the fascination of his eloquence that he persuaded the English parliament to promise him £20,000 to found a college in Bermuda—a promise which was never ratified. (See *Berkeley's Works*, edited by A. C. Fraser (1871); A. C. Fraser, *Berkeley* (1881).)

BERNARD OF CLAIRVAUX, SAINT (1090–1153). Medieval Cistercian monk who became abbot of Clairvaux in 1115. He entered into controversy with Abélard (q.v.), and although no match for him intellectually, the personal influence due to his saintly life and character more than made up for the handicap. (See J. C. Morison, *Life and Times of St. Bernard* (1884).)

BESANT, ANNIE (1847–1933). President of the Theosophical Society. She was educated in England, Germany and France; worked as a radical under Bradlaugh; and took an active part in trade unionism. Joined the Theosophical Society in 1889 and was elected president in 1907. Author of many books on eastern wisdom. See *Theosophy*.

BETHANY. The village near Jerusalem where Lazarus lived with his sisters (John xi.).

BETHEL. (1) The place, 11 miles north of Jerusalem, where Jacob slept and had a vision (Gen. xxviii.). (2) A nonconformist chapel. From Heb. *beth-el*, house of God.

BETHESDA (BETHSAIDA). A pool near Jerusalem where miraculous cures were reported (John v. 2).

BETHLEHEM. A small town, 5 miles south of Jerusalem, which has become one of the sacred places of the world owing to the traditional birth of Jesus Christ in a manger there. For a good account of present-day Palestine, see H. V. Morton, *In His Steps* (1934).

BETHLEHEMITES. (1) A Cambridge community of friars (13th C.). (2) An order of knights formed to resist the Turks (15th C.). (3) A Central American order and nursing community (17th C.) which became extinct about 1850.

BETHSAIDA. See *Bethesda*.

BEZA, THÉODORE (1519–1605). French Calvinistic theologian who became administrative successor to Calvin in 1564. Author of many works in defence of Calvin. (See H. M. Baird, *Théodore Beza* (1899).)

BHAGAVAD GITA ("THE LORD'S SONG"). Name of a poem in the 6th book of the Mahabharata (q.v.). It teaches that action performed with detachment (in disregard of its fruits) is good because it obliterates Karma (q.v.) (2nd C. B.C.). For a good verse translation, see Sir Edwin Arnold, *The Song Celestial*.

BHAKTI. See *Yoga*.

BHAVANI. Wife of Shiva (q.v.).

BIBLE. The sacred writings on which the Christian Religion is based. The Bible consists of the Old Testament and the New Testament. The O.T. is a selection of Hebrew literature taken from various sources. These writings which, in common with the N.T. scriptures, the Christian churches regard as inspired, were from very early times divided into three sections, the Law, the Prophets and the other books. Opinions differ as to the exact date when the O.T. canon was closed. The majority of scholars incline to the view that some of the Psalms and the Book of Daniel belong to the two centuries before Christ.

§ 2. The N.T. consists of a selection of writings regarded by the Catholic and other churches as of apostolic origin. Twenty-seven Greek compositions compose the canon: the Gospels of Matthew, Mark, Luke and John; The Acts of the Apostles; twenty-one epistles attributed to apostles, and the Revelation attributed to St. John. The N.T. canon was established about A.D. 350, after the Council of Nicea. The factors which led to the acceptance into the canon or rejection of a book are hard to estimate, since the critical judgment of the modern historian was not then in vogue; faith and a feeling of the value of the book's content appear to have guided the decision. The rejected (apocryphal) books of the N.T. show, for the most part, a crude and even puerile insistence upon miracles.

§ 3. With the coming of the 19th C., historical method had a profound influence on Bible study. The Higher Criticism (q.v.)—fiercely resented at first—did no harm to the Christian devotion to the Bible, but quite the reverse. The Christian conception of God, prophecy and inspiration passed to higher levels. The first chapter of Genesis gained enormously in value as it came to be regarded as spiritually and not literally true. The higher critics enabled the divine element in the Bible to shine forth more clearly than ever before. See also *Versions of the Bible.* (See A. S. Peak, *A Guide to Biblical Study* (1897); Gilbert T. Sadler, *A Short Introduction to the Bible* (1911); J. H. Gardiner, *The Bible as English Literature* (1906).)

Bible, The Breeches. The edition of Wittingham, Gilly and Sampson, of 1579, in which Genesis iii. 7 was rendered: "The eyes of them bothe were opened . . . and they sewed figge-tree leaves together and made themselves breeches." (See R. Lovett, *The Printed English Bible* (1894).)

Bible, The English. The chief English versions of the Bible are:

(1) A manuscript paraphrase of the complete Bible, dated 1290, in the Bodleian, Oxford.

(2) Versions from the Vulgate by Wicliffe (1356–84).

(3) Tyndale's version of the N.T. (1525).

(4) Miles Coverdale's version of the whole Bible (1535).

(5) King James's Bible (the Authorized Version), published 1611.

(6) The Revised Version, published in 1881.

(See B. F. Westcott, *A General View of the History of the English Bible* (1905); Samuel McComb, *The Making of the English Bible* (1910); H. W. Hoare, *Our English Bible* (1911).)

Bible, The Vinegar. Printed at the Clarendon Press in 1717, in which the heading to Luke xx. is given as "The Parable of the Vinegar" instead of Vineyard.

Bible, The Wicked. Printed by Barker and Lucas in 1632 in which "not" was omitted from the seventh Commandment, making it, "Thou shalt commit adultery."

Bible Christians. A sect of Methodists founded by William O'Brien in Devonshire in 1815. The Brienite Movement spread rapidly in England, U.S.A. and the British Empire. It was reabsorbed into the United Methodist Church in 1907.

Bible Societies. Societies for the dissemination of the Scriptures. The chief are:

(1) Society for Promoting Christian Knowledge, 1698.

(2) Society for Propagating the Gospel in Foreign Parts, 1701.

(3) Naval and Military Bible Society, 1780.

(4) Sunday School Society, 1785.

(5) British and Foreign Bible Society, 1804.

BIBLIA PAUPERUM. 15th-C. books of engravings of Scripture subjects to serve as bibles for such as could not read.

BIDDING - PRAYER. The prayer offered before the sermon in certain cathedrals and university churches, for the souls of benefactors. (A.S. *biddan* = to pray.)

BIG-ENDIANS. A religious party in Swift's Lilliput. The Big-endians are the Catholics, the Little-endians the Protestants. (A satire at the expense of orthodoxy; conscience compels the Big-endians to break their eggs at the big end: they are ready to murder the Little-endians for breaking them any other way.)

BIKKU, BIKSHU. (1) Lowest order of disciples in early Buddhism. (2) A Hindu ascetic who has renounced the worldly life.

BINATION. Celebration of Mass by the same priest twice in one day. Only permitted under exceptional circumstances. (Cath.)

BIRETTA. Catholic clergy's small cap; black for priests, purple for bishops, red for cardinals.

BISHOP. In Christian churches (East and West) a clergyman appointed to the spiritual direction of a diocese, under an archbishop, and controlling priests and deacons. In the N.T. priest and presbyter (Gr. *presbyteros*, comp. of *presbys* = old) are used interchangeably for officers administering the affairs of the congregation. By the 2nd C. the bishop had become a higher officer. (See S. G. Green, *A Handbook of Church History* (1904).)

BISHOP IN PARTIBUS INFIDELIUM. Bishops who were merely titular, without regular jurisdiction, their duty being to assist another bishop or to act as the Pope's delegate.

BISMILLAH ("IN THE NAME OF ALLAH"). Arabic formula repeated before a ceremonial act; often used as a mere exclamation.

BLACK FRIARS. See *Dominicans*.

BLACK MAGIC. The art of producing startling phenomena of a supernatural character by evil means or for evil purposes. For an interesting account of 12th-C. black magic in Tibet, see Prof. W. Y. Evans-Wentz, *Milarepa* (chap. 3).

BLACK RUBRIC. The injunction to kneel which appears at the end of the Anglican service of Holy Communion. It was formerly printed in big black type.

BLAIR, HUGH. 18th-C. Scottish divine, author of the famous sermons so popular that they earned him a pension of £200 a year. (Blair's sermons have been described by a later critic as "a bucket of warm water.")

BLAKE, WILLIAM (1757–1827). Poet, painter and seer. His life and work were inspired by visions and illuminations. Of great insight, Blake was unbalanced and brooded too much on the O.T. prophets.

BLASPHEMY. Speaking profanely or insultingly of God. An offence formerly severely punished in Christian and Moslem countries.

BLAVATSKY, MADAME. See *Theosophy.*

BOANERGES ("SONS OF THUNDER"). The name given by Christ in rebuke to James and John (Mark iii. 17).

BOAZ. The rich and respectable husband of Ruth (Ruth ii. 1).

BODHI. Wisdom in the Buddhist system. The Bodhic Path is the Path of Wisdom.

BODHISATTVA. A Buddhist term applied to one who having progressed far on the path leading to Buddahood, is destined to become a Buddha (" Enlightened One ").

BODY AND SOUL. The body is regarded by Christianity as the house of the soul. The contradistinction between body and soul which appears vividly in Plato has entered Christianity from that source. (See H. W. Robinson, *The Christian Doctrine of Man* (1913).)

BOEHME, JAKOB (1575–1624). A German mystic and visionary of peasant origin, whose works have exerted strong influence on later thinkers (Hegel, Schelling, etc.). (See Evelyn Underhill, *Mysticism* (1911).)

BOETHIUS (BOETIUS) (A.D. 480–524). Philosopher and statesman under Theodoric, put to death for his Christian orthodoxy. Famous for his *De Consolatione Philosophiae,* " a golden volume, not unworthy of the leisure of Plato or Tully " (Gibbon). (See T. Hodgkin, *Italy and Her Invaders,* vol. iii (1896) ; H. F. Stewart, *Boethius* (1891).)

BOHEMIAN BRETHREN. A reforming sect living strictly by the gospel (15th C.). It was finally absorbed by the Moravian Brethren (q.v.).

BOLLANDISTS. John Bolland, a Jesuit, in 1643 commenced the *Acta Sanctorum* or *Lives of the Saints.* His helpers (" the Bollandists ") continued the work which was interrupted in 1794 but resumed in 1845 and still continues.

BOLSENA. An Italian town near Orvieto, where the famous miracle is said to have taken place in 1263. (A priest, sceptical of transubstantiation, was convinced by seeing drops of blood on the host he was consecrating.)

BONAR, HORATIUS. 19th-C. Scottish hymn-writer and minister of the Free Church in Edinburgh. Author of " I heard the voice of Jesus say."

BONAVENTURA, SAINT (1221–74). A Catholic theologian of neo-Platonic sympathies. He was opposed to Roger Bacon (q.v.), whom he prevented from lecturing at Oxford. Bacon stressed the intellectual side of theology; Bonaventura the living power of the affections.

BONIFACE, SAINT (680–754). A Saxon scholar and preacher who went as a missionary to Germany. He attracted the attention of Charles Martel and became bishop of Mainz in 732. He was a staunch traditionist, severely reprimanding an Irish monk for affirming the newfangled doctrine of the Antipodes.

BOOTH, WILLIAM (1829–1911). Founder of the Salvation Army (q.v.).

BORA. See *Australia.*

BOSSUET, JACQUES BÉNIGNE (1627–1704). French Catholic divine of outstanding oratorical ability. His cherished dream was to bring back the Huguenots to the Catholic Church. It remained a cherished dream. (See Mrs. Sidney Lear, *Bossuet* (1874); Sir J. Fitz-J. Stephen, *Horae Sabbaticae*, vol. ii (1892).)

BO-TREE. The *ficus religiosa* of India, held sacred by Buddhists because Buddha is reputed to have attained enlightenment while meditating under it.

BOUGH, THE GOLDEN. See *Frazer, Sir James G.*

BOUPHONIA. The great spring festival in ancient Greece at which a sacred bull was sacrificed and eaten. The bull's hide was afterwards stuffed with straw to signify resurrection. (See Gilbert Murray, *Four Stages of Greek Religion* (1912).)

BOWDLER, THOMAS (1754–1825). The gentleman who published The Family Shakespeare (10 vols.) in 1818 in which expressions were omitted "which cannot with propriety be read aloud in a family."

BOWING. See *genuflexion.*

BOY BISHOP. Until the reign of Henry VIII the Christmas custom prevailed of appointing a boy as mock bishop for three weeks. He was usually selected from the cathedral choir on St. Nicholas's Day, 6 December. (See Gasquet, *Parish Life in Medieval England* (1906).)

BRAGI. Son of Odin and Frigga, corresponding to Apollo in Roman mythology (Norse myth.).

BRAHMA. Hindu Creator constituting with Vishnu and Shiva the divine triad.

BRAHMAN (BRAHMIN). A member of the highest or priestly Hindu caste.

BRAHMANAS. Prose commentaries on the Vedic texts of India.

BRAHMANISM. The religious system elaborated by the Hindu Brahmins, founded on pantheistic doctrine. According to Brahmanism the ideal life is divided into four periods: (1) The student spends several years with a teacher living a chaste life and memorizing sacred texts. (2) He returns home, marries and becomes a householder. (3) When he has a grown son he retires, alone or with his wife, to the forest and spends the time in meditation. (4) He becomes a solitary mendicant (Sannyasi) and subsists entirely on alms. This is the ideal, but a man might continue permanently in any of the four periods. (See M. Monier-Williams, *Brahmanism and Hinduism* (1891); J. C. Oman, *The Brahmans, Theists and Moslems of India* (1907).)

BRAHMA SAMAJ. An eclectic Indian theistic system founded by Ram Mohan Roy in 1830 (and reformed by Keshub Chunder Sen—1838–84) with the object of blending the best in Hindu thought with the best in other religions. Some important tenets of the Brahma creed are as follows:

(1) The book of nature and intuition supplies the basis of religious faith.

(2) Although the Brahmas do not consider any book written by man the basis of their religion, yet they do accept with respect and pleasure any religious *truth* contained in any book.

(3) The Brahmas believe that the religious condition of man is progressive.

(4) They believe that the fundamental doctrines of their religion are also the basis of every true religion.

(5) They avow that love towards God and the performance of the works He loves, constitute His worship.

(6) They recognize the necessity for public worship, but do not believe that communion with the Father depends upon meeting in any fixed place at any fixed time. (See John Robson, *Hinduism and Christianity*.)

BRASS, SEPULCHRAL. A brass monumental plate imposed on stone tombs in ancient churches.

BREIDABLIK. The Milky Way, regarded as the palace of Baldur in Norse mythology.

BREVIARY. A service book used in Greek and Catholic churches, containing the seven canonical services: (1) matins or lauds at 3 a.m. (2) prime at 6 a.m. (3) tierce at 9. (4) sexte at 12. (5) nones at 2. (6) vespers at 4. (7) compline at 7. The hours of services have always varied slightly according to circumstances.

BRIDEWELL. A medieval hospital built over St. Bride's Well in Bridge Street, London.

BRIDGEWATER TREATISES. A series of essays "On the power, wisdom and goodness of God as manifested in creation," written and published under the bequest of £8,000 left for the purpose by the 8th Earl of Bridgewater in 1829.

BRIGIT, SAINT. A culture goddess of the Irish Celts accepted as a saint under Christianity.

BROACH. A church spire without parapets (archit.).

BROAD CHURCH. A party in the Church of England that insists on greater freedom of thought. Kingsley and Maurice were Broad Churchmen.

BROOKE, FULKE GREVILLE, LORD (1554–1628). Poet, statesman and friend of Sir Philip Sidney. His poems on political and religious subjects show extraordinary depth and insight. His *Treatise of Religion* is a heart-cry for sincerity where lip-service and conventional morality usually prevail.

BROOKE, RUPERT (1887–1915). Poet, author of *Grantchester* and some of the finest and most inspired sonnets written during the Great War.

BROOKE, STOPFORD AUGUSTUS (1832–1916). Writer and Unitarian minister. Author of a useful *History of English Literature* (1894).

BROTHERS OF THE COMMON LIFE. A community founded by Gerard Groot at Deventer (c. 1380). They passed their time in study and meditation. Thomas à Kempis belonged to this community.

BROWNE, ROBERT (1550–1633). An Anglican clergyman who seceded from the Church, being unable to accept episcopacy. His followers (Brownists) developed later into Independents and Congregationalists (q.v.).

BRUNO, GIORDANO (1548–1600). One of the profoundest of European thinkers, Bruno was born at Nola, near Naples, in 1548; was educated in the Dominican monastery at Naples; lectured at Padua, Geneva, Lyons, Toulouse, Paris, Oxford and London; was burnt alive as a heretic in the Campo dei Fiori at Rome on 17 February 1600, where, in June 1889, amends were made by the erection of a statue to his memory. (See J. L. McIntyre, *Giordano Bruno* (1903).)

BUCER, MARTIN (1491–1551). German adherent of Luther. Persecution drove him to England, where he was given a chair in divinity at Cambridge.

BUCHANITES. Scottish 18th-C. fanatical sect founded by Lucky Buchan.

BUCHMANISM. See *Group Movement, The.*

BUCKE, DR. R. M. Author of *Cosmic Consciousness* (1901: Philadelphia), a book of outstanding importance for students of psychology and religious experience. (See William James, *Varieties of Religious Experience.*)

BUCKLE, HENRY THOMAS (1821–62). Historical writer and sociologist. His great work, the *History of Civilization in England*, gave offence because of the view maintained that religion, literature and government are the products and not the causes of civilization. (See A. W. Huth, *Life of Buckle* (1880).)

BUDDHA and BUDDHISM. Buddhism was evolved by Siddhattha Gotama, known to the world as Buddha, "The Enlightened." Gotama was born about 560 B.C. at Kapila, near Benares. According to tradition he was the son of a chief of the Sakiya clan who abandoned home-life when 29, and became a religious mendicant. For six years he consorted with Brahmins and practised asceticism and meditation. Suddenly while meditating under the famous Bo-tree (tree of wisdom), supreme illumination came to him. For the rest of his days he lived a retired life but pupils flocked to him.

§ 2. The essence of Buddha's teaching is contained in his statement of the Middle Path: avoidance of the two extremes of self-gratification and self-mortification and the Four Noble Truths: (1) All individual existence is misery. (2) The cause of this misery is attachment to sense perceptions. (3) The need to become unattached and passionless. (4) The need to follow the Eight-fold path, consisting in: Right Views; Right Aspirations; Right Speech; Right Conduct; Right Mode of Livelihood; Right Effort; Right Mindfulness; Right Contemplation. Buddha denied the existence of a permanent soul in man's five aggregates (*skandhas*), matter, feelings, sense-perceptions, predispositions and consciousness. Any permanent principle must be outside these, not subject to the changes which result from cause and effect (*Karma*). There is therefore a permanent something—"a non-born, a non-becoming, a non-created, a non-caused," which cannot be reached by speculation but may be attained by the saint as the result of his way of life. Buddha resolutely refused to answer the questions of merely intellectual inquirers. An adept at dialectic, he suited his discourse to his hearers' capacity. Deliverance from ignorance, sorrow and suffering was the only problem of importance and this could be attained by anyone who would follow the Path. His teaching was intensely practical and not, like Brahmanism and Christianity, tending towards theological definition and metaphysical speculation. Buddhism predominated in India till about the 10th C. A.D. (See Rhys Davids, *Buddhism* (1903); *Buddhist India* (1903); K. J. Saunders, *Gotama Buddha* (1920); Adams Beck, *The Splendour of Asia* (a popular but excellent account of Gotama).)

BUDDHISM, TANTRIC. See *Lamaism*.

BUDDHIST CANON. See *Canon, Buddhist*.

BULL AND BRIEF, PAPAL. A papal pronouncement dealing with problems of doctrine or discipline. From Latin *bulla* = seal. A papal brief is a document dealing with less important matters.

BULL-ROARER. The native Australian *turndun*, the *rhombos* of the Greek mysteries. It consists of a piece of wood attached to a string, which, when swung rapidly, produces a loud whirring sound.

BUNYAN, JOHN (1628–88). English Puritan who served with the Cromwellian forces. His *Pilgrim's Progress* is regarded as the finest Christian allegory.

BURMA, RELIGIONS OF. About 80% of the Burmese are Hinayana (q.v.) Buddhists; 6% Animists; 3% Hindus; 3½% Moslems; 2% Christians; and there are small numbers of Zoroastrians, Sikhs, Jains, Confucians and Jews. The Christian population consists mainly of Baptists and Catholics. For a sympathetic account of the Burmese, see Fielding Hall, *The Soul of a People* (1906); J. F. Smith, *A Century of Baptist Missions in Burma* (1913).

BURNET, GILBERT (1643–1715). Bishop of Salisbury under William and Mary. Chiefly remembered for his excellent *History of My Own Times.*

BUSHIDO. The knightly code of the Japanese nobility (*samurai*) from the 13th to the 19th C. The great ideals of Bushido were moral and physical courage.

BUSIRIS. A mythical Egyptian king whom strangers never visited twice since he sacrificed all who visited his realm to the gods.

BUTLER, JOSEPH (1692–1752). Anglican bishop and theologian. His *Analogy of Religion* is a masterpiece of forceful reasoning. (See Leslie Stephen, *History of English Thought in the 18th C.*)

BUTLER, SAMUEL (1612–80). Satirist, famous for his *Hudibras* (1663). He served as page to various Puritan justices, who served in their turn as subjects for satire. Hudibras made fun of the Puritans with unsurpassed wit and liveliness.

BUTLER, SAMUEL (1825–1902). Grandson of Samuel Butler, head master of Shrewsbury. He wrote *Erewhon* (1872) and *Erewhon Revisited* (1901), both excellent satires, but his finest work was *The Way of all Flesh,* a caustic satirical picture of English 19th-C. religious life, especially in the vicarages of the period.

C

CABALA, CABBALA. See *Kabbala.*

CÆDMON (d. A.D. 680). English monk of Whitby Abbey who wrote biblical narrative poems of much force and beauty.

CALIF. See *Khalif.*

CALIXTINES. German Hussite sect. (15th C.)

CALVARY. The place where Jesus was crucified. Also called Golgotha (Heb.).

CALVIN and **CALVINISM.** John Calvin was born at Noyon, Picardy, in 1509. The reformed doctrines he adopted compelled him to retire to Basle and finally to Geneva, where he died in 1564. His uncompromising zeal led to the burning of Servetus for heresy in 1553. The Calvinists finally separated from the Lutherans on a disagreement regarding the doctrine of the eucharist. Calvin's views were extreme and fanatical but served to emphasize certain truths necessary for that age. (See Williston Walker, *John Calvin* (1906); L. Penning, *Life* *and Times of John Calvin* (trans. by B. S. Berrington (1912).)

CAMALDULIANS or **CAMALDOLESE.** An order of reforming monks instituted in the 11th C. They wear a white robe and obey a rule of silence, prayer and manual labour.

CAMBRIDGE PLATONISTS. A group of 17th-C. Cambridge thinkers who sought to reconcile reason and revelation, introducing Platonism into their system. They included Richard Cumberland, Henry More and Ralph Cudworth. (See J. B. Mullinger, *Platonists and Latitudinarians*, in Cambridge Hist. of Engl. Lit. (vol. viii).)

CAMISARDS. Name given to the Huguenots who rebelled against Louis XIV, asserting the right to full religious liberty. They wore a camise (peasant's smock) over their armour.

CAMPANILE. Bell tower, usually separate from the church.

CAMPANOLOGY. The science of bells and bell-ringing.

CANAAN. The biblical name for Syria.

CANDLEMAS. The Church festival (2 Feb.) to commemorate the Purification of the Virgin and Presentation of the Infant Jesus in the Temple. In the Catholic Church the altar candles are blessed on that day.

CANDLESTICK, GOLDEN. A six-branched candlestick of gold in the Jewish tabernacle (Ex. xxv. 31).

CANON. (1) A clergyman living within the precincts of a cathedral or in a clergy house and obeying the canons (rules) of the church. A minor canon has cathedral duties, but is not a member of the chapter. An honorary canon is a non-residentiary member of the chapter. (2) That portion of the Mass between the Preface and the Paternoster. (3) A musical composition on a single theme. (4) The books of scripture accepted by the Christian Church.

CANON, BUDDHIST. The Mahayana (q.v.) form of Buddhism has no canon of scriptures. The Hinayana (q.v.) form has a scripture canon consisting of the Tripitaka or Three Baskets—the Basket of Discipline, the Basket of Sermons and the Basket of Higher Religion.

CANONESS. The lady governing a female religious community.

CANON LAW. See *Law, Canon.*

CANONICAL HOURS. See *Breviary.*

CANONIST. One skilled in canon law.

CANONIZATION. The process in the Greek and Roman churches by which suitable persons (deceased) are made saints. The first papal canonization was that of St. Ulric (993).

CANOPY. The baldachin or covering borne in processions over the priest who carries the host (Cath.).

CANTERBURY, ARCHBISHOPS OF. The following is a complete

list of the archbishops of Canterbury:

		A.D.
1.	St. Augustine	597
2.	St. Laurentius	604
3.	St. Mellitus	619
4.	St. Justus	624
5.	St. Honorius	627
6.	St. Deusdedit	655
7.	St. Theodore	668
8.	Berchtwald	693
9.	St. Tatwine	731
10.	Nothelm	735
11.	Cuthberth	741
12.	St. Breogwine	759
13.	Jaenberht	766
14.	Æthelhard	793
15.	Wulfred	805
16.	Feologild	832
17.	Ceolnoth	833
18.	Æthelred	870
19.	Plegmund	890
20.	Athelm	914
21.	Wulfhelm	923
22.	St. Odo	942
23.	St. Dunstan	960
24.	Ethelgar	988
25.	Sigeric	990
26.	Ælfric	995
27.	Ælfeah	1005
28.	Lyfing	1013
29.	Æthelnoth	1020
30.	Eadsige	1038
31.	Robert	1051
32.	Stigand (deprived 1070)	1052
33.	Lanfranc	1070
34.	St. Anselm	1093
35.	Ralph d'Escures	1114
36.	William de Corbeuil	1123
37.	Theobald	1139
38.	St. Thomas à Becket	1162
39.	Richard	1174
40.	Baldwin	1185
41.	Hubert Walter	1193
42.	Stephen Langton	1207
43.	Richard Grant	1229
44.	St. Edmund (Rich)	1234
45.	Boniface	1245
46.	Robert Kilwardby	1273
47.	John Peckham	1279
48.	Robert Winchelsey	1294
49.	Walter Reynolds	1313
50.	Simon Mepeham	1328
51.	John Stratford	1333
52.	Thomas Bradwardine	1349
53.	Simon Islip	1349
54.	Simon Langham	1366
55.	William Whittlesey	1368
56.	Simon Sudbury	1375
57.	William Courtenay	1381
58.	Thomas Arundel	1397
59.	Roger Walden	1398
	(Thomas Arundel restored)	1399
60	Henry Chicheley	1414
61.	John Stafford	1443
62.	John Kemp	1452
63.	Thomas Bourchier	1454
64.	John Morton	1486
65.	Henry Dean	1501
66.	William Warham	1503
67.	Thomas Cranmer	1533
68.	Reginald Pole	1556
69.	Matthew Parker	1559
70.	Edmund Grindal	1576
71.	John Whitgift	1583
72.	Richard Bancroft	1604
73.	George Abbott	1611
74.	William Laud (Beheaded, 1645; fifteen years' vacancy.)	1633
75.	William Juxon	1660
76.	Gilbert Sheldon	1663
77.	William Sancroft (deprived 1690)	1678
78.	John Tillotson	1691
79.	Thomas Tenison	1695
80.	William Wake	1716
81.	John Potter	1737
82.	Thomas Herring	1747
83.	Matthew Hutton	1757
84.	Thomas Secker	1758
85.	Frederick Cornwallis	1768
86.	John Moore	1783
87.	John Manners Sutton	1805
88.	William Howley	1828
89.	John Bird Sumner	1848
90.	Charles Thomas Longley	1862
91.	Archibald Campbell Tait	1868
92.	Edward White Benson	1883
93.	Frederick Temple	1897
94.	Randall Thomas Davidson (resigned 1928)	1903
95.	Cosmo Gordon Lang	1928

CANTICLE. (1) A scriptural sacred song (non-metrical) chanted in churches. (2) The canonical Song of Solomon (q.v.).

CANTILENA (also **CANTUS FIRMUS**). (1) A melody of ancient hymns and chants for church use. (2) Plainsong (q.v.).

CANTO. The leading (usually treble) melody.

CANTOR. The precentor or leader of church singing.

CANTORIS. Belonging to the cantor or precentor (gen. of L. *cantor*).

CAPA. See *cope.*

CAPITAL. The top part of a column (archit.).

CAPITAL PUNISHMENT. Death legally inflicted as a penalty for crime. The tendency to-day is for the death penalty to be further restricted. The growth of humanism is illustrated by the following facts:

(1) The Jews stoned their criminals (Lev. xx. 2).

(2) Draco's code (594 B.C.) punished every offence with death.

(3) Maurice, a pirate, was the first Englishman to be hanged, drawn and quartered (A.D. 1241).

(4) Sir Robert Peel's Acts (1824–9) abolished the death penalty in a number of cases.

(5) By the Criminal Law Consolidation Acts (1861) death was confined to treason and wilful murder.

(6) In 1865 the Commission on Capital Punishment issued their report, recommending penal servitude in place of death in certain cases.

Proposals to abolish the death penalty in England have been many times introduced into parliament but have always been negatived. (See Oldfield, *The Penalty of Death* (1901); Andrews, *Old Time Punishments* (1901).)

CAPITULARY. Belonging to a cathedral chapter. Charlemagne's laws are called capitularies (L. *capitula* = chapters).

CAPUCHINS. A Franciscan order of friars who wear pointed hoods (*capuche*). They were established in 1525 and seek to follow literally the life of St. Francis.

CAPUT MORTUUM. A skull.

CARDINAL. The highest official, next the Pope, in the Catholic Church. The original sacred college of cardinals was composed of the incumbents of Roman parishes. They began to assume the right to elect Popes about 1179. They first wore the red hat (as a reminder they ought to shed their blood for religion if required) about 1245. Paul III gave them the scarlet habit in 1464, and Urban VIII the title of Eminence in 1630. See also *Papacy, Popes.*

CARLYLE, THOMAS (1795–1881). English writer of Scottish peasant origin. His hatred of cant, commercialism and materialism gave his writings the fervour of an Israelitish prophet. His influence on his age was considerable. See Froude, *Thomas Carlyle.*

CARMATHIANS. A Mohammedan sect established by Carmath, a Shiite (q.v.) (9th C.).

CARMELITES. A Catholic mendicant order established by a crusader (Berthold) on Mount Carmel in the 12th C. St. Theresa (q.v.) reformed the

Order with the result that it split into two groups, the discalced (barefooted) and the calced (shod).

CARNIVAL. The festival in Italy and other Catholic countries at Shrovetide before Lent. (It. *carne vale* = good-bye meat!)

CAROL. A hymn of joy, especially such as are sung at Christmastide.

CARPENTER, EDWARD (1844–1929). Writer and social reformer. Ordained in the Church of England, Carpenter (owing to a change of views) legally relinquished his orders. Chief books: *Towards Democracy* (1902); *My Days and Dreams* (1916); *Pagan and Christian Creeds* (1920). He was a keen advocate of a simpler method of living.

CARTESIANISM. The system of the philosopher Descartes, who taught that consciousness alone is the basis of reality. (*Cogito, ergo sum* = I think, therefore I am.)

CARTHUSIAN. A religious order originating from the Benedictines and founded by St. Bruno of Cologne in 1086, who retired with six followers to Chartreuse in Dauphiné. Their austere rules (an ascetic diet, rough clothing and silence) were drawn up by Basil VII, their general. (See "Monasticism," *Cambridge Medieval History*, vol. i.)

CARTWRIGHT, THOMAS (1535–1603). English Puritan divine deprived of his office of Lady Margaret Professor of Divinity, Cambridge, by John Whitgift, vice-chancellor of the University, as a result of Cartwright's violent attacks on the Church of England.

CASSIODORUS, FLAVIUS MAGNUS AURELIUS (490–585). Historian, statesman and monk who served the emperor Theodoric and founded two monasteries at Squillace, Calabria. Wrote many treatises, one at the age of 93. (See T. Hodgkin, *Italy and her Invaders*, iii and iv.) George Gissing refers to him in *By the Ionian Sea*.

CASSOCK. The loose black robe worn by clergy and choristers.

CASSOLETTE. A censer or perfume box.

CASTE. The division of society into classes in India. The chief castes are: Brahmins (priestly caste), Ksatriyas (warriors), Vaisyas (soil-tillers), and Sudras (menials). There are some twenty or more distinct castes (occupational, religious, national, etc.). Expulsion from the caste results in social ostracism. (See J. C. Oman, *Indian Life, Religious and Social*.)

CATACOMBS. Subterranean dwellings used by the early Christians.

CATAFALQUE. A temporary structure placed over a coffin during a lying in state.

CATECHISM. Religious instruction in the form of question and answer. In the early Church the catechumen (q.v.) was thus instructed.

CATECHUMEN. Name given in the early Christian Church to converted Jews and heathens who were receiving instruction preparatory to baptism. With the introduction of infant baptism, the catechumenate gave way to sponsors (q.v.).

CATEGORICAL IMPERATIVE. In the ethical system of Kant the absolute command of the moral law irrespective of everything else.

CATHARIST, CATHARISM. A name adopted by various Puritan sects, especially the medieval Manicheans, who overspread Europe. In southern France they were known as Albigenses (q.v.).

CATHEDRAL. The chief church of a diocese, in which the bishop has his throne (*cathedra*).

CATHERINE, SAINT. The name of six saints in the Catholic calendar, the most famous being St. Catherine of Alexandria, who was tortured on the wheel in the 4th C.

CATHISMA. A division of the psalter in the Greek Church.

CATHOLIC. Orthodox as opposed to sectarian. The adjective is used of: (1) The Christian Church before the great Schism between East and West. (2) The Church of Rome alleged to have been founded by Christ and His apostles. (3) The Greek Church also claiming divine sanction. (4) The Church of England as a true agent of grace through its sacraments and bishops.

CATHOLIC APOSTOLIC CHURCH. See *Irving, Edward.*

CATHOLIC CHURCH. See *Roman Catholic Church.*

CATHOLIC EMANCIPATION. An Act drawn up by Peel and Wellington passed by the British parliament in 1829 for the relief of Catholics from civil disabilities.

CATHOLIC EPISTLES. The canonical epistles addressed to general readers and not to particular persons or churches (1, 2, 3 John; 1, 2 Peter; James; Jude).

CATHOLICS, OLD. The group of Catholics who refused to accept the dogma of papal infallibility promulgated in 1870.

CECILIA, SAINT. Catholic patron saint of music and the blind (Feast, 22 Nov.).

CELEBRANT. The officiating priest at the Eucharist.

CELEBRATION. Act of celebrating the Eucharist (high, with music; low, without).

CELESTINES. An order of Benedictine monks founded about 1254 by Peter da Marrone, who became Pope Celestine V and resigned after five years. Referred to by Dante as he who made "the great refusal."

CELIBACY OF THE CLERGY. The early Church held celibacy more conducive to Christian piety than marriage, but it was not till the 11th C. that celibacy was required of the clergy. The Council of Trent (1545–63) made celibacy binding on all holding major orders or taking monastic vows. In 1547 marriage was restored to the English clergy.

CELLA. The central part of a Greek and Roman temple.

CELSUS. A Platonist opponent of Christianity of the 2nd C. His books were destroyed by the infuriated Christians and we only know them from quotations in Origen's reply. His arguments rested on: The social inferiority of Christians; the crudity of their teaching; the impossibility of the deity of Christ; the foolishness of God as represented by the Christians.

CELTS, RELIGION OF THE. See *Druids.*

CEMETERY. Burying-ground, usually consecrated.

CENACLE. The room in which Jesus and His disciples ate the Last Supper. (L. *cenaculum.*)

CENOBITES, CŒNOBITES. Monks who live in community, instead of alone like hermits.

CENOTAPH. (1) An empty tomb. (2) The monument to the Unknown Warrior in Whitehall, London.

CENSER. The thurible or pan in which incense is burned.

CERBERUS. The three-headed dog guarding the entrance to Hades (L. myth.).

CEREMONIES. Religious rites. See *rite, ritual.*

CERES. The Roman name for the Greek Demeter, goddess of corn and tillage.

CERINTHUS. A Jewish Christian gnostic. (1st C.)

CHAKRA. Sanscrit term for a psychic nerve-centre. There are said to be six of these, passive in the ordinary man, but which can be activated by the practice of yoga.

CHAKRAVATIN. A yogi who has attained complete control of all his inner forces.

CHALCEDON. The fourth ecumenical council (A.D. 451).

CHALDEA, CHALDEANS. See *Babylon.*

CHALICE. A communion-cup.

CHALLACOMBE, EAST. See *Starr, Meredith.*

CHALMERS, THOMAS (1780–1847). Professor of Moral Philosophy in Edinburgh and St. Andrews and the first moderator of the Free Church of Scotland on their secession from the Established Church.

CHANCE. "A word void of sense; nothing can exist without a cause" (Voltaire).

CHANCEL. The east end of a church, usually screened from the nave.

CHANCELLOR OF A CATHEDRAL. An officer in charge of the chapter-library, seals, etc.

CHANCELLOR OF A DIOCESE. An ecclesiastical lawyer appointed to assist the bishop concerning questions of ecclesiastical law.

CHANGE-RINGING. Changes introduced in ringing a peal of bells.

CHANT. Church music adapted to the singing of unmetrical verses.

CHANTRY. A chapel endowed for the chanting of masses.

CHAPEL. A place of worship other than a regular church, or attached to a school, college, palace, etc. ; also a lesser church within a church having its own altar.

CHAPEL ROYAL. The choir attached to the chapel of a royal palace (e.g. children of the Chapel Royal, St. James's Palace).

CHAPLAIN. A clergyman attached to a private family or public service.

CHAPTER, CATHEDRAL. The canons or other clergy attached to a cathedral.

CHAPTER-HOUSE. The place where the chapter meets.

CHAPTREL. The capital of a pillar supporting an arch (archit.).

CHARACTER. See *personality*.

CHARISMATA. Supernatural powers believed by the early Christians to be given to the baptized. In all primitive religions such faculties are believed to exist. Similar powers are claimed by Faith Healers, Christian Scientists, etc., as well as by the Catholic and other churches. Though the phenomena are simple, the psychology involved is abstruse. (Gk. *charisma* = grace.) See *faith-healing*.

CHARITY. Goodwill ; the desire to do good to others. In medieval times a materialist view of charity largely prevailed, the faithful desiring to reap personal benefits by giving to the poor. An enormous increase in begging and beggary was the result.

CHARITY, SISTERS OF. Members of certain Christian sisterhoods who work among the poor.

CHARM. A trinket said to bring good fortune. See *magic, mana*.

CHARTISM, CHARTISTS. A 19th-C. movement in England to increase the political power of the manual workers. Its six points were : (1) manhood suffrage ; (2) equal electoral districts ; (3) vote by ballot ; (4) annual parliaments ; (5) abolition of property qualification for members of parliament ; (6) payment of members. Charles Kingsley was an active worker in the movement.

CHASTITY. Refraining from sexual intercourse. Religions have tended to veer between the extremes of sex activity (see *phallicism*) and sex-restraint (see *asceticism*). The pagan cults had sought to hallow and curb the sex-functions by recognizing them in religious worship. This led to much abuse, with the result that the early Christians went to the other extreme.

CHASUBLE. Priest's sleeveless vestment worn while celebrating Mass.

CHAUCER, GEOFFREY (1340–1400). England's earliest supreme poet —" the morning star of song." His *Canterbury Tales* should be studied by every student of medieval religious conditions, for here are inimitable pictures of priest and pardoner and prioress. (See G. G. Coulton, *Chaucer and His England.*)

CHERUB (pl. **CHERUBIM, CHERUBS**). A winged spirit, with human face, attendant on Yahweh.

CHESTERTON, GILBERT KEITH (b. 1874). Novelist and journalist who joined the Catholic Church in 1922. Much of his work (*Orthodoxy*, 1909; *The Thing*, 1929) shows strong Catholic tendency.

CHEVET. The apse of a church.

CHEYLA. Hindu term for the follower of a religious teacher or guru.

CHILLINGWORTH, WILLIAM (1602–44). English theologian who became a Jesuit and studied at Douai (1630). He subsequently returned to the Church of England, and became an able Anglican controversialist.

CHIME. Bells rung in harmony.

CHIMERA. A fabulous monster of Greek mythology.

CHINA, RELIGIONS OF. The chief religions of China are:

(1) Confucianism (q.v.), an ethical system based on a nature religion.

(2) Buddhism (q.v.), introduced into China in the 5th C. A.D.

(3) Ancestor-worship and pantheism, which is very strong in Chinese villages. They have many temples for the worship of mountains, streams, rocks, etc.

(4) Taoism (q.v.), a philosophic system which has developed into a religion. *Tao* (= way) signifies the way to Reality. Lao-tze (q.v.) was the founder of Taoism.

(See H. A. Giles, *Religions of Ancient China* (1905).)

CHOIR. Band of singers attached to a cathedral or church.

CHORAL, CHORALE. A simple harmony with slow rhythm: any part of the service sung by the choir (Cath.).

CHOREPISCOPUS. A country or suffragan bishop in the early Church.

CHORISTER. Member of a choir.

CHRISM, CHRISOM. (1) Consecrated oil used in christening (Cath.). (2) A white cloth laid by the priest on a newly baptized infant. (3) Also used of the child itself (chrisom child).

CHRIST. See *Jesus Christ.*

CHRISTADELPHIANS. An American Christian Millenarian sect who deny a personal devil and believe in conditional immortality. Also called Thomasites from their founder, John Thomas of Brooklyn (1805–71).

CHRISTEN. To baptize and admit into the Christian Church. See *catechumen*; *baptism*.

CHRISTIAN BROTHERS. A Catholic brotherhood founded by Jean Baptiste de la Salle (1652–1719) for furthering education. It still has an extensive membership.

CHRISTIAN ERA. See *Anno Domini*.

CHRISTIAN EVIDENCE SOCIETY. A Church of England society established in 1871 to counteract unbelief among the educated classes. Tracts, etc., are published. Headquarters: 33 and 34, Craven Street, London, W.C.2.

CHRISTIANITY. The religious systems and theologies that have developed from the beliefs of the Jewish sect called Nazarenes and Christians. Until the 19th C. Christianity was generally believed to be a new creation, something entirely unique and distinct from all religions previously known. The researches of 19th-C. scholars and thinkers (see *Strauss, Loisy, Colenso, Renan, J. G. Frazer, J. M. Robertson, Edward Carpenter*) greatly modified that view. It is now generally held that much of the content of Christianity was taught in previous religions. See *Attis, Osiris, Mithra, Mystery Religions.* "The Mysteries influenced Christianity considerably and modified it in some important respects" (Dr. Cheetham). The Egyptians celebrated the resurrection of Osiris by a sacrament in which they ate the consecrated wafer. Many Christian festivals likewise have their origin in the festivals of earlier religions (see *Christmas Day*). The light thus shed on Christian origins does not belittle Christianity but links it with the other great world religions and serves to show the progressive and evolutionary nature of religion.

§ 2. In the first or apostolic age of Christianity there was little organization and no distinction of clergymen and laymen. In the second period (1st and 2nd C.s, bishops and presbyters emerged from the general body of the faithful. Discipline and dogma began to be discussed. In the third period (3rd and 4th C.s) the Church as an organization of clergy had come into being. Dogma hardened. Salvation was held to be attainable only within the Church. Excommunication could render life torture and death an eternity of burning The bishops (many of them foolish men of great learning), alone had the right to determine questions of doctrine. The Grecian world, with its passion for abstract thought and exact definition, contributed to the intellectual ferment, with the result that theological contention took the place of primitive faith; Orthodoxy fought Arianism; Nestorian, Jacobite and Donatist wrangled one with another, seeking to define that which is incapable of definition. Persecution, rioting and angry controversy made life difficult for the philosophic and well-disposed. To try to calm the waters, a Council was called at Nicea in 325 over which the emperor Constantine presided. From this time Christianity was established as a State Church and became definitely Romanized.

§ 3. With the final break of the Empire into east and west in the 9th C., Christianity was split into two great churches—the Latin (or Roman Catholic) and Greek. The bishop of Rome, basing his claim on certain forged documents (see *Donation of Constantine*), assumed supreme headship of the Church and entered on a long contest with the emperor for political power. Upon the emergence of nationalism (13–14 C.) Christianity entered a new phase. The universal supremacy of the Roman Church was felt to be irksome and country after country threw off the yoke (see *Reformation*). The revival of classic study (see *Renaissance*) had also loosened the claims of theological dogma. A period of fierce wars and persecutions resulted, Catholic against Protestant. Spain deluged the Netherlands with blood, Calvinist thirsted for the blood of Lutheran, and the Pope went in state to return thanks for massacres such as that of St. Bartholomew (q.v.).

§ 4. With the coming of the 18th C. a better spirit manifested and religious strife was raised from the physical to the mental sphere; rationalist and theologian fought wordy battles until the claims of induction began to distract attention from theological dogma to scientific inquiry. Christianity, regarded historically, cannot escape the charge of fomenting strife and bloodshed. But the same is true of Mohammedanism and other great religions—Buddhism probably showing the cleanest record in this respect. Religion aims at the regeneration of men. But men are continually seeking the benefits (spiritual and material) of religion while shirking the regenerative process, without which the fruits cannot be enjoyed.

§ 5. Christianity has nurtured many wise and saintly souls, known and unknown: Synesius of Cyrene; St. Bernard of Clairvaux; St. Francis of Assisi; St. John of the Cross; Jakob Boehme; Lancelot Andrews; John Donne; George Herbert. The lives of these men speak loudly and will continue to speak long after the piteous cries of persecutors and persecuted have faded into silence. All religions change and evolve, as man himself changes and evolves. Will Christianity merge into some new religion, better fitted to the needs of coming generations, or will it give place to an enlightened Humanism based on philosophy and psychology? The dictionaries of the future must be consulted for an answer to these questions. See art. *Religion*, § 7. (See Adolf Harnack, *What is Christianity* (1918); W. Adams Brown, *The Essence of Christianity* (1902).)

CHRISTIAN KNOWLEDGE, SOCIETY FOR PROMOTING. A Church of England society founded in 1698 for the publishing and distribution of Bibles, Christian literature and tracts. Headquarters: Northumberland Avenue, London, W.C.2.

CHRISTIAN SCIENCE. A sect founded by an American, Mary

Baker Eddy, in 1866. She derived her ideas from Dr. Quimby, who treated her for a nervous affliction. The cult insists that matter is the opposite of infinite or Divine Mind and that all sickness, pain and evil are illusory and should be disregarded. Christian Science practitioners claim to be able to cure any and every disease from toothache to cancer by prayers for which a regular fee is charged. (See Mary Baker Eddy, *Science and Health*; M. C. Sturge, *The Truth and Error of Christian Science* (1903); Mark Twain, *Christian Science* (1907).)

CHRISTIAN SOCIALISM. A 19th-C. movement in European Protestant countries seeking to combat the crude materialistic tendencies of Socialism. Early Christian Socialist leaders were F. D. Maurice, J. M. Ludlow and Charles Kingsley. Christian Socialism stresses the moral responsibility of the individual and supports the churches.

CHRISTIAN SOCIAL UNION. An English Christian socialist association organized by Bishop Gore and Canon Scott Holland in 1889 to apply Christian ideals to social and economic problems.

CHRISTMAS. The festival of Christ's birth. It was not celebrated until the 4th C. The 6 January was at first chosen but later changed to 25 December to avoid confusion with the Baptism of Christ on that date. The fixing of 25 December was probably due to the birth of Mithra (q.v.) celebrated on the same day, marking the end of the winter solstice. The Roman Saturnalia (17 Dec.) certainly gave something of its character to the gustatory and bibulous Christian festival. (See R. H. Schauffler, *Christmas, Its Origin and Significance* (1907).)

CHRISTOLOGY. That section of theology which concerns Christ.

CHRONOLOGY. The following list gives some important dates in the history of the great religions:

	B.C.
Memphis (Egypt) built	4400
Jewish Era begins	3760
Men-Kau-Ra builds pyramids	3633
Ur-Gur, king of Ur, builds temples	3200
Indian Era begins	3102
Abraham migrates from Mesopotamia to Canaan	2300
Israelites enter Egypt	c. 1730
Exodus of the Israelites	1270
Fall of Troy (traditional)	1184
Rise of the caste system in India	1200–1000
Solomon builds the Temple	970
Lycurgus gives laws to Sparta	885
Olympian Era begins (First Olympiad)	776
Roman Era begins	753
Babylonian Era begins	747
Zoroaster born	660
Pythagoras born	582
Prince Siddattha, the Buddha, born	560
Age of Pericles in Greece	463–431
Plato born at Athens	427
Socrates died	399
Aristotle born	384
Old Testament translated into Greek at Alexandria (Septuagint)	c. 200
Julius Caesar invades Britain	55
Herod the Great made king of the Jews	43
Birth of Jesus Christ	4
	A.D.
Death of Jesus Christ	33
Founding of St. Peter's Rome (traditional)	42

	A.D.
Marcus Aurelius Antoninus, emperor and philosopher, born	121
Constantine the Great declares himself the Protector of Christianity	312
Sack of Rome by Alaric	410
Christian Era arranged by Dionysius the Little	c. 527
St. Benedict of Nursia builds his monastery at Monte Cassino	528
St. Columba builds his monastery at Iona	563
Mohammed born at Mecca	570
Augustine becomes archbishop of Canterbury	597
Mohammed's Hegira	622
First appearance of Mohammedanism in India	636
Buddhism introduced into Japan	700
Climax of Mohammedan influence: Mohammedanism supreme from the Pyrenees to the Himalayas	705–715
First Crusade	1096–1099
St. Francis of Assisi	(b.) 1182–(d.) 1226
Conquest of Constantinople by the Turks and destruction of the Eastern Empire	1453
Luther posts his 95 Theses on the church door	1517
Henry VIII assumes title of Supreme Head of the Church of England	1535
Francisco de Xavier introduces Christianity into India	1543
Accession of Akbar the Great	1556
Massacre of St. Bartholomew in France	1572
Authorized Version of the English Bible published	1611
Catholic Emancipation Act passed in England	1829
The Theosophical Society founded by Madame Blavatsky	1875
The Great War, which struck a severe blow at organized, dogmatic and formal religion all over the world	1914–1918

CHRYSOSTOM, SAINT JOHN (344–407). Patriarch of Constantinople. A powerful preacher who gave offence to the Court by his outspokenness, and was banished to the Caucasus where he died. (See F. W. Farrar, *Gathering Clouds*, for a good description of St. Chrysostom.)

CHUANG-TSE (**CHUANG-TZW**). Chinese philosopher and idealist, follower of Lao-tsze. Tao (ultimate reality), he taught, can only be reached by developing the intuition. ("Repose, tranquillity, stillness, inaction—these are the ultimate perfection of Tao.") (4th C. B.C.) See *Taoism*.

CHUCIUS (**CHU HSI**) (A.D. 1130–1200). Chinese philosopher. He taught that, despite the appearance of dualism, only reality (Li) or spirit controls all phenomena.

CHURCH ARMY. A Church of England organization established by the Rev. Wilson Carlile, D.D., in 1882, with the aim of helping the manual workers spiritually and materially. Headquarters: 55, Bryanston Street, London, W.1.

CHURCH, CHRISTIAN. The origin of the Christian Church is to be found in the Jewish groups who were followers of Jesus Christ. They had no officers, no organization, no definite doctrine. During the following centuries, bishops and presbyters were chosen for administrative purposes, thus originating the priesthood.

§ 2. By the 3rd C. the Catholic Church had come into being and Rome was gaining pre-eminence. During the Middle Ages the Church of Rome sought to step into the place left vacant by the fall of the Roman Empire (see *Empire, Holy Roman*). The Reformation put an end for ever to this dream. England separated and in America denominationalism took the place of a national Church. (See D. Stone, *The Christian Church* (1905).)

CHURCH CONGRESS. A conference of clergy and laity of the Church of England held annually to discuss religious problems.

CHURCH COUNCILS. The chief Ecumenical, or General, Councils were:

(1) First Ecumenical Council held at Nicea over which Constantine presided. It condemned Arianism and drew up the Nicene Creed (325).

(2) Council of Constantinople, at which the Arian heresy found favour (337).

(3) Council of Sardis, which finally condemned Arianism (347).

(4) Second Council of Constantinople, to consider the errors of Origen (553).

(5) Second Nicene Council, called to consider Iconoclasm (784).

(6) First Lateran Council, at which the right of investiture was settled between Pope Calixtus II and the emperor Henry V (1123).

(7) Council of Lyons, which deposed the emperor Frederick II (1245).

(8) Council of Trent; held to condemn the doctrines of the Reformers, Luther, Calvin, Zwingli (1563).

(9) Vatican Council, when the Infallibility of the Pope was promulgated (1870).

CHURCH DISCIPLINE ACT. An Act passed by the English Parliament in 1840 whereby bishops may inhibit defaulting clergy from conducting services, etc.

CHURCH FATHERS. See *Fathers, Church.*

CHURCH GOVERNMENT. There are three chief forms of government prevailing in the Christian churches:

(1) Episcopal or government by bishops, priests and deacons. See *Church, Christian; Greek Church; Church of England.*

(2) Presbyterian or government by laymen of age and experience (elders). See *Presbyterianism.*

(3) Congregational or control by vote of the church members. See *Congregationalism.*

CHURCHING. The ceremony of thanksgiving in church by a mother after the birth of a child.

CHURCH OF ENGLAND. The State Church established in England. Christianity was introduced into Britain from the Continent in the 3rd C., and the British Church thus formed joined with the missionary church sent over by Augustine in 597. Authorities differ as to whether the Church of England to-day is truly representative of the primitive British Church. The Anglo-Catholics take the view that it is; the Protestants (or Low Church) prefer to regard it as a product of the Reformation. See art. *Religion*, § 6.

CHURCH OF FRANCE. The chief events of the Catholic Church of France are:

(1) St. Pothinus preached to the Gauls (c. 160).

(2) Council of Arles, condemning the Donatists (314).

(3) St. Louis restrained Papal impositions (1269).

(4) Appeals to the Pope forbidden (1438).

(5) Disputes between Jesuits and Jansenists (1640).

(6) The archbishop of Paris resisted the dogma of papal infallibility at the Vatican Council (1870).

(7) Alfred Loisy excommunicated for his views (1903).

CHURCH OF IRELAND. The Irish Episcopal Church (United Church of England and Ireland) was disestablished under the Irish Church Act of 1871.

CHURCH OF NORTH AMERICA. In 1784, Bishop Seabury, consecrated in Scotland, became bishop of Connecticut. In 1787 two more bishops for the American Church were consecrated at Lambeth.

CHURCH, RICHARD WILLIAM (1815–90). Dean of St. Paul's in 1871, author of several books of a High Church tendency.

CHURCH OF ROME. See *Roman Catholic Church.*

CHURCH OF SCOTLAND. On the abolition of Episcopacy in 1638, Presbyterianism became the established religion. Its formulary of faith, compiled by John Knox in 1560, was finally established with the Treaty of Union, in 1707.

CHURCH WARDEN. A lay official in episcopal churches responsible for certain parochial matters.

CHURCHYARD. The consecrated burial-ground adjoining a church.

CIBORIUM. (1) A vessel containing the host. (2) A canopy over the high altar (Cath.).

CINCTURA. Moulding round a column (archit.).

CIRCUMCELLIONES. See *Donatists.*

CIRCUMCISION. Ritualistic operation of cutting off the male prepuce. It was practised among the ancient Hebrews, Egyptians and Mohammedans. (See Gen. xvii. 23–7.)

CIRCUMCISION, FEAST OF THE. A commemoration of the circumcision of Jesus (1 Jan.).

CISTERCIANS. An order of monks established in 1098 by Robert, abbot of Molesme, a Benedictine, in the forest of Citeaux in France.

CLAIRAUDIENCE. The power of hearing voices, etc., not audible to the senses. See *Spiritualism.*

CLAIRE, SAINT. A religious order for women instituted by St. Francis of Assisi (q.v.).

CLAIRVOYANCE. The power of seeing objects not visible to the senses. See *Spiritualism.*

CLEAR-STORY. See *clerestory.*

CLEMENT OF ALEXANDRIA (A.D. 150–215). An eclectic Christian scholar of Alexandria. His philosophic temper influenced Christianity considerably. He was Origen's teacher.

CLEMENT, EPISTLE OF. An epistle ascribed to Clement of Rome (q.v.). Other writings believed to be his are: two Epistles on Virginity; the Epistle to James.

CLEMENT OF ROME (c. 40–97 A.D.). A traditional disciple of St. Peter and reputed author of several epistles.

CLEMENTINES. Adherents of the anti-pope Clement VII—opposed to the Urbanists, followers of Pope Urban VI. (14th C.)

CLERGY, CLERK, CLERIC. Ministers of the Christian Church, bishops, priests and deacons. The bishops (*episcopoi* = overseers), elected from the presbyters, assumed higher functions about 330. In the 7th and 8th C.s the clergy began to possess temporal power as landowners. Their power was also greatly increased by their being regarded as the possessors of grace transmitted from the Apostles through the bishops. In the Catholic Church bishops and priests formed a higher order; minor orders being represented by exorcists, acolytes and lesser officials. (See A. R. Whitham, *Holy Orders* (1903).)

CLERESTORY, CLEAR-STORY. Upper story, usually with windows, above the nave of a church.

CLERICAL DISABILITIES ACT. An Act passed by the British Parliament in 1870 relieving priests or deacons of certain clerical disabilities upon their resigning ecclesiastical office and preferment. Under this Act, Sir Leslie Stephen (q.v.) and Edward Carpenter (q.v.) legally "unfrocked" themselves.

CLOISTER. Originally the wall enclosing a religious house, later the monastery itself and especially the quadrilateral area enclosed by the building.

CLUGNY, CLUNY, ABBEY OF. French abbey founded in 910 by Abbot Bern and actively supported by William, duke of Berry (the Pious).

CODEX. An ancient manuscript (bound), usually in large round characters (uncials).

CODEX BEZAE. A 6th-C. manuscript in the University Library, Cambridge, which belonged to Theodore Beza (1562–81). It contains the gospels and part of Acts in Greek and Latin.

CODEX SINAITICUS. A 4th-C. manuscript of the O.T. and N.T. discovered on Mount Sinai in 1859.

CŒNOBITES. See *Cenobites*.

COLENSO, JOHN WILLIAM (1814–83). Mathematician and first bishop of Natal. His work among the Zulus and their doubts of certain statements in the Pentateuch led him to a critical examination of the O.T. and he thereupon published a book of destructive criticism which occasioned fierce controversy. He was deposed and excommunicated by Bishop

Gray of Capetown, but confirmed in his see by the English Courts of Law. (See G. W. Cox, *Life of J. W. Colenso* (1888).)

COLERIDGE, SAMUEL TAYLOR (1772–1834). English poet and philosopher who liberalized Christian ideals by his insistence on moral and rational principles.

COLET, JOHN (1467–1519). Scholar and dean of St. Paul's. Founded and endowed St. Paul's School, London. (See J. H. Lupton, *Life of John Colet* (1887).)

COLLECT. A short prayer of one petition. In the Roman and Anglican liturgies the prayer preceding the gospel and epistle for the day.

COLLEGE OF CARDINALS. (Sacred College.) The senate, in the Catholic Church, of six cardinal bishops, fifty cardinal priests and fourteen cardinal deacons. The College elects the Pope and acts as a papal advisory committee.

COLLYRIDIANS. Arab heretics who offered little cakes (collyrides) to the Virgin Mary. (4th C.)

COLMAN. Irish bishop of Lindisfarne where he founded a monastery of English and Irish monks. But trouble arose because the Irish monks wandered away in summer and in winter returned for food and warmth, thus giving offence to the English brethren. See *Bede* (*Eccles. Hist.*, iv, 4).

COLUMBA, SAINT (521–97). Irish monk who went as missionary to Scotland and became abbot of Iona. His monastery there became the chief centre of Christian civilization in North Britain.

COLUMBAN, SAINT (c. 540–615). Irish monk and classical scholar who (to escape the beauty of the Irish girls) travelled to France, Switzerland and Italy. While in Burgundy he tried to reform the licentious Queen Brunehild, but was banished and fled to Rome.

COMMANDMENTS, THE TEN. See *Decalogue.*

COMMENDAM. Holding a church benefice till a suitable pastor be found. The custom of holding benefices in commendam by clerks and laymen was much abused in the Middle Ages. By an Act of William IV, bishops were forbidden to hold in commendam such livings as they held when consecrated.

COMMENDATION OF THE SOUL. An act of prayer commending the dying to the mercy of God.

COMMINATION SERVICE. An Anglican service for Ash Wednesday reciting God's threatenings to the wicked.

COMMON PRAYER, BOOK OF. The Liturgy of the Church of England. See *Liturgy, the English.*

COMMUNION, HOLY. The Christian sacrament of bread and wine. It appears to have grown out of the primitive Agape (q.v.). At first it was a commemorative meal, the Lord's Supper, held in memory of the last meal Jesus ate with his disciples. But such sacrificial meals were common to all early cults (see *Totemism*) and some of the ideas connected with them became blended with the Christian Faith. With the hardening of dogma many ideas came to be connected with the bread and wine (see *Transubstantiation : Real Presence*). Although Holy Communion is a rite observed in the Catholic, the Greek, the Anglican and Lutheran churches, the doctrine connected with it differs widely in the several churches. (See (for C. of E. doctrine) Darwell Stone, *The Holy Communion*; (for the Cath. doctrine) Cardinal Wiseman, *The Real Presence.*)

COMMUNION OF SAINTS. One of the affirmations of belief occurring in the Apostles' Creed (q.v.). The Protestants restrict its meaning to spiritual fellowship among believers on earth; the Catholics extend the meaning to include souls in purgatory and saints in heaven.

COMPLINE. The last daily service of the Catholic Church. See *Breviary.*

COMPOSITE ORDER. A blending of the Ionic and Corinthian orders (archit.).

CONCEPTION, IMMACULATE. See *Immaculate Conception.*

CONCH. An apse or semi-dome of an apse (archit.).

CONCLAVE. The body of cardinals or room in which they meet. See *college of cardinals.*

CONCORDAT. An agreement between the Pope and a secular government; the most celebrated being that between Napoleon I and Pius VII in 1801, to arrange ecclesiastical affairs in France after the Revolution.

CONCUPISCENCE. Excessive sexual desire.

CONCURSUS. The doctrine of Calvin, derived from St. Augustine, that man, previous to the Fall, was preserved in perfection by God's grace.

CONFESSION. Acknowledgment of sin to a priest. The earliest canonical age for confession in the Catholic Church is seven.

CONFESSIONAL. (1) An enclosed box or recess in which a priest hears confessions. (2) The practice of confession.

CONFESSION OF FAITH. A formulary embodying the beliefs of a church or sect. Confessions of faith are usually the result of controversy and differ from creeds in that they concern groups of believers rather than the whole church. The various Protestant bodies have frequently drawn up confessions of faith. Some famous confessions of faith are: The Confession of Dositheus (1672)—an authoritative statement by the Greek Church; The Roman Catechism (1566)—a statement of doctrine for the clergy; The First Bohemian Confession of Faith (1530)—a Protestant Confession. The famous Augsburg Confession (1530) of the Lutheran Faith.

CONFESSION, GENERAL. (1) In the Church of England a public confession of sin repeated after the minister by the congregation. (2) In the Catholic Church a private confession in which the penitent sums up past sins, including those already confessed.

CONFESSOR. (1) A priest who hears confessions (Cath.). (2) One who confessed Christianity despite persecution. (3) A title of reverence given to men of holy life (e.g. Edward the Confessor).

CONFIRMATION. The rite admitting persons to full communion in the Catholic, Greek, Lutheran, Anglican and other churches. It is administered by the bishop with imposition of hands and implies a moral strengthening by the gift of the Holy Spirit.

CONFITEOR. A form of confession in the liturgy of the Catholic Church. (L. *confiteor* = I confess.)

CONFRATERNITY. A brotherhood of laymen authorized within the Catholic Church usually for philanthropic or educational purposes (e.g. Confraternity of the Sacred Heart; of the Blessed Virgin; of the Precious Blood, etc.).

CONFUCIUS (551–478 B.C.) and **CONFUCIANISM.** Confucius (K'ung-tsze) was an official in Lu, his native state, who became one of the greatest of sages. During his life no attention was paid to his teaching. It was not until two centuries after his death that he was recognized as China's greatest teacher. He taught that virtue is natural and man by nature good. Self-control is the foundation of his system. If each does his duty, peace and equilibrium result. The proper observance of duty must bring peace between parent and child, husband and wife, brother and brother, friend and friend. The supreme virtue is "Jin." "Jin is to love all men and not to do to others what you would not wish done to you." Jin appears to include also courage, reverence, justice, loyalty and all the idealist constructive virtues. The irony of circumstance decreed that the agnostic Confucius should be worshipped as a god after his death. The chief books of Confucianism are the *Yi-King* (Book of Changes); the *Shu-King* (Book of History); the *Shi-King* (Book of Poetry). The depth of his wisdom is revealed in such sayings as: "What the superior man seeks is in himself; what the small man seeks is in others." "Learning, undigested by thought, is labour lost; thought, unassisted by learning, is perilous." "A man can enlarge his principles; principles do not enlarge the man." "The cautious seldom err." (See G. G. Alexander, *Confucius, the Great Teacher* (1891).)

CONGÉ D'ÉLIRE. Permission given by the crown to the dean and chapter to elect a bishop.

CONGREGATION. (1) A committee of bishops in conference (Cath.). (2) The Scotch reforming party in the time of Mary Queen of Scots. (3) A body of people united to worship in a church.

CONGREGATIONALISM, INDEPENDENTISM. An English Christian sect which originated with Robert Brown (c. 1580), who held that each church or congregation should be free of all others. Brown himself underwent thirty-two imprisonments and his followers were continually persecuted. Cromwell, himself an Independent, obtained for them toleration. In the 19th C. their numbers increased considerably. The Congregationalists stress social endeavour and municipal reform. (See R. W. Dale, *History of English Congregationalism.*)

CONGREGATION OF THE INDEX. The officials of the Catholic Church who prepare the index (q.v.).

CONGRESS, CHURCH. See *Church Congress.*

CONSALVI, ERCOLE (1757–1824). Cardinal and secretary to Pope Pius VII at the outbreak of the French Revolution.

CONSCIENCE. The inward contemplation of one's thoughts and actions from the moral standpoint. Conscience is the result of education (in the broadest sense), experience and the inner life. It may give good or harmful advice according to the detachment or moral condition of the individual.

CONSCIOUSNESS. The impression each has of his own existence (*Cogito, ergo sum*). " Wise men have discarded the use of all such question-begging words as space, time, cause, subject and object, matter, energy, and the like. Instead, consciousness is observed ; and immediately it becomes plain that consciousness depends on unconscious help from moment to moment. . . . That is to say . . . consciousness depends on reinforcements from processes of which it is unconscious until the completed version appear in consciousness " (Archibald Weir, *For To-day* (1933), p. 26.)

CONSCIOUSNESS, COSMIC. Psychologists are agreed that there are many degrees of consciousness and that mankind has experienced two : (1) a diffused or tribal consciousness closely akin to that of the animals. In this state he was hardly aware of the ego but identified himself entirely—or almost entirely—with his tribe. (2) With the full awakening of the ego (q.v.), strife entered his being and was reflected in discontent and tribal warfare (see *Fall of Man*). This is the consciousness experienced by the majority at the present time.

(3) There is, in history and literature, evidence that certain people have experienced a higher type of consciousness in which the union with all Being is felt and the ego tends to be obliterated. For an able exposition of the subject, see William James, *The Varieties of Religious Experience* ; Dr. R. M. Bucke, *Cosmic Consciousness.*

CONSECRATION. Setting apart for holy purposes. All religions have held certain animals, people or things sacred (see *tabu*). Christianity maintains the rite of consecration in the eucharist (q.v.), the dedication of persons to the priesthood and the setting apart of churches, cemeteries, etc.

CONSISTORY. (1) An ecclesiastical court in the Catholic Church, consisting of the Pope and cardinals; it deals chiefly with the appointment of cardinals, bishops, etc. (2) In the Lutheran Church, a court to supervise religious and educational affairs. (3) In the Church of England, a court with ecclesiastical jurisdiction within the diocese.

CONSTANCE, COUNCIL OF (1414–18). The Church Council summoned by Pope John XXIII and the Emperor Sigismund to end the schism between rival Popes; to decide as to the teaching of John Huss and to consider reform within the Church. The Council deposed the two Popes, John XXIII and Benedict XIII, and elected Cardinal Colonna Pope as Martin V. John Huss was condemned and burnt (6 July 1415). The efforts to reform the Church were successfully opposed by the cardinals and tactfully ignored by Pope Martin.

CONSTANTINE. Roman emperor converted to Christianity (for reasons of state) in 312. During the Arian controversy he strove to preserve an undivided Church. (See J. B. Firth, *Constantine the Great* (1905).)

CONSTITUTIONS OF CLARENDON (1164). The legal settlement between Henry II and Becket with regard to civil and ecclesiastical courts.

CONSUBSTANTIATION. The Lutheran doctrine of the substantial presence of the body and blood of Christ in the bread and wine of the Lord's Supper.

CONTEMPLATION. The mental state of stillness attained after prolonged meditation (q.v.). It is practised by the Yogis, the Buddhists and certain Catholic orders. See *meditation*.

CONTINENCE. Self-restraint, especially as regards sexual desire. The churches of to-day counsel moderation; the early Church advocated extreme asceticism, with evil results.

CONTRA-TENOR, COUNTER-TENOR. Alto part when sung by a male voice (in contrast to a tenor).

CONTRITION. Repentance arising from the love of God (Cath. theol.).

CONVENT. A religious community of men or women and the building they inhabit. The Egyptian monk Pachomius founded the first Christian convent (4th C.).

CONVENTICLE. Contemptuous name given to meeting-places of the dissenters in Jacobean times.

CONVENTICLE ACTS. The name given to several Acts passed by the British Parliament in the 17th C. to penalize Catholics and dissenters for the open practice of their religious rites.

CONVERSION. A change of consciousness, after which the subject finds his moral disposition and mental attitude altered. Theologians of the past ascribed conversion to an act of Grace and regarded the phenomenon as peculiar to the Christian religion. Modern psychology has proved convincingly that conversion has nothing to do with creed or dogma, but is a result of psychological and ethical law. Such changes of consciousness were experienced by certain initiates in the Greek Mysteries (q.v.) and probably in the early Masonic societies. (See Jung, *Modern Man in Search of a Soul* (1934). Also William James, *The Varieties of Religious Experience*.)

CONVOCATION. (1) The ancient ecclesiastical court of an archbishop. (2) An assembly of the clergy of the Church of England divided into an upper and a lower house and presided over by the archbishops of Canterbury and York. There is also a House of Laymen attached. (See Lothbury, *A History of the Convocation of the Church of England*.)

COPE. An ecclesiastical sleeveless vestment worn in processions, but not by the celebrant at Mass (Cath.).

COPERTINO, ST. JOSEPH OF. A Calabrian monk to whom were ascribed curious phenomena of levitation. (See Norman Douglas, *Old Calabria* (1915), chap. x. For similar levitation phenomena, see Prof. Evans-Wentz, *Milarepa*, p. 212.)

COPTS, COPTIC CHURCH. The native Egyptian Church founded in the 2nd C. Coptic Christianity is derived from the Eutychians (q.v.).

CORBAN. Anything vowed to God (Heb.).

CORDELIER. A Franciscan (wearer of a cord or girdle).

CORINTH. Greek city, renowned for wealth and luxury, visited by St. Paul in A.D. 54 (Acts xviii.).

CORONATION. The rite of crowning a sovereign. The English Coronation Service is derived from the Liber Regalis, a manuscript in the keeping of the dean of Westminster, used since the coronation of James I.

CORPORAL CLOTH, CORPORATION CLOTH. The cloth used for covering the eucharistic elements (Cath.).

CORPUS CHRISTI. A Catholic festival held on the Thursday after Trinity, in honour of the consecrated host in the Eucharist.

COSIN, JOHN (1594–1672). Bishop of Durham (1660). A ritualist of broad views and genial temper.

COSMIC CONSCIOUSNESS. See *consciousness, cosmic.*

COSMOGONY. The science of the origin of the universe. In early ages the subject was dealt with mythologically. Such theories were (1) the Cosmic Egg; (2) a struggle between chaos and cosmos; (3) creation by God's Word or Will (Gen. i.). Modern thought inclines to theories of cosmic evolution.

COSMOLOGY. The science of the universe as a whole, regarded philosophically rather than according to the old mythological views.

COTTA. A surplice.

COUNCILS, CHURCH. See *Church Councils*.

COUNTER REFORMATION. The movement of reform within the Catholic Church to counter the effect of the Protestant Reformation. Prominent ecclesiastics took part in the work, of which the chief were: Cardinal Bellarmine, Philip Neri, Vincent de Paul, Francis de Sales and Charles Borromeo. The Inquisition (q.v.) took an active share in the work, but the chief instrument of the Counter Reformation was the Council of Trent (q.v.) (1545–63). This Council introduced many reforms into the administration of the Church and many of its decrees have continued in force ever since. (See A. W. Ward, *The Counter Reformation*.)

COUNTER-TENOR. See *contra-tenor*.

COURTS, ECCLESIASTICAL. The medieval Bishop's court dealt chiefly with moral and testamentary offences. From it appeal lay to three Roman courts: the Sacred Roman Rota, the Apostolic Synatura, and the Sacred Penitentiary. In England, ecclesiastical courts came into being in the 11th C. (see *Arches Court*). They dealt with blasphemy, apostasy, heresy, schism, divorce, incest, fornication, probate of wills, etc. The formation of the Divorce and Probate Courts in 1857 relieved them of most of their functions.

COVENANTERS. Signatories of the Solemn League and Covenant, English and Scottish, of Charles I's reign. They were vowed to secure civil and religious liberty.

COVERDALE, MILES (1488–1568). An austere friar converted to Protestantism, who made the first complete English translation of the Bible (1535). (See J. J. Mombert, *English Versions of the Bible*.)

COWL. A monk's hood.

COWPER, WILLIAM (1731–1800). English poet who collaborated with John Newton in writing the Olney Hymns (1779).

CRABBE, GEORGE (1754–1832). Poet who acted as domestic chaplain to the duke of Rutland. His *Tales of the Hall* show a very high command of poetic realism. (See Alfred Ainger, *Life of George Crabbe*.)

CRANMER, THOMAS (1489–1556). Churchman who assisted Henry VIII in the work of the Reformation and was rewarded with the Primacy. He suffered martyrdom under Queen Mary. (See A. F. Pollard, *Cranmer and the English Reformation*.)

CRASHAW, RICHARD (1613–49). Poet and Catholic divine. His poetry, distinguished by exalted religious feeling, shows the influence of George Herbert.

CREATION. See *cosmogony*.

CREATIONISM. (1) The theory that the universe is the result of God's act of creation—and is not due to evolutionary process. (2) The theory that each human soul is created at birth—opposed to traducianism (q.v.).

CREDENCE-TABLE. A table to hold the eucharistic elements before consecration (Cath.).

CREDO. A creed or the musical setting for it.

CREED. A summary of religious beliefs, held by a group or a church. The Christian creeds appear to have grown out of early baptismal confessions.

CREED, APOSTLES'. A Christian creed traced to the 2nd C. and erroneously ascribed to the apostles. It became a part of public worship in the Catholic Church of the 11th C. and was soon afterwards adopted by the Church of England.

CREED, ATHANASIAN. A Christian creed erroneously attributed to St. Athanasius. It appears to have originated in Gaul or North Africa (6th to 9th C.). Authorities differ as to its authorship. Its use in the Church of England, owing to the damnatory clauses, has aroused much controversy. The Protestant Episcopal Church (U.S.A.) omits this creed from its prayer-book. (See W. A. Curtis, *A History of the Creeds* (1911).)

CREED, NICENE. A creed said to have been adopted by the Council of Nicea (A.D. 325). It more probably originated with the Council of Constantinople (381). The Nicene, in common with other creeds, grew out of heresies and the need to refute them. In this sense all creeds may be said to owe their origin to heretics. (See J. Pearson, *Exposition of the Creed* (1849).)

CREMATION. Burning of the dead, a practice forbidden in the Catholic Church.

CRIME AND PUNISHMENT. Crime may be defined as a failure or refusal to live up to the standard of conduct deemed binding by the rest of the community. Owing to changes in social conditions, certain crimes are differently regarded in different ages. That which in one age is a crime, in another may be a meritorious act. Most crimes are due to either malice, greed or lust and the percentage has been computed as follows:

Crimes of malice . . .	15%
Crimes of lust . . .	10%
Crimes of greed . . .	75%

Punishment in earlier ages was regarded as retributive, but is to-day looked upon as mainly reformative. For this reason the prison system tends to become more humane. The response to milder treatment has proved entirely satisfactory both in England and America. (See A. MacDonald, *Criminology* (New York, 1893).)

CROCKET. Ornamental carving on the angles of spires (archit.).

CROMLECH. A circular enclosure of ancient stones found in many parts of the world (e.g. Stonehenge and Carnac, Brittany) and used probably for sun-worship or ancestor-worship.

CROMWELL, OLIVER (1599–1658). Lord protector of England who defeated and deposed Charles I. His hatred of political and religious tyranny joined with his Puritan faith gave him irresistible power. The strict Puritan form of religion he upheld led to the violent reaction of the Restoration. Cromwell's character has been variously interpreted by different writers. (See Carlyle, *Letters and Speeches of O. Cromwell*; R. Tangye, *The Two Protectors* (1899); John Buchan, *Oliver Cromwell* (1934).)

CROSS. A pre-Christian religious symbol found in Egypt, India, China, Europe and America. Christianity adopted the symbol and attached new meanings to it.

CROSS, INVENTION OF THE. Festival to commemorate the finding of the "true cross" in Jerusalem by St. Helena on 3 May 328 (Cath.).

CROWN. A species of spire or lantern supported by flying-buttresses (archit.).

CROZIER, CROSIER. A bishop's pastoral staff or crook. It dates from 5th C. and is possibly derived from the Roman augur's *lituus*.

CRUCIFER. Bearer of a processional cross (eccles.).

CRUCIFIX. An image of Christ fixed to the Cross (Cath.).

CRUCIFIXION. (1) The infliction of death by nailing or binding to a cross. A penal method used by the Romans. (2) The death of Jesus Christ on the Cross.

CRUET. A vessel to hold eucharistic wine or water (eccles.).

CRUSADES. The military expeditions undertaken by medieval sovereigns to drive the infidels from Jerusalem and capture the Holy Land. The Church, in an age of pilgrimages, favoured the Crusades as an opportunity for Christian enterprise. Peter the Hermit, the 11th-C. monk of Amiens who fanned the crusading flame, appears to be legendary. The Crusades were:

(i) First Crusade (1096–9), originated by Pope Urban II, in which Jerusalem was taken by assault, 15 July 1099, and Godfrey de Bouillon made king.

(ii) Second Crusade, preached by St. Bernard in 1146, led by the emperor Conrad III and Louis VII of France, proved disastrous.

(iii) Third Crusade, undertaken in 1188 by the emperor Frederick Barbarossa. It was joined in 1190 by Richard I of England and Philip II of France. A fruitless expedition.

(iv) Fourth Crusade (1202–4), led by Baldwin IV, count of Flanders. Was moderately successful.

Between the Fourth and Fifth Crusades the curious movement known as the Children's Crusade took place (1212). The preacher of the movement was a peasant lad, Stephen of Cloyes (France). Encouraged by certain monks, he preached in Paris of an angel that had appeared to him urging him to the Crusades. A religious frenzy spread among the children of France and Germany. Thousands of boys under twelve and many girls joined the movement. They crossed the Alps by Mont Cenis and the St. Gotthard into Italy. A few took ship at Genoa and many at Marseilles. Some 5,000 of those who reached Marseilles were betrayed by merchants and sold into slavery.

(v) Fifth Crusade (1216–20), led by the kings of Cyprus and Hungary. Met with disaster in Egypt.

(vi) Sixth Crusade (1227–9), led by the emperor Frederick II, who captured Jerusalem in 1229.

(vii) Seventh Crusade (1249–54), led by Louis IX (St. Louis) of France, who was captured in 1250 and ransomed.

(viii) The Eighth and last Crusade, led by St. Louis in 1270. It was a failure, Louis dying of fever at Carthage the same year. It resulted in Christians being driven out of Syria. (See W. B. Stevenson, *The Crusaders in the East* (1907).)

CRUX. See *cross.*

CRUX ANSATA. An Egyptian symbolic cross with looped handle, signifying life, power, fertility.

CRYPT. An underground chapel or cell, often used for burial.

CUCHULAIN. A sun-god of Irish mythology.

CUDWORTH, RALPH (1617–88). The best known of the Cambridge Platonists (q.v.).

CULDEES. A fraternity of Scottish monks living at St. Andrews in the 8th C. (L. *cultores Dei* = servants of God.)

CUL-DE-FOUR. A low spherical vault (archit.).

CULT. The system of beliefs associated with a group or a deity.

CUP. See *chalice.*

CURATE. (1) The holder of a benefice who has the cure of souls (Cath.). (2) An assistant to the rector or vicar of a parish (Anglican).

CURE OF SOULS. The spiritual care of members of a parish (Cath. and Anglican).

CURIA ROMANA. The officials of the papal government.

CURSE. See *demon.*

CUSP. A projecting ornament in Gothic tracery (archit.).

CYBELE. A Phrygian goddess, symbol of the fruitful earth; wife of Attis who represents the growing and fading vegetation. Her cult was introduced into Rome in 204 B.C. and became very popular. See *mystery religions.*

CYNIC. The name given to a sect of philosophers founded by Antisthenes of Athens (5th C. B.C.) who contemned all worldly things except morality. (Gr. *kynos* = dog.)

CYPRIAN OF CARTHAGE, SAINT (A.D. 200–58). Bishop of Carthage, whose doctrine of the Church as the sole Ark of Salvation helped to build up the primacy of Rome.

CYRENAIC SECT. A school of Greek philosophy founded by Aristippus of Cyrene (365 B.C.). He taught that man's chief aim should be pleasure. Virtuous life being the highest form of pleasure, an ethical system resulted.

CYRENE. A province of Libya in N. Africa.

CYRENE, SYNESIUS OF. See *Synesius*.

CYRIL OF ALEXANDRIA (376–444). Bishop of Alexandria and one of the Fathers (q.v.). He was a stern opponent of heresy, persecuting Jews and pagans. It was due to his influence that Hypatia (q.v.) was murdered.

CYRIL OF JERUSALEM (315–86). Defender of the Nicene Creed against Arianism.

D

DAGOBA. See *Stupa*.

DAGON. A Philistine agricultural god.

DAI NICHI. The Absolute or ultimate Reality of Japanese Buddhism.

DAITYAS. The demons in Vedic religion.

DAKINI ("Sky-goer"). Fairy-like beings of Tibetan Lamaism, both good and evil.

DAKMA. Parsi towers on which dead bodies are exposed to be eaten by birds.

DALE, ROBERT WILLIAM. A 19th-C. Congregational minister; author of *The Atonement*, a mystical work on vicarious suffering.

DALMATIC. A wide-sleeved vestment worn by deacons (Cath.).

DAMASCUS. The capital of ancient Syria. St. Paul lodged there during the three days of his blindness (Acts ix. 8, 9).

DANCING. The meaningless dancing of to-day traces back to the more purposeful dancing of a primitive state of society. When the tribal system was in vogue dancing was ritualistic and expressive of the joy in war, hunting, courting, etc. Christianity retained ritual dancing until the 8th C. A.D. The Dance of the Seises (Sixes) performed by boys in Seville Cathedral, during the chief festivals, is a survival of ritual dancing. (See Reginald St. Johnston, *A History of Dancing* (1906).)

DANIEL. (1) The second son of David by Abigael (1 Chron. iii. 1). (2) The author of the Book of Prophecies. (3) The fourth son of Aaron (Ezra viii. 2).

DANIEL, THE BOOK OF. An historical and prophetical book of the O.T. Research has proved that *historically* it is quite inaccurate and was probably written at the time of Antiochus Epiphanes as political propaganda. (See Woods and Powell,

The Hebrew Prophets for English Readers.)

DANTE ALIGHIERI (1265–1321). The greatest of medieval poets. His *Vita Nuova* allegorizes and spiritualizes his love for Beatrice Portinari. The *De Monarchia* is a plea for a universal monarchy which alone could put an end to war and strife. The *Divine Comedy* describes hell, purgatory and paradise, and though it does not rise above the theology and cosmology of the time, it shows deep insight into the subtlest problems of life. (See Paget Toynbee, *A Dante Dictionary*; Edward Moore, *Studies in Dante*, 3 vols. (1903).)

DARWIN, CHARLES ROBERT (1809–82). Naturalist and physician who, on the publication of his *The Origin of Species* (1859), became world-famous owing to the fierce opposition his theories encountered from the Christian churches. Darwin's doctrine of evolution amounts to this: Since man is able to assist animals and plants to change from wild to better forms by selecting the most desirable units for breeding, it is reasonable to look for something of the sort in Nature. He came to the conclusion, after long study and observation, that Nature selects the individuals best suited for the conditions of living and rejects (i.e. destroys) those less adapted; the "struggle for existence" resulting, broadly speaking, in "the survival of the fittest." (See F. Darwin, *Life and Letters of Charles Darwin*; F. W. Headley, *Life and Evolution*.)

DATASIA, DATARY. The papal office where documents, grants, etc., are dated and despatched. The Datary is the officer in charge.

DAVID. The son of Jesse, king of Judah and Israel, and founder of the royal dynasty of Judaea (1 Sam. xvi.). (11th C. B.C.) (See T. K. Cheyne, *Aids to Devout Study of Criticism* (1892).)

DEACON. An officer in the early church whose duty it was to care for the sick. In modern usage the term covers: (1) The lowest order of clergy in Episcopal churches. (2) A secular officer in some Presbyterian churches. (3) A secular officer who assists the minister and dispenses charity. (4) In the Methodist Church the deacon is an ordained minister but not a pastor. (Gr. *diakonos* = a servant.)

DEACONESS. (1) In apostolic times a female servant of the Christian Society. (2) The nun who, in a convent, has care of the altar (Cath.). (3) In some Protestant churches, a woman who ministers to the poor and sick.

DEAN. (1) A dignitary in cathedrals and collegiate churches. (2) The president of a college. (3) The presiding judge in the Anglican Court of Arches (q.v.).

DEAN, RURAL. A deputy of the bishop or archdeacon in certain parishes (Anglican).

DEBUNK. A modern verb signifying to get rid of clap-trap (bunk or bunkum). Literary and historical works that have been "debunked" are usually unreliable, the effort to display clever modernism resulting in bias or lack of perception.

DECALOGUE. The Ten Commandments Moses (q.v.) is said to have brought down from Mount Sinai. The Decalogue became the ethical ideal for the Israelites and, as interpreted by succeeding ages, for the Christians.

DECLARATION OF INDULGENCE. An Act passed in the reign of Charles II suspending penal laws against Catholics and Nonconformists.

DECORATED. An elaborate style of Gothic architecture (14th C.). See *Architecture.*

DECRETALS. The papal decrees determining points of ecclesiastical law.

DECRETALS, FALSE. A collection of canons dealing with ecclesiastical law. It is divided into three parts: (1) Seventy letters attributed to popes of the first three centuries, all of which are spurious. (2) A collection of canons, mainly genuine. (3) A collection of skilfully blended genuine and false letters. The forgery was detected by Catholic and Protestant scholars in the 17th C. The object of the forger appears to have been to exalt the power of the Church and especially the Papacy. (See A. C. Flick, *The Rise of the Medieval Church* (1909).)

DEE, JOHN (1527–1608). English mathematician and astrologer who was patronized by Queen Elizabeth and the earl of Leicester. (See Charlotte Fell Smith, *John Dee.*)

DEFENDER OF THE FAITH. The title conferred on Henry VIII by Pope Leo X (1521) in return for his book on the Seven Sacraments written to refute Luther. With delightful irony the title was continued as a designation of the Protestant English monarchs.

DEGRADATION. In ancient canon law the withdrawing of all ecclesiastical rights and benefits from criminous clerks.

DEGREES, LAMBETH. The right of the archbishop of Canterbury to confer degrees, *honoris causa,* derives from his pre-Reformation powers as legate of the Pope.

DEICIDE. (1) The slaying of a sacred totem animal. (2) The dramatic representation in certain mystery religions of the slaying of a god.

DEIFICATION. See *Emperor-worship.*

DEISM. The belief in a god but not in revealed religion. Some prominent deists: Lord Herbert of Cherbury, the philosopher Hobbes, Voltaire.

DELPHI. See *oracle.*

DELUGE. The biblical account of the Flood (Gen. vi.–viii.). Such stories are found in most ancient literatures (Arabia, Greece, Egypt, Africa, Japan, Asia). The Deluge traditions probably arose from tidal waves and cyclones in primitive times. See also *Ark.*

Demeter. In Greek mythology the mother of Persephone. The beautiful story of the taking of Persephone to the underworld held deep meaning for the Greeks. Those who were initiated into the mysteries of Eleusis learnt from it the principle of a future life and how the seed must fall and decay before it can experience new life. Demeter was the Great Mother —or Natura. (See L. Dyer, *The Gods in Greece* (1891).)

Demiurge. A gnostic term to distinguish the creator of the universe from the supreme God.

demon and **demonology.** The word derives from the Gr. *daimon* = a spirit. Primitive people everywhere believe in demons as evil spirits. The demonology of the Jews included good and evil spirits. The early Christians regarded all the gods of paganism as demons. Jesus held the current belief of his time with regard to evil spirits. Demonology is a widespread religious cult dealing with beings malevolent and benevolent. In English, "demon" denotes malevolence, but it is not so in all languages (in German it is neutral). Demonology was known to the Jews and is practised among all primitive peoples. The phenomena associated with it continue to be examined and discussed by modern psychical researchers. (See R. C. Thompson, *Devils and Evil Spirits of Babylonia.*)

Denis, Saint. First bishop of Paris and patron saint of France. (3rd C.)

De Profundis. Psalm 130, from its opening words "out of the depths."

dervish. Persian word corresponding to the Arabic fakir and signifying a mystic ascetic. Fakirs and dervishes cultivate "magical" powers by means of concentration and ascetic practices.

Descent to Hades. The doctrine of Christ's descent to the underworld (1 Pet. iii. 19), referred to in the Apostles' Creed, is probably derived from the Jewish belief that the Messiah would preach also to the departed spirits. Osiris, in the Egyptian religion, also "descended into hell." (See L. H. Jordan, *Comparative Religion* (1905).)

Destiny. The inscrutable power believed to control human and cosmic processes. A counterpart of the subtler Eastern doctrine of Karma (q.v.).

Deutero-Isaiah. The assumed author of the later prophecies of Isaiah. (See P. K. Cheyne, *The Book of Isaiah.*)

Deuteronomy. The fifth book of the Pentateuch.

deva. (1) Beneficent spirits of light and air (Hindu and Buddhist). (2) Evil spirits and demons (Persian myth.).

devil. See *demon.*

DEVOTION. The giving up of the mind and heart to the contemplation of God. The chief (Christian) books of devotion are: The Psalms; *The Little Flowers of St. Francis*; *The Imitation of Christ* (Thomas à Kempis); *The Soul's Progress in God* (Bonaventura); *Centuries of Meditations* (Thomas Traherne); *Introduction to the Devout Life* (Francis de Sales); *The Saints' Everlasting Rest* (Baxter); *The Dark Night of the Soul* (St. John of the Cross); *Light on the Path*, by M. C.

DHAMA-RAJA. The Tibetan king of the Dead. Cf. Osiris.

DHAMMAPADA. A string of 423 Buddhist moral maxims of unsurpassed wisdom and beauty: e.g.

5. Hatred does not cease by hatred at any time; hatred ceases by love; this is its nature.

129. All men tremble at punishment, all men fear death. Remember that you are like unto them, and do not kill nor cause slaughter.

223. Let one overcome anger by love, let him overcome evil by good; let him overcome the greedy by liberality, the liar by truth.

DHARMA ("Divine Body of Truth"). Hindu term signifying the following of an ethical system of life (Rules of Right Conduct) which brings peace and ultimate deliverance from sangsara (q.v.).

DHARMAKAYA ("divine body of truth"). In Tibetan Lamaism the body of essential wisdom (*bodhi*) or complete enlightenment. The Buddha is regarded as possessing three bodies: (1) the human illusory body; (2) the body of truth or wisdom; (3) the body of bliss. Ordinary mankind could only perceive the first of these bodies.

DHYANA. Meditation; the Hindu and Buddhist practice of concentrating the mind on one idea for long periods, with the result that sense-perceptions are stilled. See *meditation*.

DIANA (ARTEMIS). The Roman moon-goddess of chastity and hunting; her worship at Ephesus was also associated with fertility.

DIAPASON. (1) A whole octave. (2) A harmony. (3) Various musical sounds in concord. (4) Two organ stops.

DIASIA. A Greek festival to commemorate the dead.

DIASPORA. Dispersion, a term applied to the post-exilic Jews dispersed among the Gentiles.

DIATESSARON. A harmony of the four Gospels to make one narrative. The first was composed by Tatian (q.v.) in the 2nd C.

DICKENS, CHARLES (1812–70). One of the greatest of English novelists. His strong humanitarian sympathies, shown especially in the *Christmas Carol, Bleak House, Oliver Twist,* rendered his work a strong force making for social reform.

DIDACHE, THE. A Christian document discovered in 1875 in a monastery at Constantinople and known also as the Teaching of the Twelve Apostles. It contains (1) moral precepts for catechumens; (2) instructions as to the Eucharist, baptism, fasting, prayer, etc.; (3) a final chapter on eschatology. It was probably written between A.D. 130 and 150. (See G. C. Allen, *The Teaching of the Twelve Apostles* (1903).)

DIES IRAE (L. "day of wrath"). A medieval Catholic hymn on the Last Judgment, so called from its opening words. (13th C.)

DIGNITARY. A high official of the church.

DIOCESAN CONFERENCE. A meeting of the clergy of the diocese, presided over by the bishop.

DIOCESE. The territory under the jurisdiction of a bishop.

DIONYSIUS THE AREOPAGITE. An Athenian Pauline convert to Christianity (Acts xvii. 34).

DIONYSIUS EXIGUUS. A learned chronologist and theologian of the 6th C. and a friend of Cassiodorus. He introduced the Christian era we now use. Cassiodorus describes him as a saintly ascetic of wisdom and simplicity, humble-minded, with rare eloquence and a fine capacity for silence.

DIONYSUS (Roman **BACCHUS**). A Greek god of fertility. His rites are important for, directly or indirectly, they appear to have influenced early Christianity. Dionysus was born of a virgin (Semele or Demeter) on 25 December (the winter solstice). He was reared in a cave and was identified with the Ram or Lamb—probably traced to the zodiacal sign. He was called Saviour. In the Mysteries the passion of Dionysus was represented, his death, descent to the underworld and resurrection. Raw flesh was distributed to the worshippers, who ate it in memory of the death of Dionysus dismembered by the Titans. (See Charles F. Dupuis, *Traité des Mystères*, ch. i.)

DIPTYCH. (1) A register of saints read aloud during the eucharist. (2) A pair of pictures on folding panels.

DIRECTORY, CATHOLIC. A Catholic book issued each year giving the regulations for the Mass and Office.

DIRGE. A funeral song or hymn.

DISCALCED. See *Carmelite.*

DISCIPLE. A follower; one who receives instruction from another. See also *cheyla.*

DISCIPLES OF CHRIST. (1) Christ's followers as described in the N.T. (Matt. xi. 2; xxvi. 20). (2) A large sect of American Protestants established by Thomas and Alexander Campbell in 1807. They boast over eight thousand churches and some six thousand ministers.

DISESTABLISHMENT and DISENDOWMENT. The annulling of the establishment of a Church as the State Church. The Irish

Church was disestablished by Act of Parliament in 1869. Private bills for disestablishing the Church in Scotland have been introduced, but without success. Proposals for disestablishing the Church of England have many times been brought forward by dissenters and others, but the problem is complicated by vested interests owing to endowment. (See J. E. C. Welldon, *The Religious Aspects of Disestablishment* (1911).)

DISPENSATION. (1) Stages of God's dealing with his creatures (e.g. Patriarchal, Christian dispensations). (2) Permission given by the Pope or some high official in the Church to break a rule or law. Catholic dispensations were ordered by the Council of Trent (1563) to be given free; in practice they are subject to four charges: tax, expenses, eleemosynary fine and alms.

DISSENT and DISSENTERS. Separation from a church. In England, Dissent made rapid progress in Elizabeth's reign (Separatists, Brownists, Presbyterians, Anabaptists, etc.). The Baptists and Quakers increased rapidly during the Commonwealth. Under the Stuarts the Dissenters suffered severe persecution until the Toleration Act (q.v.) gave them greater freedom. The Wesleyan revival (18th C.) brought fresh spirit to religion and strengthened Dissent. The power of Dissent in England is now about equal with that of the Church of England and they confront one another on the problem of Disestablishment (q.v.).

DIVINATION. The supposed magical power by which a knowledge of future or secret things is obtained. See *Spiritualism*; *dreams*; *oracle*.

DIVINE RIGHT. The doctrine that a king is God's representative and rules by God's will. Kingship having evolved from the priesthood (see *Numa*; *Moses*), the idea of divine right of kings obtained everywhere in primitive times. The English Stuarts insisted on Divine Right so stubbornly that they provoked revolution; Louis XIV of France did the same. The Russian and Prussian royal houses were wrecked largely as a result of the inflated egotism which a belief in divine right feeds.

DIVORCE. The legal dissolving of a marriage contract. Modern law allows two kinds of divorce: (1) absolute divorce (*a vinculo matrimonii*) and (2) limited divorce—"legal separation" (*a mensa et thoro*). In primitive states of society divorce appears to be common—the chief cause being sterility. Among the Greeks and Romans divorce did not involve public legal procedure until Augustus insisted on the presence of seven witnesses. Statistics show that divorce is most prevalent in the United States; Germany comes next, then France, then England.

DJINN. See *jinn*.

DOCETISM. (1) A 2nd-C. belief pronounced by the Church to be heretical. Docetism denied the human nature of Jesus

Christ and asserted that his body only *seemed* to be real. (Gr. *dokein* = to seem.) The view was held by Gnostics, Manichaeans, etc. (2) A similar doctrine arose in the later schools of Buddhism regarding the person of Buddha.

DODD, WILLIAM (1729–77). Church of England divine who was hanged for forging a bond. Dr. Johnson wrote a petition for commutation of the sentence. Dodd's *Beauties of Shakespeare* is an excellent anthology.

DOGMA. A doctrine defined and taught as resting on divine or supreme authority. The Catholic Church is the great storehouse of Christian dogma. The modified view of external religious authority, as held in the Protestant churches, causes dogma to take a secondary place.

DOGMATIC THEOLOGY. That branch of theology which expounds ecclesiastical dogmas.

DOLLY WORSHIP. A nonconformist phrase to describe the Catholic religion. (See Eric Partridge, *Slang, To-day and Yesterday*, p. 197.)

DOLMEN. A prehistoric structure (? grave) of two unhewn stones supporting a flattish stone.

DOMINIC, SAINT, and DOMINICANS (1170–1221). St. Dominic was a Castilian monk who worked in southern France among the Albigensian heretics. He founded the Dominican Order of mendicant friars with the purpose of training preachers and controversialists. The Dominican Order received papal confirmation in 1216. (See A. T. Drane, *History of St. Dominic.*)

DONATION OF CONSTANTINE. A forged 8th-C. document pretending to have been addressed to Pope Sylvester I by Constantine the Great, lending support to papal claims to terrestrial and spiritual authority.

DONATISTS. A 4th-C. sect of African Christians established by Donatus, an African bishop. The Donatists were extremely strict and held that the sacraments are valid only when administered by a priest whose life squares with his doctrine. They occasioned Constantine much trouble owing to the violence of some of their members, fugitive slaves and vagrants, called Circumcelliones (*circum cellas* = from house to house).

DONNE, JOHN (1573–1631). English poet and divine. He served as private secretary to Lord Chancellor Ellesmere and incurred his wrath by a clandestine marriage with his niece. King James I persuaded Donne to take holy orders and appointed him dean of St. Paul's, where he became famous for his eloquent preaching. See art. *Religion*, § 1. (See Izaak Walton, *Lives of John Donne*, etc.; Hugh I'A. Fausset, *John Donne.*)

DORIAN MODE. (1) An ancient Greek mode in music, simple and solemn. (2) The first of the Christian ecclesiastical modes.

DORMER. A vertical window in a sloping roof.

DORSAL, DOSSAL, DOSSEL. Ornamental cloth at the back of the altar (eccles.).

DORT (DORDRECHT), SYNOD OF. A Protestant synod held at Dort from 13 November 1618 to 25 May 1619 to which deputies were sent from all the reformed churches in Europe to settle the differences between the doctrines of Luther and Calvin as against Arminius. The Synod condemned the tenets of Arminius.

DOUAY BIBLE. The English translation of the Bible for Catholics made at the University of Douai in 1609.

DOUKHOBORS. An 18th-C. Russian community of nonconformist peasants. They claim to worship God in the spirit, and put small value in Church or dogma. They have suffered much persecution and many have emigrated to Canada. (See Aylmer Maude, *A Peculiar People, the Doukhobors.*)

DOXOLOGY. A short hymn in praise of God. Metrical doxologies usually concluded Latin hymns.

DREAMS. In primitive society an importance was attached to the dreams of sleep which seemed exaggerated until modern psychological research brought to light many vital problems connected with the dream state. It has been shown that the dream-consciousness in sleep is continuous with the waking consciousness, although in sleep the direct control of the will is absent. The researches of Freud and Jung have demonstrated that deep currents of emotional life tend to come into consciousness in the dreams of sleep. For this reason a systematic study of dreams is often of great value in gaining a deeper self-knowledge. Practically all (though few realize the fact) suffer from suppressions of various kinds which react adversely on health and well-being. The realization of these suppressions by the subject leads to their elimination and a consequent freedom which is of infinite value to health and happiness. J. W. Dunne, in his remarkable book, *An Experiment with Time* (1927), has shown that everybody dreams of events which happened in the past and also of events that take place later in time. From this fact, amply authenticated, he has advanced a theory of "serialism" with regard to time. His ideas are in line with the physicists' theory of a time-space continuum. Following this theory, Mr. Dunne claims to have proved the existence of life after death, which would appear to have resemblance in some respects with the dreams of sleep. "In our future existence," he writes, "we shall be four-dimensional beings in fifth-dimensional time, living the kind of life we glimpse now in dreams." (See also J. W. Dunne, *The Serial Universe* (1934).)

DRUIDISM. The religious system of the ancient inhabitants of Gaul and the British Isles. The

Druids formed the learned and priestly caste. The course of training for a novice was prolonged, sometimes extending over twenty years. They taught that the soul is immortal and subject to many incarnations. (See P. W. Joyce, *A Social History of Ancient Ireland* (1903).)

DRUSES. A people inhabiting the north of Syria professing a religion derived partly from the Bible and partly from the Koran.

DUALISM. (1) The doctrine of the complete separation of spirit and matter. (2) The doctrine of two distinct and opposed principles of good and evil (philos.).

DUNKERS or **TUNKERS.** A sect of German-American Baptists founded by Alexander Mack (1679–1735) who practise triple immersion and observe the Love Feast and other primitive customs. They hold the doctrine of non-resistance.

DUNS SCOTUS, JOHN (1255–1308). An Oxford Franciscan teacher, leader of the Schoolmen (q.v.), who opposed the classical studies of the Renaissance. From his followers (Dunses) the word "dunce" is derived.

DUNSTAN, SAINT (925–88). Archbishop of Canterbury who served King Edred and afterwards King Edgar as an able minister.

DURGA. See *Kali.*

DYOPHYSITES. A 5th-C. Christian sect who insisted on the two natures of Christ, human and divine.

E

EA. Babylonian god of streams and rivers; worshipped at the confluence of the Tigris and Euphrates.

EAGLE. See *lectern.*

EALHWINE. See *Alcuin.*

EARLY ENGLISH (or **POINTED**). The style of Gothic in which the pointed arch was first used in England (13th C.; archit.). Examples: Temple Church, London; parts of Winchester, Wells, Durham and Salisbury cathedrals and Westminster Abbey. See *Architecture.*

EASTER. The oldest festival of the Christian Church. The word is derived from A.S. *Eastre,* the goddess of Spring and of Dawn, and the festival derives partly from Christian and partly from pagan sources. Easter was not observed in apostolic or sub-apostolic times, and did not come into prominence until embittered controversy as to its exact date (the "quarto-deciman controversy") disturbed the Church of the 2nd and 3rd C.s.

EASTER-OFFERING. A gift (usually money) made to the parson by his parishioners at Easter.

EASTWARD POSITION. The position of the celebrant at the Eucharist, facing the altar. The High Church party in the C. of E. favour this position; the Low Church party favour the north position.

EBIONISM, EBIONITES. Contemptuous name applied to the doctrines and membership of the Jewish Christians of the early Church. They regarded the Mosaic Law as binding on Christians and denied the miraculous birth of Jesus Christ. (Heb. *ebyon* = poor.)

EBLIS. Leader of the fallen angels in Mohammedan theology.

ECCE HOMO. A picture of Christ crowned with thorns. (L., Behold the Man: John xix. 5.)

ECCLESIA. The popular assembly in ancient Athens; the term was applied to the Christian Church by the Septuagint translators.

ECCLESIASTES. A book of the O.T. tradition ascribed to Solomon.

ECCLESIASTICAL COMMISSIONS. The first ecclesiastical commission for the C. of E. was appointed by Queen Elizabeth in 1584; another was appointed in 1641 and again by James II in 1687. Ecclesiastical Commissioners (bishops, deans and laymen), for the management of Church property, were appointed in 1835 and incorporated in 1836. The law relating to them was amended in 1868.

ECCLESIASTICAL COURTS. See *courts, ecclesiastical.*

ECCLESIASTICUS. An apocryphal book of the O.T. See *Wisdom Literature.*

ECCLESIOLOGY. The science of church building and decorating.

ECK, JOHANN MAIER (1486–1543). German Catholic theologian who served as a controversialist against Luther and Zwingli.

ECKHART (EKKEHART), JOHANNES ("Meister Eckhart") (1260–1327). German mystic of Platonic and pantheistic tendencies. He entered the Dominican Order and lectured in Paris and later at Cologne. At Strassburg he came in contact with the Beguines, some of whose doctrines he adopted and systematized, with the result that he was summoned before the Inquisition. He made certain recantations and his death occurred before the matter was settled. He was the first who attempted to give a speculative basis to the Christian doctrines. (See R. M. Jones, *Mystical Religion* (1909).)

ECSTASY. A state of consciousness in which a feeling of exaltation and excessive joy is experienced. In primitive religions this experience is induced by intoxication of various kinds (see *Peyotism*). Mysticism has sought the experience, or found it without direct seeking. The phenomena of hypnotism are closely allied with it. Various religious "revivals" in England and America have led to wild manifestations of crowd hysteria and ecstasy. Many saints of all religions have experienced ecstasy See *Samadhi.*

ECUMENICAL COUNCIL. (Gr. *oikoumene ge* = the inhabited world.) A hypothetical council representing the whole Christian world. Since Christianity is split into numberless churches and sects, such a council is an impossibility. The following seven councils are usually regarded as "ecumenical": Council of Nicea (325); First C. of Constantinople (381); First C. of Ephesus (431); C. of Chalcedon (451); Second C. of Constantinople (553); Third C. of Constantinople (680); Second C. of Nicea (787).

EDDAS. The ancient Norse books of mythology. (See T. Percy, *Northern Antiquities*.)

EDEN, GARDEN OF. See *Golden Age*.

EDICT OF NANTES. The legal settlement of 1598 by which the Huguenots in France were granted privileges of worship and civic rights. It was revoked in 1685.

EDICT OF WORMS. The imperial order promulgated at Worms (1521) by which Luther and the Lutherans were put under the ban. See *Luther, Martin*.

EDMUND, SAINT. Archbishop of Canterbury in the reign of Henry III. A man of wide culture and saintly life. (See W. Wallace, *Life of St. Edmund*.)

EDOMITES. An ancient people inhabiting Edom in the south-east of Palestine.

EDUCATION, RELIGIOUS. Previous to the Industrial Revolution in England there was little education of the mass population and what there was emanated chiefly from the Church. The establishment of the S.P.C.K. (1699) led to the foundation of several "charity schools," and from this time onward elementary education spread widely in England. The Education Act of 1902, which extended rate aid to denominational schools, led to the "Passive Resistance" campaign amongst Nonconformists, who objected to the religious teaching given in Catholic and Church of England schools. A compromise was effected in 1908. Much bitter feeling has been evinced among Churchpeople and Nonconformists as to what kind of Christianity children should be taught. This is regrettable because it is probably better that children should not receive much (if any) doctrinal teaching. It is of far greater importance, as psychology abundantly demonstrates, that they shall grow up in an atmosphere of love, tolerance, freedom of thought and a complete absence of strife between parents, relatives and teachers.

EDWARDS, JONATHAN (1703–58). One of the ablest theologians of the U.S.A., for some years tutor at Yale. His philosophy was based on the Platonic teaching that the universe has no existence save in the mind or idea and that God is the only entity. (See S. E. Dwight, *Life and Works of Jonathan Edwards*, 10 vols. (1829).)

EGO. The "I" or principle of self-consciousness in man. Archibald Weir writes, in *For To-day* (1933): "No exact sense has been applied to such words as soul, self, ego, personality, or any others indicating agents controlling the physical organism. The muddle-headed habit is of long standing. It reaches back far beyond the age of the Antonines." The average person regards the "I" as that bundle of qualities that make up personality. But a very little reflection shows that the real "I" is not that bundle but a being capable of objectively contemplating it. Thus the contemplator can be pushed farther and farther back until it becomes impossible to determine what the "self" is. Eastern philosophy (see *Upanishads*), which has probed the problem more deeply than any other, has come to the conclusion that the self of each human being is continuous with the Self of the universe and is thus intimately associated with the selves of all other beings. It follows from this philosophy that the only means of reaching the universal Self is the purification of the individual self. It is the ego, regarded in its lower aspects, that serves as a screen shutting us from truth or reality. Thus the search for truth resolves itself less into an intellectual than a moral problem. A study of the Upanishads has convinced many modern thinkers that the cultivation of personality (i.e. ministering to the ego) is the great enemy to be overcome by those who would devote themselves to the search for truth. (See Edward Carpenter, *Pagan and Christian Creeds* (Appendix).)

EGYPT, RELIGION OF. Egypt is the land of two great forces: the Sun and the River Nile. From these Egyptian religion developed—the vivifying sun (Ra; Aton; Khepri; Horus) and the fructifying Nile (Osiris). These twin forces gave birth to other myths and these in turn to others, until we find an ever-increasing family of gods—Ra's daughter, Maat (Truth or Righteousness); Horus, Set, Amon, Ptah, Nefertem, Thoth (the Moon). The Egyptians believed in a life after death, but its enjoyment largely depended on the care with which the physical body was preserved by relatives. Hence arose the custom of building immense tombs and pyramids.

§ 2. Egyptian beliefs were woven around (1) the body, (2) the spirit, (3) the "Ka." The Ka was a spiritual "double" whose duty it was to bring food-offerings to the dead. The dead passed, with the setting sun, to a western land. Only kings and high officers of state accompanied Ra in his triumphal journey across the sky. With the gradual growth of culture the Egyptian religion evolved an ethical standard and Osiris developed into a judge of the dead who weighed souls in the balance. This function of Osiris causing the timid too great uneasiness, magic charms were introduced to ensure a favourable verdict.

§ 3. The worship of Ra had always taken precedence of the other cults and by 1500 B.C. his high priest had become the national chief priest wielding a power that began to rival the throne. Aware of his danger, King Ikhnaton in 1375 B.C. opposed the priestly power by introducing a reformed monotheistic religion. Aton, the Sun-god, was declared to be sole god, a god of love, with care for all his creatures. After Ikhnaton's death the forces of conservatism proved too strong and the old gods returned. An enlightened animal worship became very popular in the last centuries B.C. and the worship of Isis and her little son Horus provided a sympathetic atmosphere for the birth-stories of Christ. (See E. A. W. Budge, *A History of Egypt* (1902); G. Maspero, *Histoire ancienne des peuples de l'Orient*, vol. i (1895).)

EGYPTIAN BOOK OF THE DEAD. A manual of instructions usually interred with the mummy in ancient Egypt. It gave directions for the soul's guidance when brought before the great judge Osiris, and for its journey to rebirth (reincarnation). In many respects it closely resembles the Tibetan Book of the Dead (Bardo Thödol—q.v.). (See E. A. W. Budge, *The Book of the Dead*.)

EKKEN, KAIBARA (b. 1629). Japanese philosopher, scholar and social reformer. He adhered to to the Chu philosophy, considering it the nearest to that of Confucius and Mencius. Many of his sayings are profound: e.g. " Gods are moved by neither bribery, flattery nor familiarity, but by sincerity." " Usually men who do good reap happiness, while those who do evil reap evil. . . . Though seeking happiness, one cannot find it if Heaven wills otherwise."

ELDER. (1) A lay official in the Presbyterian Church. (2) Ordained ministers without a pastorate in the Methodist Church.

ELECTION. The predetermination of certain persons (the elect) to salvation by God's will. A doctrine held by Calvinists and Arminians.

ELECT LADY. A title which occurs in 2 John i. Authorities differ as to whether John was addressing a lady or a church—a doubt not usually found in familiar correspondence.

ELEMENTS. The eucharistic bread and wine (theol.).

ELEUSINIA. See *Mystery Religions*.

ELEVATION OF THE HOST. The holding up of the eucharistic elements for worship (Cath.).

ELIJAH. An Israelitish prophet also called " the Tishbite "—possibly from the place of his birth. He sternly opposed the idolatry of King Ahab (1 Kings xvii. 1).

ELISABETH, SAINT (1207–31). Wife of Louis IV of Thuringia, who renounced her position to live a life of asceticism and service among the poor and sick. She was canonized in 1235. (See Charles Kingsley, *Saint's Tragedy*.) (Not to be confused with the Virgin Queen.)

ELISHA. The disciple who succeeded Elijah as prophet. (See 2 Kings iv., vi., viii.)

ELLWOOD, THOMAS (1639–1713). A Quaker friend of John Milton. He wrote an autobiography giving interesting details of Milton's life.

ELOHIM. Hebrew name for God; used in many passages of the O.T. instead of Jahweh. This has led some scholars to the conclusion that the Pentateuch was composed at two widely different periods, the "Elohistic" portions being the more primitive.

ELOI, SAINT (588–689). Apostle of the Belgians and patron saint of goldsmiths.

ELUL. The twelfth month of the Jewish civil year.

ELYSIUM. The Greek mythological home of the blessed. See *heaven*; *Paradise*.

EMANATION. The doctrine that regards the universe as issuing from God continually instead of regarding creation as an act in time.

EMANCIPATION, CATHOLIC. See *Catholic emancipation*.

EMBALM. The practice of preserving a dead body from decay by injecting drugs. The Egyptians believed the welfare of the dead depended on the preservation of their physical bodies. See *Egypt, Religion of*.

EMBER-DAYS. The three fast days (Wednesday, Friday, Saturday) in each quarter, following the first Sunday in Lent, Whitsunday, Holy Cross Day (14 Sept.) and St. Lucia's Day (13 Dec.). Ember days are appointed for the ordination of clergy (C. of E.).

EMBOLISM. A prayer for deliverance from evil, inserted after the Lord's Prayer. (Gr. *embolismos* = put in.)

EMERSON, RALPH WALDO (1803–82). American man of letters. One of the deepest thinkers the U.S.A. have produced. His mystical interpretation of life had a profound influence on the religious thought of Europe and America. (See Oliver Wendell Holmes, *Ralph Waldo Emerson* (1885); *Emerson's Journals*.)

EMINENCE. The title given since 1631 to cardinals, formerly styled Most Illustrious (Cath.).

EMPEROR-WORSHIP. Worship of the Roman Emperor became a prominent state function during the first three centuries of our era. It appears to have arisen in the eastern provinces where divine honours were paid to certain Roman officials. The new cult became established at Rome in the reign of Augustus. The Senate, while encouraging the provincials' deification of rulers (living or dead), restricted Emperor-worship in Rome to such emperors as had been officially apotheosized by decree of the Senate. The honour was bestowed on Julius Caesar in 62 B.C. The early Christians came into conflict with the state by refusing to take part in Emperor-worship.

EMPIRE, HOLY ROMAN. The official title given to the German Empire from 962 to 1806 when the imperial title was resigned by Francis II of Hapsburg.

ENCRATITES. A 2nd-C. ascetic sect founded by Tatian (q.v.).

They abstained from marriage, meat and wine.

ENCYCLICAL. (1) A letter from the Pope to the bishops condemning errors or advising a course of conduct in times of stress. (2) A letter sent round to a number of people.

ENCYCLOPEDISTS. The writers (Voltaire, Rousseau, Grimm, Diderot, d'Alembert, Montesquieu and others) who contributed to the first French Encyclopedia (1751–80)—*Encyclopédie ou Dictionnaire raisonné des Sciences, des Arts, et des Métiers.* The work was directed mainly at undermining the influence of the Church in France which at that time blocked the way to liberal thought and scientific research.

ENDOWMENT. Money or property given to an institution for its upkeep.

ENERGUMEN. One possessed by an evil entity. See *possession, demoniacal.*

ENGLISH CHURCH. See *Church of England.*

ENGLISH CHURCH UNION. A society formed within the Church of England in 1860 with the object of upholding High Church doctrine and ritual and to assist clergy prosecuted for unlawful ritualistic practices.

ENNEAD. A group of nine lesser gods, presided over by a chief god, in ancient Egyptian cities.

ENOCH. Father of Methuselah. In the Biblical account he was translated to heaven without suffering death (Heb. xi. 5).

ENOCH, BOOK OF. An apocalyptic work which disappeared about the 8th C. An Ethiopic version was discovered in 1773.

ENTABLATURE. That part of a design that rests on the capitals (archit.).

ENTHRONE. To install a bishop in his see.

ENTHUSIASM. See *Revivals,* § 2.

EPACTS. Nineteen numbers used for fixing the date of Easter by indicating the moon's age at the beginning of each civil year in the lunar cycle.

EPHESUS, COUNCIL OF. An ecumenical council held at Ephesus in 431. It excommunicated Nestorius (q.v.) for his denial that the divinity and humanity of Christ were enacted in a single person.

EPHOD. A vestment worn by Hebrew priests (Exod. xxviii.).

EPHRAIM THE SYRIAN, SAINT. A Mesopotamian saint of the 4th C. A.D. He was widely known as a poet, commentator, preacher and apologist.

EPICLESIS, EPIKLESIS. That part of the prayer used in the Eastern Church whereby the elements (water, bread, wine and oil) are consecrated.

EPICTETUS. Stoic Greek philosopher. The kernel of his teaching was that the highest wisdom consists in distinguishing what is ours from what is not ours. Nothing, he decided, is truly ours except our will. (Cf. *In Memoriam*—"Our wills are ours to make them thine.") Each man has within him a guardian spirit or genius. The perfect man knows no anger in the face of provocation and his peace of mind is such that it cannot be broken.

EPICURUS, EPICUREANISM (342–270 B.C.). Greek philosopher of Samos and founder of the Epicurean philosophy. In his famous garden at Athens he gathered a school of disciples (men and women) about him. The community lived a plain and simple life. His teaching was of the most intimate and personal kind and he avoided publicity and public life. The epicurean wisdom is best summed up in the sentence. "We cannot live pleasantly unless we live wisely and nobly and righteously." (See H. Sidgwick, *History of Ethics* (1902); Evelyn Abbott, *Hellenica* (1898); A. E. Taylor, *Epicurus*.)

EPIPHANIUS (320–403). Bishop of Constantia, noted for his orthodoxy. His Panarion (medicine-chest) refutes eighty heresies.

EPIPHANY. (1) The manifestation of a god. (2) The Christian festival commemorating Christ's manifestation to the Magi (6 Jan.).

EPISCOPACY. Church government vested in bishops. See *bishop*.

EPISTEMOLOGY. The philosophy of knowledge.

EPISTLE. A didactic letter, especially those written by early Christians to encourage their comrades in the faith. The N.T. Epistles are as follows :—

Epistle to the :	*Written from :*	*Date (approx.).* A.D.
Galatians	Thessalonica or Corinth	51–53
1 Thessalonians	Corinth	52–54
2 Thessalonians	Corinth	52–55
1 Corinthians	Ephesus	56
2 Corinthians	Macedonia	57–59
1 Timothy	Macedonia	56–59
Titus	Colosse or Macedonia	56–59
Romans	Corinth	58
James	Judea	61
Philemon	Rome	61–63
Colossians	Rome	61–62
Ephesians	Rome	61–62
Philippians	Rome	62
Hebrews	Rome	62–63
Jude	(Uncertain)	64
2 Timothy	Rome	61–62
1 Peter	Babylon	66
2 Peter	(Uncertain)	68
1, 2 and 3 John	Ephesus	70

EPISTOLER, EPISTLER. Reader of the liturgical epistle in the communion service.

EPITHALAMION, EPITHALAMIUM. A song or poem in celebration of marriage. One of the finest epithalamia in the language is Edmund Spenser's "Epithalamion." See also *Song of Solomon*.

EQUITY. (1) Fair play, justice. (2) Technical legal procedure intended to moderate the rigour of the common law in the interests of fair dealing, and to prevent too strict adherence to the literal text.

ERA. A series of years reckoned from a certain point. The chief historical eras, other than the Christian era, are :

	B.C.
(1) Biblical era (dated by Bishop Usher) from Creation	4004
(2) Jewish era	3761
(3) Era of Constantinople .	5508
(4) Era of Nabonassar . .	747
(5) Era of the Seleucidae (used by the Maccabees)	312
(6) The Grecian Olympiads.	776
(7) Roman era (reckoned from the founding of Rome — *anno urbis conditæ*)	753
	A.D.
(8) The Mohammedan era, dated from the Hegira	622

ERASMUS, DESIDERIUS (1466–1536). A Dutch scholar and man of letters of outstanding importance in the Reformation. He was brought up in a monastery but disliked the life intensely and only under pressure from his guardian became an Augustinian canon. His interest was in letters and literature rather than theology. After much opposition he became a student at Paris University and took a degree in theology. His wit, humour, enormous learning and literary enthusiasm gave him a position somewhat akin to Voltaire's in a later age. With cutting satire he trounced the stupidity of the monks. But Erasmus, though he fought the clergy, respected the Church. His letters are among the wittiest and most vivid ever written. So sharp was his pen and so enormous his energy that after his time the Catholic Church was never again quite the same. He opened the door to more liberal and rationalist views and whipped much somnolent stupidity from the cloister. (See biographies by S. Knight (1726) ; J. Jortin (1760) and R. B. Drummond (1873) ; also *Erasmus's Letters* translated by F. M. Nichols (1904).)

ERASTIAN. A follower of Thomas Erastus (1524–83), a Swiss physician who denied the Church's right to inflict excommunication. The word has come to mean extreme subservience of the Church to the State, though Erastus never held or taught such a doctrine.

ERIGENA, JOHN SCOTUS. A 9th-C. Neo-Platonic Irish philosopher and theologian of very enlightened views. He taught that creation is not an act in time but a continual process outside the time-factor. (See F. D. Maurice, *Medieval Philosophy*, pp. 45–79.)

EROS (L., *Cupid*). God of Love in Greek mythology. The cosmic Eros born of the world-egg laid by Time (Chronos) in the bosom of Chaos was the originator of all created beings.

ESCHATOLOGY. The doctrine concerning last things, i.e. death and the after-state. See *future life.*

ESDRAS, BOOKS OF. The name of six Jewish books. The most important are the Apocryphal I and II Esdras. I Esdras was probably written in the 4th C. B.C. and the apocalyptic II Esdras about A.D. 100.

ESOTERIC DOCTRINE. The knowledge of laws, forces and causes below or above the threshold of normal consciousness.

ESSENCE. The real nature of a thing. The word constitutes one of the intellectual straws so frequently split by early theologians. (Was the Son of the same essence (*homoousios*) as the Father, or of a similar essence (*homoiousios*).)

ESSENES. A Jewish monastic and ascetic sect of the early Christian era. They probably derived their doctrine from Persian, Buddhist or Pythagorean sources. The early Christians appear to have been influenced by the Essenes in various points of life and doctrine. (See Edward Schürer, *The Jewish People in the Time of Christ.*)

ESTABLISHED CHURCH. See *Church of England.*

ESTHER (Persian for "a star"). Daughter of Abigail and cousin of Mordecai. See *Esther, Book of.*

ESTHER, BOOK OF. The 17th book of the O.T. It is of Persian origin; 19th-C. scholarship has found in it much Babylonian and Persian mythology.

ETHELRED. See *Ælred.*

ETHERIC BODY. A term used in theosophy (q.v.). The difference between a plant and a stone is mainly due to the plant having a physical and an etheric body, whereas the stone only has a physical body. The etheric body roughly corresponds to what science calls the magnetic field and is closely connected with glandular activity. It is the mainspring of physical energy, the substance from which dreams are woven. It is condensed in ectoplasm and is the cause of most of the phenomena of spiritualism. It is said to rest above the physical body during sleep, like a cloud. It is the force in man which corresponds to the plant kingdom in nature.

ETHICS. The science or philosophy of moral conduct. The origin of morality, lost in the sands of time, must be dug out by psychological and sociological research. As soon as man gained self-consciousness (see *ego*; *Fall of Man*) he entered on a period of strife with himself and with others. The ego, gradually built up by civilization, led him to self-gratification, and this in turn to pain and a seeking for deliverance. Might is Right was the doctrine of all early (and a good many late) civilizations, and the individual was tempted to believe that his own happiness (which he identified with gratification of desire) must be pursued at all hazards. The resulting strife gave birth to moral codes and theological systems: Osiris with the scales in Egypt; the Laws of Manu in India; Jahweh promulgating the Law on Mount Sinai, modified in later times by insistence on the need for kindness, truth and honesty. In India the subtle Hindu discovered the law of Karma which teaches that every thought and deed sets forces at work that vibrate through successions of lives. St. Paul bore witness to the same law. Buddha tamed the ego in his followers by showing them its true nature and how its shuts off the individual from divine influxions. Confucius insisted on the folly of doing to others that which each dislikes or resents when done to himself. For the Western world the greatest ethical teachers are Plato and Aristotle. Plato held the cardinal virtues to be: Wisdom; Courage; Self-control; Justice. Only by man's pursuit of these *in himself* can the anarchy resulting from lust and passion in the world be stayed. Aristotle, less of the poet and more of the scientific thinker, carried forward the work of Plato into new fields but added little to Plato's ideal conceptions. With the spread of Christianity in the West, ethics became blended with religious thought and dogma. Problems of sin, redemption and union with God occupied medieval thinkers, of whom the greatest were Abélard and Aquinas. The "mean" or middle way which Greek philosophers advocated, gave place to the more metaphysical and extreme views of saints and mystics. The 18th C. in Germany brought ethics back to a more rationalistic basis (see *Spinoza*; *Kant*) and in England ethical thought was ably represented by Thomas Hobbes (q.v.), Cudworth, Cumberland, etc. The doctrine of evolution tended to direct the attention of ethics towards the origins of morality, and the discovery of psychology as a science (see *Freud*; *Jung*; *Psycho-analysis*) to provide the tools for investigation. At the present time the conditions of social life are changing so rapidly that ethical standards will need to be frequently reconsidered. The simple belief certain theologians have held that there is one immutable "Right" and one immutable "Wrong," is found by the deepest thinkers to be without foundation. The good customs of one age frequently appear as the vices of the next. But the spirit of man orients itself to changing conditions, and though codes and customs pass, the supreme qualities of courage, wisdom, love and truth have never been, will never be, regarded as "out of date" by any genuine system of ethics. (See L. T. Hobhouse, *Morals in Evolution*; H. Sidgwick, *Outlines of the History of Ethics*.)

EUCHARIST. See *Communion, Holy*.

EUCHITES. (1) A 4th-C. Mesopotamian mystic sect. (2) An 11th-C. sect of Thracian dualists.

EUCHOLOGION. The prayer-book of the Greek Church.

EUDEMONISM (EUDŒMONISM). An ethical system in which the pursuit of happiness is the purpose of morality; according to Hobbes egoistic happiness, according to Mill, altruistic. (Gr. *eudaimonia* = happiness.)

EUGENICS. The science of race improvement by attempted judicious mating and application of the laws of heredity. Eugenics, first studied by Sir Francis Galton, is at present an infant among the sciences, but the collection of much useful data has led to interesting and valuable theories. By the elimination of undesirable qualities in childhood far-reaching benefits should result to mankind. But owing to the subtlety of the phenomena involved great caution is required in the study and application of eugenics. (See F. Galton, *Hereditary Genius* (1892).)

EUHEMERISM. Mythology regarded as having its origin in history. According to this view the gods of early religions were men of outstanding qualities to whom divine worship was offered after their death. From Euhemerus, a 4th-C. B.C. Sicilian philosopher.

EUNOMIANISM. A form of Arianism enunciated by Eunomius (4th C.), who held that God could not beget a son without introducing duality into the Godhead.

EUNUCH. A desexualized man. Some of the mystery cults were served by castrated priests, and Mohammedan rulers employ eunuchs as guardians of the harem.

EUSEBIUS OF CAESAREA (260–340). An ecclesiastic of vast erudition and the father of ecclesiastical history. At the Council of Nicea (325) he supported Orthodoxy against Arianism.

EUTHANASIA. The theory that in cases of fatal disease involving extreme pain a person may be painlessly killed. The Christian churches have consistently opposed this view despite the obvious cruelty sometimes involved. Many hold the opinion that, with the necessary legal safeguards, euthanasia should be made lawful.

EUTYCHES, EUTYCHIANISM. Eutyches was a 5th-C. archimandrite (q.v.) of Constantinople who taught that Christ's human nature was merged in the divine at the time of his birth, thus giving him one divine nature and not a divine and a human nature.

EVANGELICAL. That type of Christianity which stresses the authority of Scriptures rather than of a church.

EVANGELICAL ALLIANCE. An international association of Protestants founded in London in 1846 for the promotion of Protestant liberty to safeguard evangelicalism against "the encroachments of Popery and Puseyism." International conferences are held from time to time.

EVANGELIST. An author to whom one of the four Gospels is ascribed. See *Matthew*; *Mark*; *Luke*; *John*.

EVE. The name given by Adam to his wife (Gen. iii. 20).

EVE. The evening before a festival (eccles.).

EVENSONG. An Anglican evening service appointed to be said or sung daily.

EVIL. In ethics, that which hinders or prevents the realization of the good. The origin of evil has given rise to many theories. Some of the great religions, Christianity, Zoroastrianism, etc., trace evil to a dark power, Devil or Satan, leading mankind astray. Buddhism and Stoicism, on the other hand, take a more rationalistic view and trace evil to uncontrolled desire. Evolution sees in evil atavistic tendencies, i.e. the persistence of animal qualities in man. The aim of all the great religions is to eradicate these evil propensities. At a certain stage in human development a law would appear to come into force prompting and impelling allegiance to a life of higher ideals (see *regeneration*; *initiation*; *conversion*). Such a change undoubtedly took place in the case of St. Paul, Mohammed, St. Francis and certain of those who experienced initiation into the pagan mysteries. The single-minded pursuit of philosophy or prolonged concentration on work of various kinds has sometimes led to similar results. The history of religious experience should be studied for a better understanding of the problems involved. (See G. Lowes Dickinson, *The Meaning of Good.*)

EVODIUS. First bishop of Antioch.

EVOLUTION. The idea of evolution, i.e. the theory that plants and animals are derived from earlier forms that were unlike them, is not new, nor was it discovered, as is popularly believed, by Charles Darwin. Certain early Greek and Hindu thinkers were well aware of the ideas that underlie evolution. Nevertheless, on the complacent 19th-C. theologian the theory of evolution burst like a bombshell. Accustomed to regard Genesis as strictly historical and literal, Darwin's theory seemed to him the negation of Christianity, although Darwin's work concerned only physical organic changes. Christian dogma has since then, in great measure, adjusted itself to evolutionary theory. The application of psychology to some of the spiritual problems which evolution raises will probably, in the future, yield a rich harvest to religious thought. (See Charles Darwin, *The Origin of Species*; Joseph McCabe, *The Story of Evolution.*)

EWE-LAMB. A poor man's one possession (2 Sam. xii,).

EWIGKEIT. Eternity (Ger.).

EXARCH. (1) A bishop of the Eastern (Byzantine) Church. (2) An ecclesiastical inspector in the Greek Church.

EX CATHEDRA. From a bishop's chair. The Pope's official utterances are so termed and are regarded as binding on all Catholics.

EXCOMMUNICATION. Expulsion from fellowship in a church. The practice of excommunication appears to have grown up gradually in the Catholic Church until in the Middle Ages it was the most powerful weapon of the papacy. Minor excommunication involved suspension from taking the sacraments and could only be removed by submission and penance. Major excommunication decreed banishment and, in the case of a king, loss of his crown. With the coming of the Reformation, excommunication rapidly lost its terrors.

EXEGESIS. Interpretation, generally used of Scripture. Exegesis takes different forms in different ages. Late Greek thought applying exegesis to Homer found allegorical meaning beneath the simple narrative; Origen and others applied similar methods to Christian Scriptures. Medieval theologians wallowed in allegory, Aquinas easily finding four meanings in the simplest Scripture texts. With the Reformation a more rationalistic method came in which developed into modern critical exegesis.

EXEMPTION. An order from some high official of a Church whereby a person is relieved from the authority of a lesser officer.

EXODUS. The second book of the O.T. describing the going of the Israelites from Egypt to Palestine under the leadership of Moses and Aaron. (See A. H. McNeile, *The Book of Exodus* (1908).)

EXOMOLOGESIS. A full or public confession of sin (Cath.).

EXORCISM. The expelling of evil spirits from people or places by religious or magical formula. The phenomena out of which exorcism arose among primitive peoples are still met with but are usually given a psychological or pathological interpretation. Practically all primitive religions regard demoniacal possession as an adequate explanation of sickness and insanity. Much ignorance on spiritist phenomena prevailed in primitive society and still prevails in civilized countries. So determined were the 19th-C. scientists to free themselves from this incubus of ignorance that they plunged into the deep sea of negation, denying all hauntings, apparitions, etc., or attributing them to trickery. The rite of exorcism is still retained in the Catholic liturgy both in baptism and in cases of "possessed" persons and haunted localities. Many of the phenomena of possession are today considered psychologically under the terms "ego," "inhibition," "suppressed complex," etc.

EXPECTATION-WEEK. The time between Ascension Day and Whitsunday spent by the apostles in prayer, in expectation of the coming of the Holy Spirit.

EXPOSITION. In the Catholic Church the setting forth of the eucharistic elements for worship.

EXTREME UNCTION. A Catholic sacrament for anointing the dying with oil; said to receive authority from James v. 14. See also *viaticum*.

EZEKIEL. A Jewish prophet, made captive by Jehoiachin, king of Judah. His prophecy forms the 26th book of the O.T. In style, Ezekiel is impetuous, vigorous and a master of invective. (See J. Skinner, *Ezekiel* (*Expos. Bible*) (1895).)

EZRA. A Jewish priest and scribe at the time of the Jews' return to Palestine (c. 458 B.C.). Author of the canonical book of Ezra. There is also an extensive Ezra literature of which the chief books are the Third and Fourth Books of Ezra (or in their Greek form, 1 and 2 Esdras (q.v.). (See S. R. Driver, *Literature of the O.T.*)

F

FABER, FREDERICK WILLIAM (1814–63). English hymn-writer who, with Newman (q.v.), went over to the Catholic Church. Best remembered for his fine hymn, "The Pilgrims of the Night."

FABRIC. A church structure.

FABURDEN. A kind of counterpoint consisting of thirds and sixths added to a canto fermo (mus.).

FACULTIES, COURT OF. A court established by Henry VIII whereby the archbishop of Canterbury was given power to grant facilities and dispensations.

FAIRY. A non-human being akin to the nymphs and naiads of the Greeks. Stories of fairy-folk are found in the primitive records of all nations and races. Certain people, gifted with supernormal or clairvoyant powers, appear to have the faculty of seeing them. One theory propounded is that they belong to a race akin to the human but in a much lower evolutionary stage than the human. Anatole France wrote: "What is there absurd in assuming their (i.e. the fairies') existence? It is the contrary hypothesis, little as people imagine it, which is repugnant to reason. For the chances are that all the forms of life do not come within our senses, and that we are not constituted in such a way as to be able to comprehend the whole scale of beings." Expressed in terms of psychology, fairies may be regarded as forces of the unconscious alike in man and in nature which under certain conditions appear in human consciousness. Occultists and psychologists are agreed that they belong to the amoral order and are therefore dangerous. (See Evans Wentz, *The Fairy Faith in Celtic Countries*; Maurice Hewlett, *The Lore of Proserpine*.)

FAITH. Supreme confidence in the reality of that which is not proved or is incapable of proof. The Christian churches have required in their followers faith in matters of doctrine and dogma. The Catholic religion stresses the need for faith in the Church's guidance of each individual member. The Protestant churches have diverted the allegiance of faith from the Church to the Scriptures and the soul's relationship to God. For the Protestant theologians, faith took on three aspects: (1) Intellectual comprehension of Scripture (*notitia*). (2) Admission that it is the truth (*assensus*). (3) Personal trust in God (*fiducia*). The moderns tend to regard faith as a spiritual adventure in search of truth rather than the acceptance of a body of doctrines.

FAITH-HEALING. The belief, supported for Christians by James v. 15, that bodily illness may be cured by prayer or faith in the healing power of God. Faith-healing and "miraculous" cures are not peculiar to any one religion, church or faith. It has been practised in all ages, in all countries by all religions. The crutches left by grateful cripples at Lourdes (q.v.) find their equivalent in the plaster casts of arms, legs, etc., left by grateful devotees in the pagan temples of Greece and Rome. The scientific temper of to-day finds the explanation of many cures of the kind in Suggestion (q.v.). A committee appointed in 1924 by the archbishop of Canterbury to consider problems of spiritual healing, deprecated "extravagant claims" for faith-healing and emphasized the need to consider *spiritual* rather than *physical* results. In 1934 St. Stephen's Church, Brighton, was set aside exclusively for faith-healing, Dr. Bell being appointed by the bishop of Chichester to take charge. The sufferers treated may remain under their own doctors, Dr. Bell believing that the best results are obtained when religion, psychology and medicine work together. See *Psychotherapy*; *Psycho-analysis*.

FAKIR. A Hindu religious mendicant.

FALASHAS. An Abyssinian Jewish sect with a religion based on primitive Judaism.

FALDISTORY. A bishop's seat in the chancel.

FALDSTOOL. (1) A bishop's armless chair. (2) A desk at which the litany is said or sung in English churches.

FALL OF MAN. The Biblical doctrine that Adam, having eaten the forbidden fruit, was expelled from the Garden of Eden and condemned to toil, suffering and death. Similar myths are found in all the great religions. Modern thought tends to regard them as pointing to a pre-self-conscious period; a time of innocence and happiness (see *Golden Age*), before the sexual rites and religious ceremonies of primitive peoples had lost their naïve and child-like character. With the coming of self-consciousness to mankind, sex came to be regarded as the Serpent ever tempting to destruction. Such a view was false, but it was a necessary stage through which man had to pass in order to reach higher levels of consciousness. His goal being complete consciousness and full manhood, as exemplified in the Buddha and the Christ.

FALSE DECRETALS. See *Decretals, False.*

FANA. The last stage in Sufi mysticism in which the devotee finds absorption in God or Reality. Cf. *Nirvana.*

FANATICISM. Excessive religious zeal. Fanaticism, the canker in all religions, is caused by lack of balance in the individual. (L. *fanum* = temple.)

FANON. (1) A napkin used by the celebrant at Mass. (2) A cope, worn by the Pope over the alb.

FAN-TRACERY. Tracery rising from a capital and spreading fanlike over the surface of a vault (archit.).

FARSE. An explanation, in the vernacular, of the Latin epistle.

FASTING. Abstaining from food. The origin of fasting by the religious probably derives from disinclination for food at certain seasons (e.g. funerals and times of mourning). It was very early discovered that fasting tends to exalt the higher faculties at the expense of the more animal propensities. The Amalzulus have an axiom, "the continually stuffed body cannot see secret things." Fasting as a religious exercise is not so much practised as it used to be, but the purely physical benefits of fasting are beginning to be brought to the notice of the medical profession by the general public, nature healers and others.

FATALISM. The belief that all events are the result of inexorable, unalterable law. See *Nemesis*; *Kismet.*

FATE. The power which orders events. The Greek poets appear sometimes to reconcile Fate with the will of Zeus, sometimes to regard Fate as an independent and higher power. Sophocles and Euripides insist on a mysterious force that rules and determines men's lives. In Hesiod the web of Fate is spun by the three sisters, Clotho, Lachesis and Atropos. The Christian doctrine of Predestination is akin to the classic belief in Fate. See also *Karma.*

FATHERS, CHURCH. The leading Churchmen of the first five centuries are so styled; the chief are:

§ 2

1st C. (Greek)

		A.D.
Clement of Rome	d.	100
Ignatius	d.	115
Polycarp	d. c.	169

§ 3

2nd C. (Greek)

		A.D.
Justin Martyr	d. c.	166
Irenaeus	d. c.	200
Athenagoras	d. c.	170

§ 4

3rd C. (Greek)

		A.D.
Clement of Alexandria	d. c.	217
Hippolytus	d.	230
Origen	d. c.	253

§ 5

3rd C. (Latin)

		A.D.
Tertullian	d. c.	220
Minutius Felix	d. c.	255
Cyprian	d. c.	258

§ 6

4th & 5th C.s (Greek)

		A.D.
Eusebius	d. c.	340
Athanasius	d.	373
Ephrem Syrus	d. c.	378
Basil	d.	379
Cyril of Jerusalem	d.	386
Gregory Nazianzen	d.	389
Macarius	d. c.	391
Gregory Nyssen	d. c.	394
Epiphanius	d.	403
John Chrysostom	d.	407
Cyril of Alexandria	d.	444
Theoderet	d.	457

§ 7

(Latin)

		A.D.
Arnobius	d. c.	320
Lactantius	d. c.	330
Ambrose	d.	397
Jerome	d.	420
Augustine	d.	430

Fatiha. The opening words of the Koran, used as a daily prayer by Mohammedans.

Faun. A spirit of the fields, partly human in form (L. myth.).

Fear. Dread of possible happenings. Fear has played an active part in the growth of religion. To the early Christian, death meant physical burning in hell if he did not embrace the faith. This in later years became spiritualized into the dread of cleansing purgatorial pains. The field of fear has of late shifted from the hereafter to this life. Very few to-day share Hamlet's dread of "that sleep of death," but multitudes suffer from fear-complexes connected with earth life. Fear, like all destructive emotions, should be faced. If this is done deliberately it dies, and by concentrating on its opposite (courage) evolutionary progress can be made.

Feast, Festival. A day commemorating some religious event. The chief Christian festivals are: Easter (The Resurrection)—on the Sunday after the full moon of the spring equinox; Christmas (25 Dec.), the Birth of Christ; Epiphany (6 Jan.), the visit of the Magi; Circumcision (1 Jan.); Presentation (2 Feb.); Annunciation (25 March); Assumption (15 Aug.); All Saints' (1 Nov.); All Souls' (Cath.) (2 Nov.); Immaculate Conception (Cath.) (8 Dec.). Festivals are more tenacious of life even than the religions of which they form part. Many Christian festivals derive from pagan feasts of a similar character; thus Christmas has many features in common with the Roman Saturnalia (q.v.) and Easter with various festivals celebrating the vernal equinox.

Febronianism. A German 18th-C. movement in the Catholic Church to limit the administrative power of the Pope. Johann Hontheim (Febronius) founded it.

Federal Council. A meeting in New York in 1905 of representatives of evangelical denominations with the aim of promoting interdenominational co-operation. Since then annual meetings have been held and much social work undertaken.

Feet-washing. A custom arose in the church of the 11th C. whereby royal persons washed the feet of poor folk on Holy Thursday. It derived probably from John xiii. 1–17, and is still observed in certain branches of the Catholic and Protestant churches.

FÉNELON, FRANÇOIS DE SALIGNAC DE LA MOTHE (1651–1715). Archbishop of Cambrai and author of the *Adventures of Telemachus*, written for Louis XIV's grandsons. He was an eminent literary critic, inclined to mysticism, and an intimate friend of Madame Guyon (q.v.) the Quietist.

FERETORY. A shrine for carrying relics in processions.

FERIAL. A holiday that is neither a fast nor a festival.

FESTILOGY, FESTOLOGY. A treatise on ecclesiastical festivals.

FESTIVAL. See *feast.*

FETISHISM. Belief in the possession of magical powers by material objects. Fetishism is found in all forms of primitive religion. Charms, amulets, stones, and trees are believed by primitive races to possess magical powers. The mistletoe of the Druids and the Jewish ark of the covenant are probably survivals of fetishism. So (according to some authorities), are Christian relic-worship and the eucharist.

FIFTH MONARCHY MEN. A fanatical sect of Cromwell's time who believed that Jesus Christ was about to descend from heaven and set up the fifth universal monarchy (Dan. ii. 44). They rose in rebellion several times and were finally suppressed in 1661 and their leader, Thomas Venner, executed.

FIGURED-BASS. The bass part written with figures beneath it to indicate the harmony: also *thorough-bass*

FILIOQUE. A clause inserted into the Nicene Creed at Toledo in 589 asserting that the Holy Ghost proceeds from the Son as well as from the Father. The clause was rejected by the Eastern Church and so has always stood in the way of reconciliation between the Roman and Greek Churches. The "Filioque Controversy" was much debated in the London of 1870, when the problem of reunion between the Greek and Catholic churches was discussed by high authorities. Kinglake, witty author of *Eothen,* said London ladies took an interest in the subject because they believed a "Filioque" was a clergyman's baby born out of wedlock.

FINIAL. The foliage at the top of Gothic spires, gables, etc. (archit.).

FIORETTI. The name given (Little Flowers) to a delightful collection of legendary tales of St. Francis of Assisi (q.v.). The manuscript dates from 1390.

FIRE-WORSHIP. Primitive man has everywhere held fire as sacred —both the hearth-fire and the heavenly fire (the sun; lightning). Fire-worship was represented in ancient Rome by the cult of Vesta (Hestia) (q.v.). There a perpetual hearth-fire was tended by the Vestal Virgins. The Parsis of India (q.v.) are the present-day representatives of the Persian fire-worship introduced by Zoroaster. See also *Beltane*.

FIRST CAUSE. The originator of the Universe. Reason seeks a First Cause, hoping thereby to get nearer Reality, but when the First Cause is reached the cause of the First Cause is still to seek. It is therefore more logically and intellectually satisfying to regard the Universe not as a Creation but as existent fact.

FIRST-FRUITS, FIRSTLING. The first yield or profits regarded in primitive ages with awe as of supernatural origin. From this arose the custom of Annates (q.v.).

FISH. Among early Christians the fish was a favourite symbol of their Faith. The origin of the sign is obscure, but it seems probable that it came from Pisces, the Zodiacal Fish which at that period was the sign of the spring equinox.

FISTULA. The tube through which the eucharistic wine was at one time sucked from the chalice (Cath.).

FIVE CLASSICS, THE. The Sacred Scriptures of Confucianism (q.v.) which are divided into five books.

FIVE MILE ACT. The Act of 17 Chas. II c. 2 (Oct. 1665) forbidding Nonconformist ministers who refused the non-resistance oath to come within five miles of any parish or town where they had formerly preached under penalty of £40. The Act was abolished by William III in 1689.

FLABELLUM. A fan to swat troublesome flies during Mass (Cath.).

FLAGELLANTS. Certain Italian fraternities who practised voluntary scourging. (13th C.)

FLAMBOYANT. The latest style of Gothic in France (15th–16th C.s) corresponding to Perpendicular in England (archit.).

FLAMEL, NICHOLAS (1330–1418). A noted French alchemist whose life and work caused much discussion in the time of Charles VI of France. Flamel appears to have been a mystic as well as an alchemist to whom success in the transmutation of metals was accredited. His biography was written by Lenglet du Fresnoy.

FLÈCHE. A slender spire rising from the intersection of nave and transept, as in Notre Dame (archit.).

FLOOD. See *Deluge*.

FLORIATED, FLOREATED. Decorated with floral carvings (archit.).

FLORILEGIA. An anthology of quotations from early Christian writers.

FONT. The vessel used for baptismal water in churches.

FOOL. In primitive ages fools (i.e. mentally deficient persons) were regarded as being specially favoured by the gods. It was probably due to this belief that the king's fool of the Middle

Ages owed his licence (e.g. Queen Elizabeth's Pace; Heywood of Henry VIII—probably the "Yorick" of Hamlet). The child-like simplicity of certain saints shows us folly in its highest and best aspect—that indicated by Christ when He said: "Except ye become as little children ye cannot enter the kingdom."

FORGIVENESS. Ethically forgiveness is an attitude of the mind and heart in which the offended party renounces all claims for damage and cleanses his mind of ill-feeling. ("Draw the curtain of Night upon injuries. Shut them up in the tower of oblivion, and let them be as though they had not been"—Francis Bacon.) The Catholic Church teaches that God's forgiveness is only granted to the individual through the Church and usually through the sacraments. The Protestant churches look for God's forgiveness in the Atonement (q.v.). The continually maintained attitude of goodwill to all beings which the great religions insist upon would obviate the need of forgiveness among men.

FORMALIST. One with an exaggerated reverence for forms, rituals and ceremonies. The Pharisees were the formalists of the gospel age. It would be invidious to determine which classes or professions are the formalists of our own.

FORMARIANS (FOMORIANS). The old gods of pre-Celtic Ireland, of equal or greater beauty than the Celtic gods who took their places. They were peaceful gods of the harvest, but came to be regarded as in opposition to the Celtic gods and so were associated with darkness, evil and death.

FORTUNATUS, VENANTIUS (c. 530–600). A charming epicurean bishop of Poictiers who loved learning and wrote Latin verses of delightful freshness and simplicity. He was born at Trieste, studied at Ravenna and, in old age, settled as a friend of Radegund (ex-wife of Lothair I of Neustria) at her convent at Poictiers. (See Jack Lindsay, *Medieval Latin Poets*; Helen Waddell, *Medieval Latin Lyrics*.)

FORTY-TWO ARTICLES. The Articles of the Church of England ratified by the bishops and privy council in 1553. Three were afterwards eliminated. See *Articles, Thirty-Nine*.

FOSSOR. A gravedigger.

FOX, GEORGE (1624–91). Founder of the Society of Friends (Quakers). He was born at Drayton, Leicestershire, and in his youth experienced unusual psychological and religious experiences. Owing to his attacks on the clergy (he frequently interrupted divine service) he was much persecuted and frequently imprisoned. His Journal is of great interest to the student of mystical literature. (See Hodgkin, *Life of George Fox* (1896).)

FOX, JOHN (1516–87). Canon of Salisbury and author of *The Book of Martyrs*. He was in early life tutor in the family of Sir Thomas Lucy of Charlecote. (He does not refer anywhere to Shakespeare.) Fox's sympathy was with the Reformed Faith, but he was careful and accurate in his handling of facts.

FRANCE, CHURCH OF. See *Church of France.*

FRANCIS OF ASSISI, SAINT (1182–1226), and **FRANCISCANS.** Francis of Assisi was son of a merchant, Pietro Bernadone. His education appears to have been slight but sufficient. His temper in youth was impetuous and adventurous, gay and winning. During an illness he experienced conversion (q.v.), from which period his life became totally different—bent on the pursuit of the ideal of love for all beings. He was determined to follow the precepts of Jesus literally, and probably no man ever made a more courageous attempt to do so or with more startling results. His personal influence was so compelling that he became the focus of a religious revival which spread throughout Europe. The Order of Franciscans was sanctioned by Innocent III in 1209. Extreme asceticism joined with a joyous mysticism were the elements of a character simple and direct yet subtle when subtlety was required, that fascinated, and has continued to fascinate, mankind. The Order passed through many vicissitudes. In 1907 Pius X united various groups of Franciscans into the Order of Brothers Minor. There is a second order for women—Poor Clares (from Santa Chiara). And a third order for laymen aspiring to the ideals of Franciscan piety. (See Sabatier, *Vie de S. François* (Engl. trans., L. S. Houghton, 1901); Abel Bonnard, *Saint Francis of Assisi* (trans. by Florence Simmons, 1930); D. H. S. Nicholson, *The Mysticism of St. Francis of Assisi* (1923).) See also *Religion*, §§ 1, 6.

FRANCIS DE SALES, SAINT (1567–1622). Bishop of Geneva, son of M. de Boisy, comte de Sales. Francis was educated at Annecy and Paris. He became a noted preacher and a man of great influence owing to his saintly life. His *Introduction to a Devout Life* (pub. 1609) was widely read throughout Europe. (See Leigh Hunt, "The Gentleman Saint" (*The Seer*, pt. ii).)

FRANKEL, ZACHARIAH. See *Reformed Judaism.*

FRATER, FRATRY. A refectory or chapter-house.

FRATERY. A religious fraternity.

FRATICELLI. Friars of the Franciscan Order who insisted on practising the ideal of Poverty originated by St. Francis. They were persecuted by the Church and condemned by a Papal Bull of 1317.

FRAVASHI. The Persian or Zoroastrian counterpart of the Greek daimon, the Roman genius and the Christian angel or higher self. The fravashi was also regarded as a part of the soul and became united with it after death.

FRAZER, SIR JAMES GEORGE (b. 1854). Fellow of Trinity College, Cambridge, and author of *The Golden Bough* (1890–1915), the fullest and most comprehensive work on mythology and comparative religion published. The work is a storehouse of facts and is probably more cathartic, as regards Christian orthodoxies, than is generally realized.

FREE CHURCH FEDERATION. The leaders of various dissenting Churches of Britain arranged a series of congresses (1892–5) at Manchester, Leeds, etc., which resulted in the formation of the National Council of the Evangelical Free Churches in 1896. The objects of the Council are to facilitate co-operation among the Free Churches, to establish local councils, etc. The organization does good work in furthering Protestant interests.

FREE CHURCH OF SCOTLAND. A body that seceded from the national church of Scotland in 1843, headed by Thomas Chalmers. The secession arose out of the question of the right of patrons to nominate to benefices. The Free Church claims a right of vote for parishioners. In 1900 a union was effected between the Free Church and the United Presbyterian Church.

FREED-STOOL. See *frith-stool.*

FREEMASONRY. The society of Freemasons is an ethical and benevolent organization with an ancient and highly elaborate ritual. It professes no religious dogmas save the belief in God and immortality to which every brother, on "initiation" (admission), is required to subscribe. The ideal of a reasonable life and a charitable attitude to all men is upheld by ceremony and instruction. Authorities differ widely as to the whence, and when, of the society's origin. Some have found in it traces of the ancient Mystery Religions, Gnosticism and the Rosicrucian and other occult mystical associations. But the esoteric meaning of the ritual used does not evoke much interest to-day. The first decided traces of the Craft of Masonry appear in the 16th C. The present organization dates from the "revival" in 1717, when four London Lodges formed the Grand Lodge of England from which all organized Freemasonry as known to-day originated. All the Lodges and Grand Lodges in both hemispheres trace their origin to England and are run on a similar basis of Three Degrees, controlled by Grand Lodges. There are many grades in Freemasonry, but the difficulty of obtaining admission to the higher grades increases as progress is made. A claim has recently been put forward that Freemasonry was established (or entirely reorganized as an ethical society) by Francis Bacon, some of whose works, notably the *New Atlantis*, show undeniable traces of Rosicrucian or Masonic influence. (For this view, see Alfred Dodd, *The Personal Poems of Francis Bacon* (1930).) See also George Thornburgh, *Freemasonry ; When, Where, How ?* (1914).

FREETHINKER. See *rationalist.*

FREE WILL. Freedom to choose between alternatives. Moral philosophers have from early ages debated the problem whether man has free will or not. The Determinists or Necessitarians argue that a man's behaviour is the result of temperament, habits, environment, etc. The advocates of free will maintain that moral responsibility ceases entirely unless man has free will and that consciousness itself testifies to freedom.

FREUD, SIGMUND (b. 1856). The pioneer of psycho-analysis. Freud was born of Jewish parents in Moravia. He studied medicine in Vienna and Paris. At Paris he made the acquaintance of Charcot and Janet, who were studying hypnotic phenomena, and whose experiments had demonstrated the existence of the unconscious mind. Freud set up as a nerve specialist in Vienna, at first using hypnosis. His studies finally led him to the system of psycho-analysis associated with his name. (See Geraldine Coster, *Psycho-analysis for Normal People*.)

FREYIA ("**LADY**"). Also called Mardoll ("Shining over the Sea") and Menglodh ("Ornament loving" or "Necklace glad"). Freyia, like Frigg, was the wife of Odin. She was a beautiful and beneficent goddess of love, of marriage and death. Her chariot was drawn by cats as symbols of fecundity and she wore a robe of feathers in which she flew over earth and sea. With her brother Freyr she was associated with the return of spring. (Norse myth.)

FRIAR. A member of one of the mendicant orders in the Catholic Church. The chief mendicant orders are: Franciscans (Grey Friars, Friars Minor); Dominicans (Black Friars, Friars Major, Friars Preachers); Carmelites (White Friars); Augustinians (Austin Friars).

FRIAR'S LANTERN. The will-o'-the-wisp (*ignis fatuus*).

FRIARY. A monastery.

FRIDAY, GOOD. The Friday before Easter that commemorates Christ's Crucifixion. (From Frigga, wife of Odin.) (Norse myth.)

FRIENDS, SOCIETY OF. A Christian sect originated by George Fox (q.v.) c. 1648. The nickname "Quakers" was thrust upon them. The Friends dispense with sacraments and liturgies, maintaining that the soul finds God best in quietness. Instead of attending services and sermons, they meet together and sit in silence. They refuse to take oaths or to bear arms in time of war. They take an active part in reform movements and mission work and have a membership of some 20,000 in England and some 125,000 in America. (See T. E. Harvey, *The Rise of the Quakers*; J. F. Rowntree, *The Society of Friends*.)

FRIGG ("**THE BELOVED**"). Wife of Odin and goddess of love, marriage and the home (Norse myth.). She was probably identical at one time with Freyia (q.v.). From this goddess we derive Friday (Lat. *Dies Veneris*).

FRITH-STOOL, FREED-STOOL. A chair in the sanctuary, near the altar (eccles.).

FRONTAL. (1) A pediment over door or window (archit.). (2) An embroidered covering for the altar (eccles.).

FRUMENTIUS (c. 300–c. 360). A native of Phoenicia who founded the Abyssinian Church.

FUGUE. A musical composition in which the subject is given out in the first part and taken up by an answering second part, during which the first part continues as an accompaniment. Bach was probably the greatest composer of fugues.

FULBERT OF CHARTRES (d. 1029). A great teacher of the 11th C. and the author of some fine Latin poems. (See Jack Lindsay, *Medieval Latin Poets* (1934).)

FULLER, THOMAS (1608–61). Chaplain to Charles II and noted antiquary, chiefly remembered for his *Worthies*. As an historian his work is entirely unreliable. "He would sit patiently for hours listening to the prattle of old women, in order to obtain snatches of local history, traditionary anecdote, and proverbial wisdom; and these he has worked up in his work entitled *The Worthies of England*." *Chambers' Cyclopedia of English Literature* (vol. i, p. 376). To Fuller we owe the apocryphal story of "the wit combats" between Shakespeare and Ben Jonson at "The Mermaid." (Fuller was only eight years old in 1616—the year of Shakespeare's death.)

FUNERAL. The ceremonies connected with burial. See also *mummy*.

FUNG-SHUI. The Chinese science of orientation to the forces of Nature. According to this belief the sites of houses, graves, temples, etc., must be chosen by doctors of this science, which is a mingling of astrology, geomancy and magic.

FUTURE LIFE. The phrase used for life after death. A belief in the continued existence of the dead is found amongst nearly all primitive tribes. The early Greeks regarded the dead as shadowy wanderers in an Underworld. Many of them underwent painful purifying processes. Early Jewish belief was vague, but the Israelites appear to have believed in a future life for the righteous. The Christian belief in a future state is derived in part from earlier ideas—Greek, Roman, Egyptian, Semitic. In different ages the Christian belief has taken different forms. Christ taught the certainty of a future life ("In my Father's house are many mansions") but discouraged inquisitive seeking for details, as also did Buddha. The brutal conditions of the Middle Ages led to the gross conceptions of extremes of pleasure (for "the good") and of pain (for "the wicked") which we see depicted in the frescoes of the Renaissance. (See R. H. Charles, *A Critical History of the Doctrine of a Future Life*; R. J. Thompson, *The Proofs of*

Life After Death (1906) (opinions collected of the world's most prominent thinkers).)

§ 2. For the modern philosophic mind tending to the view that Time and Space can have no existence in Reality, *timeless being* takes the place of the older conceptions of immortality. Consult also articles, *Heaven*; *Purgatory*; *Hell*. (See Archibald Weir, *Light; A Philosophy of Consciousness; The Dark*; J. W. Dunne, *The Serial Universe* (1934).)

G

GABARS, GHEBERS, GUEBRES, GIAOURS. The name given to the Zoroastrians of Persia. For centuries they suffered persecution from the Mohammedans. In 1854 their co-religionists, the Parsis of India, came to their assistance and their position (owing also to greater tolerance from Persia) was immensely improved.

GABRIEL. The angel of death of Jewish mythology. In medieval romance he is the second of the seven spirits that stood before God's throne. In Milton he is the chief of the angelic guards of Paradise. Longfellow (Golden Legend) makes him the angel of the moon.

GABRIOLE, IBN (A.D. 1020–70). Writer on ethics and religion; also of hymns. Influenced by Plato.

GAD. (1) One of the Israelitish tribes (Gen. xxx. 9–11). (2) A prophet-friend of David (1 Sam. xxii. 5). (3) An early Semitic goddess of fortune.

GALATIA. A province of Asia Minor. Paul's Epistle to the Galatians was written about A.D. 51.

GALILEE. (1) One of the Roman divisions of Palestine. (2) A porch at the west end of certain abbeys where the clergy ministered to women and dispensed charity (eccles.).

GALILEO (1564–1642). Italian mathematician who taught that the earth moves round the sun and was persecuted by the Catholic Church for his "obstinacy" in affirming it.

GALL, SAINT. A famous abbey (Switzerland) founded in the 7th C. Hraban Maur was a famous abbot of St. Gall.

GALLICAN CONFESSION. A Huguenot Confession of Faith drawn up at La Rochelle in 1559.

GALLICANISM. The spirit of nationalism in the French Church—opposed to Ultramontanism or subjection to the personal authority of the Pope.

GALLIO, JUNIUS ANNAEUS. The Roman proconsul of Achaia in A.D. 53 who refused to take action when a Jewish clamour was raised against Paul (Acts xviii. 12–17). (See, for an imaginative reconstruction of the times, Anatole France, *The White Stone*.)

GALTON, SIR FRANCIS. See *eugenics*.

GAMALIEL. A learned Jewish rabbi to whom St. Paul went for instruction (Acts v. 34; xxii. 3).

GAMBLING. The staking of money on an uncertain event as in horse-racing, football, etc. Gambling is usually condemned in England because it tends, in the unbalanced, to become a mono-mania. But so equally may anything from church-going to cigarette-smoking. There is nothing inherently "wicked" in gambling; the evils resulting derive from the lack of self-control in the individual.

GANDHARVA. A Hindu god of the upper air and of fire.

GANDHARVAS. Semi-divine musicians of India's heaven.

GANESA (GANESHA). An elephant-headed Hindu god of wisdom. Son of Shiva and Parvati.

GANGES (GANGA). The sacred river of India. The myth of the Ganges is told in the Ramayana (q.v.).

GARGOYLE. A projecting spout in form of a grotesque figure. (Goth. archit.).

GARTH. An enclosure or garden in a cloister.

GARUDA. The Hindu god of birds, half-man, half-eagle.

GATHAS. A section of the Zoroastrian scriptures, containing prayers and hymns.

GAUTAMA. See *Buddha*.

GAYATRI. A verse of the Vedas held in utmost reverence by Hindus ("We meditate on that desirable Light of the divine Savitri, the sun who governs our holy rites").

GAZA. The Philistine city from which Samson carried away the gates (Judges xvi.).

GEB. Father of Osiris (Egypt. myth.).

GEHENNA. A valley near Jerusalem where in early times human sacrifices were offered to Moloch. The name was afterwards given to the place of punishment of the dead. See *hell.*

GEIGER, ABRAHAM. See *Reformed Judaism.*

GEMARA. The second portion of the Talmud. It forms a commentary on the first part, the Mishna.

GENERAL. The head of a religious order (Cath.).

GENERAL ASSEMBLY. The highest court of the Presbyterian Church in Scotland, Ireland and the U.S.A.

GENESIS. The first book of the Bible, describing creation: believed to be a composite work owing to the varying names (Yahweh and Elohim) used for God. (See S. R. Driver, *Genesis.*)

GENEVIÈVE, SAINT (c. 422–512). Patron saint of Paris (3 Jan.).

GENIUS. The guardian angel of Roman mythology. The genius familiae is a household spirit; the genius loci is attached to a place. See also *Fravashi.*

GENIZAH. A chamber in synagogues for sacred relics, etc.

GENTILE. A biblical word for a non-Jew. (Lat. *gentilis* = of the same clan, or nation.)

GENTLEMAN OF THE CHAPEL-ROYAL. A lay singer in the royal chapel. (Usually applied to St. James's Palace Chapel.)

GENUFLECTION. The bending of the knee in reverence before an altar, etc. (Cath.).

GEORGE, SAINT. Gibbon (*Decline and Fall*) wrongly assumed that George of Laodicea (murdered in the reign of Julian) was the Christian soldier martyred under Diocletian. Gibbon's George was the fellow Gregory Nazianzen said would "sell himself for a cake." St. George was, according to legend, a Roman officer who suffered death (c. 303) rather than carry out Diocletian's order to persecute Christians. Many legends gathered about his name, e.g. the Dragon story, which probably derived from pagan mythology. The English Crusaders in Palestine were greatly impressed by the stories of St. George. They said that a mysterious warrior on a white horse was seen in battle after battle aiding their cause. King Richard used the name of St. George for his battle-cry and returned to England with the ideal warrior, St. George, for England's patron saint. (See H. V. Morton, *In the Steps of the Master.*)

GERAH. The smallest Hebrew coin, worth about 1½*d.*

GERATOLOGY. The science of the phenomena of decadence. (Gr. *geros* = old age; *logia* = discourse.)

GERHARD, JOHANN (1582–1637). The Lutheran theologian who met the Catholic dogma of an infallible Church with the Protestant dogma of an infallible Bible.

GERSON, JEAN CHARLIER DE (1363–1429). French ecclesiastic who tried to mend the papal schism at the Councils of Pisa (1409) and Constance (1418).

GETHSEMANE. An olive garden near Jerusalem, the scene of the Agony of Jesus Christ (Matt. xxvi. 36).

GHAZALI. See *Al-Ghazali.*

GHEBERS. See *Gabars.*

GHETTO. The Jewish quarter in medieval cities. Ghettos were established in most European cities in the 11th C. and continued until the 19th.

GHOST, HOLY. The third person of the Trinity (q.v.).

GIANTS. The folk-lore of primitive ages everywhere bears witness to an early race of giants. Genesis refers to the Nephilim (Gen. vi. 4), the Rephaim and the Anakim, gigantic men of early times. Greek mythology bears witness to the Gigantes, the Centaurs and the Titans.

GILBERTINES. An order of canons and nuns established at Sempringham (Lincolnshire) by Gilbert (1131–48).

GILGAMESH. The hero of a religious epic of ancient Babylonia.

GINN. See *jinn*.

GIPSIES (GYPSIES), RELIGION OF THE. The gypsies, a race of (possibly) Egyptian origin which appeared in Europe in the 14th C., usually conform to the religion of the country they inhabit. If they have any religious traditions of their own, which is doubtful, these take the form of superficial occult knowledge, fortune-telling, etc. For a good account of gipsy life and thought, see the books of George Borrow.

GIPSY SMITH. A noted evangelical preacher (b. 1860). He assisted General Booth in his missionary work. (See *Gipsy Smith, his Life and Work, an Autobiography*.)

GIROVAGI ("WANDERERS AROUND"). A class of wandering monks in the early Christian centuries. St. Benedict (480–544) in his Rule complains of "the last and worst kind of monks who spend their life in travelling up and down; always wandering, never stable."

GLANVILLE, JOSEPH (1636–80). Anglican divine strongly influenced by the Cambridge Platonists. Author of the *Vanity of Dogmatizing*, in which occurs the story of the scholar gipsy on which Matthew Arnold based his famous poem.

GLASSITES. A Christian sect founded by John Glas (1695-1773). Glas was deposed from his ministry in the Church of Scotland in 1730 for maintaining that a congregation is subject to no foundation save that of Christ. Glassites are also known as Sandemanians from Robert Sandeman, Glas's son-in-law.

GLEBE. Land belonging to a parish church or benefice.

GLORIA. A doxology. The Greater Doxology is the gloria in excelsis (Glory be to God on high); the Lesser Doxology is the Gloria Patri (Glory be to the Father, and to the Son, and to the Holy Ghost, etc.).

GLOSS. An explanatory comment inserted in the margin of ancient manuscripts.

GNOME. A goblin or earth-spirit in medieval folk-lore.

GNOSTICISM. The Gnostics are sometimes regarded as a Christian heretical sect, but research has proved that Gnostic societies were scattered about the Hellenistic world before, as well as after, the birth of Christianity. They appear to have been of Indian origin. There seems little doubt that outside Palestine, Christianity itself was a Gnostic community (see Reinach, *A Short History of Christianity*). The Fourth Gospel was, in the early centuries, attributed to the Gnostic Cerinthus. The cause of the triumph of Christianity over the Gnostic societies seems to lie in its more easily intelligible and simpler doctrines. Whereas Gnosticism appealed mainly to the learned men of outstanding ability, Christianity, when Hellenized and Romanized, became a state religion which the average man could profess without moral or intellectual strain. The *gnosis* (knowledge) claimed by the Gnostics did not derive from the intellect (*nous*) but from a deepening of the intuition (*psyche*) as a result of meditation and ascetic practice. Yet Gnosticism itself was an intellectual religion. The central doctrine of all the Gnostic brotherhoods was the duality of the universe —matter opposing spirit, light confronting darkness. From this resulted a reconciliation of opposites by means of a system of emanations and the victory of a Perfect Man. From God proceeded a lower world, from this a lower, and so on, until a material world wholly or partly evil came into being. Above all these emanations exists the Great Mother of the Gods under whom rule seven world-creating planetary powers. Another prominent doctrine is that of the Primal Man or Son of Man who is the real, ultimate, perfect or complete man, of whom all men are incomplete copies. The Primal Man has raised himself out of matter to completeness and by his efforts mankind (his members) still imprisoned in matter will be set free. There seems no doubt that much Christian doctrine, especially the doctrine of redemption by a Saviour God, was influenced—if not directly inspired —by Gnostic belief. In Gnosticism, salvation is a myth, an allegory or figure and not, as in orthodox Christianity, an historical event. The General Councils which made Gnosticism a heresy expelled from orthodox belief much valuable teaching of an esoteric nature. (See G. T. Sadler, *The Gnostic Story of Jesus Christ* (1914); G. R. S. Mead, *Thrice-Greatest Hermes*; C. W. King, *The Gnostics and Their Remains*.)

GOBLIN. A mischievous sprite of folk-lore.

GOD. The Supreme Being, creator, preserver and destroyer of the universe. In a primitive state of society men have everywhere believed in a multitude of spirits or gods. The belief in one supreme God appears to have grown up as a result of: (1) Conquest of one tribe or nation by another, and the enforced worship of "the true God" (i.e. the conqueror's); (2) the necessity of accounting for the creation of the universe and the probability of one creator outweighing the claims of many. When the evolutionary stage of belief in one God has been reached there is still wide diversity of view as to the nature of God, since man tends always to create God in his own image. To the Hebrews Yahweh was a God of power, anger, love and a rather crude righteousness. The Egyptian Osiris was a stern judge of living and dead. To the Hindus God (Brahma) is the soul (*âtman*) of the universe, akin to man's own soul. Brahma is beyond all material manifestations; and the world, as men experience it through the senses, is illusion (*mâya*). The Christian conception of God is a development of the Jewish idea of Yahweh. Love (goodwill) to all beings is his chief attribute and the sufferings of men are a cleansing process. If men will co-operate, seeking to follow his laws, they serve their own interests —which are His (" In His will is our peace," Dante). If they refuse, then the iron gauntlet of correction (war, disease, restlessness, boredom) falls upon them. The Christian doctrine of the Trinity (q.v.) arose from Hellenistic influences in the 2nd C. To the modern mind there seems little difference between the conception of God and that of the Ether. Both are equally symbols of the unknown. The idea of a personal God symbolizes the ideal Being—or Higher Self—latent in man as the oak is latent in the acorn. The enormous value of concentrating on this ideal is obvious to anyone acquainted with the elements of psychology. All ideals to which man aspires are latent in the soul. Cf. Shelley, " The mind creates that which it contemplates." (See J. R. Illingworth, *Personality Human and Divine*; Floyd B. Wilson, *The Man of To-morrow* (1914).)

GODESCALUS. See *Gottschalk.*

GODFATHER and **GODMOTHER.** The man and woman who sponsor a child at baptism.

GOETHE, JOHANN WOLFGANG VON (1749–1832). German poet, dramatist and philosopher and probably the greatest man Germany has produced. His crowning achievement was " Faust " —the poetic epitome of his vast experience. Goethe reveals the most universal type of genius and the vivid personal impression he made is testified by Napoleon's words after meeting him, " Voilá un homme ! " His greatest work was his own life, in all its fullness, richness and creativeness. For obvious reasons he is belittled in the Germany of to-day (1935). (See J. R. Seeley, *Goethe* (1894); S. Dowden, *New Studies in Literature* (1895); and various studies by the late Professor J. G. Robertson.)

GOLDEN AGE. The belief in a far-distant age when mankind lived a blissful existence such as he has never known in later periods is a heritage from all primitive peoples. It is found in classic myth and Hebrew legend (Gen. iii. 8). Modern thinkers have found in these stories reference to man's condition before he became acutely aware of his personal ego, the development of which involved him in a Fall (q.v.) from the state of innocent happiness—akin to that experienced by the lower animals. (See Edward Carpenter, *Pagan and Christian Creeds*, chap. ix.)

GOLDEN LEGEND (LEGENDA AUREA). A collection of the lives of the Saints written by Jacobus de Voragine, a Dominican, about 1260.

GOLDEN NUMBER. The number of any given year in the Metonic Cycle (q.v.). The golden number ranges from one to nineteen.

GOLDEN ROSE. A rose of wrought gold blessed by the Pope annually on the 4th Sunday in Lent.

GOLGOTHA. The place near Jerusalem reputed to be the scene of Jesus' crucifixion. Also called Calvary (the Grecized form of Heb. *Golgotha* = a skull).

GOLIARD. Name for a medieval monk who amused his superiors at table by telling funny stories.

GOLIATH. The Philistine giant whom David slew (1 Sam. xvii.).

GOMARIST. A follower of Francis Gomarus, a fierce opponent of the Armenians. (16th–17th C.s.)

GOOD. The desirable, a term capable of wide application. The moral problem of good and evil has been one of the subjects discussed by philosophy and religion since man was a thinking being. Difficulty has been found in harmonizing theism with the evil in the world. Probably the best explanation is the Hindu doctrine of *mâya*, teaching that all sense-impressions are deceptive in character, a doctrine strongly reinforced by modern scientific thought. See also *Ethics*.

GOOD FRIDAY. The Friday preceding Easter, kept as a fast-day in memory of Christ's crucifixion.

GOOD-WORKS. See *merit*.

GORE, CHARLES (1853–1932). Anglican bishop of Birmingham. A high-churchman. Author of *Roman Catholic Claims* (1889), etc.

GORGON. One of the three sisters (Stheno, Euryale and Medusa) with snakes in place of hair, whose terrible appearance turned the beholder to stone (Gr. myth.).

GORHAM CONTROVERSY. In 1849 the bishop of Exeter refused to institute the Reverend Cornelius Gorham to the vicarage of Brampford Speke because he denied that spiritual regeneration was conferred by baptism. After two years' controversy the Privy Council decided in favour of Mr. Gorham.

GOSPELS, THE. The four canonical Christian gospels, or accounts of Jesus' life are Matthew, Mark, Luke and John. Matthew's Gospel was probably written at Antioch in the 1st C. Mark's Gospel, probably written in Rome, appears to form the basis for Matthew and Luke. Luke used parts of Matthew (or Matthew's sources) but introduced new matter peculiar to himself. The Gospel of John probably dates from the early 2nd C. and shows strong Hellenistic influence. These four gospels gradually displaced the many gospels of the early Christians. See *Apocrypha*; *N.T.*

GOTTSCHALK (GODESCALUS) (c. 808–67). A monk (oblate) in the German monastery of Fulda in the time of Abbot Hrabanus Maurus. Having studied Augustine, he carried the Augustinian doctrines too far and was accused of heresy. Gottschalk was a vigorous thinker and accomplished poet, author of the beautiful *Ut quid jubes, pusiole*. (See Jack Lindsay, *Medieval Latin Poets* (1934).)

GOTHIC. An order of architecture which began about the 9th C.

A.D. and spread throughout Europe. Its chief feature is the pointed arch.

GOTHS. A war-like and brutal nation inhabiting the country between the Caspian and Baltic seas in the 3rd C. A.D. The Ostrogoths became masters of Italy at the fall of the Roman Empire. The Visigoths conquered Spain.

GRAAL. See *Grail.*

GRACE. (1) A theological term for the divine life in man aiding him in the struggle for perfection. The doctrine has meant different things to different people in different ages. According to the Protestants grace is a personal relationship of the soul to God ; the Catholics define grace as "a metaphysical potency" acting mainly through the sacraments ; St. Augustine insisted that man's salvation is due exclusively to grace, but Pelagius held that grace merely reinforced human virtue ; Calvin denied that grace was extended to all men, he limited its working to himself—and the other elect. (2) A prayer offered before or after a meal. The custom (now honoured only by the clergy) dates from the 3rd C. (3) In terms of psychology grace is an influence from the superconscious that sometimes accompanies or follows states of humility, repentance and unselfishness. Its effects are ennobling and regenerative.

GRADUAL. (1) The anthem (in the Mass) between epistle and gospel formerly sung from the steps (*gradus*) of the altar. (2) The book containing the anthem.

GRAIL (GRAAL), THE HOLY. The name of various legends connected either with the chalice out of which Jesus drank at the Last Supper, or in which Joseph of Arimathea caught some of the sacred blood of Jesus. The legend, which took a markedly mystical meaning, may be the result of Christian influence on Celtic myth or an infusion of Celtic myth into Christianity. It is first found in the French romances of the 12th C. The name has become a symbol for any high spiritual adventure.

GREECE, RELIGION OF. The ancient Greek religion consisted of a loosely held anthropomorphic polytheism with a deeper core of mysticism. In Homer the Olympic gods reflected a patriarchal state of society, the gods being little superior to men save in strength and longevity. In a later age (8th–6th C.s B.C.) the desire for a more intimate, personal religion was met by the Mysteries (q.v.) of Dionysius, Demeter and Persephone. The Eleusinian Mysteries of Demeter constituted the strongest religious force in the ancient world, inculcating a high morality and inspiring the initiate with lofty ideals. (See L. Campbell, ***Religion in Greek Literature*** (1898) ; Jane Harrison, ***Religions of Ancient Greece.*** (Naomi Mitchison has written some excellent novels of life in ancient Greece.)

GREEK CHURCH. The eastern branch of the early Christian

Church, known also as "The Holy Orthodox Catholic Apostolic Eastern Church." It is distinguished from the Catholic (or Roman Catholic or Latin Church) by its refusal to accept the Papacy. The name "Greek" is due to its having arisen in the Greek-speaking parts of Europe and Asia. It is the national church of Russia and of modern Greece. To this Church belonged all the great Church Fathers, from Polycarp to John of Damascus (8th C.). It is also the Church of such outstanding theologians as Clement of Alexandria, Origen, Basil, Chrysostom and the two Basils. The final break with Rome, the result of political jealousies and theological differences, came in 1054 when Pope Leo IX excommunicated Michael Cerularius and the whole Eastern Church. The ostensible cause of the schism was the Filioque controversy (q.v.), the Roman Church, without consulting the Eastern Church or getting the sanction of an ecumenical council, having added to "proceeding from the Father" (in reference to the Holy Ghost) the words "and the Son" in the Apostles' Creed. In the Greek Church a married priesthood is allowed, but bishops are chosen from the celibate monastic orders. The ritual is more elaborate than in the Catholic Church. (See Adrian Fortiscue, *The Orthodox Eastern Church* (1907); F. G. Cole, *Mother of all Churches* (1908).)

GREGORIAN CHANT. A chant introduced by Pope Gregory I (6th C.), which was an improvement on the Ambrosian Chant.

GREGORY THE GREAT (590–604). The first Pope of this name. By reforms, by taking a prominent part in politics and by missionary activity he steadily advanced the power of the Papacy. Gregory is gratefully remembered by the English for his discerning (or flattering ?) description of them—"Angels, not Angles." See *Papacy and Popes*.

GREGORY THE ILLUMINATOR (250–333). The founder of the Armenian Church.

GREGORY OF NAZIANZUS (329–90). A distinguished theologian of the Greek Church (q.v.). He endeavoured to define many indefinable church dogmas.

GREGORY OF NYSSA (330–98). Theologian of the Greek Church, brother of Basil the Great. Became bishop of Nyssa and helped to formulate the Christian doctrines of the Trinity.

GREGORY OF TOURS, SAINT (538–94). Bishop of Tours and author of many books of history, martyrology, etc.

GREGORY THAUMATURGUS. A bishop of Neo-Caesarea in Pontus to whom many miracles were attributed. (3rd C.)

GREMIAL. The cloth laid on the bishop's knees to protect his vestments from the oil during ordinations.

GREY FRIARS. See *Franciscans*.

GRILLE. The grating shutting off nuns in a convent from friends visiting them.

GRINDAL, EDMUND (1519–83). Archbishop of Canterbury under Elizabeth ; a robust Protestant and the "gentle Shepherd Algrind" of Edmund Spenser's *Shepherd's Calendar*. (See Gee, *Elizabethan Clergy*.)

GRISAILLE. Decorative painting to imitate bas-relief.

GROIN. The curve formed by the crossing of two arches (archit.).

GROSSETESTE, ROBERT (c. 1175–1253). Learned churchman and bishop of Lincoln. He was a zealous reformer, and supporter of the ecclesiastical against the civil power under Henry III and Edward I.

GROUP MOVEMENT, THE. A Christian sect founded by an American minister, Frank N. D. Buchman, and introduced into England as the Oxford Groups. Buchman, after much lecturing and travel, founded the First Century Christian Fellowship in 1921. The Group Movement is revivalist in its nature and advocates the public confession of sin by members of the group. It had a considerable vogue in Oxford in 1933–4. A noted divine referred to it as "spiritual exhibitionism." (See Russell, *For Sinners Only*.)

GUARDIAN ANGEL. See *genius.*

GUEBRES. See *Gabars.*

GUEUX (BEGGARS). The name taken by a confederation of Dutch nobles in 1565 to resist the introduction of the Inquisition into the Netherlands by Philip II of Spain.

GUNPOWDER PLOT. A plot formed by certain Catholics to blow up the English Houses of Parliament. It was arranged for 5 November 1605, but detected in time. The leaders were Robert Catesby and Guy Fawkes.

GURU. Hindu term for a spiritual teacher.

GUYON, JEANNE MARIE BOUVIER DE LA MOTHE (1648–1717). French Quietist and friend of Fénelon (q.v.) who gained a large following as a result of her personal charm and eloquence. (See T. C. Upham, *Life of Madame de Guyon* (New York, 1854).)

GWYNN. A Celtic god of the underworld, son of Nudd and king of the Welsh fairies. His symbol was an owl.

GYMNOSOPHISTS ("naked philosophers"). The name given by Greek writers to certain Hindu philosophers who lived on a minimum of food and wore no clothes.

GYPSIES. See *Gipsies.*

H

HABIT. The tendency acquired of performing certain actions or harbouring certain thoughts. Habits may develop from instincts, and therefore the control of instincts as well as the formation of habits are of great importance in attaining a well-ordered life. The Hindu doctrine of Karma stresses the importance of habits. "Sow an act and reap a habit; sow a habit and reap a character; sow a character and reap a destiny." Most of the opinions and beliefs held by mankind are due to inherited or acquired habits of thought and the prejudices to which these give rise.

HADES. The world of the dead in Greek mythology, divided into Elysium for the blest and Tartarus for the wicked.

HADITH. The traditional sayings of Mohammed.

HADJ, HAJJ. The pilgrimage of Mohammedans to Mecca or Medina. (Ar. "a pilgrimage.")

HAFTERAH. A portion of the Jewish scriptures read on the Sabbath in the Synagogue, after the reading from the Pentateuch.

HAGGADA. A literary and poetical Rabbinical commentary on the O.T. which together with the Halasha (q.v.) forms the Midrash (q.v.).

HAGIOGRAPHA. The last of the three Jewish divisions of the O.T.: comprehending Psalms, Proverbs, Job, Daniel, Ezra, Nehemiah, Ruth, Esther, Chronicles, Canticles, Lamentations, Ecclesiastes.

HAGIOLATRY. The worship of saints.

HAGIOLOGY. The literature which has gathered about the lives of the Saints.

HAGIOSCOPE. An oblique opening (squint) in the chancel wall of a church affording a view of the high altar.

HAIL MARY. See *Ave Maria.*

HAJJ. See *Hadj.*

HALACHAH, HALAKAH, HALASHA. That part of the Midrash (q.v.) which deals with Hebrew legal precepts.

HALEVI, JEHUDAH BEN SAMUEL (c. 1085–1143). The greatest medieval Jewish poet. His chief work, Cuzari, was a defence of the Jewish religion against Christianity and Mohammedanism. He wrote many exquisite hymns. (See Mrs. H. Lucas, *The Jewish Year.*)

HALLAJ (AL-HALLAJ). A Mohammedan mystic, put to death at Bagdad for asserting "I am Reality" and insisting on the potential deity of man.

HALLEL. The Psalms (cxiii.–cxviii.) sung at Jewish festivals.

HALLELUJAH, HALLELUIAH. A Jewish doxology at the end of certain psalms, used also in Christian worship. (*halelu* = praise ye; *Jah* = Jehovah.)

HALLOW. To make holy.

HALLOWE'EN. The evening before All Saints' Day (All Hallows).

HALLOWMAS. The feast of All Saints (1 Nov.). See also *All Saints' Day.*

HALO. See *nimbus.*

HAMADRYAD. The spirit of a tree, expressed as a wood-nymph (Gr. myth.).

HAMARTIOLOGY. The branch of theology which treats of sin. (Gr. *hamartia* = sin; *logia* = discourse.)

HAMMURABI CODE. In December–January 1901–2 French excavators at Susa in Mesopotamia discovered fragments of an inscribed pillar. Almost the whole inscription (The Hammurabi Code) was pieced together and is now in the Louvre, Paris. Hammurabi was 6th king of the first Babylonian dynasty (2123–2081 B.C.) and his code shows a very highly developed civilization in Babylonia. The intention of his code was "to cause justice to prevail in the land, to destroy the wicked, to prevent the strong from oppressing the weak, to enlighten the land and to further the welfare of the people." The Code proves that Hebrew civilization was largely derived from Babylonia.

HAMPTON COURT CONFERENCE. A meeting summoned by James I to settle differences between the Anglican Church and the Puritans. Largely owing to James's pedagogic attitude, little was effected. But to this conference the magnificent "authorized version" of the Bible owes its inception.

HANDS, LAYING ON OF. A rite observed in the Christian and other religions (see *ordination*). The custom of touching to cure scrofula by the Stuart and earlier kings is probably akin, in origin, to the Christian rite. In all ages certain persons have possessed the gift of healing (or ameliorating) disease by touch. (See *Memoirs of Edward, Eighth Earl of Sandwich.*) In primitive times such persons were venerated as possessing supernatural power or mana (q.v.).

HANUKKAH. A Jewish festival on 25 December (Kislev), also called the Feast of Lights. It celebrates the rededication of the Temple in 165 B.C. following the Jewish victory over the Syrians. Probably also connected with the winter solstice.

HAPI. The Egyptian god of the Nile, a male figure with female breasts.

HARMONY OF THE GOSPELS. A collation of parallel passages from the four gospels to demonstrate similarities and dissimilarities.

HARPY. A hostile winged monster of Greek mythology, possibly a personification of the winds.

HARUSPEX. An Etruscan priest from whom the Roman augur was derived. He foretold the future from animal entrails.

HARVEST FESTIVAL. A feast of the ingathering of crops observed from remotest ages. The Feast of Pentecost (q.v.) was observed as the Jewish harvest festival. The Roman Cerealia was held in honour of Ceres. The Druids celebrated harvest on 1 November. In pre-Reformation England harvest commenced on Lammas Day (1 August) when loaves of bread were presented in church. Many old customs derived from worship of the Corn-spirit still linger in remote places. (See J. G. Frazer, *The Golden Bough* vols. i and ii.)

HASIDAEANS, HASIDIM. A strict Jewish sect of Palestinian scribes. (3rd and 2nd C.s B.C.)

HASSOCK. A cushion to render kneeling in church less irksome.

HATHA YOGA. The branch of Hindu Yoga (q.v.) which deals mainly with physical health.

HATHOR. An ancient Egyptian mother-goddess of love. She is represented as a woman with a cow's head. Identified by the Greeks with Aphrodite.

HATRED. A negative, destructive emotion, the antithesis of goodwill. Such emotions can be overcome if the sufferer will calmly face and watch them as soon as they arise within him. But to do this he must be keenly aware of his inner conditions. Anger never arises from *external* conditions but always from *internal*. See also *anger*.

HEARSE, HERSE. The carriage in which the dead are conveyed to the grave.

HEATHEN. One who is not a Christian, a Mohammedan or a Jew. Used abusively of religions other than one's own. (A.S. *haethen* = dweller on the heath; cf. L. *paganus* = a rustic.)

HEAVEN. The place, or state, of God and the blessed. The Greek Elysium was the abode of gods and heroes. The wicked passed to Hades, a land of mist and darkness. The Hebrew Sheol appears to have been a similar abode. In N.T. times heaven became the dwelling-place of God and the angels; Gehenna (hell) being the place of the wicked. Christianity, though at certain periods stressing the belief in heaven and hell, has always been vague in its definitions. The greatest Christian thinkers have insisted that "heaven" and "hell" are states of the soul and not localized places. The orthodox Christian belief that the individual (ego) is somehow absorbed in God, yet maintaining individuality, compares unfavourably with the far deeper teaching of Buddha that the ego is finally lost and merged in something much greater—the universal Self, or Reality. See *Nirvana*.

HEBDOMAD. The group of angels or divine planetary emanations in the gnostic system.

HEBDOMADARY. The member of a convent who officiates in the choir, etc., for a week.

HEBER, REGINALD (1783–1826). Anglican bishop of Calcutta and author of many beautiful hymns ("From Greenland's Icy Mountains"; "Holy, holy, holy, Lord God Almighty," etc.).

HEBREWS. See *Judaism*.

HEDONISM. The ethical doctrine that happiness is the highest good.

HEGEL, GEORG WILHELM FRIEDRICH (1730–1831). German philosopher who taught that Reality is to be found only in consciousness. (See W. T. Harris, *Hegel's Logic* (1890).)

HEGIRA, HEJIRA. Mohammed's flight from Mecca (15 July A.D. 622) from which the Mohammedan era is dated.

HELL. The abode of the wicked after death. In medieval theology hell was a place of physical burning or, as in Dante, of intense cold. Modern theologians regard hell as the state or condition of the unrepentant wicked. (See, for an account of the Buddhist hell, Prof. Evans-Wentz, *The Tibetan Book of the Dead.*)

HELLENISM. (1) The civilization of ancient Greece. (2) The later Greek culture which spread over Europe and had a deep influence on Christianity.

HENRY VIII (1509–47). King of England during whose reign the Church of England separated from Rome. The cause of his renunciation of allegiance to Rome was the Pope's refusal to sanction his divorce from Catherine of Aragon in 1529.

HERA (L. Juno). The wife of Zeus and goddess of fertility (Gr. myth.).

HERACLITUS. Greek philosopher who taught that the universe is pervaded by reason and that matter is in a state of perpetual flux. (6th C. B.C.)

HERBARTIAN. A follower of the German philosopher and educationist Herbart who taught a pluralistic realism. (18th–19th C.s.) See F. H. Hayward, *The Student's Herbart* (1902); F. H. Hayward, *The Secret of Herbart.*)

HERBERT, GEORGE (1593–1633). English poet; friend of Bacon, Donne and Walton. Author of some of the finest sacred poetry in the language. (See A. G. Hyde, *George Herbert and His Times* (1907).)

HERBERT OF CHERBURY, EDWARD, 1ST LORD (1583–1648). Brother of the above. Philosopher and metaphysician. His aim was to account for religion without any supernatural origin. His *Ancient Religion of the Gentiles* has been called "the Charter of the Deists."

HERCULES. A Greek hero sometimes identified with the Sun-god, and regarded by the Greeks as a saviour who laboured for the good of mankind. The chief of his twelve labours were: The descent into Hades and taming of Cerberus (conquest of death); slaying the Nemean Lion (victory over the passions); cleansing of the Augean stables (destruction of evil habits); the gathering the apples of the Hesperides (acquisition of wisdom).

HERESY. Any doctrine opposed to the authorized teaching of the church or society of which one is a member. The Catholic is a heretic to the Protestant, and vice versa. The word derives from the Greek *hairesis* = choice, and indicates one who makes his own choice.

THE CHIEF CHRISTIAN HERESIES OF THE EARLY CENTURIES

1st C.

The Simonians (from Simon Magus).
The Cerinthians.
The Ebionites.

2nd C.

The Basilidians.
The Valentinians.
Gnostic Brotherhoods.
Nazarenes.
Cainites.
Marcionites.

3rd C.

The Patripassians.
The Novatians.
The Sabellians.
The Manicheans.

4th C.

The Arians.
The Apollinarians.
Collyridians.
Seleucians.
Jovinianists.
Bonosians.

5th C.

The Pelagians.
The Nestorians.
Eutychians.

6th C.

The Predestinarians.
The Agnoetae.
The Monothelites.

When a heretical sect becomes large and powerful enough it ceases to be "a heresy" and becomes "a church." The number of heresies to which the great religions have given birth is largely due to the desire of scholars and theologians to label and define such portions of experience as transcend intellect.

HERETIC. The upholder of heresy.

(It is an heretic which *makes* the fire,
Not he which burns in't.
Winter's Tale.)

HERMAS, THE SHEPHERD OF. A Christian Scripture (uncanonical) of the 2nd C. A.D. ascribed to Hermas, brother of Pius, bishop of Rome. The work consists of visions, parables, etc., and is sharply critical of the Roman Christians. English translation by Dr. C. Taylor (1906).

HERMES. (1) A Greek god of sleep, dreams and death, identified with Roman Mercury. As the "Conductor of dreams" the Greeks offered him the last libation before sleep. He was regarded as the messenger of the gods and conductor of souls to Hades. (2) The Egyptian god, Thoth identified with the Greek Hermes and known as Hermes Trismegistus (thrice-greatest). He was regarded as the originator of religion, magic, art, alchemy and science. (3) During the 3rd C. the name Hermes was used as a pseudonym to cover various writings of a neo-Platonic, Judaistic and theosophical nature. (See G. R. S. Mead, *Thrice Greatest Hermes* (1907).)

HERMIT (EREMITE). One who retires from society for purposes of devotion. (Gr. *eremos* = solitary.)

HERO. In Greek mythology a being superior to men but inferior to gods. Such beings are also found in the early civilizations of China, Japan, Persia, etc. Among primitive people a teacher or helper stands out so forcibly from the rank and file that he becomes, in his lifetime or after death, a hero or a god. See *euhemerism*.

HEROD ANTIPAS. Son of Herod the Great. He is referred to in the Gospels as " Herod," and Christ is reported as having applied the epithet " fox " to him (Luke xiii. 32). Herod was represented as a swaggering bully in old plays—hence Shakespeare's " it out-herods Herod " (*Hamlet*).

HERRICK, ROBERT (1591–1674). One of England's greatest lyric poets. He held the living of Dean Prior (Devon) for many years; was ejected during the Commonwealth but reinstated in 1662. In his poetry he was particularly happy in blending Christianity with the best feeling of paganism.

HESTIA. See *Vesta*.

HESYCHAST. A mystic quietist sect of the Greek Church. (14th C.)

HEU T'U. The earth regarded as a god in the State religion of China.

HEXATEUCH. The first six books of the O.T., i.e. the Pentateuch and Joshua.

HIBBERT LECTURES, THE. A lectureship endowed in 1878 under the Hibbert Fund, to deal with the origin and development of religion. Many renowned scholars have contributed to the series.

HIERARCHY. Government by priests as in Israel in the time of Moses and Aaron.

HIERONYMITES. The name of several orders of hermits in the 13th and 14th C.s.

HIEROPHANT. A priest as revealer of sacred things. (Gr. *hieros* = sacred, *phaenein* = to show.)

HIGH ALTAR. The principal altar in a church or cathedral.

HIGH CHURCH PARTY. A section within the Church of England that exalts the authority of the priesthood, the sacraments, confession, etc. It derives, through the Oxford Movement (q.v.), from Elizabethan times when Whitgift and Bancroft supported Romanism in the Church of England in defiance of Puritan opinion.

HIGHER CRITICISM. A term applied to the critical examination of Scripture, which seeks to determine problems of date, authorship, authenticity, etc.

HIGH PRIEST. A chief priest, especially in the ancient Jewish Church.

HILARIUS (HILARY). (1) A pupil of Abélard at Paris who became canon of Ronceray. He was an accomplished Latin poet and wrote hymns in metrical Latin. See the delightful verses to an English Boy charmingly translated in Jack Lindsay's *Medieval Latin Poets* (p. 158). (2) A 4th-C. bishop of Poictiers who vigorously opposed Arianism.

HILDEBRAND. See *Gregory the Great*.

HINAYANA. See *Mahayana*.

HINCMAR (805–82). An accomplished scholar at the court of Louis the Pious; appointed archbishop of Reims by Charles the Bald.

HINDUISM. The religious beliefs and customs of the Hindus, peculiar to some 217,000,000 of the people of India. While Brahmanism is the term applied to the priestly aspect of Hindu life, Hinduism is generally used to describe its social and popular religious aspects. There is no single authoritative Scripture of Hinduism, but in its place a mass of unrelated religious literature—the Puranas, the Tantras, etc. Truth is regarded as enshrined in the votary, meditation on the sacred texts serving to evoke it. The belief in Karma (q.v.) and reincarnation (q.v.) permeate Hindu life and thought. Western activity, in its many forms, finds no response in the Hindu who experiences greater satisfaction in the search for God and the soul.

In Hinduism religion and morality have little connection. The religious teachers (*sadhus*), of whom there are over five million wandering about India, do not all inculcate (or practise) morality. Mystical states and an exalted devotion to God are what the Sadhu aims at. He may claim, and frequently does, that he is "above good and evil," but is not prevented thereby from committing actions contrary to an average ethical standard. The chief gods of the Hindu pantheon are Vishnu, the creator and sustainer; Shiva, the destroyer, and the post-Vedic Brahma. Hinduism, despite its persistent cultivation of the inner life and its deep intuitional philosophy, is in the main a negative force, owing to its invertebrate neglect of the moral law and its too great detachment from material conditions. (See A. Barth, *The Religions of India* (1882); Sir John Strachey, *India.*) For Indian philosophy, see under *Mimansa, Nyaya, Sankhya, Vaiseshika, Vedanta, Vedas, Yoga.*

HITTITES. A people of ancient Israel inhabiting the highlands of Asia Minor with their capital at Boghaz-Kerii. Their religion appears to have been borrowed chiefly from Egypt and Babylon.

HOBBES, THOMAS (1588–1679). One of the greatest of English philosophers; a friend (possibly amanuensis) of Francis Bacon, Ben Jonson and Lord Herbert of Cherbury. His political philosophy, expressed in his *Leviathan*, inclined to the belief that all human action springs from varying degrees of selfishness. (See Leslie Stephen, *Life of Thomas Hobbes* (1904).)

HOLDHEIM, SAMUEL. See *Reformed Judaism.*

HOLY CITY. Usually Jerusalem, but the epithet is also applied to Rome, Mecca, Benares, etc.

HOLY COAT. A seamless garment preserved at Treves reputed to be the coat of Jesus.

HOLY COMMUNION. See *eucharist.*

HOLY FAMILY. A picture or representation of the infant Jesus with Joseph and Mary.

HOLY GHOST (HOLY SPIRIT). The third person of the Trinity (q.v.). (See H. B. Sweete, *The Holy Spirit in the Ancient Church.*)

HOLY GRAIL. See *Grail, Holy.*

HOLY OF HOLIES. The inner chamber of the Jewish tabernacle which only the high priest might enter.

HOLY JOE. (1) The circular low-crowned hat worn by clergymen (slang). (2) A pious person or, among sailors, a parson (slang). (See Eric Partridge, *Slang*, p. 198.)

HOLY OFFICE. See *Inquisition.*

HOLY ORDERS. Ordination enabling to serve in the Christian ministry. The Church of England, since the Reformation, recognizes three orders: bishops, priests and deacons. The Catholic Church recognizes seven orders: priests, deacons, subdeacons (major orders); acolytes, exorcists, readers and doorkeepers (minor orders); the office of bishop being included in the priesthood. The Eastern churches, Russian, Greek, Armenian, etc., maintain five orders: bishops, priests, deacons, subdeacons, and readers. In the Church of England the age for the diaconate is 21, for the priesthood 24, for the episcopate 30. The Catholic Church requires the subdeacon to be not less than 22, the deacon must be 23, the priest 25 and the bishop 30. In the Church of England clergy of all degrees may marry; in the Catholic Church celibacy is required of all in major orders. In the Eastern churches a secular priest may be married before ordination, but if his wife dies he may not remarry.

HOLY-ROOD. The cross in Catholic churches over the chancel entrance.

HOLY SEE. See *Papacy.*

HOLY SEPULCHRE. The rock-tombs (two) in Jerusalem where the body of Jesus is supposed to have lain.

HOLY SPIRIT. See *Holy Ghost.*

HOLY THURSDAY. See *Ascension, Feast of the.*

HOLY WATER. Water blessed by a priest (Cath.).

HOLY WEEK. The week before Easter.

HOLY WRIT. The Scriptures.

HOMILETICS. That branch of theology which deals with the writing and delivery of sermons. See *preaching.*

HOMILY. A sermon or hortatory discourse.

HOMOIOUSIOS. Greek adjective meaning "of like substance." The word was adopted by the moderate party among the Arians (q.v.) of the 4th C. to define the relationship of the Son to the Father. But the word was rejected by the orthodox party at the Council of Nicaea in 325 and the adjective *homoousios* ("of the same substance") substituted in its place.

HOOD. A head covering, forming part of the cloak worn by medieval laymen and monks. When hats came into fashion the hood continued as part of the monk's habit. See *vestments*.

HOOKER, RICHARD (1533–1600). Anglican clergyman and author of the *Laws of Ecclesiastical Polity*. The work was written to defend episcopacy against Puritanism.

HORUS. The hawk-headed sun-god of ancient Egypt, son of Hathor, or, according to others, of Osiris. The hostility between Horus and Set symbolized the conflict between Light and Darkness. The Greeks identified Horus with Apollo.

HOSANNA. A shout used by the ancient Hebrews in praise of God.

HOSEA. A minor prophet of the O.T. Nothing, save vague traditions, is known of his life. The Book of Hosea belongs to the 8th C. B.C. It is strongly emotional in character. (See W. R. Harper, *Amos and Hosea* (1905).)

HOSPITAL. The earliest establishment devoted solely to nursing the sick appears to be the monastery of St. Sorore in Siena in 9th C. A.D. The Hospitallers and Knights of St. John were active in establishing hospitals during the Crusades. The latter established a hospital in Jerusalem about 1048.

HOSPITALLERS. A medieval religious order open to both sexes. The Hospitallers were Augustinians who took an additional vow to tend the sick and poor.

HOST. The circular wafer consecrated in the eucharist (Cath.). The word derives from the Latin *hostia* = an animal slain in sacrifice. The Christian eucharist is thus linked etymologically with earlier pagan religious rites of a similar character.

HOURS, CANONICAL. See *Breviary*.

HOUSEL. (1) The eucharist. (2) The act of taking the eucharistic bread and wine. (A.S. *husel* = sacrifice.)

HOUSELING-CLOTH. A cloth to prevent crumbs falling, used by the priest in celebrating the eucharist.

HUGO OF ST. VICTOR. French mystical philosopher and a monk of the abbeys of St. Victor at Marseilles and Paris. (11th–12th C.s.)

HUGUENOTS. Name given to the French Protestants of 16th and 17th C.s. Suggested derivations of the word are: (1) Ger. *eidgenoss* = confederate; (2) diminutive of Hugo, the name of some French Calvinist; (3) the gate of King Hugo, a meeting-place of the Protestants in Paris. Fierce persecution of the Huguenots in France continued throughout the 16th and 17th C.s. In 1535, 1,500 Huguenots, including John Calvin, fled from France. Peace was in sight when the Massacre of the Huguenots on St. Bartholomew's Day, 1572, again set fanaticism ablaze. By the Edict of Nantes (q.v.) in 1598, religious and political liberty was granted the Huguenots, but in 1685 Louis XIV revoked the Edict and 400,000 Huguenots emigrated to Europe and America. It was not until 1801 that the legal rights of the Protestants in France were recognized. (See Henry M. Baird, *History of the Rise of the Huguenots.*)

HUITZILOPOCHTLI. The chief god of the Aztecs of Mexico to whom they annually offered human victims. (See W. H. Prescott, *History of the Conquest of Mexico.*)

HUMANISM. See *Renaissance.*

HUME, DAVID (1711–76). English philosophical writer who aroused keen opposition in ecclesiastical circles by his *Natural History of Religion* in which he denied or ignored any supernatural element. His *History of England* attained immense popularity and introduced a more philosophic method of writing history. (See Hill Burton, *Life of David Hume* (1846).)

HUMERAL. A scarf worn by the priest at certain parts of Mass and Benediction.

HUMILIATI. A Catholic religious order open to men and women who devoted themselves to the service of the poor (15th–16th C.s). The order still exists in Italy.

HUNTINGDON'S CONNECTION, COUNTESS OF. A Methodist sect founded by the Countess of Huntingdon (1707–91) for evangelical preaching.

HUS, JOHN (1370–1415). Bohemian reformer who paved the way for the Reformation. His sympathies with Wycliffe aroused the suspicions of the Catholic Church and in 1411 he was put under a ban. This did not deter him from continuing his work. He was condemned by the Council of Constance and burnt at the stake in 1415. (See Count Lützow, *The Life and Times of John Huss* (1909).)

HUXLEY, THOMAS HENRY (1825–75). English biologist and writer on evolution, psychology and ethics. His views gave offence to Bishop Wilberforce (q.v.) and Mr. Gladstone, who objected to his belief that cosmic processes have no moral ends, moral purpose being of exclusively human origin. (See Leonard Huxley, *Life and Letters of Thomas Henry Huxley* (1900).)

HYACINTHE, FATHER (1827–1912). A French monk, Charles Loyson by name, excommunicated for his liberal views. He organized a free Catholic Church in Paris.

HYKSOS. Shepherd kings and probably the earliest invaders of Egypt. They worshipped Seth (q.v.) and have been identified with (1) the Arabs, (2) the Israelites, (3) the Syrians, (4) a Tartar race. (c. 2000–1700 B.C.)

HYMN. A song of praise to God. The ancient Greeks sung a *hymnos* or song to the gods and heroes at festivals. The Hindus, from early times, had their Rigveda, a collection of hymns of praise and prayer. The Egyptians and Hebrews included sacred songs in the temple ritual. Hilary (4th C.) introduced Latin metrical hymnody, but after his time hymn-writers turned mainly from quantitative to accentual verse. Luther and the reformers laid stress on the need for psalm-singing and the singing of Protestant hymns. In England, Isaac Watts in his *Hymns and Spiritual Songs* (1707) gave a more modern form to the medieval hymn and the Wesleys carried on his work. The evangelical hymn of the Methodist reformers was modified by the more literary influences of the Oxford Movement (q.v.). (See John Julian, *Dictionary of Hymnology* (1907).)

HYPATIA (A.D. 370–415). Alexandrian mathematician and philosopher, daughter of the philosopher Theon. She became the head of a Neoplatonic school in Alexandria, where her eloquence, modesty and beauty allied with keen intellectual gifts attracted a large number of pupils. Synesius of Cyrene was among her friends and scholars. Owing to the fanaticism of Cyril, bishop and patriarch of Alexandria, the Christians were incited to attack her, with the result that she was murdered by the Christian mob in March, 415. (See Socrates, (*Hist. ecclesiastica*, vii, 15; also Charles Kingsley's novel, *Hypatia*.)

HYPERDULIA. The worship paid by Catholics to the Virgin Mary, a little less than that paid to God (described as *latria*) and a little more than that paid to the saints (described as *dulia*).

HYPERION. Son of Uranus and Ge and father of the Sun-god Helios—the source of light and beauty.

HYPNOTISM. A sleep-like condition induced by artificial means. See *mesmerism*.

HYPOSTASIS. The essence or real substance of each of the three persons of the Godhead (Cath. theol.).

HYSSOP. An aromatic plant of Palestine referred to in John xix. 29.

HYSTERIA, RELIGIOUS. A neurotic condition of emotional excitement. It has often been produced by the magnetic type of preachers such as Savonarola (q.v.); John Wesley and others, Christian and non-Christian.

I

IBAS. Bishop of Edessa condemned by the Fifth Synod of Constantinople for Nestorian views. (5th C.)

IBLIS. Chief of the evil spirits in Mohammedanism; originally an angel. Pride caused him to fall.

ICARUS. Son of Daedalus, the mythical inventor. Icarus flew with the wings his father made him till the sun melted their wax fastenings and he fell into the sea. " The succeeding part of the fable of Daedalus and Icarus is plain, concerning the use of mechanic arts, whereto human life stands greatly indebted, as receiving from this treasury numerous particulars for the service of religion, the ornament of civil society, and the whole provision and apparatus of life; but then the same magazine supplies instruments of lust, cruelty and death. For not to mention the arts of luxury and debauchery, we plainly see how far the business of exquisite poisons, guns, engines of war and such kind of destructive inventions, exceeds the cruelty and barbarity of the Minotaur himself " (Francis Bacon, *Wisdom of the Ancients*).

ICON. A pictorial representation of Christ or a saint in the Greek Church.

ICONOCLASTS. An image-smashing party in the Greek Church who opposed the worship of icons. (8th–9th C.s.)

ICONOSTASIS. A wall in Byzantine churches separating choir from nave.

IDEA. In the teaching of Plato an archetype of the many varieties of existence in the universe, belonging to the supersensible world where alone Reality is found.

IDEALISM. (1) The doctrine that all reality is in its nature psychical—due to the perception of ideas. (2) The search for the highest and best. Carlyle, Emerson and Ruskin are examples of idealists in this sense. Idealism in religion and philosophy stands opposed to materialism. The Catholic and most Christian churches only favour idealism up to a point, since the idealist usually relies on experience rather than any traditional body of doctrine.

IDHUN. Goddess of eternal youth and wife of Bragi (Norse myth.).

IDOL. An image or person too much honoured. Francis Bacon (*Novum Organum*, I, 38) distinguishes four popular idols: (1) of the nation or tribe; (2) of the den or cave (fallacies due to personal causes); (3) of the forum (those due to the influence of words and phrases); (4) of the theatre (those due to misconceptions of philosophic systems). By all these " idols " men's minds are led astray so that they fail to reach Truth.

IDOLATRY. Most primitive forms of religion reveal the worship of physical objects—stones, trees, etc. Later, as in Egypt, the desire for worship turned towards animals. It seems probable that animal-worship gave place, at a later stage, to worship of exceptional men. Thus, owing to changing conditions, the worship of one age tends to become the idolatry of the next.

IGNATIUS. Bishop of Antioch and the author of letters to various churches, the authenticity of which has been questioned by scholars. Ignatius is regarded as one of the Apostolic Fathers. He is said to have suffered martyrdom in the Roman Colosseum c. 107. (See G. Krüger, *Early Christian Literature*.)

I.H.S. A monogram to indicate Jesus Christ. Probably derived from an error in latinizing the first three letters of the Greek word for Jesus.

IKHNATON. Ruler of Egypt, 14th C. B.C., who introduced religious reforms based on a mystical monotheism. He established his cult under a new priesthood but the forces of conservatism proved too strong at his death and the old gods returned.

ILLUMINATI. Various mystical brotherhoods have been so named:

(1) The Alombrados of Spain (16th C.).

(2) The Guérinets of France (17th C.).

(3) The Mystics of Belgium (18th C.).

(4) The German order of Illuminati founded in 1776 and aiming at the establishment of a religion consistent with reason. The German Illuminati probably derive from the Rosicrucians (q.v.).

ILLUMINATION. The name given to a psychological experience to which many of the saints and mystics testify. When oxygen and hydrogen are combined in certain proportion the result is a new element, water. Similarly when the subject and object of the mind unite through concentration, the result is a new equilibrium of consciousness, or illumination. The knowledge that arises in an illumined mind is derived from intuition, not from reason. Its marks are lucidity and intensity of vision, great discernment, and the ability to grasp simple principles in complex situations. Illumination was experienced by certain initiates in the Greek Mysteries. Reitzenstein (*The Hellenistic Mystery Religions*) refers to the illumination (*photismos*) which attended initiation and salvation. Dr. Bucke (*Cosmic Consciousness*) describes a similar experience. "All at once . . . I found myself wrapped in a flame-coloured cloud. . . . Directly afterwards there came upon me a sense of exultation, of immense joyousness accompanied or immediately followed by an intellectual illumination impossible to describe. I saw . . . that the foundation principle of the world, of all the worlds, is what we call love, and that the happiness of each and all is in the long run absolutely certain." (See William James, *The Varieties of Religious Experience*, Lectures xvi and xvii.) See also under *initiation*.

IMAM. (1) The calif or head of Shiite Islam regarded as the spiritual successor of Mohammed. (2) The officer who leads the devotions in Mohammedan mosques.

"IMITATION OF CHRIST, THE" **("IMITATIO CHRISTI").** A famous devotional work of medieval Christianity, usually ascribed to Thomas à Kempis (1380–1471), a canon regular of Mount St. Agnes in Zwolle. The book, which has had an enormous influence perhaps second only to the Bible, has also been ascribed to John Gerson (1363–1429), chancellor of the University of Paris; and to John Gersen, abbot of a Benedictine monastery at Vercelli in the 12th C. (See F. R. Cruise, *Thomas à Kempis* (1887); also his *Who was the Author of the Imitation?* (1898).)

IMMACULATE CONCEPTION. The dogma that the Virgin Mary was conceived without "original sin" was first enunciated by St. Bernard and was maintained by Duns Scotus and his followers. It was not received into the Catholic Church as an article of faith until 1854 (Pius IX).

IMMANENCE. The belief that the intelligent creative principle of the universe pervades the universe itself. It is contrasted, on the one side, with transcendence, which regards the divine power as acting apart and above, and on the other with pantheism, which holds that God and the universe constitute a single entity.

IMMORTALITY. The survival of personality after death believed in, with variations and modifications, by many religions. See also *Future Life* and *Timeless Being*.

IMMURE. To bury alive in a wall. The Roman Vestal Virgins who broke their vows were thus put to death. In medieval times defaulting nuns appear to have been punished in the same way. The remains of immured nuns have been found at Coldingham Abbey and other places.

IMPANATION. The Lutheran doctrine that the body of Christ is united with the consecrated bread in the eucharist. See also *consubstantiation*.

IMPLICIT FAITH. In the Middle Ages the lower orders of clergy and the laity were regarded as too ignorant to understand the mysteries of the faith. They were required to accept whatever the Church taught by "implicit faith."

IMPOSITION OF HANDS. See *hands, laying on of.*

IMPOSTOR, RELIGIOUS. One who imposes on others either knowingly or as a result of self-deception. Some noted religious imposters were:

1. The Spaniard Gonsalvo Martin who pretended to be the angel Michael. He was burnt by the Inquisition in 1360.

2. George David, son of a waterman of Ghent, proclaimed himself the Son of God. He taught that only the body could be defiled by sin. Many became his followers, especially women. He died at Basle in 1556, promising to rise again in three years, but failed to do so.

3. Sabbata Levi, a Jew of Smyrna, proclaimed himself to be Jesus Christ in 1666.

4. William Hacket, an Englishman, proclaimed himself to be Jesus Christ and was executed for blasphemy in 1591.

5. Joanna Southcott, proclaimed she had conceived the Messiah. She had many followers at the time of her death (27 Dec. 1814).

Owing to the crudeness of the popular conception of Christianity and the low average of human intelligence, religious impostors continue to appear frequently and to gain large followings. The genuine religious leaders of the world have never made exalted claims on their own behalf, although such claims have frequently been made for them *by their followers* and usually after their death. They have always observed and respected the moral law. Humility, strict honesty, forbearance under persecution and love (expressed in the form of goodwill to all men), have formed the bedrock of their lives and teaching. The religious charlatan, sooner or later, reveals the mainsprings of his activity—pride and egoism.

INARI. The goddess of vegetation in Japanese Shintoism.

INCARNATION. The orthodox Christian doctrine of the union of the divine nature with the human in the person of Jesus Christ.

INCENSE. Odour of spices burned in churches and temples. The custom prevailed in ancient Babylon, Egypt and Rome.

INDEPENDENTS. See *Congregationalism.*

INDEX EXPURGATORIUS. A list of books issued by the Catholic Church which must be read only in expurgated editions.

INDEX LIBRORUM EXPURGANDORUM or LIBRORUM PROHIBITORUM. A list of books issued by the Catholic Church which the faithful are forbidden to read under pain of excommunication.

INDIA, RELIGIONS OF. See *Hinduism.*

INDICTION. A cycle of fifteen years adopted as part of their chronological system by the Popes.

INDRA. A Hindu god of war and fertility, slayer of Vritra, the demon of drought. His home is the fabulous Mount Meru, supposed to lie north of the Himalayas, where dwell also the Apsaras or nymphs.

INDUCTION. Introduction of a clergyman to an ecclesiastical office.

INDULGENCE. The Catholic doctrine that after absolution divine justice still requires satisfaction on earth or in purgatory. By receiving an indulgence this satisfaction can be made on earth. Indulgences have never been abolished and are classified as (1) Plenary (remitting all punishment); (2) Partial (remitting a portion); (3) Temporal (granted for a time); (4) Perpetual (lasting till revoked).

INDULT. A papal licence authorizing something to be done which is not sanctioned by the law of the Church. Not to be confused with indulgence (q.v.).

INFALLIBILITY OF THE POPE. The doctrine of the Catholic Church, promulgated by the Vatican Council of 1870, that the Pope, when speaking *ex cathedra,* is preserved from error in everything regarding faith and morals.

INFANTS, UNBAPTIZED. See *Limbus.*

INFIDEL. (1) One, born in a Christian country, who disbelieves in the Christian revelation. (2) A disbeliever in divine revelation.

INFRALAPSARIANISM. The doctrine held by St. Augustine and revived by Calvin that God, having created the world for his own glory, permitted the Fall and then "elected" from among the fallen a multitude of vessels of mercy (the Elect). He sent His Son for the redemption of these, but left the rest of mankind to suffer punishment for their sins. The doctrine should be distinguished from the Supralapsarianism of the strictest Calvinists and the Sublapsarianism of the more moderates.

INGE, WILLIAM RALPH (b. 1860). Recently dean of St. Paul's. A distinguished scholar and modernist of sceptical temper. The author of many books on Christian mysticism and of a great number of ephemeral articles in the daily press. His most important work is *The Philosophy of Plotinus* (1918).

INHIBITION. (1) The checking of one mental process by another. " Few people . . . realize how constantly this factor of inhibition is upon us, how it contains and moulds us by its restrictive pressure almost as if we were fluids pent within the cavity of a jar " (William James). (2) The official prohibition of a priest to perform his sacred office.

INITIATION and **INITIATES.** Initiation is the term given to a psychological crisis resulting in increased awareness, in a deeper and wider consciousness. The crisis is frequently accompanied by visual or auditory experiences of an unusual nature which possess a symbolic significance similar to dreams.

In primitive and medieval times initiation was induced by certain rites or ceremonies during which the neophyte was subjected to unexpected and often terrifying ordeals. Many primitive tribes still use these methods successfully. The initiatory ceremonies held by modern masonic and similar societies are largely anachronistic survivals, because they very rarely, if ever, induce the psychological crisis referred to.

Nowadays initiation is usually caused by an unexpected mental or emotional shock or by following a system of mental and spiritual training under the guidance of a proficient teacher.

In the absence of such a teacher, the crisis may result in an unbalanced mind, for initiation involves the passage from one state of mental equilibrium to another.

Psychological treatment, if *sufficiently constructive* (psychoanalysis is not), may induce initiation into a higher order of consciousness, and will probably do so more frequently in the future.

There have always been initiates of various attainment in the world. The following are the chief degrees :

1. Initiate (sometimes used generically but properly applied to the first degree) : One who has " entered the stream " of a wider and deeper consciousness. One who has experienced the lower levels of illumination, of

which there are many degrees varying in scope and intensity. Initiates have a tremendous capacity for work. Examples: Widely known geniuses, such as H. G. Wells, Bernard Shaw, Roosevelt, Bismarck.

2. Adept. An advanced initiate. One who can control his thoughts, desires and sensations and, through such control, has developed supernormal knowledge, skill and power. No true adept will claim to possess such knowledge and power, which belong to the collective nature of man. He will put them into his work. The work, to the discerning, reveals the man. Adepts have a far-reaching influence on their age. Examples: Merlin, Leonardo Da Vinci, Napoleon, Julius Caesar, Blake.

3. Saint. The true saint is a spiritual genius who thinks nothing of himself. He becomes a channel for the higher creative powers in the collective unconscious of the race. A saint is the personification of morale, good-will, co-operation. Examples: St. Francis of Assisi, St. John of the Cross, Meister Eckhardt.

4. Master. One whose consciousness has become identified with the deepest springs in life in the super-conscious. A Master combines and transcends the qualities of saint, adept and initiate. All Masters are essentially equal, but they differ in manifestation according to the requirements of the age they live in and their means of rational expression.

A Master is one who is beyond idolatry. He is idea in being and activity, the personification of cosmic will and law. His consciousness transcends ideas, but he selects, adapts and energizes ideas that inspire and transform his age.

Examples: Jesus, Buddha, Lao-tsze, Plato, Socrates, Apollonius of Tyana, Pythagoras, Krishna, Zoroaster, Mohammed. (See Rudolf Steiner, *Initiation and its Results*; Geraldine Coster, *Yoga and Western Psychology* (1934).)

Innocents' Day or **Childermas.** A festival in memory of the massacre of the babies by Herod, kept by the Catholic Church on 28 December and by the Greek Church on 29 December. There appears to be no historical evidence to bear out the N.T. reference to such a massacre. In the Middle Ages, Childermas was kept as a children's festival with the appointment of a boy-bishop and other ceremonies.

Inquisition or **Holy Office.** A medieval Catholic tribunal for the trial of heretics. The court first came into prominence under Gregory IX. Its officers were chosen almost entirely from the Dominicans; its activities were carried into all European countries except England and Scandinavia. Proceedings were conducted in secret and the defendant allowed no legal adviser or witnesses. He was not permitted to know who had informed against him. Torture was applied by lay officials outside the court. Punishment ranged from fasts, prayers and pilgrimages, to a life-sentence of imprisonment or to burning at the stake. The goods of the convicted were confiscated. The

Inquisition was finally abolished in Spain in 1820. (See H. C. Lea, *History of the Inquisition*.)

INSPIRATION. A term applied to the exalted influence found in all sacred scriptures and in the finest and deepest poetry. Various views have been held with regard to the inspiration of the Jewish and Christian Scriptures. The older view inclined to the belief that every word the O.T. and N.T. writers used was literally and historically true. The influences of science and rationalism modified this belief. Modern thinkers tend to regard inspiration as an inflow from the unconscious or, as Bacon termed it, divine influxions.

INSTALLATION. The induction of a canon into his cathedral stall or of a minister into his pastorate.

INSTITUTION. (1) The ritual with which a priest is assigned a cure of souls by his bishop. (2) The origination of the Eucharist or Lord's Supper.

INTENTION. One of the three necessities for the validity of a sacrament, the others being form and matter (schol. theol.).

INTERCESSION. Pleading or praying for another. The Catholic and Greek churches insist on the importance of intercession. Angels, saints and the Virgin Mary "offer up their prayers to God for men." The Protestant churches do not approve this seeking for the Saints' intercession. Christ, they affirm, is man's sufficient and only mediator with God.

INTERDICT. A decree of the Pope forbidding the clergy to perform their sacred functions. In the Middle Ages interdict was a powerful papal weapon. When a prince was put under an interdict, the clergy of his realm were forbidden to perform their clerical duties except to baptize infants and confess dying penitents. In 1170 Alexander III put England under interdict, and when King John was excommunicated by Innocent III (1208) England lay under an interdict for six years. The power of the interdict gradually dwindled with the coming of the Renaissance and the Reformation.

INTERMEDIATE STATE. The condition of the dead immediately after death. See *Purgatory*; *Future Life*.

INTERSTICE. The time required in the Catholic Church between promotions of its officers from one degree to another.

INTOLERANCE. Anger or irritation bred by opinions or beliefs which differ from one's own. Intellectual narrowness and a too close imprisonment in the ego are the chief causes of intolerance. The saintly temper (St. Catherine of Siena, St. Augustine, Luther, Calvin) frequently evinces intolerance owing to an unbalanced zeal; so also does the artistic temper by pampering its ego under the name of "artistic temperament."

INTONATION. The opening phrase of a plain-song melody, sung by the officiating priest or a chorister.

INTRADOS. The lower surface of an arch (archit.).

INTROIT. The part of the Mass immediately following the Confiteor and sung as the priest approaches the altar.

INVENTION OF THE CROSS. See *Cross, Invention of the.*

INVESTITURE. In medieval ecclesiastical history the ceremony of conferring an office or benefice. The famous investiture controversy between Pope Gregory VII and the emperor Henry IV (see article *Papacy*, § 2) led to open war (1075 to 1085). The emperor and Pope each claimed the right of investing bishops and abbots with the cross and ring. A compromise was effected in 1122 by the Concordat of Worms which arranged for the Pope to confer on ecclesiastics their right to perform religious functions and the emperor their political rights.

INVITATORY. The antiphon to the Venite or 95th Psalm (*Venite, exultemus Domino*).

INVOCATION. The act of calling upon God as in certain public prayers, e.g. the Litany. The custom of invocatory prayer is of great antiquity. It was used by the Babylonians, Egyptians, Greeks and Romans. Philosophically God can be no more in one place than in another, for He belongs to a realm transcending time and space. But the invocational prayers assist the mind in concentration and induce favourable states of consciousness.

INVOCATION OF SAINTS. See *intercession.*

IPSAMBUL. See *Abu Simbel.*

IRENAEUS (c. 135–200). Bishop of Lyons, and pupil of Polycarp of Smyrna. The author of many theological treatises, the chief being *Against Heresies.* (See Bethune-Baker, *An Introduction to the Early History of Christian Doctrine* (1903).)

IRENICON. The deacon's litany at the beginning of the Greek liturgy.

IRENICS. That branch of theology which seeks to minimize differences between opposing creeds, its antithesis being polemics.

IRVING, EDWARD (1792–1834). A gifted preacher of the Scottish Presbyterian Church. Owing to his doctrines regarding the humanity of Jesus Christ he was excommunicated by the London Presbytery in 1830. In 1832 he founded the Irvingite or Holy Catholic Apostolic Church. His claims to apostolic "gifts" and healing powers aroused keen controversy. (See Mrs. Oliphant, *Life of Edward Irving* (1862).)

ISAAC. The son of Abraham and Sarah and one of the Israelitish patriarchs. (See Gen. xvii., xxi., xxvi.) Reputed to have died at the ripe age of 180 (Gen. xlix.)

ISAGOGICS. The preliminary science which serves as an introduction to exegesis. (Gr. *eisagōgē* = an introduction.)

ISAIAH. The greatest of the O.T. prophets. The date of his writings is a subject of controversy among scholars, but the events referred to appear to assign them to the reigns of Uzziah, Jotham, Ahaz and Hezekiah. (See S. R. Driver, *Isaiah, His Life and Times.*)

ISAIAH, ASCENSION OF. An early Christian apocalyptic book of Jewish origin. (A.D. 3rd C.)

ISHMAEL. The son of Abraham by Hagar (Gen. xvi. 11).

ISHTAR (ESTHER). The Babylonian goddess of love and fertility, identified with Aphrodite and Venus.

ISHVARA. The Saviour God of the Hindu pantheon in the popular cults, Brahma being the more philosophical aspect of the Supreme Being.

ISIDORE OF SEVILLE (560–636). Spanish ecclesiastic and author of the *Encyclopedia of the Sciences*, a work which served through dark ages to keep alive some memory of classical culture. (See Migne, *Patrologia Latina*, 81–84.)

ISIS. A fertility goddess of the ancient Egyptians, wife of Osiris and mother of Horus. The mysteries of Isis were very popular at the time of the rise of Christianity. For an account of them, see *The Golden Ass* of Apuleius.

ISLAM. The name used by the Mohammedans for their religion (See *Mohammed*). (Ar. *islam-salama* = to submit to God.)

ISMAILIS. A neo-Platonic sect of Shiite Mohammedans established by Abdallah ibn Maymun in the 9th C. A.D. The Ismailis supported the Karmatian revolt in Mesopotamia which threatened the supremacy of the Abbasids. They claim that Ismail (c. 770) was the seventh and last of the Imams (q.v.). Groups of Ismailis continue in Arabia, Egypt and India.

ISRAEL, RELIGION OF. In the earliest times the worship of the Israelites did not differ from that of other primitive tribes. Necromancy, ancestor-worship, witchcraft and fierce blood-feuds occupied much of their time. Their civilization was decidedly lower than that of Assyria and Babylon at the same period. It was not until the time of Moses (q.v.) that conditions began decidedly to improve. When Moses led his tribes into Canaan he brought with him some of the culture of Egypt. Moses was the real founder of Hebrew religion which he based on a sounder system of hygiene and ethics. Under his influence the primitive Baal cults gave way to the more enlightened worship of Yahweh. With the coming of the Hebrew prophets (c. 8th to 6th B.C.) the idea of Jewish nationalism was born. Yahweh became established as the Israelitish God of war, destined to triumph over all who worshipped other gods. But since no nation, however warlike, can win every time, defeats at the hands of Assyria caused the Jewish faith to waver. The prophets thereupon insisted that Assyria was

Yahweh's scourge for Israel's sins. This skilful manœuvre, joined with the insistent teaching that Yahweh was a god of Righteousness, carried the fortunes of the Israelites still further. But the prophets were bound by the narrow ideal of nationalism: they preached a Messianic triumph for Jewry and for the world, a rule of Righteousness of the kind they approved. The inexorable movement of events undermined these aspirations; other, less racial and more humanistic forces mingled with the teaching of the later prophets—Isaiah and the writers of the wisdom literature. The Israelites, with their narrow orthodoxy and bitter ecclesiastical feuds, could never establish an empire. Their hopes faded before the majesty of Rome, and the best (and some of the worst) of their religious aspirations passed into that Jewish sect out of which Christianity grew. (See T. K. Cheyne, *Traditions and Beliefs of Ancient Israel.*)

ISRAFIL. The Islamic angel of music. At the end of the world he will sound the Resurrection Trumpet.

ISUMBRAS, SIR. A hero of medieval romance, so proud and wilful that he brought down many punishments upon his head. He became penitent and humble; his afflictions turned into blessings. There is deep meaning as well as much beauty in the fable.

ITE, MISSA EST. The closing words of the Catholic Mass ("Go, the congregation is dismissed").

ITHURIEL. One of the angels appointed by Gabriel to search Paradise for Satan who had effected an entrance.

ITIHASAS. The two great Hindu epics—the Ramayana and Mahabharata are so called.

IXION. A king of the Lapithae who was bound to a revolving wheel in Hades for presuming to imitate Jove's thunder.

J

JACA. The devil of Cingalese mythology.

JACOB. Son of Isaac and Rebecca and twin-brother of Esau (Gen. xxv., xxvii., xxviii.).

JACOBIN. A French Dominican, so called from their monastery of St. Jacques, Paris. The French revolutionaries were called Jacobins from their meetings in the hall of this monastery.

JACOBITE. (1) An adherent of King James II and his descendants. (2) A member of the Syrian Monophysite Church founded by Jacobus Baradaeus. (A.D. 6th C.)

JACOB'S-LADDER. The ladder which Jacob saw in his dream (Gen. xxviii. 12).

JACOBSON, ISRAEL. See *Reformed Judaism.*

JACOB'S-STAFF. A pilgrim's staff, from the allusion to the patriarch Jacob (Gen. xxxii. 10).

JAGANNATH or **JUGGERNAUT.** An immense image of Vishnu kept in the temple at Puri in Orissa. At an annual festival the image is drawn through the streets by crowds of devotees. In earlier days many of these are said to have flung themselves under the wheels of the car in ecstatic devotion.

JAHWEH, JAH. See *Yahweh.*

JAINS. A Hindu sect of nonconformists to the Brahmanical system. The sect, of which there were in 1901, 1,334,140 members, grew out of the philosophical speculations prevailing in the valley of the Ganges in the 6th and 5th C.s B.C. The system was established by Maha-vira, also called Jina, the conqueror, a contemporary of Gotama, the Buddha. The Jains are divided into two parties, the Digambaras (sky-clad), who go naked, and the Svetambaras or white-robed. But the practice of nakedness has been almost abandoned; the Digambaras being sky-clad only at meal-times. Their system teaches that everything (even minerals, fire and water) has a soul (*jiva*) and approximates closely to the modern scientific views of the ultimate atoms. They maintain that the answer to every speculative question is "yes and no" (*Syad-vada*). Thus you may maintain the eternity of the world from one point of view and deny it from another. The Digambaras carry their ascetic practices so far that they even deny themselves the pleasure of washing their teeth, for fear of injuring the poor microbes. (See Hopkins, *Religions of India,* pp. 280–96.)

JAMES. (1) One of the brothers of Jesus Christ.

(2) His two apostles—"the Greater" and "the Less."

(3) The first Bishop of Jerusalem—possibly James the Less.

(4) Title of a N.T. epistle, traditionally ascribed to James the Less.

JAMES, HENRY (1843–1916). American novelist of great distinction. His work is the subtle creation of a mind keenly interested in psychology.

JAMES, WILLIAM (1842–1910). Brother of above; professor of philosophy and psychology. His *The Varieties of Religious Experience* (Gifford Lectures) is the standard English work on the psychology of religion.

JAMSHID. King of the Genii whose golden cup contained the elixir of life (Pers. myth.).

JANNAB. The Mohammedan garden of Paradise.

JANNES and **JAMBRES** (or **JAMNES** and **MAMBRES**). Pharaoh's magicians who imitated some of Moses' miracles (2 Tim. iii. 8, 9).

JANSENISM. The evangelical doctrine (derived from St. Augustine) preached by Cornelius Jansen (1585–1603), bishop of Ypres. Both Augustine and Jansen taught the perversion and inability to do good of the natural human will, unaided by Grace—which is overwhelming and irresistible. Jansenism, after much controversy, was condemned in 1713 by Clement XI in his bull Unigenitus—which the French Church rejected. See also *Port Royal.*

JANUARIUS, SAINT. The patron saint of Naples whose blood, preserved in a tube, is believed by the faithful to liquefy every year on 19 September.

JANUS. The Roman god of beginnings. He had two faces, looking to the future and the past.

JAPAN, RELIGIONS OF. The chief religions of Japan are Shinto, Confucianism and Buddhism. Shinto is a mingling of nature-worship with ancestor-worship. It teaches no definite code of morals. Human beings are regarded as virtuous by nature, each man's conscience being his best guide. The dead pass to another world where they influence the lives of their survivors and must be propitiated by ritual worship. Shinto has become mingled with Buddhism which entered Japan from Korea in A.D. 552. Japanese Buddhism is divided into thirteen sects, the most scholarly of these being the Zen Sect (q.v.), in which truth is reached by pure contemplation. These various doctrines of Shinto and Buddhism have been the occasion of much strife, with resultant wars (12th–16th C.s) during which even the monks fought. But there has never been persecution with stake and rack as among Christians.

§ 2. Confucianism has always remained a moral code for scholars and the literary class, a practical philosophy rather than a religion. Christianity entered Japan in the 16th C., but was almost immediately stamped out. It re-entered the country in 1858, the first Christian Church being built at Yokohama in 1862, by a small band of Catholic Fathers. The Japanese Catholic church now numbers somewhere about 75,300 members. The Greek Orthodox Church was established by Father Nicolai in 1861. The Anglican Church was established in Japan in 1859 and in conjunction with the Episcopal Churches of America and Canada supports a number of missions. There are also many Christian sects, Baptist, Congregational, Society of Friends, Salvation Army, etc., at work in Japan. (See F. Brinkley, *Japan* (12 vols., 1904.)

JATAKAS. A collection of Buddhist folk-lore, sayings of the Buddha, tales of his infancy, etc.

JEHAD, JIHAD. A holy war of Mohammedans inculcated as a duty by the Koran on Islamic unbelievers.

JEHOIAKIM. Eldest son of Josiah and brother of Jehoahaz, king of Judah (2 Kings xxiii. 36).

JEHORAM or JORAM. A king of Judah, son of Jehoshaphat (2 Kings viii. 16, 21).

JEHOSHAPHAT. Son and successor of Asa, king of Judah (1 Kings xv. 24). Also *Josaphat.*

JEHOVAH. A corruption of the Hebrew word for God. It arose (A.D. 14th C.) from a mistaking of the consonants of the name Yahweh and of the vowel points of the name Adonai.

Jehu. Son of Nimshi and grandson of Jehoshaphat, remembered for his furious driving (2 Kings ix. 20) and for his ruthless massacre of the worshippers of Baal (2 Kings x.).

Jeremiah. The last pre-exilic prophet of Israel (6th C. B.C.). His Prophecy constitutes the twenty-fourth book of the O.T. It is a stern denunciation of the people for their idolatry and corruption. The fate of the holy city is told in language of great beauty.

Jericho. A remote city of Palestine to which David's servants were sent while their beards were growing. (See 2 Sam. x. 4, 5.)

Jeroboam. A king of Israel, son of Nebat and father of Nadab (1 Kings xi. and xii.).

Jerome (Hieronymus) c. A.D. 340–420). The most eminent Christian scholar of the early church. He was born at Strido in Dalmatia, of well-to-do Christian parents and educated at home, afterwards proceeding to Rome, where he studied law and philosophy. By temperament Jerome was a scholar, thirsting for knowledge. His ardent temper led him into many controversies and disputes. The narrowness of the Christian outlook of his time persuaded him that the study of pagan literature was sinful. Yet the uncouthness of the Christian scriptures repelled him. Christ appeared to his troubled mind in a dream. "Jerome," he said, "you care more to be a Circeronian than a Christian." Thereupon Jerome resolved that "David was to be henceforth his Simonides, Pindar and Alcaeus, his Flaccus, Catullus and Severus." With this resolve he became a hermit for a time, studying Hebrew and engaging in fierce controversy on Arianism. In 382 Jerome was summoned to Rome by Pope Damasus, who wished to make use of his vast scholarship. At Rome he speedily became a focus of intellectual life. A group of widows and maidens met together to study the Scriptures with him. He taught them Hebrew and spoke eloquently in favour of the celibate life. On the death of Damasus, scandalized relatives of these ladies began to gossip. Difficulties increasing, he left Rome. Two wealthy Roman ladies, Paula and her daughter, Eustochium, followed him. After travelling in Egypt they all returned to Palestine and settled at Bethlehem, where Paula built three monasteries for nuns and one for monks. Jerome presided over the fourth monastery and there produced his Latin translation of the Scriptures which developed into the Vulgate (q.v.). He produced many other literary works and died at Bethlehem in 420. His letters are of great value for the ardent character they reveal and for their history of his times. (See E. L. Cutts, *Life of St. Jerome* (Fathers for English Readers Series); C. Martin, *Life of St. Jerome* (1888).)

JERUSALEM. The capital of the kingdom of Israel from David's time until the accession of Rehoboam (933 B.C.). After that time it became the capital of Judah till the Jewish state came to an end in 586 B.C. The city has had a varied history, having been held by Hebrews, Greeks, Persians Romans, Arabs, Turks, Crusaders, French and English. (For a good account of the historic Jerusalem, see Kinglake, *Eothen* (chap. xvi); also H. V. Morton, *In the Steps of the Master* (1934).)

JESSE. (1) Father of David and so ancestor of Jesus Christ (Isa. xi. 1, 10). (2) A large branched candlestick formerly used in churches.

JESSE-WINDOW. A window in stained glass representing a genealogical tree of Christ's descent from Jesse.

JESUS CHRIST. The Messianic title of "Christos" applied to Jesus of Nazareth is found first in the writings of Paul. No trustworthy material for a "life" of Christ exists, though this has not deterred countless scholars and historians from writing such biographies. The earliest records deal mainly with the ministry of Jesus, emphasizing the Messianic claims. Mark's gospel appears to be the earliest and most reliable. He tells us that Jesus lived at Nazareth and was the son of a carpenter. That he became a follower of John the Baptist, was baptized by him and went for a while to meditate in the desert. He returned to work amongst men and his life henceforth may be divided into (1) his ministry in Galilee; (2) a period of wandering; (3) the journey to Jerusalem, arrest and crucifixion.

§ 1. (1) During the first period of his ministry Jesus was living in the house of Simon Peter at Capernaum. Here he gathered around him twelve staunch followers who became the Apostles (q.v.) He taught that the Kingdom of Heaven, or of God, was at hand and urged men to prepare for this new age by a change of heart and of will. Righteousness was to be the keynote of the new age and he stressed the need for humility and the humble virtues. The freshness of his teaching and the readiness and assurance with which he spoke, so much in contrast with the learned and laboured expositions of the Rabbis, attracted crowds of eager listeners. Miraculous healings appear to have accompanied his teaching and the atmosphere of excitement which prevailed no doubt assisted these while possibly leading to some exaggeration. From Capernaum his work extended into surrounding regions.

(2) A period of wandering followed. The cause of his leaving Capernaum is not clear. It may have been due to the hostility of Herod Antipas or of the Rabbis. We get glimpses of him near Tyre and Sidon; and at Caesarea and Philippi. His teaching continued and became mingled with hints of Messianic claims either made by himself or repeated by his disciples. The idea too that he would accomplish his work by suffering and death became more and more a part of his teaching.

(3) Jesus returned southward, and after a short stay at Galilee set out with his disciples to keep the Passover at Jerusalem. This was of the nature of a challenge and resulted from his casting aside all reticence with regard to his Messianic claims. The priests and pharisees saw in him a dangerous rival who was gaining a popularity which threatened their power. They bribed Judas, one of the twelve, to betray Jesus secretly. Events followed rapidly. He ate a last meal with the disciples and retired to the Garden of Gethsemane—the scene of a fierce inward struggle. He was taken before the Sanhedrin and then before Pilate, the Roman governor, and charged with treason and blasphemy. Pilate was unable to save him from priestly hatred and he was crucified. The accounts of the Resurrection are confused, but from very early days it was believed he rose on the third day and appeared to Peter (1 Cor. xv. 4–8). It seems probable that the disciples had some supernormal experience which convinced them that Jesus had survived death.

§ 2. Certain critics have held the view that the Jesus story as told in the Gospels is legendary or mythical (D. F. Strauss, Bruno Bauer, Emilio Bossi, J. M. Robertson). Many strong arguments have been adduced in support of this view and it is undoubtedly true that " there is much to be said on both sides." Perhaps Edward Carpenter's position will commend itself to the more thoughtful at the present time: " Personally I must say I think the ' legendary ' solution quite likely, and in some ways more satisfactory than the opposite one—for the simple reason that it seems much more encouraging to suppose that the story of Jesus (gracious and beautiful as it is) is a myth which gradually formed itself in the conscience of mankind, and thus points the way of humanity's future evolution, than to suppose it to be the mere record of an unique and miraculous interposition of Providence, which depended entirely on the powers above, and could hardly be expected to occur again. . . . Certainly the difficulties in the way of regarding the Gospel story (or stories, for there is not one consistent story) as *true* are enormous " (*Pagan and Christian Creeds*, p. 211). The problem is of less importance than it used to be since it has become more widely realized that the fundamental truths of religion are based on inner experience and not on the researches of scholars and the views of theologians.

JESUS, SOCIETY OF (JESUITS). A Catholic religious order founded by Ignatius Loyola (q.v.), page to Ferdinand V of Spain. He renounced the military for the ecclesiastical profession and established his society at Paris in August, 1534. It received papal approbation in 1540. The society is founded upon military principles. There are six grades of officers. The novice has to undergo a strict retreat, in solitary confinement. In this way his real character is tested. Subsequent discipline insures a high degree of efficiency. Jesuit activities are directed chiefly to missionary enterprise and education. There are estimated to be about 20,000 members in all parts of the world. (See Guettée, *Histoire des Jésuites* (Paris, 1859); G. B. Nicolini, *History of the Jesuits* (1884) (written from the Protestant point of view).)

JESUS, SON OF SIRACH. The author of the apocryphal Ecclesiasticus.

JEWISH ERA AND CALENDAR. The Jews date from creation, which they place 3,760 years, 3 months before the Christian era. The Jewish year consists of either twelve or thirteen months of 29 or 30 days. The ecclesiastical year begins with Nisam; the civil year with Tisri, following the new moon of the autumnal equinox. The calendar is as follows:

CIVIL YEAR

	Begins
Tisri	30 Sept.
Marchesvan	30 Oct.
Chislev	28 Nov.
Thebet	27 Dec.
Sebat	25 Jan.
Adar	24 Feb.
Nisan or Abib	24 March
Ijar	23 April
Sivan	22 May
Thammuz	21 June
Ab	20 July
Elul	19 Aug.

JEWISH NOVELISTS AND WRITERS (ENGLISH). Disraeli, 1st Earl of Beaconsfield (1804–81), occupies a high place; as novelist he is brilliant and romantic. Israel Zangwill (1864–1926) will be remembered for his *Children of the Ghetto* (1892). Other distinguished Jewish writers are: Gilbert Cannan, "G. B. Stern" (Mrs. Geoffrey Holdsworth) and Louis Golding. (See article "Yiddish" in Eric Partridge's *Slang*, p. 266.) Sir Sidney Lee, author of the *Life of Shakespeare* and an official *Life of Queen Victoria*, was born a Jew, but changed his praenomina of "Solomon Lazarus" for "Sidney" while taking his degree at Oxford in 1883.

JEWS. See *Israel*; *Bible* (*O.T.*); *Semitism*.

JEW, THE WANDERING. A legendary Jew said to have insulted Jesus on his way to execution, and doomed as a punishment to walk the earth till Christ's second coming. In some versions his name is Kartaphilos, Pilate's porter; in others Ahasuerus, a cobbler.

JEZEBEL. Wife of Ahab. She introduced Baal-worship and had an evil reputation. (See 1 Kings xviii.)

JINN, DJINN, GINN. Spirits, fairies or goblins of Mohammedan mythology. They are translated genii in the *Arabian Nights*.

JIZO. A Japanese god of Chinese origin who protects little children.

JNANA-MARGA. The way of salvation by knowledge—the knowledge varying with the system (Hindu theol.).

JOAB. Nephew of David and commander-in-chief of his army. He slew Abner (2 Sam. iii. 27) and conspired against David (1 Kings ii. 28).

JOACHIM OF FLORIS (c. 1145–1202). A Calabrian monk and mystic of wide influence during the Middle Ages. (Rudolf Steiner describes him as "a great initiate of the Middle Ages.") He was born in Calabria, near Cosenza, and after years of ascetic life and contemplation, founded the monastery of San Giovanni in Fiore, on Monte Nero, in the massif of La Sila. Joachim and the Joachimites divided the history of humanity into three ages: the Age of the Father, of the Son and of the Spirit, or the Age of Preparation, the Age of Study, and the Age of the Spirit. Dante held Joachim in great reverence (Para. xii. 140–1). (See H. C. Lea, *History of the Inquisition of the Middle Ages*, vol. iii, ch. 1 (1888).)

JOAN OF ARC (1411–31). French peasant girl who claimed divine inspiration and encouraged her countrymen to throw off the English yoke. She fell into the hands of the English, was handed over to the Inquisition and then burnt as a heretic. In 1909 she was beatified by the Catholic Church and in 1920 she was canonized. (See Andrew Lang, *The Maid of France*; Anatole France, *Life of Joan of Arc*.)

JOAN, POPE. A woman said to have reigned as Pope between the Pontificates of Leo IV and Benedict III (847–55), and to have died in child-birth during a papal procession at Rome. A statue was erected to her memory on the spot and not removed until Luther's time. The story was accepted as true until the 15th C. Leibnitz and later historians deny Joan's existence. It is impossible to determine the truth or falsehood of such traditions. Joan's claims to the papal chair are certainly as good as those of St. Peter the Apostle. (See the present writer's romance, *When Joan was Pope* (1931).)

JOB, BOOK OF. A canonical book of the O.T. and the finest and most literary creation of Hebrew poetry. The book is concerned with the problems of suffering and evil and the writer reveals himself as philosopher as well as poet. Unlike most of the Israelitish literature which concerns itself almost entirely with national or Judaistic interests, the Book of Job enters a far wider world of human inquiry and strikes notes which vibrate beyond the narrow boundaries of race and creed.

Scholars differ as to the date of composition. It certainly belongs to the age of Jewish philosophical inquiry and has much in common with the Wisdom Literature (Ecclesiastes, Ecclesiasticus, Proverbs, the Wisdom of Solomon). The most probable date would appear to be the 4th C. B.C. (See Cheyne, *Job and Solomon*; Dawson, *Wisdom Literature*.)

JODO. A Buddhist sect founded by Honen in Japan (c. A.D. 12). He appealed to the masses by abandoning philosophy and elaborate ritual and teaching the sufficiency of grace.

JOEL, PROPHECY OF. Forms the twenty-ninth book of the O.T. The writer appears to have been contemporary with Isaiah. The prophecy is short but vigorous and vivid. (See Driver, *Joel and Amos* (1897).)

JOHANAN, BEN ZAKKAI. A great Rabbi of the 1st C. A.D. and contributor to the Mishna (q.v.).

JOHN. (1) Surname of Mark. (2) The evangelist and disciple whom Jesus loved, son of Zebedee. (3) Father of the apostle Peter. (4) A presbyter mentioned by Papias.

JOHN, ST., GOSPEL OF. The Gospel which passes under the name of "St. John's" is clearly of Judeo-Alexandrian authorship. Baur dates it at 160–70, Keim at 130, Renan at 110–15 and Harnach at 80–110. Irenaeus stated that its author lived in the time of Trajan (53–117) and published his gospel at Ephesus. Abbé Loisy has well summed up the book's significance: "What the author was, his book, in spite of himself, tells us to some extent; a Christian of Judeo-Alexandrine formation; a believer, without, apparently, any personal reminiscence of what had actually been the life, preaching and death of Jesus; a theologian far removed from every historical pre-occupation though he retains certain principal facts of tradition without which Christianity would evaporate into pure ideas; and a seer who has lived the gospel which he propounds. . . . To find his book beautiful and true, we need but take it as it is and understand it." (See F. C. Burkitt, *The Gospel History*; E. F. Scott, *The Fourth Gospel*.)

JOHN THE BAPTIST. The "forerunner" of Jesus in the Gospel story, son of the priest Zacharias and his wife Elizabeth. Preached in the "wilderness of Judaea" near the Dead Sea, his chief theme being the coming of the Messianic Kingdom and the need for repentance. He was popularly regarded as a prophet. His ministry was brought to an end by imprisonment in the fortress of Machaerus by command of Herod Antipas whose evil life he denounced and he was executed about the year A.D. 28. (See especially Margaret Goldsmith, *John the Baptist*, 1935.)

JOHN OF THE CROSS, SAINT (1542–91). Spanish mystic of the Carmelite Order. He endured severe imprisonment owing to his reforming zeal. He was beatified in 1674 and canonized in 1726. His lyrical verses breathe a spirit of rapturous ecstasy. Some of his poems have been excellently translated by Arthur Symons in *Images of Good and Evil*.

JOHN OF DAMASCUS, SAINT (c. 700–54). The last of the Greek Fathers, author of *The Fount of Knowledge*, a doctrinal work, and of many fine hymns.

JOHN THE SCOT. See *Erigena, John Scotus*.

JONAH. An O.T. prophet born at Gath-hepher in Zebulun and possibly the author of the Book of Jonah, a post-exilic book. The Book of Jonah contains much symbolism and mythology. The "great fish" that swallowed the prophet probably symbolizes Tiamat, the Dragon of Chaos. (See C. H. H. Wright, *Biblical Studies.*)

JORAM, JEHORAM. King of Israel who succeeded Ahaziah (2 Kings iii.).

JORDAN. The river which bounded Judea in the east.

JOSAPHAT. See *Jehoshaphat.*

JOSEPH. (1) Son of Jacob and Rachael (Gen. xxx. 24). (2) A wealthy disciple of Jesus who lived at Arimathea (Matt. xxvii. 57, 59). (3) The husband of Mary, mother of Jesus (Matt. xiii. 55).

JOSEPHUS, FLAVIUS (c. A.D. 37–100). Famous Jewish historian, born and educated at Jerusalem where he became a Pharisee. He led an unsuccessful rebellion against Rome, but his life was spared by Vespasian. His *Jewish Antiquities*, a history of the Jews, which reaches to the time of Christ's ministry, makes no mention of Christ except the passing reference to Jesus as " a wise man, if indeed one should call him a man," but this has been held by many scholars to be undoubtedly a later interpolation by Christians disappointed at his silence.

JOSHUA. (1) The son of Nun, an assistant of Moses (Exod. xxiv. 13). (2) Book of Joshua is the sixth of the O.T. and is probably the work of several authors. (See S. R. Driver, *Literature of the O.T.*)

JOSIAH. King of Judah (O.T.), son and successor of King Amon (2 Chron. xxxiv.).

JOWETT, BENJAMIN (1817–93). English scholar and theologian. Master of Balliol 1870. His contribution to the famous *Essays and Reviews* (1860) gave offence to the Tractarians and he was much persecuted in consequence. (See Abbott and Campbell, *Life and Letters of Benjamin Jowett* (1897).)

JUBILATE. (1) The 66th Psalm, from the opening words Jubilate Deo. (2) The 3rd Sunday after Easter, on which the psalm is sung. (3) The 100th Psalm.

JUBILEE. (1) The Jewish year of rest, marked by certain customs, observed by the ancient Israelites every fiftieth year. (2) A year of indulgence for pilgrims observed in the Catholic Church every twenty-fifth year.

JUDAISM. See *Israel, Religion of,* and *Reformed Judaism.*

JUDAS ISCARIOT. The apostle who betrayed Jesus. A legendary figure. The gospel traditions regarding him are at variance. (See Matt. xxvii. 3, 10, and Acts i. 18, 19.)

JUDAS MACCABAEUS. A leader in the Jewish revolt against the Syrian Antiochus IV (Epiphanes). Antiochus persecuted the Jews for their religion. The Jews under Judas Maccabaeus rose in revolt and defeated the Syrians in three battles (166 and 165 B.C.). The history of the Maccabees is given in five books of that name (two included in the Anglican Apocrypha). Four of the books are accounted canonical by the Catholic Church.

JUDE. One of the Apostles of Jesus, brother of James the Less, called also Judas (Matt. xiii. 55; Jude i. 1).

JUDGMENT, DAY OF. The belief in a final assize when God would allot to men their rewards and punishments is found in many primitive religions. Among the Egyptians Osiris was regarded as the judge of the dead. The Jewish idea of judgment had respect chiefly to a Day when the enemies of Israel and of Yahweh would be for ever overthrown. From Judaism the belief in a Day of Judgment passed to Christianity. In so far as such a Judgment is believed in to-day by Christian thinkers it has assumed an ethical and psychological rather than an historical and eschatalogical aspect.

JUDITH, BOOK OF. An apocryphal book of the O.T. telling how the Jewess Judith saved her countrymen from the Assyrians by assassinating their general Holofernes.

JUGGERNAUT. See *Jagannath.*

JULIAN THE APOSTATE (A.D. 331–63). Roman Emperor (nephew of Constantine the Great) who gave up Christianity in favour of Paganism. He refused to persecute Christians but encouraged the old worship in the pagan temples.

JUNO. Wife of Jupiter and representative of the female principle (Rom. myth.). Identified with the Gr. Hera.

JUPITER (JOVE). The supreme saviour God of Roman mythology and religion. He was regarded as the protective deity of the Latin people and philosophically as the world-essence. Corresponds to Zeus (Gr. myth.). (See J. B. Carter, *The Religion of Numa*, p. 160 *seq.*)

JUSTIFICATION. A religious term borrowed from the law courts. It arose out of the belief in a final Day of Judgment (q.v.) and has been used with different significations. To St. Paul justification meant acquittal from the pains of hell by the acceptance of Jesus as the Messiah. Luther regarded justification as an inner assurance of salvation given by faith to the believer. To the Calvinists justification was the result of "election": certain persons (i.e. Calvinists) had been chosen from the beginning of the world for "eternal life," the rest being destined for hell and torment. The Catholic theologians regard justification as incomplete unless it includes also sanctification or a high degree of moral purification.

JUSTIN, MARTYR. Christian apologist of the 2nd C. Author of an Apology for Christianity addressed to the emperor Antoninus, and the *Dialogue with Trypho*, an anti-Jewish apologetic. He suffered martyrdom at Rome in A.D. 165. (See J. Donaldson, *A Critical History of Christian Literature*; F. Watson, *Defenders of the Faith.*)

K

KA. A term used in the religion of ancient Egypt; of doubtful interpretation. It appears to have several meanings: (1) the "double" of a human being or the subtle essence from which he draws life; (2) the spiritual part freed at death and represented by an image of the person such as are found in Egyptian tombs; (3) the guardian angel or genius who rejoins the individual at death.

KAABA, CAABA. An Arab temple at Mecca containing the sacred Black Stone which Moslem pilgrims kiss.

KABBALA, CABBALA. The secret science of the Jewish rabbis. It interprets the Jewish Scriptures in a mystical sense based on oral tradition. Its chief books are the Sefer Yazirah (Book of Creation) and the Zohar, believed to be the work of a 14th-C. Spaniard, Moses de Leon. (See A. E. Waite, *Doctrine and Literature of the Kabbalah* (1902).)

KADDISH. A Jewish form of prayer and thanksgiving used at funerals.

KALA CHAKRA. The wheel of time (Sans.).

KALAM. The Moslem scholastic theology.

KALEVALA. The great Finnish epic, collected and put together by Dr. Lönnrot in 1835.

KALI. The Hindu goddess of destruction, wife of Shiva.

KALPA. A day of Brahma (represented as 4,320 years), in which the world passes from creation to destruction.

KAMA, KAMADEVA. The Hindu god of love, or desire, whose ten fetters have to be broken by the Buddhist disciple.

KAMI. The Japanese term for the life-power in all objects. Cf. *mana*; *numen*.

KANT, IMMANUEL (1724–1804). One of the greatest of German philosophers. Kant began as a rationalist, but this led him to a critical analysis of the processes of human thinking. In his *Critique of Pure Reason* (1781) he showed that since our knowledge is limited to experience, it is useless to seek a knowledge of things in themselves as distinguished from reality-as-we-know-it. In ethics he taught the need to obey "the categorical imperative," i.e. the absolute unconditioned command of the moral law, irrespective of every ulterior end or aim ("Act from a maxim at all times fit for law universal"). (See John Watson, *Philosophy of Kant Explained* (1908); Archibald Weir, *A Student's Introduction to Critical Philosophy* (1906).)

KARAITES. A Jewish sect founded by Anan ben David in Babylon (c. A.D. 750). It insists on the literal interpretation of Scripture unbiased by rabbinical commentaries.

KARENS. One of the native races of Burmah. Their religion is animistic.

KARMA. A Sanscrit word meaning work or act. In Hindu doctrine, Karma constitutes the sum-total of a man's acts in past lives, which determines his future lives. (Sow an act and reap a habit, sow a habit and reap a destiny.) The doctrine of Karma is frequently emphasized by St. Paul ("Whatsoever a man soweth, that shall he also reap"). The law of Karma is said to act and re-act like the swing of a pendulum. Thus (crudely expressed) A murders B; in their next lives B kills A; in the following life A kills B again. This continues until A or B kills that in *himself* which caused him to kill the other. The law then becomes modified. The aim of the Buddhist is so to live that by following the Eightfold Path (q.v.) no bad Karma is sown. The trials and sufferings which enter the lives of many saints are a result of aspiration which causes the evil Karma of past lives to be precipitated.

KARMA-MARGA. In Hindu theology the way of salvation (or path to reality) by work performed without attachment, and by the happy performance of duty.

KEBLA. See *Kibla*.

KEBLE, JOHN (1792–1866). English divine and poet who took an active part in the Oxford Movement. Remembered for his saintly character and for his *Christian Year*, religious verses of delicate poetic feeling. (See J. D. Coleridge, *Life of John Keble* (1869).)

KEMPIS, THOMAS À (1380–1471). Dutch theologian, by name Thomas Hemerken. He was born in Kempen, educated at Deventer and entered the Convent of Mount St. Agnes at Zwolle (1399). He wrote chronicles of the convent and a life of Groot. The famous anonymous *Imitation of Christ* has been ascribed to his pen.

KENOSIS. Theological term applied to Christ's laying aside his divine attributes when he became incarnate. From Philippians ii. 6, 7—"who being in the form of God . . . emptied himself (*eauton ekenose*), taking the form of a servant."

KEN, THOMAS (1637–1711). Bishop of Bath and Wells and chaplain to Charles II. He was one of the Seven Bishops sent to the Tower by James II owing to their petition to the king against the Declaration of Indulgence, which granted freedom to Dissenters. Author of several fine hymns and many devotional works. (See J. L. Anderdon, *The Life of Thomas Ken*.)

KESHUB CHUNDER SEN (1838–84). A leader of the Brahma Samaj (q.v.); a Hindu eclectic movement for religious reform.

KETUBAH. The Jewish marriage contract stating the amount settled by the groom on his bride.

KEYS, POWER OF THE. The power claimed by the popes as the alleged successors of St. Peter, to grant or refuse absolution. (See Matt. xvi. 19.) Protestants apply the passage in Matthew to bishops, clergy or members of a Christian communion.

KHALIF (CALIF). The title assumed by the successors of Mohammed as the political and religious leaders of Mohammedanism. The title is now claimed by the sultans of Turkey. (Ar. *Khalifah* = successor.)

KIBLA (KEBLA). The term applied by Moslems to Mecca as the place towards which the worshipper prostrates himself in prayer.

KIDDUSH. The Jewish ceremony of blessing a holy day or sabbath.

KINGDOM OF GOD. A term used (also Kingdom of Heaven) in the N.T.; of varying significance. It derives from the Israelitish belief that the nation of Israel would become paramount and institute a universal rule of Righteousness under Yahweh. (With this belief was mingled the apocalyptic hopes of a Messiah (q.v.).) Jesus Christ introduced new values into these conceptions, raising and spiritualizing them. In Christ's teaching the Kingdom of God symbolizes a state of society in which inward loyalty to God (the highest Ideal) is supreme and the law of love (goodwill to men) actually prevails. It was this state that men were to seek first and before all else to set up within themselves. Modern views tend towards an externalization of the N.T. teachings. The social aspects of life are felt to be of supreme importance in the Western World. Good-will between men and nations; arbitration to take the place of civil and international strife; better sanitary conditions; an ever more and more enlightened system of education—these are recognized as the foundation-stones of the Kingdom of God. So much is the need for "service" insisted upon by the churches that the true inwardness of Christ's teaching tends to be obscured. The health of the whole can only be ensured by the health of each member. Modern man conceives it his duty to save his brother; he forgets that for the blind to lead the blind results in disaster. It is the duty of each by eliminating the ego to gain enlightenment—"the Kingdom of Heaven is ***within you***."

KINGSLEY, CHARLES (1819–75). English novelist, poet and divine. He was regarded as the advocate of "muscular Christianity," a religion of a cheerful, manly and robust type. His *Hypatia* and *Westward Ho!* are distinguished for their fine prose style. He was opposed to the Oxford Tractarian Movement (q.v.) and insisted on the need for a broader Christianity as a force to ameliorate the social conditions of his time.

KISMET. A Turkish word signifying fate or destiny.

KISS OF PEACE. A kiss of greeting exchanged between members of the early Christian Church.

KNIGHTS OF COLUMBUS. A Catholic order organized in America in 1882 to promote catholicism in the northern states of the U.S.A.

KNOX, JOHN (c. 1514–72). Scottish reformer, son of an East

Lothian peasant. He entered the Catholic priesthood but changed his views and became a Protestant. His career was chequered owing to his extreme views; he spent several years as an exile in France. In 1559 he returned to Scotland, where his zeal as a preacher marked him for leadership. Widely different views have been taken of his character. But all agree as to the forcefulness of his personality. "This one man," wrote Queen Elizabeth's ambassador, "is able in one hour to put more life in us than five hundred trumpets." He profoundly influenced the religious life of Scotland. (See Thomas McCrie, *Life of John Knox* (1813); also (for a less favourable view) Andrew Lang, *John Knox and the Reformation* (1905).)

KOBOLD. An earth-spirit of German folklore.

KOHELETH ("THE PREACHER"). Term applied to Solomon (Eccles. i. 12).

KOL NICHE. A Jewish liturgy famous for the beautiful melodies to which it has been set. It is used on the Eve of the Day of Atonement and dispenses from unperformed vows.

KORAN, ALCORAN. The Mohammedan Scriptures. The Koran is a small book, about the size of the Christian N.T. consisting of 114 sections (*surahs*). The book is a collection of prayers, homilies, prophetical utterances and legislative enactments. It was made in the 7th C. A.D. some fifteen years after Mohammed's death. Moslems believe every word of it to be inspired by God. The Jewish and Christian influences in the Koran are very marked and appear to have come in by oral communications from Jews and Arabs. In style, the Koran is prosaic, though at times it reaches a fine and simple eloquence. Probably the best English translation is that of Rodman (Everyman series). See also *Mohammed.*

KOSHER. The meat of animals killed and dressed according to Jewish ritual law.

KRISHNA. Krishna appears to have been a deified hero. In the Bhagavad-gita, as an incarnation of Vishnu, he reveals the way of religious devotion (*bhakti*). There are many Krishna cults throughout northern India.

KUNDALINI. A term used by the Hindu yogis to define a principle of life held by them to reside at the base of the spine. By certain long-continued ascetic practices, only disclosed by teacher to pupil orally, this power is said to move up the spine and quicken certain psychic centres with the result that supernormal powers are awakened. See *Yoga.*

KWANNON. A Buddhist goddess of love and mercy worshipped in China and Japan.

KWEI. A Chinese collective term for disembodied spirits of many kinds.

KYRIE ELEÏSON ("LORD HAVE MERCY"). A form of prayer

used in the Catholic and Greek liturgies. In the Mass it immediately follows the introit.

L

Labadists. A sect of Protestants established by Jean de la Badie (1610–74). The Labadists were extreme in their views and ascetic in their lives.

Laban. The father of Rachel and Leah, wives of Jacob. Laban deceived Jacob by exacting seven years' service in addition to the seven agreed upon as preliminary to marrying Rachel (Gen. xxix.).

labarum. The standard adopted by Constantine after he became a Christian. It was an adaptation of the Roman military standard and bore the monogram ☧, the initial letters of the word Christos, in Greek characters.

Labyrinth. In classic myth, Daedalus was an ingenious artist of evil mind. He constructed many inventions of an objectionable nature, his greatest achievement being the Labyrinth at Cnossos in which the monster Minotaur was kept. Probably the finest interpretation of the myth is that by Francis Bacon: "The Labyrinth contains a beautiful allegory, representing the nature of mechanic arts in general; for all . . . mechanical inventions may be conceived as a labyrinth, which, by reason of their subtlety, intricacy, crossing, and interfering with one another, and the apparent resemblances they have among themselves, scarce any power of the judgment can unravel and distinguish; so that they are only to be understood and traced by the clue of experience. It is no less prudently added, that he who invented the windings of the labyrinth, should also show the use and management of the clue; for mechanical arts have an ambiguous or double use, and serve as well to produce as to prevent mischief and destruction; so that their virtue almost destroys or unwinds itself" (*Wisdom of the Ancients* (XIX), Daedalus).

Lacordaire, Jean Baptiste Henri (1802–61). French Catholic ecclesiastic, associated with Lamennais (q.v.) as an advocate of liberty against Ultramontanism (q.v.). A frequent preacher at Notre Dame, where he exerted a powerful influence.

Lactantius of Nicomedia (c. 260–330). Latin Father and author of Christian apologetics, his chief work being *The Divine Institutes*.

Lady chapel. A cathedral chapel dedicated to the Virgin Mary.

Lady Day. See *Annunciation, Feast of the*.

laity. The people as distinguished from the clergy.

Lakshmi. Vishnu's wife, a goddess of creative energy (Hindu myth.).

Lamaism. The politico-religious form of Buddhism prevalent in

Tibet and Mongolia. Lamaism stands to primitive Buddhism somewhat in the same relationship as Catholicism stands to primitive Christianity. In primitive Buddhism stress was laid on the importance of ethical and mental self-culture as leading to a change of heart and deliverance from the sufferings of life. With the growth of Lamaism in Tibet in the 7th C. A.D. there came a development from primitive simplicity. The effort towards self-culture, which mankind invariably shirks, was neglected in favour of a ritualistic system built up around the worship of saints and angels. This Tantra system, with its belief in rites and ceremonies, charms and incantations, seemed to the masses far superior to the slow conquest of egoism and ignorance. They embraced it eagerly. Witchcraft, magic and sorcery flourished like luscious weeds. It was not until the 15th C. A.D. that a reformer arose, Tsong-Kapa, the Luther of Tibet and founder of the famous monastery of Kunbum. After eight years of meditation he came forward as a public teacher. As a result of his influence Lamaism was drastically purged. He opposed the Tantra system and the many superstitions it had encouraged. Meantime the Lāma or High Priest of Tibet had gained complete spiritual and temporal sovereignty over the country. And after the reforming work of Tsong-Kapa had been completed, his two followers, abbots of the great monasteries of Gedun Dubpa, near Lhasa, and of Tashi Lunpo, became known as the Dalai Lama and the Tashi Lama and ruled jointly over the churches and state. Their successors have continued to exercise the same sovereignty. The Tibetan Church has a clergy of many ranks and degrees and the great yearly festival at Lhasa is as magnificent as anything that Rome can show. The political control of the Dalai Lama is confined to Tibet, but the Buddhist churches of China and Mongolia acknowledge his spiritual authority. About 1760 Tibet became self-isolated and Protestant missions have found it an exceedingly difficult country to work in. (See L. A. Waddell, *The Buddhism of Tibet*; H. H. Francke, *History of Western Tibet*.)

LAMBETH ARTICLES. The nine Calvinistic articles of faith drawn up at Lambeth in 1595. They were never ratified owing to Queen Elizabeth's opposition.

LAMBETH CONFERENCES. Assemblies of Anglican bishops which have met at Lambeth Palace each decade since 1867 to discuss the affairs of the Church of England.

LAMB OF GOD. In early Christian symbolism as found in the Roman catacombs and elsewhere, the lamb figures as the representation of Jesus Christ. The origin of the symbols is obscure. The most probable explanation appears to be that which connects the lamb (or ram) with the zodiacal spring sign. The bull was the religious symbol of earlier Persian and Phrygian cults (see *Mithra*).

Owing to the precession of the equinoxes at the time of the appearance of Christianity the sun was in the sign of Ares in the spring quarter. Hence the Ram or Lamb would become the symbol of the risen Saviour. (See E. Carpenter, *Pagan and Christian Creeds*, chap. iii.)

LAMENNAIS, HUGHES FÉLICITÉ ROBERT DE (1782–1854). French priest whose adoption of liberal ideas led to his severance from the Catholic Church.

LAMMAS. The old English Feast of First-fruits observed on 1 August. (A.S. *Loaf*, mass.)

LAMPETER COLLEGE. The chief college of Wales founded by Bishop Burgess in 1822.

LAMPS. In the 12th C. lamps began to be used with ritualistic significance in Catholic churches. The Hindus observe a feast of lamps. The ancient Greeks had a similar festival.

LANCET. A high narrow window terminating in a double or triple pointed arch (eccles. archit.).

LANFRANC (d. 1089). Archbishop of Canterbury under William the Conqueror, noted for his able church government and educational reforms. (See Hilaire Belloc, *William the Conqueror*.)

LANG, ANDREW (1844–1912). A writer on history and folk-lore of wide rather than deep research.

LANGLAND, WILLIAM (c. 1330–1400). English writer of whose life little is known. His great work (though some scholars think it a composite production) was "The Vision of Piers Plowman," a religious poem, pointing out the abuses of the time and suggesting remedies. In the poem the simple peasant, Piers, becomes gradually transformed into the Christ. The value of the poem resides largely in its vivid descriptions. (See H. Morley, *English Writers*; Jusserand, *A Literary History of the English People*.)

LANGTON, STEPHEN (d. 1228). Archbishop of Canterbury in the reign of King John. His appointment as primate was one of the causes of the dispute between King John and Innocent III.

LANGUET, HUBERT (1518 – 81). French Huguenot writer and diplomatist. He entered the service of Augustus I, elector of Saxony. Languet was a scholar of wide learning and rare enlightenment, as is testified by his letters to his friend Sir Philip Sidney. (See S. A. Pears, *Letters of Philip Sidney and Hubert Languet* (1845).)

LANTERN. The structure imposed on a dome or tower to admit light.

LANTERN-LAND. The name given by Rabelais to an imaginary land of literary, medical and ecclesiastical charlatans (*Pantagruel*, v, 33).

LAODICEAN. An indifferentist in religious matters (see Rev. iii. 14–18).

LAOKIUM. A Chinese quietist philosopher of the 7th C. B.C.

LAO-TSZE (c. 604–524 B.C.). Chinese philosopher, author of the *Tao-Teh-King* and founder of the religion called Taoism. His Chinese designation may be translated "the Venerable Philosopher"—a name vulgarized by many Westerners into "the Old Boy." Lao-Tsze's teaching inclined more to mysticism than that of his contemporary Confucius. The *Tao-Teh-King* is a short book, about half the length of St. Mark's Gospel. It deals with the attainment of Teh (Virtue) and with Tao, which is best translated by "The Way"—though it has other meanings. "No English word," writes Dr. Chalmers, "is its exact equivalent. Three terms suggest themselves—the Way, Reason and the Word. . . . Were we guided by etymology, 'the Way' would come nearest to the original . . . but this is too materialistic." Tao appears to be the symbol of a way, road or path pursued by the individual in his passage through life. His actions must be free from all selfish motive. In the processes of nature a similar detachment is seen at work: "All things spring up without a word spoken, and grow without a claim for their production. They go through their processes without any display of pride in them; and the results are realized without any assumption of ownership." Again and again the Philosopher insisted on the need for Humility (chap. viii); gentle compassion, economy and humility are the three virtues he most prizes. And in chapter lxiii he rises to sublime heights: "It is the way of Tao not to act from any personal motive, to conduct affairs without feeling the trouble of them, to taste without being aware of the flavour, to account the great as small and the small as great, to recompense injury with kindness." And the book closes with the finest of all benedictions: "It is the Tao—the Way—to benefit and not to injure; it is the Tao—the Way—to do and not to strive." The Taoism of to-day has degenerated from a fine philosophy to a poor religion, a religion in which the weeds of superstition, convention, lip-service, spiritualism, etc., flourish. (See Dr. Chalmers, *The Speculations on Metaphysics, Polity and Morality of "The Old Philosopher," Lao-Tsze* (1868); Sir Robert Douglas, *Confucianism and Taoism*; Lionel Giles, *Taoist Teachings*.)

LAPSED, THE. The term applied in the early Christian Church to those who, during persecution, fell away from the faith.

LAPUTA. Swift's imaginary island (*Gulliver's Travels*) inhabited by scientific speculators and doctrinaires who lost sight of practical affairs.

LARËS and PENATËS. In the Roman Religion (q.v.) the Larës were: (1) the protective gods of roads and streets; (2) the souls of virtuous ancestors who protected the home. Their images were kept in the family shrine or *lararum*. The Penatës were the household gods whose office it was to promote wealth and prosperity. The Lar Familiaris was the spirit of the founder of the house and the protector of his descendants.

LARVAE. The ghosts or mischievous spirits of ancient Rome.

LAST DAY. See *Judgment, Day of.*

LAST SUPPER or LORD'S SUPPER. See *Communion, Holy.*

LATERAN, THE. The Church of St. John Lateran at Rome, built on the site of the palace of Plautius Lateranus (1st C. A.D.)

LATERAN COUNCILS. Five ecumenical councils of the Western Church held in the Lateran in 1123, 1139, 1179, 1215 and 1512–17.

LATIMER, HUGH (c. 1490–1555). English bishop who, with Cranmer and Cromwell, assisted Henry VIII in his contest with the Pope. He was burnt at Oxford as a heretic in Mary's reign.

LATITUDINARIANS. A group of liberal and philosophical 17th-C. churchmen who tried to bring about the union of nonconformist sects with the established church.

LATRIA. The worship offered to God alone; as distinguished from " dulia," worship given to saints and angels, and from " hyperdulia," worship given to the Virgin (Cath. doc.).

LATTER DAY SAINTS. See *Mormonism.*

LAUD, WILLIAM (1573 – 1645). High-church archbishop of Canterbury and supporter of Charles I's doctrine of Divine Right. His extreme high-church views led to suspicions and he was impeached and executed on the false charge of popery. (See C. H. Simkinson, *Life and Times of Laud*; John Evan, *Charles I* (1934).)

LAUDS. The second of the Catholic canonical offices. See *Breviary.*

LAURA. An early form of Egyptian, Palestinian and Syrian monastery in which each monk lived in an isolated hermitage.

LAVABO. (1) The ritual washing of the celebrant's fingers at Mass during the recital of the psalm (xxvi.) *Lavabo manus meas in innocentia.* (2) The stone basin in monasteries for washing the hands.

LAW, CANON. The body of law which has grown up in the Catholic and derivative churches based on the Bible, tradition, decrees of councils, ecumenical, general and local decrees of diocesan and national synods, etc.

LAW, JEWISH. The corpus of laws found in Exodus, Leviticus, Numbers and Deuteronomy. It deals with matters of hygiene, ritual and ethics.

LAWRENCE, SAINT. Patron saint of curriers. Tradition says he was broiled on a gridiron during the persecutions of Valerian.

LAYING ON OF HANDS. See *hands, laying on of.*

LAY-READER. A layman in the Church of England officially appointed to preach or take part of a service.

LAZARISTS. A Catholic order founded by St. Vincent de Paul in 1624 to help the sick and poor. St. Vincent was canonized in 1737.

LAZARUS. (1) A disciple of Jesus Christ, who resided with his two sisters at Bethany. The gospels record how Jesus raised him from death after he had been three days in the tomb (John xi. 1–44). (2) The name of a beggar in one of the parables of Jesus (Luke xvi. 20).

LEAVEN. A substance to promote fermentation, used in bread-making. The Jews, associating it with defilement, forbade its employment in making bread for ritualistic use.

LEBANON. A range of mountains in Syria north of Palestine, famous for its cedars. (Cf. Keats, "from silken samarcand to cedar'd Lebanon.")

LECTERN. A church reading-desk from which the Scriptures are read.

LECTIONARY. A book containing the Scripture lessons to be read in churches.

LECTOR. (1) A minor order (preliminary to the priesthood) in the Catholic Church. (2) A Scripture reader in the early church. (3) The priest or layman who reads the lessons in church services.

LEE, SIR SIDNEY. See *Jewish writers.*

LEGATE. (1) A deputy representing the Pope. (2) An honorary distinction conferred on certain Catholic archbishops.

LEGEND, THE GOLDEN. See *Golden Legend.*

LEIBNITZ, GOTTFRIED WILHELM (1646–1716). German philosopher of the Idealist School. The universe, in his system, becomes an unbroken series of monads ("the very atoms of nature") in varying states of consciousness. In Leibnitz's philosophy the world is "the best of all possible worlds." The great difficulty of his system lies in the existence of evil—especially moral evil. His explanation—a rather tame one—is that moral evil was "permitted, not willed by God." (See Bertrand Russell, *A Critical Exposition of the Philosophy of Leibnitz* (1900).)

LEIGHTON, ROBERT (1611–84). Professor of Divinity in the University of Edinburgh and archbishop of Glasgow. A man of such broad views and sanguine temper that he tried to bring about an ecclesiastical union of the churches in Scotland.

LEMURËS. The spirits of the dead (Rom. myth.).

LENT. An annual fast of forty days, from Ash Wednesday to Easter, observed by the Catholic, Anglican and other Christian churches. It commemorates Christ's fast (Matt. iv. 2). In Latin, *quadragesima* (fortieth).

LETHË. A memory-obliterating river of Hades whose waters the souls of the dead must taste that they may forget their earth-lives (Class. myth.).

> "Lethe and Eunoe—the remembered dream
> And the forgotten sorrow—bring at last
> That perfect pardon which is perfect peace."
> LONGFELLOW.

LEVELLERS. The extreme left of Cromwell's followers. They gave trouble in the parliamentary army in 1647, and were finally suppressed by Cromwell in 1649.

LEVIATHAN. The huge animal referred to in Job xli.—possibly the sea-serpent. It has been identified with the mythical Tiamat of Babylonian mythology.

LEVITATION. The floating in air of heavy bodies; a phenomenon caused by the operation of unknown forces. See *Spiritualism*; *Siddhis*.

LEVITE. An inferior order of priesthood in the ancient Jewish Church. The levites were the reputed descendants of Levi, son of Jacob and Leah.

LEVITICUS. The third book of the O.T. See *Bible*.

LIBER PONTIFICALIS. A book containing biographies of the early popes, from Peter to Nicholas I (d. 867).

LIBERTARIAN. One who believes in Free-will as opposed to Necessity. Libertarianism has three aspects: (1) Theological: Does the will of God allow freedom for the will of man? (2) Psychological: Is man's will free or the result of converging forces—heredity, environment, etc.? (3) Scientific: Is man's will free or is his action the result of the chemical and organic activity of his bodily organism?

LIBERTINES. (1) A Jewish religious party (Acts vi. 9). (2) A party at Geneva, opposed to Calvin's moral reforms. (3) A sect of Reformers in France and Holland (16th C.) of pantheistic tendency. (4) In ethics, those who indulge their appetites without restraint.

LIBRARIES. The most famous libraries in history are:

(1) The Alexandrian library founded by Ptolemy Philadelphus (284 B.C.). It was partially destroyed in 47 B.C. when 400,000 books are said to have been lost.

(2) The library of Apellicon sent to Rome from Athens by Sylla (86 B.C.).

(3) Library at St. Mark's, Venice, established by gifts from Petrarch (A.D. 1352).

(4) The Vatican Library, founded by Pope Nicholas V (1447).

(5) The Bodleian Library, Oxford, founded by Thomas Bodley in 1598 (opened 1602).

(6) The Bibliothèque Nationale, at Paris. Begun in reign of Louis XI but not properly formed until 1724. It contains over 3,000,000 printed books and thousands of MSS.

(7) The British Museum Library (incorporating the Cottonian Library of 1598) was established in 1753.

(8) The Library of Congress, at Washington, D.C., U.S.A.

LICENCE, MARRIAGE (or **SPECIAL LICENCE**). In England, a marriage licence (in lieu of banns) may be granted by the archbishop, bishop or other authority, the marriage to be solemnized in the church of the parish in which one of the parties has resided fifteen days previously. Marriage must be celebrated within three months after banns or licence and between the hours of 8 a.m. and 6 p.m.

LICENTIATE. (1) In the Catholic Church a friar authorized to perform certain functions independent of the local priest. (2) In Protestant churches a layman licensed to preach.

LICHGATE. A churchyard gate with a porch under which the coffin can rest at funerals. (A.S. *lic* = corpse.)

LIDDON, HENRY PARRY (1829–90). English divine and canon of St. Paul's Cathedral (1870). Scholar, high churchman and eloquent preacher.

LIFE, ETERNAL. See *future life*; *Timeless Being*.

LIGHTFOOT, JOSEPH BARBER (1828–89). Bishop of Durham (1879) and Lady Margaret Professor (1875). The greatest English scholar, grammarian and textual critic of his time.

LIMBO (LIMBUS). In Catholic theology a rather vague region, not heaven but assuredly not hell to which are assigned: (1) Those who have not (through lack of opportunity) accepted Christ. (2) The pious "pagan" souls who died before the time of Christ. (3) The souls of unbaptized infants. No very definite description has been given of Limbo. Limbus Fatuorum is the Fool's Paradise where irresponsible fools who cannot be received into heaven and would not benefit from purgatory, continue in irresponsible cheerfulness.

LINGA, LINGAM. The penis or phallus, symbol of the Hindu god Shiva as representing the generative powers of nature. It is everywhere found in Hindu Saivaite temples and its female counterpart, the *yoni*.

LINGARD, JOHN (1771–1851). English historian. His chief work, the *History of England* (8 vols., 1819–30), was thought to be written from the Catholic point of view, Lingard being a Catholic priest. But it is now regarded as in the main impartial.

LITANY. A penitential and intercessory prayer in which brief supplications by the priest are followed by short responses from the congregation. Mamertus, bishop of Vienne (5th C. A.D.), is believed to be the first to have used processional litanies in times of sickness. The English litany dates from the reign of Henry VIII.

LITURGY. The ritual services of a church or (as in the Greek Church) the order for celebration of the eucharist. There are six main groups of liturgies—four eastern and two western in origin—as follows:

Eastern

I. *The Syrian Rite.* The chief liturgies of this group are the Clementine liturgy derived from the eighth book of the Apostolic Constitutions; the Greek liturgy of St. James and the Syriac liturgy of St. James.

II. *The Egyptian Rite.* This group includes the Coptic liturgies of St. Basil, St. Gregory and St. Cyril; the Ethiopian and Abyssinian.

III. *The Byzantine Rite.* To this group belong the Armenian liturgy, the Greek liturgies of St. Basil and St. Chrysostom; also the Greek liturgy of St. Peter.

IV. *The Persian Rite.* This includes the liturgies of Nestorius and Theodore of Mopsuestia. Many liturgies of this group have been lost.

Western

V. *The Roman Rite.* The only liturgy of this group is that of the Catholic Church (Church of Rome). Other uses have sprung from this rite, as in France and England.

VI. *The Hispaño-Gallican Rite.* This is a group of Latin liturgies which have mostly been superseded by the Roman rite. They used to prevail in Spain, France and northern Italy. Authorities differ as to their origin.

LITURGY, THE ENGLISH. The earliest English liturgy, that of the Celtic Christians, appears to be of Hispaño-Gallican (see above) origin. The Sarum (Salisbury) use, derived from this via the Anglo-Saxon and Anglo-Norman uses, gained precedence of the York, Hereford and other forms. The English Reformation resulted in the Prayer Book of Edward VI (1549). This book was revised several times until the final revision in 1662. The main sources from which it was compiled were: (1) The breviary, missal and other office books. (2) The Mozarabic Missal. (3) Eastern liturgies (St. Chrysostom, St. Basil, etc.). (4) Lutheran and Genevan service books. (5) Original compositions of the compilers of the Prayer Book (some of the Collects for Saints' Days, that for the Royal Family—written by Whitgift, etc.). The American and Irish Prayer Books are derived from the English.

LIVINGSTONE, DAVID (1813–73). British explorer. The London Missionary Society sent him to Africa in 1858. He did extensive pioneer work among the natives and his influence as a devout Christian was widely felt. He opened Central Africa to missionary work. (See W. G. Blackie, *Life of David Livingstone.*)

LOCKE, JOHN (1632–1704). English philosopher who traced all knowledge to sense-impressions, and our reasoning thereon. His great work was the *Essay on the Human Understanding* (1690). Though not profound, Locke was a sensible, clear-minded thinker whose work reveals the influence of Descartes and Bacon. (See H. R. Fox-Bourne, *Life of John Locke* (1876).)

LODGE, SIR OLIVER (b. 1851). A leading scientist of his time, author of *Life and Matter* (1905); *Atoms and Rays* (1924); *The Reality of a Spiritual World* (1930). In the face of much opposition, due to the mass "thinking" of a materialistic age, he asserted his belief in the genuineness of much spiritualistic phenomena of which he had made a first-hand study. He thus compelled scientists to admit the existence of these new fields of inquiry.

LOGIA. (1) The name, believed to have been first applied by Papias of Hierapolis (2nd C. A.D.) to a collection of Jesus' sayings. Some scholars have found in the Logia the common source used by the authors of Matthew and Luke; others incline to the view that the Logia is the source only of such sayings of Jesus as are peculiar to Matthew. (2) The collections of the sayings of Jesus discovered by Grenfell and Hunt (1897 and 1903) known as the Oxyrhynchus Papyrus and ascribed to the 3rd C. A.D. (Gr. *logia* = sayings.)

LOGOS. A term originally used by the Greek Stoic philosophers to describe the all-pervading life-principle of the universe. When the translators at work on the Septuagint (q.v.) came to the Hebrew word *memra* (used in the sense of the creative word of Yahweh), they translated the term into the Greek *logos*. So the Logos, in Alexandrian theology, came to incorporate the ideas of the Word of Jehovah and the life-principle of Stoicism. This development was carried further when the author of the Fourth Gospel, writing in Alexandria, applied the term to the historic Jesus ("The Word became Flesh"). Thus the Hebrew *memra*, in its Messianic aspect, became fused with the Greek life-principle and out of this fusion came the Logos–Christ. The term gradually faded out of liturgical use owing to the action of the Council of Nicea (325 A.D.), when the word "Son" was substituted for "Logos." Analogies to the term Logos are found in the Chinese Tao and the Hindu Brahma. (See E. F. Scott, *The Fourth Gospel*, chap. v (1906).)

LOISY, ALFRED FIRMIN (b. 1857). French Catholic theologian of strongly modernist views. In 1908 Loisy held a government lectureship at the École des Hautes Études Pratiques, where he lectured on Genesis and the Gospels. Trouble with the Catholic Church commenced with his publication of *L'Évangile et l'Église* (Eng. trans. 1903), in which he advocated the adaptation of the Gospel to the changing needs of humanity. There was enough historical criticism in it to arouse Catholic fears and in 1903 Cardinal Richard publicly condemned the book. The Pope refused to interfere directly, but on the elevation of Cardinal Sarto to the papacy as Pius X, a papal decree of the Index was issued condemning five of Loisy's books, including the *Religion d'Israël*, in which Loisy's mystical intuitions found perfect expression. Thereupon Loisy resigned his lectureship and returned soon afterwards to his native Lorraine, where he continued to publish books of modernist views. In March 1903 the Holy Office pronounced the major excommunication against him, whereupon Loisy wrote: "I have aimed at establishing principally the historical position of the various questions, and secondarily the necessity for reforming more or less the traditional concepts." The chief cause of the Church's unqualified condemnation of Loisy's position was his insistence that Jesus Christ himself believed in the proximity of his second coming; it follows from this that it is extremely unlikely that Christ (believing in his immediate return) would have founded the Church and the Sacraments. In consequence of this view the Catholic Church was confronted with a highly difficult situation. (See Paul Desjardins' *Catholicisme et Critique* (Paris, 1905).)

Lokayata. A Hindu materialist philosophy no longer found in India. It taught that true knowledge is the result of sense-perception. The universe is the result of combinations of the four elements and man's psychic life has a purely materialist origin.

Loki. The Norse god of strife. He has been identified with fire as being both beneficent and malevolent.

Lollards. The followers of Wycliffe (q.v.), a sect of strict Puritans.

Lord's Day. See *Sunday*.

Lord's Prayer. The prayer Jesus taught his disciples (Matt. vi. 9–13; Luke xi. 2–4).

Lord's Supper. See *Communion, Holy*.

Lord's Table. (1) The ordinance of the Lord's Supper. (2) The table or altar on which the sacred elements are laid.

Lot. Son of Haran and nephew of Abraham (O.T.). His wife was turned to "a pillar of salt" (Gen. xix. 26).

Lourdes. A place of pilgrimage for Catholics in southern France. In 1858 the Virgin Mary is said to have appeared to a young peasant girl. Many miraculous cures are reported to have taken place there. (See J. R. Gasquet, *The Cures at Lourdes* (1895), and (for the sceptical view) Zola, *Lourdes* (Paris, 1894).)

love. In English the word "love" does duty for many emotional conditions. It is applied to (1) sex-love; (2) desire; (3) kindness, springing from egoistic motives; (4) reverential devotion; (5) good-will pursued for its own sake. This last is the true expression of the highest love as exemplified in Christianity, Paganism and other great religions. (See Plato, *Symposium*, and St. Paul, 1 Cor. xiii.)

Love Feast. See *agapē*.

Low Church. That section of the Church of England which, holding evangelical views, minimizes sacerdotal claims.

LOW SUNDAY. The first Sunday after Easter.

LOYOLA, IGNATIUS, SAINT. See *Jesus, Society of.*

LUCIAN THE MARTYR (c. 250–312). Presbyter of Antioch and teacher of Arius and Eusebius.

LUCIFER. See *Satan.*

LUCRETIUS (c. 98–55 B.C.). Roman poet of rationalizing temper. In his *De Natura Rerum* he sought to emancipate from superstition. He believed in the gods, but not as interfering in the affairs of mankind.

LUKE. The author to whom one of the gospels and *The Acts* are ascribed. Believed to have been a physician. See *Gospels.*

LULL, RAYMOND (1236–1315). Philosopher, missionary, mystic and martyr. He was born and educated in Palma, Majorca. At the age of 30 he had a vision of Christ which changed his life and caused him to go as missionary among the Arabs. He wrote many interesting books of a literary nature. *Blanquerna* (1283) describes a Platonic Utopia. (See Havelock Ellis in *Contemporary Review* (May 1906).)

LUSTRE, LUSTRUM. The five-yearly ritual purification (lustration) of the Roman people by one of the censors.

LUTHER, MARTIN (1483–1546). German religious reformer, chief instigator of the Protestant Reformation and the greatest man (with the possible exception of William the Silent, prince of Orange (q.v.)) in the history of Protestantism. Martin was born of peasant parentage and educated at the University of Erfurt. In 1505 he entered an Augustinian monastery. While there he underwent spiritual and psychological experiences which altered the direction of his life. He was appointed Professor of Philosophy at Wittenberg University (1508), and a few years later was sent to Rome on university business. Having become convinced of the need for faith, sincerity and honesty of life, the impression Rome made upon him was profound and lasting. He saw everywhere outward display and verbal professions covering inward deceit and corruption. He returned to Wittenberg knowing a great deal more about the Catholic Church. The abuse of selling Indulgences (q.v.) was then rampant in the Church. Luther protested, but without attracting attention. He thereupon nailed his 95 theses against Indulgences on the church door at Wittenberg (31 Oct., 1517). It was an act of defiance, a throwing down of the gage to Rome. Going further, in a disputation with John Eck at Leipzig, Luther denied the divine right of the Papacy and proceeded to publish appeals to the German nation (*Liberty of a Christian Man*, etc.). It was now obvious that he must either be burnt at the stake or prevail. A Bull excommunicating him was published in Germany (12 Sept., 1520). Luther's reply was to burn the Bull publicly on 12

December. He was summoned before the Diet of Worms where the greatest ecclesiastical trial of medieval times took place. Before his accusers he spoke his mind freely and with magnificent courage. On his return from the Diet (they were afraid openly to condemn him) he was "captured" by the friendly elector of Saxony and carried off to his castle of Wartburg. A few years later Luther returned to Wittenberg and continued the work of the Reformation, by tongue and pen, until his death. By his steadfast courage in the face of extreme personal danger he had won freedom for the spiritual and intellectual development of mankind and forced reforms upon the Catholic Church. (See Preserved Smith, *Life and Letters of Martin Luther* (1911); R. B. Ince, *Martin Luther* (1922).)

LUTHERANS and LUTHERAN CHURCHES. The Lutheran Church originated with Luther's life and work, but has undergone many changes since. Until 1580 (when the Form of Concord was adopted) continual doctrinal disputes arose among the Lutherans. In the 17th and 18th C.s the Lutheran Free Churches spread widely, becoming established in Scandinavia, Denmark, Holland and U.S.A. The Lutheran Churches hold the Scriptures to be the inspired and infallible authority in all questions of faith, life and doctrine. (See Schaff, *History of the Creeds of Christendom.*)

LYTE, HENRY FRANCIS (1793–1847). Devonshire clergyman and hymn-writer. Probably his best-loved hymn is "Abide with me."

M

MA-ARIB. The Jewish name for evening prayer (*minha* = afternoon prayer, and *shaharit* = morning prayer).

MAAT. Daughter of Re or Ra, the Sun-god; she was goddess of truth and justice (Egypt. myth.).

MACCABEES. Name of a distinguished Jewish family of the 2nd C. B.C. In the Jewish revolt against Antiochus IV (Epiphanes), king of Syria (175–164 B.C.), who tried to force Hellenism upon the Jews, the family of Maccabees stood out prominently as leaders. (See F. Henderson, *The Age of the Maccabees* (1907).)

MACCABEES, BOOKS OF. The name given to several apocryphal books of the O.T. The chief are: I. Maccabees giving an account of the Palestinian Jews under Syrian rulers. II. Maccabees giving a less satisfactory account of the same events. III. Maccabees written with Jewish propagandist intentions. IV. Maccabees, an Egyptian work showing strong Hellenistic influences. (See Fairweather and Black, *Maccabees* (Camb. Bible for Schools).)

MACEDONIA. A district of ancient Greece, south of Thrace and north of Thessaly.

MADONNA. See *Virgin Mary*.

MAESTRO DI CAPELLA. Master of the choir at St. Peter's, Rome.

MAGI. (1) The priests in the ancient Persian Zoroastrian religion. (2) The name applied to the " wise men " who came from the East to Bethlehem in the Birth Stories of Jesus. See *Zoroaster*.

MAGIC. This term has become synonymous in the West with trick performances of conjuring owing to the extremely materialistic habits of thought prevailing. The stream of modern theosophy which commenced with Madame Blavatski's *Isis Unveiled* and has been kept flowing by such books as Dr. Evans-Wentz's *Tibetan Yoga*, Ossendowski's *Beasts, Gods and Men*, Dr. Jacolliot's works on Indian thought, etc., has considerably modified this view. The work of the mesmerists, hypnotists and suggestionists has shown too that the power of mental force is much wider and deeper than our grandfathers supposed. In certain primitive lands magic is still openly and successfully professed. Tibet has its lamas who make a livelihood from the supply of magical incantations to drive away hail from growing crops. In view of the evidence available he would be a bold man and a foolish who categorically denied the practice of genuine " magic."

§ 2. In the East a distinction is drawn between Black Magic, as practised by followers of the Left-hand Path, and White Magic, as practised by followers of the Right-hand Path. The Right-handers pursuing knowledge with a view to helping mankind and the Left-handers seeking to gain power and wealth. Unfortunately for the public, Black Magicians never label themselves as such but leave their dupes to make the discovery for themselves. Occultists assure us that the ascetic training for both branches of the magic art is very similar for a considerable period. The combination of egoism and occult power seems invariably to lead to the practice of Black Magic.

§ 3. From one point of view, magic may be defined as the science of to-morrow. To the " poor Indian " a wireless set may savour of magic just as the phenomena of hypnotism and suggestion would have been ascribed to magic or witchcraft in the 15th C. To set a law in motion does not necessarily require that it shall be understood. Hence the magic of to-day is, in many instances, the not-yet-understood science of to-morrow. The fact that certain primitive tribes have, in their ignorance, ascribed natural processes like birth and death to the magic worked by friends or enemies, is apt to mislead the Western research student. He jumps to the conclusion that magic has no existence save in superstitious minds. As Sir Isaac Newton pointed out, we only know a few handfuls of the laws of nature ; there are doubtless hundreds that we do not know. Is it not probable that some of these may be known to gifted individuals who may thereby produce startling effects whose causes are not understood and therefore ascribed to magic, in the popular sense? For further information, consult Franz Hartmann, *Magic, White and Black*, and Julian Franklyn, *A Survey of the Occult* (1935).

MAGNIFICAT. The song of the Virgin Mary (Luke i. 46–55).

MAHABHARATA. One of the two great religious and philosophical epics of India, the other being the Ramayana. It celebrates the struggles of the Bharata family for princely power. The Bhagavad Gita (q.v.) forms part of Book VI. The poem, which is of unequal value, is about eight times the length of the Iliad and Odyssey combined. An English edition was published by Pratap Chundra Roy (1883–94). (See W. Hopkins, *The Great Epic of India* (1902).)

MAHADEVA ("GREAT GOD"). A term applied to Shiva (q.v.).

MAHATMA ("GREAT-SOULED ONE"). In esoteric Buddhism and Theosophy, an adept. See *initiation*.

MAHAVASTU. The portion of Buddhistic literature connecting the Mahayana (q.v.) with the Hinayana.

MAHAVIRA. Member of a Jain family, contemporary with Gautama, and their last great leader. At the age of 30 he became an ascetic monk who sought and attained enlightenment. See also *Jains*.

MAHAYANA ("GREAT VEHICLE"). The name given to the later popular Buddhism and its literature. Its chief features being garish temples, crude images, noisy festivals and fussy ceremonial. It forms a contrast with the Hinayana ("Little Vehicle"), the primitive Buddhism and Buddhist literature of the select few. (See T. Rhys Davids, *Buddhism*.)

MAHDI. The Moslem equivalent of the Jewish Messiah, who is to appear in the "last days" and will convert all the world to Islam. Many Mahdis have appeared, notably the one who overthrew the Egyptian power in the Soudan (1884–5), but the triumph of Islam has not followed.

MAHOMET. See *Mohammed*.

MAIMONIDES. The name given to the learned Spanish Rabbi Moses Ben Maimon (1135–1204). He studied medicine, religion and philosophy and became so attached to Saladin (whose physician he was) that he refused a similar position at the English court offered him by Richard I. He advocated reason in faith and toleration in theology. His great work was *The Guide* (translated by M. Friedlander, 1905).

MALACHI. The last in chronological order of the O.T. books. The prophecy appears to be anonymous, the title having been supplied by the compiler. It probably dates from about the 6th C. B.C. (See Driver, *The Minor Prophets* (1906).)

MAMERTINE PRISON. The ancient prison beneath the church of St. Giuseppe dei Falegnami in

Rome where, tradition says, Peter and Paul were imprisoned.

MAMMON. A word derived from the Syriac *mamona* = riches. It occurs in Luke xvi. 9–13 and Matthew vi. 24.

MANA. A word used by the natives of the Pacific islands signifying the life-force in all beings animate and inanimate. This force can be assimilated by touch or by eating: "You devoured the holy animal to get its *mana*, its swiftness, its strength, its great endurance" (Gilbert Murray, *Four Stages of Greek Religion*).

MANËS. Ancestral ghosts of the dead (Rom. myth.).

MANICHEISM. A synthetic religious system built up out of Christian, Buddhist and Zoroastrian elements, by the Persian, Mani of Ecbatana (b. c. 216 A.D.). Mani's purpose was to establish an eclectic faith which should become the world religion—a splendid dream, doomed to failure. He was banished from Persia by Shahpur, probably owing to the hostility of the Persian priesthood. He returned to Persia under Baham I (273–6), but only to be put to death. Manicheism spread rapidly and was welcomed by many thoughtful minds (St. Augustine was for nine years a Manichean), but was finally suppressed by persecution instigated by the Church Fathers. The Manichean religion was simple in its worship and of a markedly ascetic character. (See Ernest Rochat, *Essai sur Mani* (Geneva, 1897).)

MANIPLE. A eucharistic vestment worn over the left arm in the Catholic, Greek and Armenian churches.

MANNA. The food supplied to the Israelites in the Wilderness (Exod. xvi. 15). From Heb. *man hu* = what is it?

MANNING, HENRY EDWARD (1807–92). English cardinal and theologian. One of the ablest of the Tractarians (q.v.). He joined the Catholic Church in 1851. For a spirited short biography in "the Strachey manner," see *Eminent Victorians* by Lytton Strachey (1926).

MAN, SON OF. A title which is first found in pre-Christian Gnostic writings, applied to the Gnostic Saviour. The term crept into Christianity by way of Judaism. In Gnostic doctrine the Son of Man is the Perfect or Complete Man of which mankind are feeble copies and into whose likeness they will ultimately grow. The same idea is found in the Greek Mysteries. Cf. Pindar: "Be of good cheer, O initiates in the mystery of the liberated god; for to you out of all your labours and sorrows shall come Liberation." (See Gilbert T. Sadler, *The Gnostic Story of Jesus Christ* (1919).)

MANTRA. (1) The first division of the Hindu Veda. (2) An ancient Hindu song or chant which, in consequence of the way it is sung, is said to produce supernormal results. The yogis of India and Tibet are said to be able to produce curious phenomena by the use of such mantras. The philosophy behind it concerns the law of vibration. Since every organism has its own vibratory rate, variations in substance can be produced by altering the vibration.

MANU. The equivalent of Noah in Hindu mythology.

MANU CODE (INSTITUTES OF MANU). A Hindu code of laws. The original work is lost, but an adaptation in verse was drawn up about the 1st C. A.D. The purpose of the Code was to bring back Hinduism, from the popular forms of Buddhism then prevalent, to the old Vedic rites and sacrifices. The Code deals with civil and criminal law, religious rites and social and domestic duties. (See A. Barth, *Religions of India.*)

MARA. The embodied evil principle in Hindu and Buddhist speculation.

MARCION and MARCIONISM. Marcion of Sinope (Pontus) was the founder of a reform movement within Christianity (2nd C. A.D.). Marcion objected to the O.T. on the grounds that it revealed a God of Anger and War. He taught that Yahweh was an inferior being whom he styled the Demiurge. The supreme God (of whom Demiurge was ignorant) revealed himself in Jesus. For the same reason Marcion wanted the O.T. thrust out of the canon. (See A. Harnack, *History of Dogma.*)

MARCUS AURELIUS ANTONINUS (121–80 A.D.). Roman Emperor to whom the Meditations ("To Himself") have been ascribed. These Meditations take a very high place in the religious scriptures of the world. (See P. B. Watson, *M. Aurelius Antoninus* (1884). And (for an excellent modern exposition) *For To-day*, by Archibald Weir (1934).)

MARDUK (MERODACH). The chief god worshipped in Babylon, creator of the world and destroyer of the monster Tiamat (primeval chaos).

MARK, GOSPEL OF. See *Gospels.*

MARONITES. A Syrian group of Catholics living on the slopes of Mount Lebanon in semi-independence of the Catholic Church. They claim to have been established by St. Maron (c. A.D. 400).

MARPRELATE CONTROVERSY. A series of lively pamphlets exchanged between the English bishops and Puritans in 1588–9.

MARRIAGE. (1) The union of man and woman as husband and wife. (2) The ceremony, religious or civil, which establishes the relationship. The forms of marriage and their attendant customs differ in every age and country. The chief kinds of marriage are:

(1) Polygamy—or the union of one man with several women, more correctly termed polygyny. This form of union, found among certain anthropoid apes, has prevailed in all stages of society from the most primitive to the most civilized. It is favoured by Mohammedanism and by Mormonism.

(2) Polyandry, or the union of one woman with several men, is rare. It is found in some parts of India and Tibet, the cause usually being a scarcity of women.

(3) Monogamy or the union of one man and one woman has become the prevalent form of marriage and in Christian countries has ousted all other forms.

Owing to obsolete laws, broader religious views and changed social and economic conditions, marriage tends to be less stable than in the preceding age. Divorce is more readily and widely sought and more easily obtained. There are, broadly speaking, two views on divorce. That held by the conservative temper which advocates the maintenance of marriage no matter how unhappy the home may be owing to incompatibility; and the view held by those of modernist tendency who think that, if the harmony which marriage should bring is impossible, then the marriage tie, in the interests of the parties and of any children involved, had better be dissolved. (See Westermarck, *History of Human Marriage* (1901).)

MARS. The God of War (L. myth.).

MARTHA. Sister of Lazarus and Mary (John xi. 1).

MARTINEAU, JAMES (1805–1900). English idealist philosopher and unitarian theologian.

MARTIN OF TOURS, SAINT (c. 316–400). Bishop of Tours, recognized as the patron saint of France.

MARTYR. One who suffers death for his belief. The Roman martyrology giving a complete list of Catholic martyrs was first published in 1583. Most martyrs, though showing splendid courage, have been fanatical and unbalanced, a truth emphasized by a modern philosopher when he said: "Better a mild criminal than a successful martyr."

MARY MAGDALENE. A follower of Jesus originally residing in the village of Magdalen (Magadan). There is no gospel evidence connecting Mary Magdalene with the prostitute who anointed Christ's feet (Luke vii. 37). For a charming story of Mary Magdalene, reverently treated, see Anatole France, *Balthasar* (Laeta Acilia).

MARY THE VIRGIN. See *Virgin Mary*.

MASORAH, MASSORAH. A collection of critical notes on the O.T. arranged by Jewish scholars between the 6th and 11th C.s A.D.

MASS. The Catholic celebration of the Eucharist (q.v.). High Mass requires the co-operation of at least three clergy; the shorter form, Low Mass, may be celebrated by one priest. The Catholic Church teaches that the Mass is the sacrifice of the body and blood of Jesus Christ and is identical with the sacrifice on the Cross. It benefits the whole church and especially the celebrant and the faithful who are present. (See A. Fleury, *The Missal Explained* (1916).)

MASSITES. "A Low Church invention for those members of the Anglican Church who believe in transubstantiation" (Eric Partridge, *Slang*, p. 198).

MATINS. (1) The Catholic office said at dawn. See *Breviary*. (2) The Anglican service of Morning Prayer.

MATTHEW, SAINT. The apostle of Jesus Christ, also called Levi, traditionally believed to be the author of the first gospel. This is unlikely in view of the unmistakably composite nature of the gospel. See *Gospels*.

MAUNDY THURSDAY. The Thursday before Good Friday.

MAURICE, FREDERICK DENISON (1805–72). Anglican clergyman who exercised wide influence as leader of the Christian Socialists. He was one of the founders of the Working Men's College and author of many books on theology.

MAURISTS. Members of the Benedictine Congregation of St. Maur, established in 1618 at the abbey of St. Maur-sur-Loire, near Saumur. They are famed for their scholarly contributions to theology and literature. Name derived from Maurus, a disciple of Benedict.

MÂYA. The Hindu term for illusion. It is applied to the world of sense-perception as distinguished from Reality, the One or Brahma.

MAYNOOTH COLLEGE. The Catholic college founded in Ireland in 1795, and designed for the education of Catholic students intending to enter the priesthood.

MAZDA (AHURA MAZDA). The supreme god of the Zend-avesta. See *Zoroaster*.

MAZDAKISM. The doctrine of a Persian heretical sect founded by Mazdak (6th C. A.D.). The movement had communistic and socialistic tendencies which caused its leader to become unpopular and finally to be put to death by King Kobad.

MAZZAH. Hebrew term for unleavened bread.

MECCA. The religious capital of Islam, in Arabia. Moslems turn towards it when they pray.

MEDIATOR. See *Atonement*.

MEDICINE MAN. A term applied to the shamans (q.v.) and witch-doctors of primitive tribes, especially the N. American Indians. The skill and knowledge of many of these men are such as to put our physicians in the shade. They show great ability in the management of wounds and fractures. Many of our drugs and herbs are derived from the practice of ancient medicine-men. "The main point is to grasp that by his special initiation and the rigid taboos which he practises—not to speak of occasional remarkable gifts, say of trance and ecstasy, which he may inherit by nature and have improved by art—he *has* access to a wonder-working power" (R. R. Marett, *Hibbert Journal*, Oct. 1918).

MEDINA. A city of central Arabia reverenced by Moslems as the burial-place of Mohammed.

MEDITATION. A term often misused for prolonged thought. Meditation, in the psychological and exact sense, connotes—as in the Hindu *dhyana* and the Buddhist *jhana*—cessation of thought. It has been the chief means of attaining purification and enlightenment in all the great religious systems. " Just as understanding is aroused by speech or thought, so soul-perceptions and experiences belonging to cosmic consciousness are aroused by meditation and by the impact of people who meditate, on their fellows. . . . It follows philosophically that we can never understand the world unless we first understand ourselves, or only in the exact proportion as we understand ourselves. Hence the wise of all ages have meditated. When, by meditation, the mind acquires one-pointedness, it becomes an immensely powerful engine which will enable us at will to contact spheres of consciousness inconceivable to a three-dimensional mentality—spheres of beauty, wisdom, joy, infinite and inexhaustible, the Treasure House of the Ages, the Source of all genius, the cradle of all wisdom, deeply hidden in every heart and mind. . . . The first step is to check the vagaries of the mind by calmly focussing it on one idea or on a series of related ideas. Or we may just watch the erratic behaviour of the mind as it jumps like a monkey from branch to branch. By quietly watching we gradually learn to control it " (Meredith Starr). It should be added that prolonged meditation should not be practised without first consulting an experienced teacher. Otherwise, lack of mental balance and other undesirable results are likely to ensue.

MEGIDDO. A city of ancient Palestine near the river Kishon (Judges v. 19).

MEGILLOT. A Hebrew term for the five scrolls (Ruth ; Lamentations ; Song of Songs ; Ecclesiastes ; Esther) read in the synagogue on the feasts of Passover, Pentecost, Tabernacles and Purim.

MELANCHTHON, PHILIPP (1497–1560). German reformer whose name, Schwarzerd, was Grecized. He was educated at Heidelberg University and became Professor of Greek at the University of Wittenberg where he became a friend of Luther. His scholarship, mild temper and conciliatory spirit won him many friends. As one of the leaders of the Reformation (q.v.) he ranks next after Luther. (See J. W. Richard, *Philipp Melanchthon* (1898).)

MELCHITES (" ROYALISTS "). The name applied to supporters of the Orthodox creeds at the Byzantine Court in the 5th C. They opposed Nestorianism.

MELCHIZEDEK. King of Salem—Salem being possibly the earlier Jerusalem. He blessed Abraham in the name of the supreme God. His blessing of Abraham led, in later literature (Psalms and Gospels), to his being regarded as a type of the Messiah. Mystery surrounds him since he is described as "without father" and " having neither beginning of days nor end of life."

MELIORISM. The doctrine (to be distinguished from optimism) that the world tends to improve. It is the ethical expression of the theory of evolution and was advocated by William James.

MEMRA. The Hebrew term translated as " Logos " in the Septuagint. See also *Logos.*

MENAION. The breviary of the Greek Church. It contains prayers, hymns and brief biographies of the saints and martyrs.

MENCIUS (385–289 B.C.). The Latin name for Mang-Tsze or Mang the Philosopher, a Chinese moral teacher who ranks next to Confucius. Mencius was a fearless teacher who took delight in lecturing the great and the important. His estimate of " the Great Man " is a searching commentary on life, yesterday, today and to-morrow : " To dwell in love, the wide house of the world, to stand in propriety, the correct seat of the world, and to walk in righteousness, the great path of the world ; when he obtains his desire for office, to practise his principles for the good of the people, and when that desire is disappointed, to practise them alone ; to be above the power of riches and honours to make dissipated, of poverty and mean condition to make swerve from the right, and of power and force to make bend—these characteristics constitute the great man. . . . The great man is he who does not lose his child-heart. . . . When one by force subdues men, they do not submit to him in heart. When he subdues them by virtue, in their hearts' core they are pleased, and sincerely submit." (See H. B. Hutchinson, *The Mind of Mencius* (1882) ; *Mencius*, trans. by Leonard Lyall.)

MENDELSSOHN, MOSES. See *Reformed Judaism.*

MENDICANT ORDERS. The Mendicant or Begging orders of monks arose in the 13th C. as a protest against the wealth and worldliness of the Catholic Church. The Mendicant Order of Dominicans was founded in 1216, the Franciscans in 1223, the Carmelites in 1245. Mendicancy, which has practically died out in the West, still flourishes in the East, owing to more primitive views of life and a less rigorous climate.

MENNO, MENNONITES. Menno (1492–1559) was a Dutch evangelical reformer who combined baptist views with a fanatical zeal for reform. Many of his followers emigrated to U.S.A., where they established a Mennonite Church.

MENOLOGION. The book of festivals of martyrs and saints compiled by the Greek Church.

MENORAH (" CANDLESTICK "). The ritual candlestick used in the Jewish synagogue.

MENTAL RESERVATION. Term applied in Catholic theology to the withholding of certain words necessary to convey the speaker's full meaning. (Thus a priest may assume ignorance of a crime learnt through confession.)

MERCURY. The Roman god of merchants and merchandise (*merx*). His worship was introduced into Italy by Greek settlers. In the streets of Rome where shops abounded, little shrines and images of Mercury were set up. On 15 May the shopkeepers sprinkled their heads with water from Mercury's spring and entreated him to take away the guilt of their misdeeds. Mercury was also the messenger of the gods, identified with the Greek Hermes.

MERCY-SEAT. The golden lid covering the Jewish Ark of the Covenant. It formed a kind of throne on which God was supposed to sit to receive supplications.

MERIT. A term used in Catholic doctrine to define that which is conferred on man by grace. There is also "a treasury of merits," the surplus virtue amassed by the saints, which may be dispensed by the Church.

MERLIN. A famous bard and magician of Welsh tradition. There was probably a substratum of truth beneath the medieval legends of Merlin. (See Malory's *Morte d'Arthur* and Layamon's *Brut*.)

MERODACH. See *Marduk*.

MESMER, MESMERISM. Franz Anton Mesmer (1733–1815), a German physician who practised healing, very successfully, by hypnotic methods. He settled in Paris where his cures attracted the attention and evoked the professional jealousy of the doctors. Patients flocked to him and many received benefit. Psychology has not yet been able to formulate a satisfactory theory to account for the striking success of his methods. (See R. B. Ince, *Franz Anton Mesmer* (1920).)

MESSIAH. The Jewish and Christian term for a world-saviour. In O.T. times, the hope of a Messiah took the form of a political aspiration. The Jews expected the coming of one who should deliver them from oppression. In later times the Messianic hope became more ethical and less political. With the coming of Christianity many Messianic prophecies of the O.T. were strained to bear a fanciful religious meaning. Jesus Christ took the old Messianic ideas and gave them new life and significance. How far he identified the title with his own mission is a debatable point. He swept aside the political significance of the term and urged men to prepare for the coming of the Messianic Kingdom—a rule of fraternity and justice in which humility, gentleness, mutual forgiveness and right-doing should be practised. Had it not been for this new interpretation he gave to the Jewish doctrine it would undoubtedly long ago have faded from memory. (Heb. *mashiach* = anointed.)

METAMORPHOSIS. Change of shape. Folk-lore everywhere preserves stories of men changed into beasts. The werwolf, berserk and vampire are examples. (See Apuleius, *The Golden Ass.*)

METAPHYSICS. The science which studies the first principles of nature and thought. The chief metaphysicians are: Socrates (What is the Good? the Beautiful? What is Wisdom and Justice?); Plato and Aristotle; Plotinus; Bacon; Locke; Hume; Spinoza; Kant, who taught that ultimate Reality ("the-thing-in-itself") is beyond the reach of human knowledge; Hegel; Fechner—the pioneer of psychology; Caird; Green; Bradley; W. K. Clifford; Bergson; J. M. E. MacTaggart; A. N. Whitehead; Archibald Weir; Bertrand Russell.

METEMPSYCHOSIS. See *transmigration*; *reincarnation.*

METHODISM. The Christian sect founded by John Wesley (1703–91). Methodism originated with a group of Oxford students (1729–35) termed Methodists in consequence of their careful, methodical pursuit of study and religious observance. Towards the end of the 18th C. the Church of England had lost grip owing to the slackness prevailing among clergy and laity. In 1738 John Wesley experienced conversion (q.v.) and henceforth he and his brother Charles and George Whitefield became active preachers and religious reformers. Their success was immense; startling revivalist phenomena resulting from their teaching. At first Wesley's followers were members of the Church of England, but the apathy or hostility of the Church led to the formation of a separate establishment in 1784. The movement spread to America, Canada and Australia. The Methodist doctrine is evangelical and Arminian, its polity a mingling of presbyterian and episcopalian elements. The ideal is "entire sanctification." Membership in 1929 (Great Britain and Ireland) was: Wesleyan Methodists, 547,628; Primitive Methodists, 225,861; United Methodist Church, 156,945; Independent Methodists, 10,943; Wesleyan Reform Union, 11,461. (See J. F. Hurst, *A History of Methodism* (7 vols., 1902).)

METONIC CYCLE. The lunar cycle (19 years), after which the new and full moon occur again on the same day of the year as at its beginning.

METROPOLITAN. The bishop of a metropolis (i.e. chief cathedral city) who presides over the other bishops of the province; called also archbishops in the Catholic Church.

MEZUZAH. A piece of parchment which the Jews fasten to the door-post. On it is inscribed the Biblical verses Deuteronomy vi. 4–9 and xi. 13–21. Its origin is the Biblical command in Deuteronomy vi. 9.

MICHAEL. (1) The archangel and prince of the celestial armies. (2) A medieval saint usually represented with scales to weigh the souls of the dead.

MICHAELMAS. St. Michael's festival (29 Sept.).

MIDRASH. The Hebrew commentary on the O.T. It is divided into Haggada (moral and poetical exposition) and Halakha (expositions of the law). Parts of the Midrash date from the 12th C. A.D.

MIHTI or MOHTI. Chinese philosopher of the period succeeding Confucius. He considered the cause of suffering to be selfishness, and its cure the application of love or good-will. If each would sacrifice his ego for the sake of others a new social order of peace and happiness would arise. Mihti has been called " the Christ of China."

MILAREPA, JETSÜN (b. A.D. 1052). The greatest saint of Tibet. His biography is of great interest for the student of religion. Beginning life as a student of Black Magic, Milarepa later became a Buddhist devotee who experienced a very severe initiation in the mountains of Tibet. He finally attained " the greatest of all great successes that can ever fall to the lot of mortal man." (See Prof. W. Y. Evans-Wentz, *Milarepa* (1928).)

MILITARISM. See *Peace Movements.*

MILL, JOHN STUART (1806–73). English political economist. He advocated Utilitarianism (q.v.) (" actions are right in proportion as they promote happiness "). (See L. Courtney, *John Stuart Mill* (1889).)

MILLENARIANISM. The ancient Jewish belief that the Messiah (q.v.) will reign over the earth for a thousand years. (See Revelations xx. 2.) This belief was one of the many doctrines Christianity inherited from Judaism. It is of apocalyptic type and has been blended at different ages with a variety of other teachings. St. Augustine spiritualized it and certain modern sects (Irvingites, Millerites, Plymouth Brethren, etc., etc.) have given it a fanatical interpretation. The ideal, regarded in a broad sense, is a fine one. " It is quite possible to conceive an imaginary society in which there should be no aggressiveness, but only sympathy and fairness . . . such a society on a large scale would be the millennium " (William James, *Varieties of Religious Experience*). (See F. C. Burkitt, *Jewish and Christian Apocalypses.*)

MILLER, WILLIAM (1782–1849). Founder of the Adventists in America who look for the immediate Second-Coming of Christ and the " End of the World."

MILMAN, HENRY HART (1791–1868). Anglican clergyman and dean of St. Paul's. Author of some inferior poetry; also of *The History of Latin Christianity* (1856)—an important contribution to research. Byron referred to Milman as " a kind of moral me."

MILTON, JOHN (1608–74). English poet of strongly Protestant and liberal views. His *Paradise Lost* is one of England's greatest epics. Not even the narrow and fanatical Hebrew material in which he worked could damp the fire and splendour of his poetic vision.

MIMAMSA (PURVA-MIMAMSA). A Hindu reactionary movement dating from about the 7th C. A.D. against philosophic doctrines. It insists on the need for Vedic rites and sacrifices.

MINERVA. Roman goddess of wisdom, identified with Greek Pallas Athene. Her festival, the quinquatrus (fifth day of the Ides), fell on 19 March.

MINHA. The Jewish daily afternoon service.

MINIMS. A strict order of mendicant friars founded by St. Francis of Paola, Calabria (1416–1509).

MINISTER, MINISTRY. See *orders, holy*; *Church, Christian.*

MINOR CANON. See *canon, minor.*

MINOR PROPHETS. The twelve prophets from Hosea to Malachi inclusive.

MINUCIUS FELIX. Christian apologist (2nd C.).

MINYAN. The quorum of ten required for worship in the Jewish synagogue.

MIRACLE. All religions incorporate many stories of magic and wonder-working, sudden cures, unexplained healing, etc. A miracle has thus come to be regarded as an event not to be explained by the action of natural forces. The Christian miracles of N.T. times occurred in a wholly unscientific age, hence much uncertainty arises as to their nature. The problem is further confused by the zeal of the faithful to prove their doctrines true by the testimony of miracles. The present tendency of the West is to stress too much our knowledge of "the laws of nature" and to dismiss all miracles as the result of fanatical credulity. The Catholic Church insists on the reality of miracles. Protestants incline to the view that though miracles happened in the past, they do not occur to-day—a somewhat illogical and arbitrary assertion. It seems probable that our knowledge of psychology and metaphysics is at present too elementary to elucidate many of the phenomena regarded as "miraculous."

MIRACLE-PLAY. A medieval form of drama founded on the O.T. and N.T. or on lives of the saints. See also *morality play.*

MIRIAM. Sister of Moses and Aaron in O.T. She rescued the infant Moses when exposed among the bulrushes (Exod. xv. 21).

MISERERE. (1) The 50th psalm of the Vulgate (51st in A.V.). (2) A hinged folding seat in a church stall.

MISHNA, MISHNAH. A division of the Talmud comprising the oral law; the other division, the Gemara, is a commentary on the Mishna. See *Talmud.*

MISSAL. The book containing the Catholic liturgy for Mass throughout the year.

MISSIONS, CHRISTIAN. Early missions form part of the history of Christianity (q.v.), Christianity being essentially a missionary religion. As soon as Europe had been Christianized, Christianity looked to the east and west for further fields of activity. The chief Catholic missions have been: (1) The Portuguese missions to West Africa and the East Indies (15th and 16th C.s). (2) The Spanish missions to South America (15th and 16th C.s). (3) The French missions to N. America, India, Ceylon and Japan (16th C.). The chief Protestant missions were: (1) English missions in N. America (17th C.). (2) Dutch missions to the E. Indies (17th C.). (3) The activities of the Church Missionary Society and other English societies (19th C.). The problem of Christian missions is a more difficult one to-day owing to a better knowledge of the excellent work done by non-Christian religions such as Buddhism, Mohammedanism, etc.

MITHRA, MITHRAS. A Persian god of light worshipped at Rome in the early Empire. Rites and secret mysteries were connected with his worship which, in many aspects, resembled those of Christianity. Mithra was a Mediator, born in a cave and followed by twelve disciples. Baptism and a kind of eucharist were parts of Mithra worship. It seems probable that certain of the Mithraic rituals and doctrines passed to Christianity. (See W. J. Pythian-Adams, *Mithraism* (1915).)

MITRE. The head-dress worn by bishops and archbishops.

MIXED CHALICE. The chalice containing mixed wine and water, in the Christian eucharist.

MIXED MARRIAGE. Marriage between a Catholic and a Protestant. See *Ne Temere.*

MOABITES. The people of Moab, the district east of the lower Jordan and the Dead Sea (O.T.).

MOABITE STONE. A slab of black basalt discovered in 1868 in Moab with an inscription in Hebrew-Phoenician letters recording the revolt of Mesha, king of Moab, against the king of Israel (2 Kings iii.). Now in the Louvre.

MODALISM. The doctrine of Sabellius that Father, Son and Holy Ghost are not three distinct persons but only three different modes of manifestation.

MODE. The method of dividing the octave for melodic purposes (mus.).

MODENA, LEON. See *Reformed Judaism.*

MODERNISM. A liberal movement of the 19th C. within the Catholic Church. The leaders of the movement were Alfred Loisy (q.v.) and Louis Duchesne. The Modernists adopted the belief that critical scholarship is the ultimate court of appeal in matters of faith. Pope Pius X condemned this view in his decree of 1907, *Lamentabili sane exitu*, and again in his encyclical *Pascendi Dominici regis*, in which he characterized the movement as "the synthesis of all heresies." The Modernist movement spread to England, where it was supported by Father George Tyrrell (q.v.), and to Italy, where Romolo Murri defended it.

MOHAMMED and MOHAMMEDANISM (also **MAHOMET** and **MAHOMETANISM**). Mohammed (A.D. 570-632), "the Praised One" (his original name was Kutam), was an orphan of Mecca brought up by his grandfather and afterwards by a rich, kindly and generous uncle. When his uncle incurred financial losses the boy had to earn his living. He became a shepherd and afterwards a conductor of caravans travelling between Damascus and Jerusalem. The widow Kadijah (fifteen years his senior) fell in love with the handsome lad, with his gleaming white teeth, dark complexion and aquiline nose, so quick and gentle by nature. Mohammed was a contemplative lad and mystical experience came to him early. He often retired to a cave for prayer and meditation. "I see a light," he said to Kadijah, "I hear the tinkling of bells in my ears and a sound like the swarming of bees." For a time he was troubled, fearing possession or madness. Kadijah reassured him. "No evil thing has happened to thee; thou dost not return evil for evil, thou art kind to relatives and friends. Rejoice, thou wilt be the prophet of prophets." His mystical experiences deepened. In a state of trance or extreme physical disturbance, revelations came to him. These were eagerly written down by followers and became the Koran (q.v.).

At Mecca, Mohammed's claims were met by mocking or persecution. He denounced the idolatry of the current worship; the low morality of the shopkeepers and merchants; the foolish and vulgar lives of the rich; the practice of infanticide and other abuses. As a consequence his family or clan was boycotted for three years and his followers maltreated. Abu Talib, the head of his family, warned him it might be impossible to protect him and begged that he would give up teaching. He replied: "Were I to be offered the sun in my right hand and the moon in my left to induce me to abandon my undertaking, the offer would be futile, for I will not rest until the Lord carry his cause to Victory, or till I die for it."

He continued to hurl curses at the wicked after the manner of Christ denouncing the Pharisees: "O beware of the time to come, when the stars shall fall from the sky . . . when the children's hair shall grow white with anguish . . . when men shall be scattered as moths in the wind. And then Allah shall cry to hell: Art thou full? And hell shall cry to Allah: More! Give me more!"

Mohammed quitted Mecca (The *Hegira* = "emigration" rather than "flight") for Yathrib (later called Medina). The outer change was accompanied by an amazing inner adaptation. Other measures were needed. The fierce Arabs about him could be controlled only by the sword. From the preacher and teacher Mohammed became the Cromwellian commander. The change was one of the most striking religious history affords. Having set the affairs of Medina in order, he led a crusade, winning all Arabia to accept his message of reform.

It is frequently objected that Mohammed did not preach a high standard of morality. This is true. But Mohammed was eminently practical. He introduced far-reaching improvements; abolished drunkenness and insisted on reform of the marriage-laws. The personal influence for good he wielded is probably without parallel in the history of religion: "The words which he preached to jeering crowds twelve hundred years ago are now being studied by scholars or devotees in London and Paris and Berlin; in Mecca, where he laboured, in Medina, where he died, in Constantinople, in Fez, in Timbucktoo, in Jerusalem, in Damascus, in Bassora, in Baghdad, in Bokhara, in Cabul, in Calcutta, in Pekin; in the steppes of Central Asia, in the islands off the Indian Archipelago, in lands which are as yet unmarked upon our maps, in the oases of thirsty deserts, in obscure villages situated by unknown streams" (W. Reade, *The Martyrdom of Man*).

Mohammed founded a Semitic religion blended of Arabic, Jewish and Christian elements. It spread with the rapidity and persistence of fire. Twice it seemed likely that Mohammedanism would become the religion of Europe; in 732 when Charles Martel met Abdur-Rahman in battle and defeated him; again in 1683 when John, king of Poland, defeated the Mohammedan army at Vienna.

The Koran requires belief in: (1) One God, Allah. (2) In angels and in the inspired Koran. (3) In the four great prophets—Moses, David, Jesus and Mohammed. (4) A future life involving a Day of Judgment and an after-state of happiness or misery. It insists on the practice of four cardinal virtues: (1) Prayer: (2) Almsgiving: (3) Keeping the Fast of Ramadan for the prescribed month when no food may be eaten during the day: (4) Making a pilgrimage to Mecca. As Christ was the embodiment of Love so was Mohammed the embodiment of Will. (See Carlyle, *Heroes and Hero-worship*; R. Bosworth Smith, *Mohammed* (1873); D. S. Margoliouth, *Mohammed and the Rise of Islam* (1905).)

MOHTI. See *Mihti*.

MOKSHA (also **MUKTI**). Hindu term for salvation.

MOLINISM. The doctrine of the Spanish Jesuit Molina (16th C.) that predestination and free-will are not mutually antagonistic since God knows that man will co-operate or react in the desired way.

MOLOCH. A Phoenician god to whom human sacrifice was offered.

MONASTICISM. Christian monasticism arose in the East with the Cenobite monks of Egypt (4th C.). (See *Pachomius*.) Jerome, Ambrose and Augustine of Hippo carried the movement further. The Benedictine Rule (founded by Benedict of Nursia, 6th C.) became predominant in the 12th C., the Order controlling 37,000 monasteries. The Military Orders (Templars, Hospitallers, etc.) originated from the Crusades. The chief mendicant orders were the Franciscans and Dominicans (q.v.).

MONISM. The philosophic theory which traces all being to one principle in contradistinction to dualism (matter and spirit).

MONK. One dedicated to the religious life in a monastery.

MONOPHYSITISM. The doctrine (condemned in A.D. 553 by the Fifth General Council of Constantinople) that Christ had but one nature, and not two—human and divine.

MONOTHEISM. The belief in one God only.

MONOTHELITES. Those who held that Christ had only one will. They were adjudged heretical by the Lateran Synod of 649.

MONSIGNOR. A Catholic title formerly given only to cardinals but now bestowed on all the higher ecclesiastics.

MONSTRANCE. A stand shaped like a candlestick used in Catholic churches to present the consecrated host for adoration.

MONTANISM. A 2nd-C. heresy advocated by the Phrygian prophet, Montanus. Montanus was a strict legalist and ascetic and advocated the return to primitive strictness of life. (See G. G. Selwyn, *The Christian Prophets* (1900).)

MONTE CASSINO. An isolated hill between Rome and Naples where St. Benedict established his monastery in the 6th C. In 1866, at the dissolution of monasteries, Monte Cassino was spared and became a national monument with the monks as custodians.

MONTHS, HEBREW. See *Jewish calendar*.

MOODY, DWIGHT LYMAN. American revivalist (19th C.) who with Ira D. Sankey organized a popular evangelical campaign in U.S.A. and England.

MORALITY. See *ethics*.

MORALITY PLAY. (Also mystery and miracle play.) The mystery play originated in 9th-C. dramatic representations of simple scenes from the N.T. (the Marys at the Tomb, etc.). Such plays increased in number until by the 12th and 13th C.s they were played in the vernacular and became the staple dramatic diversion of the people, akin to the cinema of to-day. Much of the fun was broad and coarse. With the dawn of secular drama (16th C.) the mystery plays declined in popularity (the Decennial Oberammergau play is a survival). The Morality or Morality Play was a development of the mystery or miracle play and dealt, in allegorical form, with the conflict between the virtues and the vices. The Morality survived almost to the end of Queen Elizabeth's reign. (See E. K. Chambers, *The Medieval Stage*.)

MORAL THEOLOGY. Ethical as distinguished from doctrinal theology.

MORAVIANS. A small but zealous sect of Protestants established in Moravia and Bohemia in the 15th C.

MORDECAI. A captive Jew at the Court of Ahasuerus (Esther ii. 5).

MORE, HANNAH (1745–1833). English writer and philanthropist. She assisted in establishing the Religious Tract Society. Author of *Cœlebs in Search of a Wife* (1809).

MORE, SIR THOMAS (1478–1535). English humanist statesman, author of the *Utopia*. He refused to accept Henry VIII as head of the English Church and was put to death on a vamped charge of treason. Canonized by the Catholic Church in 1935. (See Christopher Hollis, *Sir Thomas More* (1935).)

MORMONISM. An American sect founded in 1830 by Joseph Smith, whose *Book of Mormon* was, he alleged, translated from certain writings of a supernatural being, by name Mormon. The book, poor in style and content, appears to have been a fabrication of his own. The scandals in which he became involved led to his being shot. The sect continues, practising polygamy and preaching fanatical doctrines at Salt Lake City. They call themselves Latter Day Saints.

MORTAL SIN. Wilful violation of God's law which separates the soul from God (Cath. theol.).

MORTIFICATION. Bringing the passions and appetites to subjection by an ascetic life.

MORTMAIN, STATUTES OF. Various Acts of Parliament restricting the giving of property to religious houses.

MOSES. The Jewish lawgiver and prophet who led the Israelites from Egypt to Palestine. (See W. Robertson Smith, *Prophets of Israel*.)

MOSES, ASSUMPTION OF. An apocalyptic work of the 1st C. A.D.

MOSLEM. See *Mohammedan* and *Mohammedanism*.

MOSQUE. A Mohammedan place of worship.

MOTET. (1) A sacred cantata of several movements. (2) A choral composition with Biblical text.

MOTHER OF GOD. A term applied to Mary, the mother of Jesus (Cath. theol.).

MOTU PROPRIO. A papal decree of binding authority issued by the Pope himself (Cath. theol.).

MOZARABIC LITURGY. A liturgy used by the Christians of Toledo

(Spain) while under the dominion of the Arabs.

MOZETTA. A short hooded cape worn by popes, cardinals, bishops and abbots.

MUFTI. An expounder of Islamic law in Turkey.

MUKTI. See *moksha*.

MÜLLER, FRIEDRICH MAX (1823–1900). Philologist and Orientalist; professor at Oxford. His critical studies of Indian philosophy exercised considerable influence on Western philosophic thought.

MURATORIAN CANON. A list of N.T. writings drawn up apparently about A.D. 170 and edited by Muratori, who discovered it (1740). It includes 4 gospels, Acts, 13 Pauline epistles, 1 John, Jude, the Apocalypse.

MUSIC, CHURCH. From the 1st until the 11th C. the only form of church music was the unaccompanied chant. About the 11th C. the contrapuntal chant was used, sometimes accompanied, and based on the medieval scale system. Towards the end of the 16th C. the modern major and minor scales came into use for solo and chorus music with instrumental accompaniment. It was not until the Reformation that congregational singing came into vogue. (See Walford Davies and Harvey Grace, *Wisdom and Wit of Church Music* (1935).)

MUT. An ancient Egyptian mother-goddess.

MUTAZILITES. A reforming and rationalizing Mohammedan sect of the 9th and 10th C.s.

MYSTERY RELIGIONS. The word "mystery" in this connection is derived from the Gr. *Myein* = to close the eyes and *mystes* = one initiated. The idea involved appears to be closing the eyes to sense-perceptions in order that inner enlightenment may result. There has probably never been an historical age when mystery religions, recognized or unrecognized, did not play their part in leavening the mass of the materialist ideas of the multitude. The chief ancient mysteries were: The Greek Orphic, which appeared in Greece about the 7th C. B.C. The Orphic mysteries were of a theosophic nature. They taught that the physical body is the soul's prison. To attain enlightenment the initiate had to undergo purification of heart and the practice of an ascetic life. The Eleusinian Mysteries had a wide influence in Greece and, later, throughout the Roman Empire. There were two great festivals of initiation: the "Lesser Mysteries" in February and the "Greater Mysteries" in September. A period of purification preceded the initiatory rites which took place in the hall (*telesterion*) from which the public were excluded. What precisely was practised in the *telesterion* is not known since death was the penalty for revealing initiation secrets. Probably some kind of emblematic dramatic performance was enacted and powerful psychic forces appear to have been at work. At their best period the Greek Mysteries were undoubtedly a powerful influence inspiring the desire for a good life, sincerity, purity and brotherhood. Illumination (Φωτισμός) was the objective of initiation (see Reitzenstein, *Hellenic Mystery Religions*). This would probably mean that perception passed from the physical to the psychic plane, enabling the faculties of the mind to operate by intuition instead of by ratiocination. The doctrine of a future life, or perhaps more accurately of Timeless Being (q.v.), was part of the initiatory process. "Happy," wrote Pindar, "is he who has seen the Mysteries before he goes below the hollow earth: that man knows the true end of life and its source divine." The Dionysiac Mysteries appear to have been of a more emotional type, but the teaching was in essence the same; as was that also of Cybele and Attis. The later Egyptian cult of Isis and Osiris appears to have emphasized the same teaching of a deathless life. The debt which Christianity owes to the ancient Mysteries is hard to estimate precisely. But the existence of that debt is beyond all question. "The Mysteries influenced Christianity considerably and modified it in some important respects" (Dr. Cheetham, *The Mysteries, Pagan and Christian*). It is probable that Masonic ritual is an anachronistic survival from the ancient Mysteries, but the inner meaning and the psychic forces behind the movement have faded. (See also Farnell, *Cults of the Greek States*; and (for the esoteric side) John M. Pryse, *The Adorers of Dionysus* (1925).)

MYSTICISM. The generic name given to a type of religion which aims at direct experience of God or Reality. In all religions, East and West, mysticism has had its exponents. The mystic is usually more or less in revolt against ecclesiasticism, ritualism and the routine formality of worship. He is individualist and will not be satisfied with anything but direct experience of Reality. The influence wielded by such men as St. Francis of Assisi and St. John of the Cross is due to the changed consciousness for which the mystic works and which he sometimes attains. The change results in the release of subconscious powers and an extraordinary quickening of the intuition. It is true that the ecstasy of the mystic may be misleading in so far as he tries to translate it into words. But for himself the experience is genuine and since the testimony of all the great mystics is, in the main, in agreement, no wise man would venture to deny its reality. The three stages of the Mystic Way are Purgation, Illumination, and Union with the Self (called in the Buddhist system Nirvana). But the mystic may experience intimations of these stages (or states) concurrently. The outstanding mystics of the West are: Plotinus (A.D. 205–65); Dionysius the Areopagite (5th C.); John Scotus Erigena (A.D. 810–880); St. Francis of Assisi (1182–1226); Meister Eckhart (1260–1327); John Tauber

(1330–61); Thomas à Kempis and (more ecclesiastically minded) St. Teresa (1515–82); St. John of the Cross (1542–91); St. Francis de Sales (1567–1622). Also (with strong Protestant bias) Jacob Boehme (1575–1624); George Fox (1624–91); William Law (1686–1761). (See Rufus M. Jones, *Studies in Mystical Religion* (1909); William James, *The Varieties of Religious Experience*; Evelyn Underhill, *Practical Mysticism*; Sir Francis Younghusband, *Modern Mystics* (1935).)

MYTHOLOGY. The collection of legends and fables handed down from primitive times. The most beautiful, poetic and significant of such stories are those of early Greece. (See (for the Cupid and Psyche myth) Apuleius, *The Golden Ass*; and for an interesting interpretation of certain myths, Francis Bacon's *Wisdom of the Ancients.*)

N

NAAMAN. A Syrian general (O.T.) who applied to the prophet Elisha for relief from the leprosy with which he was afflicted. (See 2 Kings v. i.)

NABONASSAR. Founder of the Chaldean or Babylonian kingdom and the first of his dynasty.

NABOTH. An Israelite of Jezreel whose vineyard King Ahab coveted. Naboth refused to sell, and Jezebel, Ahab's wife, solved the problem by causing Naboth to be stoned to death (1 Kings xxi.).

NAGAS. Hindu serpent-worshippers (*naga* = serpent). See *serpent.*

NAG'S HEAD CONSECRATION. On the passing of the Act of Uniformity in Elizabeth's reign difficulty arose concerning the consecration of Matthew Parker as archbishop of Canterbury, all the bishops having resigned their sees. Parker was finally consecrated by four of the deposed bishops at Lambeth. Romish writers wickedly asserted that Parker had been consecrated at the Nag's Head Tavern, Cheapside. The story was refuted by Burnet.

NAHUM, PROPHECY OF. The 34th book of the O.T. It is of high poetical value and appears to date from the 7th C. B.C. The writer was probably a native of Nineveh. (See A. B. Davidson, *Nahum, Habakkuk and Zephaniah* (1896).)

NAIADS. Nymphs of fountains, lakes and streams (Gr. myth.).

NANAK, BABA. See *Sikhs, Religion of the.*

NANDI. A goddess of joy (Hindu myth.).

NANTES, EDICT OF (1598). A decree of Henri IV of France, granting freedom of worship to Huguenots. Louis XIV repealed it in 1685.

NARAKA. The Hindu hell. It has eight divisions for the punishment of different kinds of sinners.

NARTHEX. A portico in early Christian churches (archit.).

NASI. President of the Jewish Sanḥedrin.

NATURE and NATURE-WORSHIP. Nature may be defined as the established order and growth of all things in the universe. Man's attitude to Nature varies with varying conditions of culture and consciousness. To the Hebrews and early Christians Nature, in the objective, scientific and mystical sense, did not exist. When they thought of the matter at all they conceived of man and animals as "living"; trees, plants, stones, etc., as "dead." The ancient Greeks were wiser and more intuitive. Their thought was clearly voiced by Marcus Aurelius when he exclaimed: "O Natura, from thee are all things, in thee are all things, to thee all things return." In the Greek mysteries of Persephone, Nature as a living force is clearly recognized. All things are pulsating with life, no matter how inert they appear to the senses. The same truth was taught in the Orphic Mysteries.

The modern is at great disadvantage in understanding Nature and natural processes. Relying on pure intellect, he reaches a region where pure intellect is not enough, and his impoverished condition fails to respond to that

Sense sublime—
Of something far more deeply interfused,
Whose dwelling is the light of setting suns,
And the round ocean, and the living air,
And the blue sky, and in the mind of man:
A motion and a spirit, that impels
All thinking things, all objects of all thought,
And rolls through all things.

(See Rudolf Otto, *Naturalism and Religion*; Max Müller, *Natural Religion*; Dr. William Temple, *Nature, Man and God* (1935).)

NAVE. The middle of a church, between the two aisles.

NAYLER, JAMES (1617–60). Quaker theologian, writer and preacher.

NAZARITES. A sect of Jewish ascetics of N.T. times who took a vow against strong drink, etc.

NAZARENES. (1) Followers of Jesus of Nazareth—a title bestowed in contempt. (2) An early Christian sect (1st to 4th C.s). (3) A sect of primitive Christians in U.S.A.

NAZARETH. A town of ancient Palestine some 60 miles north of Jerusalem. Jesus Christ spent much of his time there—hence the title "Jesus of Nazareth" (Mark xvi. 6).

NEBUCHADNEZZAR. King of Babylon c. 600 B.C. (2 Kings xxiv. 1).

NECKHAM, ALEXANDER (1157–1217). Foster-brother of Richard Cœur de Lion and a noted scholar and lecturer in Paris and in England. Became abbot of Cirencester and wrote several works in Latin verse (*De Naturis Rerum*; *De Contemptu Mundi*).

NECK-VERSE (Psalm lxxi. 1). "Have mercy upon me, O God, according to thy lovingkindness . . ." So called because it was the trial verse of those claiming Benefit of Clergy. If they could read it the justice said *Legit ut*

clericus and they were set at liberty.

NECROLATRY. Worship of the dead. See *ancestor-worship.*

NECROMANCY. Divination by questioning the spirits of the dead. It was a method used among all primitive people; in Greece and Rome and by the Jews and early Christians. The spiritualists of to-day continue the practice. See *Spiritualism.*

NEGRO CHURCH OF AMERICA. The first Negro churches were established in U.S.A. in 1776. The work of education among the Negroes hardly began before the Proclamation of Emancipation. They have now some hundreds of schools and colleges.

NEHEMIAH, BOOK OF. The O.T. book of Nehemiah properly forms part of the book of Ezra. Little is known of the author. See *Ezra.*

NEMESIS. The goddess of vengeance or retributive justice (Gr. myth.). See also *Karma.*

NEOPHYTE. (1) A person recently initiated. See *Mystery Religions.* (2) A newly baptized person in the early Church. (3) A newly ordained priest or monk (Cath.).

NEO-PLATONISM. A system of philosophy which combined Platonic with Oriental and Christian elements. It originated at Alexandria (3rd C. A.D.) with Ammonius Saccas and was developed by Porphyry, Plotinus, Proclus and others. (See C. Bigg, *Neoplatonism*; Thomas Whittaker, *The Neoplatonists.*)

NEPTUNE. God of the sea (L. myth.).

NEREIDS. Sea nymphs (Gr. myth.).

NERGAL. Babylonian sun-god, regarded in the two aspects of benevolence and malevolence.

NERI, SAINT PHILIP. See *Oratorians.*

NESTORIUS and NESTORIANS. Nestorius was patriarch of Constantinople from A.D. 428 to 431. He denied the union of divinity and humanity in the single personality of Christ. Christ, he said, had two natures, human and divine. He objected to the term Theotokos ("Mother of God") applied to the Virgin Mary, which, he asserted, wrongly inferred that God, the Logos, had been born of the Virgin. Nestorius was condemned and deposed at the Council of Ephesus in 431.

NE TEMERE. A decree of Pope Pius X promulgated in 1907. It announced that baptized Catholics can be married only before a Catholic priest and two witnesses. A non-Catholic who marries a Catholic must promise not to interfere with the other partner's practice of religion and to rear children of the marriage in the Catholic faith.

NEW ENGLAND THEOLOGY. A type of Christianity cultivated in the Congregational churches of U.S.A. from 1750 to 1900. Its aim was to harmonize Christian theology with reason.

NEW JERUSALEM, CHURCH OF. The Church established by the followers of Emanuel Swedenborg (q.v.).

NEWMAN, FRANCIS WILLIAM (1805–97). Scholar and theologian, brother of Cardinal Newman. Both brothers had an evangelical upbringing. Francis William developed towards eclecticism and scepticism. His chief book was *Phases of Faith* (1850). (See I. G. Sieveking, *F. W. Newman* (1909).)

NEWMAN, JOHN HENRY (1801–90). A clergyman of the Church of England who became one of the leaders of the Oxford Movement (q.v.). Coming in conflict with the ecclesiastical authorities, he retired to his parish at Littlemore. In 1845 he joined the Catholic Church. He was made a Cardinal in 1879. Many fine hymns were written by him, the best known being " Lead, kindly Light." (See E. A. Abbott, *Life of J. H. Newman*; Lytton Strachey, *Eminent Victorians*.)

NEW TESTAMENT. See *Bible* (*N.T.*).

NEW THOUGHT. A somewhat vague term to cover religious views (supposed to be " new ") of an eclectic type. Theosophy in England and the writings of Emerson, R. W. Trine and Orison Swett Marden in U.S.A. all contributed to the New Thought Movement. Its distinguishing features are vigorous optimism, a re-affirmation of the best in all religions and philosophies and a distaste for traditional ecclesiastical dogmatism.

NEWTON, JOHN. Anglican clergyman who collaborated with William Cowper in composing the Olney Hymns (" Glorious things of thee are spoken," etc.).

NICEA. See *Church Councils*.

NICENE CREED. See *Creeds*.

NICHIREN (A.D. 1222–82). A reformer of Buddhism in Japan. A man of saintly life who emphasized the need for meditation and a high ethical standard of conduct.

NICODEMUS. A well-to-do Pharisee who became a follower of Jesus Christ (John iii. 1).

NICODEMUS, GOSPEL OF. An apocryphal gospel containing *The Acts of Pilate* and *The Descent of Christ to the Underworld*. See *Apocrypha* (*N.T.*).

NIETZSCHE, FRIEDRICH WILHELM 1844–1900). Brilliant German philosopher of iconoclastic views. Highly emotional by temperament, he became less and less balanced until his reason gave way and he died insane. He was in continual revolt against the ideas of his time. He attacked Christianity because he thought it encouraged the weakling and degenerate. He attacked the State because it cramped individual development. He attacked democracy for its subservience to authority. He preached a doctrine of " the Superman " and the " Will to power." Though his writings were brilliant they lacked depth and subtlety. His contemporary influence was out of all proportion to his importance as a thinker. (See A. M. Ludovici, *Who is to be Master of the World? An Introduction to the Philosophy of Friedrich Nietzsche* (1909).)

NIMBUS. A halo or aura of light surrounding the heads of saints in religious paintings.

NIMROD. The founder of Babel (Gen. x. 8–10).

NINEVEH. The capital of Assyria (2 Kings xix. 36) and rival of Babylon.

NIRVANA. In Buddhism the supreme condition of being. It is consciousness unobscured by the darkness of unconsciousness. From the emotional aspect it is pure bliss unaffected by sorrow. "There is, disciples, a Realm devoid of earth and water, fire and air. It is not endless space, nor infinite thought, nor nothingness, neither ideas nor non-ideas. Not this world nor that is it. I call it neither a coming nor a departing, nor a standing still, nor death, nor birth; it is without a basis, progress or a stay; it is the ending of sorrow" (Gautama, the Buddha).

NOAH. Legendary Jewish patriarch, the ninth in descent from Adam (Matt. xxiv. 37). In medieval legend, Noah's wife entered the Ark unwillingly after a quarrel with her husband.

NOCTURNE. A service in the early church at midnight and daybreak.

NOMINALISM. The view that regards ideas as mere names—not (as Plato taught) realities. See also *Occam, William of.*

NON-COMMUNICATING ATTENDANCE. The practice of certain Anglican "high churches" for the congregation to be present during celebration of Holy Communion while not partaking of the sacraments.

NONCONFORMITY. Refusal to accept certain doctrines. Nonconformists are those who, disagreeing with the doctrines of the Church of England, have set up churches of their own. The passing of the Act of Uniformity in 1662 led to the withdrawing of some 2,000 clergy from the Church of England who refused to use the Book of Common Prayer. The term Nonconformist was applied to these men and was gradually extended to include other dissenting bodies. The Toleration Act of 1689 relieved Nonconformists from much oppressive legislation. Further privileges were extended to them throughout the 18th and 19th C.s. In 1871 the barriers against them at Oxford and Cambridge were swept away and in 1880 they obtained the right of burial in consecrated churchyards.

NONES. See *Breviary.*

NONJURORS. A group of clergy, English and Scottish, who refused to swear allegiance to William and Mary in 1689, holding themselves still bound by their oath of allegiance to the deposed King James II.

NON-RESISTANCE. The doctrine of those who regard warfare as unjustified under any circumstances. Such an attitude is usually based on Christ's teaching in the Sermon on the Mount (Matt. v.), which is the severest condemnation of war—private, public, civil and international—ever expressed and the most completely and persistently disregarded by all Christian nations, churches and sects with the exception of the Quakers.

NORMAN ARCHITECTURE. The round-arched style prevailing in England from 1066 to c. 1200.

NORNS. The three Scandinavian Fates, Urd, Verdande and Skuld (Past, Present and Future). They determine the destinies of men. Cf. the Greek sisters—Clotho, Lachesis and Atropos.

NOTRE DAME. The magnificent cathedral of Paris, begun in 1163.

NOVATIAN and NOVATIANISM. Novatian was the first antepope, a Roman presbyter elected Pope in 251 in opposition to Pope Cornelius. The schism arose out of Novatian's protest against the readmission to the Catholic Church of those who had lapsed during the Decian persecutions. Novatian suffered martyrdom under Valerian.

NOVENA. A nine-days' devotion with intent to obtain a request from the Virgin or a saint (Cath.).

NOVICE. One who has entered a convent or monastery but not yet taken the vows.

NOWEL (NOËL). Synonym for Christmas, of French derivation.

NUDISM. A health movement advocating exposure of the body to light and air. Many nudist colonies have been established recently in England, America and on the Continent. Unlike the Gymnosophists (q.v.), they practise no particular philosophy except the pursuit of physical health and—since sunlight, in excess, can be as hurtful as, in moderation, it can be beneficial—they frequently miss it.

NUMBER, GOLDEN. See *golden number*.

NUMEN. Roman term for the life, power or spirit in all things. There were gods (*numina*) of trees, rivers, fields, etc. Cf. *mana*.

NUN. A female member of a religious house who takes certain vows.

NUNC DIMITTIS. The Song of Simeon (Luke ii. 29–32) which forms part of the Anglican liturgy.

NUNCIO. A papal ambassador. See *legate*.

NUT. In ancient Egypt the sky-goddess, separated from Geb, her husband (the earth), by Shu (the air).

NYMPHS. Fairy beings who inhabit mountains, rivers, trees, etc. (Gr. myth.). See Maurice Hewlett, *The Lore of Proserpine*, for a delicate handling of fairy faith.

NYAYA. The Hindu system of logic.

O

OATH. See *vow.*

OBIISM. The practice of sorcery among the negroes of the W. Indies and U.S.A.

OBIT. A register of deaths in a monastery.

OBLATE. (1) One devoted to a monastery but not under its vows. (2) A child handed over to a monastery to be reared as a monk (Cath.).

OBLATION. Gifts of bread and wine offered for the eucharist in the early Church were called the *Great Oblation.* The offertory was called the *Lesser Oblation.*

OBSESSION. (1) In psychology, an idea that obstinately persists in the mind. (2) In spiritualism, control of the medium by an external entity.

OCCAM (or **OCKHAM**), **WILLIAM OF** (c. 1280–1349). A Franciscan who taught Nominalism (q.v.). Occam held that scientific verification of faith is impossible, theology not being a science but an infused faith.

OCCULTISM. Esoteric doctrine or knowledge of laws, forces and causes below or above the threshold of normal consciousness. Magic, alchemy, astrology are branches of occultism. Theosophy and Brahmanism enter the territory of the occult at certain points, so also does science when concerned with psychic phenomena, and all religions in so far as they deal with the phenomena of mysticism. (See Julian Franklyn, *A Survey of the Occult* (1935).

OCKHAM. See *Occam.*

OCTAVE. (1) The eighth day after a festival, counting the feast-day itself (Cath.). (2) An interval of twelve semi-tones (mus.).

ODIN (**WODEN**). The saviour-god of Norse mythology. He was, by his own desire, hanged on a tree for the salvation of men. "I know I was hanged upon the tree shaken by the winds for nine long nights. I was transfixed by a spear; I was vowed to Odin, myself to myself" (Havamal). (See *Dictionary of Non-Classical Mythology* (Everyman series); Carlyle, *Heroes and Hero Worship.*)

OFFERING. A ritual sacrifice. The Israelites, in common with other primitive tribes, had an elaborate system of ritual sacrifices—bloody and bloodless, meat-offerings, drink-offerings, burnt-offerings, etc. (See S. A. Cook, *Religion of Ancient Palestine.*)

OFFERTORY. (1) Money collected at a religious service. (2) The verses or anthem sung while the collection is made. (3) The prayers said by the priest over the sacred elements in celebrating Mass.

OFFICE. A religious service with prescribed liturgy.

OFFICE, HOLY. See *Inquisition.*

OIL, HOLY. Consecrated oil for the service of religion. Holy oil is used in the Catholic Church at baptism, confirmation and for anointing the sick. See *extreme unction.*

OLD CATHOLICS. The title taken by a number of Catholics in Munich and other parts of Germany and Switzerland who separated from the Catholic Church in 1870. They objected to the new dogma of papal infallibility promulgated by Pope Pius IX. (See W. J. S. Simpson, *Roman Catholic Opposition to Papal Infallibility* (1909).)

OLD TESTAMENT. See *Bible* (*O.T.*).

OLIVES, MOUNT OF (OLIVET). The hill, planted with olives, which overlooked Jerusalem. Here Jesus rested with His disciples on the way to Gethsemane. The olive has been a symbol of peace from remote antiquity.

OLIVETANS. An order of Benedictine monks founded in 1313 by Bernard Tolomei at Monte Oliveto, near Siena.

OLYMPUS. A mountain in Thessaly, the traditional abode of the Greek gods.

OM. A mystic symbol of India on which the Hindus of all sects meditate. It is also spelt " aum " and in this form symbolizes many speculations connected with the number three —the three worlds, the three bodies of the Buddhas, etc. In this small word the Hindus find a symbol of infinite subtlety and power; it is a key to Reality, the divine creative force or Logos, the all-creating vibration out of which natural phenomena arise. (See F. A. Barth, *The Religions of India*; Talbot Munday, *Om* (a romance, but written with a sympathetic understanding of Hindu thought).)

ONTOLOGY. The philosophy that treats of pure being (Gr. *on, ontos* = being). Kant saw that it was futile to attempt to define Pure Being or Reality, and since his time the old " ontological argument " of theologians such as Augustine, Anselm, etc., has fallen into disuse. Modern philosophy realizes that there is no possibility of contact with that-which-is, by means of the knowing process or sense perceptions.

OPHITES. An early sect of Gnostics (q.v.) who, in common with the Egyptians and Babylonians, attached religious and symbolic importance to the serpent (Gr. *ophis*). Their doctrines were a mingling of pagan and Christian thought. (See King, *The Gnostics and Their Remains* (1887).)

OPUS OPERATUM. A term used in Catholic theology to indicate the grace which flows from the sacramental act (*ex opere operato*) independent of the faith of those who receive or the merit of him who administers.

ORACLE. Among the ancient Greeks the god or goddess

worshipped in certain temples was believed to answer questions of worshippers. The Oracle of Delphi was the most famous. Similar phenomena are claimed by the Spiritualists (q.v.) to-day. See *divination*; *clairaudience*.

ORANGE, WILLIAM PRINCE OF (1533–84). A German prince who was the soul of the resistance of the Protestant states of the Netherlands against the cruel oppressions of the Catholic Philip II of Spain and his general, Alva. William, nicknamed "the Silent" (a curious misnomer), was one of the most lovable and most heroic characters the 16th C. produced. His religious tolerance was extraordinary (in a religious man) and his courage has probably never been surpassed. He was assassinated by an agent of Philip II in 1584. (See Ruth Putman, *William the Silent* (1911); Frederick Harrison, *William the Silent*.)

ORATORIANS. Congregations, oratories, in the Catholic Church first established by St. Philip Neri (1515–95) to assist the Counter-Reformation (q.v.). Members take no vows and are free to leave at any time.

ORATORIO. A sacred story set to music and performed by soloists, chorus and full orchestra. So called from the Oratory of the Church of Sta Maria in Vallicella, Rome, where such performances first took place. (16th C.)

ORDEAL. A method in ancient and medieval times of determining the guilt or innocence of an accused person by the test of fire, water, etc. If the fire burnt or he failed to float in water he was adjudged guilty, since God had not attested otherwise.

ORDERS, HOLY. See *holy orders*.

ORDERS, RELIGIOUS. Societies of men or women living under a religious rule. They are found in many religions, e.g. Buddhism, Christianity, Shintoism, etc. St. Basil established a house of Christian monks in 359. St. Benedict built his monastery on Monte Cassino in 529. In the 13th C. many orders were formed—Franciscans, Dominicans, Carmelites, etc. See *monasticism*.

ORDINAL. (1) An annual guide for the canonical services throughout the year (Cath.). See *Breviary*. (2) In the Anglican Prayer Book the liturgy for ordination of bishops, priests and deacons.

ORDINARY, AN. A bishop is so called by right of his jurisdiction within his diocese.

ORDINARY OF THE MASS. The fixed order for saying Mass.

ORDINATION. Admission to the Christian ministry by the laying on of hands of a bishop in the Catholic, Greek and Anglican churches. Such laying on of hands is not practised in dissenting churches.

OREAD. A mountain nymph (Gr. myth.).

ORENDA. A word used among the Iroquois Indians for the life-force in all objects. Cf. *mana*; *numen*.

ORIGEN (A.D. 182–251). The most distinguished theologian of the early church, of deep and wide influence. He taught at Alexandria and Caesarea. His death at Tyre was hastened by tortures inflicted under Decius. He was influenced by Greek philosophy, especially Plato, and by Gnosticism (q.v.); he was in fact a speculative philosopher first and a theologian afterwards. Many of his views came to be regarded as heretical, e.g. the pre-existence of the soul, the eternal creation of the world and his gnostic interpretation of the Fall. He was a prolific author and an indefatigable worker. (See H. F. Hort, *Six Lectures on the Ante-Nicene Fathers* (1895); S. P. Black, *Early Christianity* (*Paul to Origen*).)

ORIGINAL SIN. The orthodox Christian doctrine of the depravity of man's nature due to the transmitted sin of Adam. Ideas derived from the theory of evolution have made it hard for a number of Christians to accept this doctrine. The Buddhist view that man's ego is the result of many births in many forms, is more in line with modern scientific thought than the Christian doctrine of original sin.

ORMUZD (**ORMAZD**; **AHURA MAZDA**). The supreme God of the early Persians, holy, merciful, eternal, creator of the world. By later development he became the good principle as opposed to the bad (Ahriman). (See A. V. W. Jackson, *Religion of Ancient Persia* (Religions A. and M.).)

ORNAMENTS. C. of E. Prayer Book term for all the articles used in the church services.

ORPHEUS. " The fable of Orpheus . . . seems to hold out a picture of universal philosophy. . . . For the labours of Orpheus exceed the labours of Hercules, both in power and dignity, as the works of knowledge exceed the works of strength. . . . Philosophy making men forget their unbridled passions and affections . . . so that they soon after build themselves habitations, form cities, cultivate lands, plant gardens. . . . So that they may not improperly be said to remove and call the trees and stones together " (Francis Bacon, *Wisdom of the Ancients*). Cf.

> Orpheus' lute was strung with poet's sinews,
> Whose golden touch could soften steel and stones,
> Make tigers tame and huge leviathans
> Forsake unsounded deeps to dance on sands.
>
> *Two Gentlemen of Verona*, iii. 2.

ORPHISM. See *Mystery Religions*.

ORPHREYS. Rich embroidery attached to vestments (eccles.).

ORTHODOXY. The affirmation of beliefs and dogmas believed to be eternally true by a church or party.

OSCULATORY. A tablet containing a picture of Christ or the Virgin which was kissed by the priest or the people.

OSIRIS. Ancient Egyptian saviour-god, and god of the dead. "The old Egyptians celebrated the resurrection of Osiris by a sacrament, eating the sacred cake or wafer after it had been consecrated by the priest, and thereby becoming veritable flesh of his flesh" (W. Williamson, *The Great Law*). See also *Egypt, Religion of*, § 2.

OSTIARIUS. The doorkeeper of a church or monastery (Cath.).

OVERALL, DR. JOHN. Dean of St. Paul's during the reign of James I. "Overall and Lancelot Andrews . . . were the most learned men of a generation in which extensive reading was more general among the higher clergy than it has ever been since" (Mark Pattison in *Ency. Brit.*). They both assisted in preparing the Authorized Version of the Bible (1611). Dr. Overall's wife was reputed "the greatest beauty of her time in England and had the loveliest eyes that ever were seen, but wondrous wanton." To her were written the delightful verses:

Downe lay the shepherd swaine so sober and demur,
Wishing for his wench again so bonny and so pure,
With his head on hillock lowe and his arms akimboe,
And all was for the loss of his hye nonny nonny noe.

OWEN, JOHN (1616–83). English Nonconformist divine, an able preacher and man of wide learning. Chosen to preach before parliament the day after King Charles's execution, he fulfilled his delicate task with admirable tact and without directly mentioning the event. (See James Moffatt, *The Golden Book of John Owen* (1904).)

OWEN, ROBERT (1771–1858). The first English Socialist. His aim was to establish society on a co-operative basis. (See Frank Podmore, *Life of Robert Owen*.)

OXFORD MOVEMENT. A 19th-C. movement in the Church of England directed to rousing the Church to greater activity and introducing many doctrines and practices of the Catholic Church (e.g. the Real Presence, the Eucharistic Sacrifice, Auricular confession, etc.). The leaders of the movement were a group of Oxford men: Froude, Palmer, Mozley, Keble, Percival, Ward, Pusey and Newman. Petitions were presented to the archbishop of Canterbury and a series of "Tracts for the Times" was published, dealing with doctrine and worship and inspired by Romanizing tendencies. Tract No. 90 (seeking to prove that the Thirty-Nine Articles are capable of an interpretation entirely in harmony with Catholic dogma) produced a violent storm. Many who had joined the movement seceded. Newman, followed by many friends, joined the Catholic Church. The result of the agitation was the coming into being of the modern High Church Party advocating a nearer approach in doctrine and ritual to Rome. (See R. W. Church, *The Oxford Movement*; G. H. F. Nye, *The Story of the Oxford Movement* (non-controversial).)

OYOMEI. The Chinese philosophy of Wang Yang Ming (q.v.). (15th C.)

P

PACHOMIUS (292–346). Egyptian monk and founder of the cenobite or monastic system. He organized many monasteries.

PACIFIST. One who believes that all controversies can and should be settled by mutual agreement without recourse to violence. Christ and Buddha condemned anger and the violence to which it leads. Pacifism gained enormous impetus from the Great War, which was a vivid object-lesson on the stupidity, futility and barbarity of war. For proof, see the spate of "war-books" (novels, etc.), published between 1927 and 1931. See *War, Fundamental Causes of.*

PAGAN and **PAGANISM.** Term applied by the early Christians to those who refused to adopt the new faith. (From *paganus* = a rustic, a heathen or heath-dweller, the country-folk being slower to change their habits of worship than the town-dwellers.)

PAINE, THOMAS (1737–1809). English democrat and rationalist. Author of *The Rights of Man* and *The Age of Reason.* (See M. D. Conway, *Thomas Paine.*)

PALESTINE EXPLORATION FUND. English society founded in 1865 for the conducting of scientific research in the Holy Land. Headquarters: 2 Hinde Street, Manchester Square, London, W.1.

PALEY, WILLIAM (1743–1805). English theologian. His *Evidences of Christianity,* a long ago out-of-date Christian apologetic, was, until recently, one of the chief subjects for the entrance examination to Cambridge University.

PALL. (1) A chalice-cover (Cath.). (2) The cloth covering a coffin.

PALLIUM. A white scarf with six black crosses worn by the Pope and by certain archbishops on whom it is bestowed.

PALM SUNDAY. The Sunday before Easter commemorating Christ's entry into Jerusalem when palm-branches were strewn in his way by the multitude.

PAN. The pastoral god of ancient Greece, representing Nature (Gr. *pan* = all). "This fable is perhaps the noblest of all antiquity and pregnant with the mysteries and secrets of nature. Pan, as the name imports, represents the universe. . . . Echo makes a most excellent wife for Pan, as being no other than genuine philosophy, which faithfully repeats his words . . . thus representing the true image and reflection of the world without adding a tittle" (Francis Bacon, *Wisdom of the Ancients*).

PANTHEISM. The doctrine that Nature and the Universe are manifestations of God. Pantheism regards creation not as an act in time but as an extratemporal process. Brahmanism and Neo-Platonism, which look upon the world as an aspect of the Infinite, tend towards pantheism. Spinoza (q.v.) is regarded as the greatest of modern pantheistic philosophers. (See John Hunt, *Pantheism and Christianity* (o.p.).)

PAPACY and POPES. The Christian Church began as a simple democratic society held together by common beliefs. It grew into a powerful religious monarchy ruled by the bishop of Rome. During the first three centuries, in place of the Papacy, we find five patriarchates, those of Constantinople, Rome, Jerusalem, Alexandria, and Antioch. The gradually acquired primacy of Rome arose out of the following circumstances:

1. The political and geographical position of Rome as the chief seat of government in the ancient world.

2. The invasion of Italy by the barbarians, Alaric and Attila, and the veneration with which popes like Innocent I and Leo the Great, who withstood them, came to be regarded.

3. The missionary zeal of Rome which resulted in converted Saxons, Germans, Gauls, etc., making pilgrimage to "The Holy City."

Gregory the Great (Pope from 590 to 604) is the earliest bishop of Rome to whom the name Pope can be justly applied.

By the 8th C. it looked as though the Pope would become firmly established as head of a Church extending from Antioch to the British Isles. This was prevented by rivalry and difference of opinion between the bishop of Rome and the Byzantine or Eastern Church. The Eastern Church denounced the use of images as idolatrous. Rome made this the *casus belli.* It resulted that in the 11th C. the Christian Church split into the Greek or Eastern Church and the Latin, Roman or Catholic Church.

In the West, however, the power of the Papacy steadily increased. Two famous documents, the Donation of Constantine and the False Decretals, became foundation-stones of the papal claims. The Donation of Constantine was a fabrication asserting that Constantine the Great bestowed on the Pope and his successors the sovereignty over Italy and the countries of the West. The False Decretals declared that the bishop of Rome had exercised sovereign power as early as the 1st and 2nd C.s. Both documents are now acknowledged by all scholars, Catholic and Protestant, to be forgeries.

Assisted by these documents and by the importance of Rome as the great European Court of Appeal, the Papacy had attained, in the 10th C., a world-wide power.

§ 2. When Otto the Great (mid 10th C.) established "the Holy Roman Empire," the two world powers, emperor and priest, entered upon the struggle for supremacy that lasted for centuries.

It came to a swift climax when Gregory VII (Hildebrand) by reforms within the Church and a vigorous policy of interference, raised the Papacy to a paramount position in Europe. "The time has gone by," it was boasted by one of the popes of this period, "when the Church could say, 'Silver and gold have I none.'" "Yes," came the quick rejoinder, "and the time has gone by when Peter could say, 'Arise and walk.'"

Henry IV of Germany opposed the policy of Gregory. He was put under an interdict with the result that he had to sue for pardon to the Pope; he was compelled to do it thoroughly, standing in sackcloth for three days in the snow outside the Pope's Apennine castle at Canossa. Henry had his revenge when he drove Gregory to exile and to death at Salerno.

The power of the popes continued to increase and it was not until Philip the Fair of France opposed Pope Boniface VIII (1294–1303) that the world-power of the Papacy began to crumble. Philip declared that the Pope had no political authority in France. Excommunication was threatened, but the Pope died before it could be put in force. In 1309 Philip the Fair removed the papal chair from Rome to Avignon, where it remained until 1378.

§ 3. From this "Babylonian captivity" in France the Papacy never completely recovered. In 1378 the Roman factions elected their own Pope and thus the Church had two representatives of St. Peter—one at Avignon and the other at Rome. In 1409 a general council assembled at Pisa to consider the situation. Both popes were deposed and another, Alexander V, was elected. But the deposed pontiffs refused to accept the council's ruling and now there were three pontifical representatives of St. Peter. It was therefore found necessary in 1414 to call another council. It met at Constance. Two of the claimants were successfully deposed and one resigned. A new pope, Martin V, was elected, and the Christian world was again united under a single head. But these events had destroyed the universal reverence for the Holy See. Kings and princes were henceforth the Pope's equals, not his vassals.

§ 4. The activity of the Papacy was perforce confined more and more to the spiritual sphere. Even this was greatly weakened by the Protestant Reformation which deprived the Pope of about half of his supporters. Nevertheless, despite Modernism (q.v.) and Scientific enquiry, the Papacy is still an active power in the Western world. "The Papacy," wrote Macaulay grandiloquently, "was great and respected before Saxon had set foot on Britain, before the Frank had passed the Rhine, when Grecian eloquence still flourished in Antioch, when idols were still worshipped in the temple of Mecca. And she may still exist in undiminished vigour when some traveller from New Zealand shall, in the midst of a vast solitude, take his stand on a broken arch of London Bridge to sketch the ruins of St. Paul's."

Anatole France took a different view. Two fictitious characters projected into the year A.D. 2270, discuss religion:

"'To mention France only, we have the religion of humanity, positivism, Christianity, and Spiritualism. In some countries there are still some Catholics, but they are few and split up into sects, as the result of schisms which occurred in the 20th C., when Church and State drifted apart. For a long time now there has not been any Pope.'

"'You are mistaken,' said Michel. 'There is still a Pope. It is by a mere chance that I know of him. He is Pius XXV, dyer, Via dell' Orso, in Rome.'

"'What!' I exclaimed, 'the Pope is a dyer!'

"'What is there surprising about that! He must perforce have a trade, just as everybody else.'

"'But his Church?'

"'He is recognized by a few thousands in Europe.'"

(*The White Stone.*)

Perhaps Macaulay's breezy optimism requires to be balanced by Anatole France's subtle pessimism; or vice versa, according to the point of view. (See James Bryce, *The Holy Roman Empire*; Gregorovius, *History of Rome*; Hallam, *Middle Ages*; Ranke, *History of the Popes*.)

PAPAL STATES (States of the Church). The former temporal possessions of the popes. These were taken away in 1870 on the foundation of the kingdom of Italy. The Pope now possesses only the papal territory in Rome, the Lateran and his country estate at Castel Gandolfo.

PARABLE. A story told to illustrate a doctrine.

PARABOLANUS. A lay assistant in the early Eastern Church.

PARACLETE. The Holy Ghost as comforter and advocate (see John xiv. 16, 26).

PARADISE. See *heaven*.

PARAMITA. The six supreme Buddhist Perfections: love of truth; patience; kindness; courage; balance; unattachment.

PARASCEVE. The eve before the Jewish Sabbath; sometimes applied to Good Friday.

PARISH. The district under one pastor.

PAROUSIA. The N.T. Greek word for Christ's Second Coming.

PARSIS (**PARSEES**). The descendants of the Zoroastrians who fled to India from Persia in the 7th C. during the Mohammedan conquest of Iran. They are monotheists who worship Ormazd, the Good Principle and acknowledge Zoroaster as his prophet. Their Scripture, the Avesta, insists on the need for "good thoughts, words and deeds." See also *Zoroaster*. (See D. F. Karaka, *History of the Parsees*.)

PARSON. Colloquial term for a priest or clergyman. (In American underworld slang he has many other names: e.g. Bible ranter, Fire-escape, Galway, Hallelujah-peddler, Heaven-reacher, Holy-roller, and the brutal Mission-squawker. (See Eric Partridge, *Slang*, p. 30.)

PARSONS, ROBERT (FATHER PARSONS) (1546–1610). English Jesuit priest and political agitator. He became rector of the English College at Rome in 1597. One of the reputed authors of the famous *Leicester's Commonwealth*.

PARVATI. Wife of Shiva (q.v.) (Hindu myth.).

PASCAL, BLAISE (1623–62). French mystic and philosopher. God, he taught, is known through the heart. Famous for his *Pensées*. (See St. Cyres, *Blaise Pascal* (1909).)

PASCH. The Jewish Passover: Easter.

PASCHAL CANDLE. A candle blessed and placed on the Altar the day before Easter (Cath.).

PASCHAL CONTROVERSY. The dispute in the early Church concerning the proper time to celebrate Easter.

PASCHAL LAMB. The lamb slain and eaten at the Jewish Passover.

PASSION OF CHRIST. The sufferings of Jesus during his last days on earth: the agony in the Garden, the betrayal by Judas, the haling before Caiaphas and the Sanhedrin, and then before Pilate, Pilate's washing of hands before the crowd, the scourging and mocking, the journey to Golgotha and Crucifixion. "A chain of causes, which because we cannot follow them might—in the loose language of common life—be called an accident, determined that the part of the dying God in the annual play should be thrust upon Jesus of Nazareth, whom the enemies he had made in high places by his outspoken strictures were resolved to put out of the way" (Sir J. Frazer, *The Golden Bough*, vol. ix—"The Scapegoat"). (Sir James Frazer there deals with the Mystery-plays of earlier religions.)

PASSIONISTS. A Catholic order instituted in Italy (1920) and devoted to the Passion of Christ.

PASSION MUSIC. Music to which words describing the sufferings of Christ are set.

PASSION OFFICES. Special offices to spread devotion for the passion of Christ (Cath.).

PASSION PLAY. See *morality play*.

PASSION SUNDAY. The second Sunday before Easter.

PASSION WEEK. The fifth week in Lent, beginning with Passion Sunday.

PASSOVER. The annual Jewish feast to commemorate the passing of the destroying angel over the Israelites when he slew the first-born of the Egyptians. It lasts a week and begins 15th of Nisan (roughly April).

PASTOR. A clergyman (literally shepherd).

PASTORAL EPISTLES. Those in N.T. to Timothy and Titus.

PASTORAL THEOLOGY. The theology which treats of the pastor's duty to his people.

PATEN. The plate used for the Eucharistic bread.

PATER NOSTER. See *Lord's Prayer*.

PATH, THE NOBLE EIGHTFOLD. The *via sacra* of the Buddhists leading to Nirvana or Enlightenment. This is the middle way —or way of perfection—and has eight stages:

1. *Right Understanding.* (Truth must be sought before all else.)
2. *Right Resolution.* (The determination to attain the highest degree of wisdom.)
3. *Right Speech.* (All words which are not kind, pure and true are forbidden, no matter in what situation a man may be.)
4. *Right Conduct.* (Deeds and words must not spring from likes or dislikes: but only from desire to further the law of love unfailing and goodwill to all.)
5. *Right Living.* (Choosing, as far as may be, a right means of getting a living; avoiding those which entail cruelty to man or beast.)
6. *Right Effort.* (The continual need for going forward in the Path and not resting or falling back: harmony with the great law of life will help Right Effort.)
7. *Right Meditation.* (The mind must be at peace, free of illusion and distortion: this state is attained by Meditation.)
8. *Right Rapture.* (The only true bliss is that of Nirvana—the peace which passes all understanding; and the goal of all effort.)

PATIMOKKA. A code of 227 rules to regulate the life of Buddhist monks.

PATMORE, COVENTRY (1823–96). Catholic poet. Patmore was a civil servant in the British Museum. Best known for his "Angel in the House"—a poem in praise of married love. (See Edmund Gosse, *Coventry Patmore.*)

PATMOS. An island in the Ægean Sea (modern Patimo or Patmosa), whither John the Evangelist is said to have been banished by Domitian and where he wrote the book of Revelation.

PATRIARCH. (1) The head of a family among the early Israelites. (2) The highest officer in the early Christian Church. There were five patriarchates (before the Papacy came into being), situated at Rome, Jerusalem, Antioch, Alexandria and Constantinople. (4th C.)

PATRICK, SAINT (c. 389–461). Traditional patron saint of Ireland.

PATRIMONY OF ST. PETER. The temporal dominions of the Pope. See *Papacy*.

PATRIPASSIANS. An anti-Trinitarian sect of the 2nd and 3rd C.s. They denied the existence of three persons in the Godhead.

PATRISTICS (PATROLOGY). The study of the Church Fathers (q.v.).

PATRON. One who holds the right to appoint to an Anglican benefice.

PATRON SAINTS. Saints regarded as affording special protection to persons, churches, localities, etc.

PATTISON, MARK (1813–84). Scholar who, for a time, assisted the Oxford Movement (q.v.). Remembered for his excellent *Life of Isaac Casaubon.*

PAULICIANS. A dualistic Eastern sect founded c. 660 which allegorized the Christian doctrines and emphasized the Pauline doctrine of the Christ within.

PAUL, SAINT (d. c. A.D. 64). The chief apostle of the early Christian Church. He was born at Tarsus (Cilicia) of Jewish parents. While preparing at Jerusalem to become a rabbi, he came in touch with the Christians whom he violently disliked, taking a share in the persecution of Stephen. Suddenly, near Damascus, he experienced a vision which converted him to Christianity and changed his life. This appears to have been a psychological experience akin to that of Mohammed and many of the saints. Thereafter he entered on a missionary career, preaching in Damascus, Syria and Cilicia, Asia Minor and Greece. He was imprisoned at Caesarea and at Rome and put to death during the reign of Nero. It was due to Paul that Christianity, blended with Greek ideas borrowed from the Mystery Religions (q.v.), ceased to be a Jewish sect and became a world-wide movement. His frequent use of the Mystery language (e.g. " buried with Christ " ; " planted in the likeness of his death," etc.) points to the likelihood that he was an initiate in the Mysteries. "The hellenistic religious literature *must* have been read by him ; he uses its terms and is saturated with its thoughts " (Reitzenstein, *The Hellenistic Mystery Religions*). (See Percy Gardner, *The Religious Experience of St. Paul* ; F. A. Spencer, *Beyond Damascus : A Biography of Paul the Tarsian* (1935).)

PAUL AND THECKLA, ACTS OF. See *Apocrypha* (*N.T.*).

PAX. (1) The kiss of peace (Rom. xvi. 16). (2) An osculatory (q.v.).

PEACE MOVEMENTS. International peace congresses in Europe began with those held in London in 1843, in Paris in 1849 and in Frankfort in 1850. The first International Conference was held at The Hague in 1899. To this conference twenty European countries, four Asiatic, and two American sent delegates. This conference set up a Permanent Court of Arbitration (The Hague Tribunal). It recommended Commissions of Inquiry and all possible offices of mediation. A second Peace Conference was held at The Hague in 1907 which agreed on the necessity for a Court of Arbitration. The Great War put an end to all such attempts, but on 10 January 1920 the League of Nations came into being when peace with Germany was ratified. Its Charter or

Covenant contains 26 Articles, many of which are directed to the prevention and settlement of disputes between nations. Fifty-five nations are members of the League. Japan and Germany withdrew in 1933. The U.S.S.R. was admitted in 1934 and the U.S.A., although refusing to join, co-operates with the League in many of its activities. The League consists of:

(1) An Assembly which meets annually at Geneva and is composed of three representatives from each Member State.

(2) A Council which meets three times a year. Great Britain, France, Italy and U.S.S.R. are permanent members and ten other States are elected annually as temporary members.

(3) A Permanent Court of International Justice, consisting of fifteen judges and four deputy judges, selected for their high legal and moral authority. It sits permanently at The Hague and has already dealt successfully with forty-three disputes.

The work of the League covers a wide ground and deals with many philanthropic and constructive efforts. Viscount Cecil, K.C., is President of the League, and Professor Gilbert Murray, LL.D., is Chairman of the Executive Committee. Headquarters: 15 Grosvenor Crescent, London, S.W.1. See also *War, Fundamental Causes of.*

PEACOCK, REGINALD (c. 1395–1460). English theologian and bishop of Chichester. He came into conflict with his superiors on the subject of the Infallibility of the Church and narrowly escaped the stake. His chief work is *The Repressor of over-much weeting (blaming) of the Clergy* (1455)—a fine example of 15th-C. English. (See John Lewis, *Life of Peacock* (1820).)

PEARSON, JOHN (1613–86). English theologian who became bishop of Chester in 1673. His chief work is the *Exposition of the Creed* (1659), one of the finest productions of English theology.

PECTORAL CROSS. A cross worn by bishops during Mass (Cath.).

PELAGIUS and PELAGIANISM. Pelagius was a Christian monk (c. 360–420) who worked in Rome. He and his followers denied the doctrine of original sin. Pelagianism was condemned by Pope Innocent I.

PENANCE. A Catholic sacrament by which absolution, following confession and satisfaction, is given. See *Absolution.*

PENATÊS. The domestic gods of ancient Rome, worshipped by the householder and his family. Also see *Larês.*

PENITENTIAL. A Catholic book of rules to guide priests in their office as confessors.

PENITENTIAL PSALMS. Psalms suitable for penitents (Psalms vi., xxxii., xxxviii., li., cii., cxxx., cxliii.).

PENN, WILLIAM (1644–1718). English Quaker who founded Pennsylvania, U.S.A. (See Mrs. C.

Grant, *William Penn* (1907), and the *Life* by C. E. Vulliamy.)

PENTATEUCH. The first five books of the O.T.

PENTECOST. (1) Jewish festival held on the fiftieth day after the Passover to commemorate the giving of the Law. (2) Christian festival to commemorate the descent of the Holy Ghost at the Feast of Pentecost (Acts ii.).

PERFECTIONISM (PERFECTIBILITY). The belief that a man may live without sin (yielding to the lower nature), thus attaining moral perfection. The doctrine is taught or inferred in all the great religions, but they differ as to how far divine grace (Tao, Shakti, Buddhi) is necessary. See art. *Religion*, § 7.

PERICOPE. An official selection from the epistles and gospels to be read in churches on Sundays and holy days.

PERPENDICULAR STYLE. The ecclesiastical architecture (14th to 16th C.s) which followed the Decorated style in England.

PERSEPHONE (L. Proserpine). The daughter of Demeter, the earth-mother of Hellenic religion. See *Mystery Religions*.

PERSIA, RELIGION OF. See *Zoroaster*.

PERSON. One of the three hypostases (individualities) in the Christian Trinity.

PERSONALITY. "Personality is the space-time factor which expresses or obstructs individuality. The word is derived from the L. *persona* = a mask. Individuality is essentially calm, steadfast, dynamic and unchanging, although its expression may constantly change. It is the vehicle of Self and responds to monitions from the eternal. The ego is the link between personality on the one hand and individuality and the Self on the other, between the space-time world of change and the unchanging beyond. In evolution the personality reflects the ego, and later (as the ego gradually becomes purified) the Self or Spirit, through the medium of individuality. The selfish, separative and destructive elements of personality are derived from the ego. Ego and personality are products of time and space. The unpurified ego separates consciousness from the whole. It isolates the person. As a result, personality, *especially if strong*, reflects the vices instead of the virtues of individuality. Instead of charity, we have bigotry; instead of the sage, the fanatic. Obstinacy masquerades as will, desire as love, self-interest as sincerity. The personality at this stage is narrow, constricted, selfish" (Meredith Starr).

PETER, ACTS OF. Two apocryphal works, the Catholic Acts and the Gnostic Acts attributed to St. Peter. The Apocalypse of Peter is also ascribed to him. See *Apocrypha* (*N.T.*).

PETER DAMIAN, SAINT (c. 1006–72). Italian Benedictine who did much to reform the monastic life of his time.

PETER, EPISTLES OF. Two N.T. books traditionally ascribed to the apostle Peter. They were addressed to the Jewish Christians scattered abroad (*diaspora*). There is not sufficient external or internal evidence to determine the authorship. (See Prof. Bigg, *Peter and Jude*.)

PETER, GOSPEL OF. An apocryphal gnostic gospel. (2nd C.)

PETER THE HERMIT (d. 1151). A French priest from Amiens said to have aroused crusading enthusiasm in France. Believed by some historians to be a legendary figure. See *Crusades*.

PETER LOMBARD (c. 1100–60). Bishop of Paris and eminent theologian. His *Sentences*, a collection of patriotic sayings, had immense popularity.

PETER, PREACHING OF. A 2nd-C. forgery represented as the work of Peter. It defends Christianity against paganism and Judaism.

PETER, SAINT. The fisherman of Bethsaida who became Jesus' disciple, his name being changed from Simon to Cephas or Peter (Rock). Jesus stayed with Peter and his wife at their house in Capernaum while he was teaching in Galilee. The famous passage in Matthew xvi. 17–19 is beset with critical difficulties. That the Christian sect in its infancy survived was due largely to the strong faith and enthusiasm of Peter who was the first to believe that Jesus had "risen from the dead" (1 Cor. xv. 5). Of his later life nothing is known save the tradition that he suffered martyrdom at Rome under Nero—probably about A.D. 64.

PETER'S PENCE. An English tax of one penny paid to the Pope on St. Peter's Day (1 Aug.) and collected from all families possessed of thirty pence yearly rent in land. It was first collected by Ina (c. 725) and was abolished by Henry VIII in 1534.

PEYOTISM. A religious system of the Red Indians of the northern plains, U.S.A. Peyote is a cactus found in the Rio Grande and used as a ceremonial and medicinal drug. It produces marked spiritual exaltation and is said to be harmless in its effects. Out of its use has grown a church with ritual and officers. (See Vincenzo Petrullo, *The Diabolic Root* (1935).)

PEYYUT. A Jewish liturgical poem added to the regular service on holy days.

PHALLICISM, PHALLISM. Sex-worship, symbolized in the male organ or phallus. Sex-worship of various kinds entered into the pre-Christian and pre-Jewish religions. The extreme asceticism of early Christianity probably resulted from a desire for "reformation" in this respect. Phallicism was a recognized part of the religion of Greeks, Romans and Phoenicians. The worship of the lingam or phallus as a symbol of creative power continues in Hindu temples. (See Edward Carpenter, *Pagan and Christian Creeds*, chap. xii.)

PHARAOH. Egyptian word signifying "sun" and applied to their kings. After the subjugation of Egypt the word "Ptolemy" was substituted for "Pharaoh."

PHARISEES. A Jewish religious sect of 2nd C. B.C. Strict in their observance of the Law and external religious devotion. Their terrible denunciation by Jesus Christ was due to the externality and rigid traditionalism of their religious life and practice.

PHENICIA (PHOENICIA). A province of ancient Syria bordering the Mediterranean and including the seaports of Tyre and Sidon.

PHERENICE. See *Berenice*.

PHILEMON, EPISTLE TO. An epistle of St. Paul to Philemon of Colosse concerning his slave Onesimus. Onesimus had run away and become a Christian. Paul wrote his letter to conciliate Philemon and win pardon for the defaulting slave. (See M. R. Vincent, *Philippians and Philemon* (International Critical Commentaries).)

PHILISTINES. Ancient inhabitants of S.W. Palestine, hostile to the Israelites.

PHILO (c. 20 B.C.–A.D. 50). A learned Jewish scholar of Alexandria. He endeavoured to reconcile Judaism with Greek ethics and philosophy.

PHILOSOPHY. The science of being or the knowledge of the causes and laws of phenomena. Pythagoras first used the term philosopher about 528 B.C. Philosophy may be classified as (1) Moral or Ethical; (2) Intellectual; (3) Natural and Inductive. The chief *Ancient Schools* of Moral and Intellectual philosophy and their approximate dates are: Pythagorean (c. 500 B.C.); Platonic (374 B.C.); Peripatetic (Aristotelian) (334 B.C.); Sceptic (Pyrrho, 334 B.C.); Cynic (Diogenes, 330 B.C.); Epicurean (306 B.C.); Stoic (Zeno, 290 B.C.); Neo-Platonic — combining Christianity with Platonism (Ammonius Saccas, d. A.D. 243) and the Alexandrians Plotinus, Porphyry and Jamblichus (d. A.D. 333).

The chief *Modern Systems* are: Rational and Inductive (Bacon, c. 1624); Cartesian (Descartes, c. 1560); Perceptive (Locke, c. 1690); Idealistic (Berkeley, c. 1710, and Leibnitz); Transcendental (Kant, Hamilton, etc., 1770–1860); Absolute Idealism (Hegel, 1810–30); Utilitarian (Bentham, Mill, etc., 1790–1873); Positivism (Comte, 1830); Evolutionary Realism (Darwin, Herbert Spencer, etc., 1873); Philosophy of Consciousness (including the unconscious), Archibald Weir (Self, 1926).

The chief Inductive philosophers are: Thales (c. 600 B.C.); Pythagoras (590 B.C.); Ptolemy (A.D. 150); Ben Musa and the Arabians (c. A.D. 800); Roger Bacon (1266); Copernicus (1543); Kepler (1618); Francis Bacon (*Novum Organum*, 1620); Newton (1687); Laplace (1775); Faraday (1831); Einstein (b. 1879).

PHOENICIA. See *Phenicia.*

PHOTIUS (c. 820–91). Patriarch of Constantinople. A man of great learning who contested the rival claims of Rome under Pope Nicholas I.

PHYLACTERY. (1) A little box containing passages of Scripture on parchment worn on the left arm by Jews during divine service. (2) A case for relics used by the early Christians.

PIETISTS. A sect of German religious reformers led by Philip Spener (1635–1705). They emphasized the need for Bible study and practical Christianity.

PILATE, PONTIUS. Roman procurator of Judea (appointed A.D. 26). He was in office at the trial of Jesus Christ. See Sir James Fitzjames Stephen, *Liberty, Equality and Fraternity*, for an interesting discussion of the part taken by Pilate in the trial of Jesus.

PILGRIMAGE. A journey to a shrine or sacred place, the motive being religious. The chief Buddhist shrines are: Kapilavastu (birthplace of Buddha), Benares (where, under the Bo-tree, he attained Enlightenment), and Kusinagara (where he attained Nirvana). In Islam the pilgrimage to Mecca is required once of all Moslems. The chief places of Christian (Catholic) pilgrimage are: Rome, Lourdes (France), and many local shrines in Italy, France, Germany, etc.

PILPUL. A Rabbinical method of studying a sacred text (Heb.).

PIR. A religious mystic guide in Islam; equivalent to the Hindu *guru* (q.v.).

PISA, COUNCIL OF. A general council held in 1409 to effect reforms in the Church and to settle the great Schism which had produced two rival popes. See *Papacy*, § 3.

PISCINA. A basin on the south side of the altar for cleansing sacred vessels.

PITAKA. A collection of Buddhist Scriptures (lit. "basket"). See *Buddhism.*

PLAIN-SONG. The singing in unison used in the Christian Church of the West from the earliest times and still used in all Catholic churches. It is of a droning, recitative character.

PLATO and **PLATONISM** (428–347 B.C.). The greatest of ancient Greek philosophers, who presided over a philosophic school at Athens for forty years. He left forty-two dialogues, and twelve letters have been ascribed to him. Plato taught a philosophy of dualism. The world consists of transient phenomena perceived by the senses and a permanent invisible world of Reality (the world of Ideas). To fulfil his nature best, man must strive to live in the world of Ideas, and to do this he must overcome passion and appetite. In so far as he is successful in his efforts he will be able to live in the world of Ideas (or the world of the Beautiful and the Good). Like Buddha, Plato taught the doctrine of transmigration of souls (reincarnation), and ultimate release from re-birth, and re-absorption in God. See also *Philosophy*; *Neo-Platonism*. (See Walter Pater, *Plato and Platonism* (1901).)

PLOTINUS (205–70). Neo-Platonic mystical philosopher of Alexandria. He combined the Platonic philosophy with Oriental doctrines of Emanation and Neo-Pythagorean principles. See also *Philosophy*. (See T. Whittaker, *The Neo-Platonists* (1901); Rufus M. Jones, *Studies in Mystical Religion* (1909).)

PLURALISM. (1) The holding of more than one benefice at the same time. (2) A philosophic or religious system which recognizes more than one ultimate Principle. See *polytheism*.

PLYMOUTH BRETHREN. A religious sect of somewhat restricted outlook originating at Plymouth (c. 1830). (See W. B. Neatby, *History of the Plymouth Brethren* (1902).)

POLEMIC THEOLOGY. Exposition of doctrine that seeks to refute (alleged) errors of other beliefs. When a Church is powerful enough to be ruthless, opposing beliefs become "heresies." When it loses power it has recourse to polemics.

POLYCARP, bishop of Smyrna (c. 107); said to have suffered martyrdom at Smyrna in A.D. 155. See *Church Fathers*.

POLYGAMY. See *marriage*.

POLYTHEISM. The belief in a plurality of gods held by the Greeks, Romans, Hindus, etc.

POMA (POME). Small globe filled with hot water, on which the celebrating priest warms his hands in cold weather (Cath.).

PONTIFF (PONTIFEX). (1) Roman high priest (pontifex). (2) A bishop, especially the Pope (Cath.).

PONTIFICAL. (1) Office book of episcopal ceremonies. (2) (pl.) The official robes of priest, bishop or Pope.

PONTIFICAL MASS. Mass celebrated by a bishop wearing his full vestments (Cath.).

POOR CLARES (NUNS OF ST. CLARE). A sisterhood founded by St. Francis (c. 1212). See *Francis of Assisi, St.*

POPE. See *Papacy and Popes*.

PORSON, RICHARD (1750–1808). English scholar of very great distinction. Fellow of Trinity, Cambridge, and Professor of Greek. Son of the parish clerk of E. Ruston, Norfolk. (See J. S. Watson, *Life of Richard Porson* (1861).)

PORTIFORIUM (PORTFORY, PORTUARY). A breviary.

PORTIUNCULA. The church St. Francis built with his own hands. See *Francis of Assisi, St.*

PORT ROYAL DES CHAMPS. A Cistercian convent near Paris, founded in 1204. Famous as the retreat of the Jansenists, Arnaulds, Pascal, Lancelot, etc. See *Jansenism*. The building was pulled down in 1710.

PORTUARY. See *portiforium*.

POSEIDON (L. Neptune). God of the sea in ancient Greece. (See Jane Harrison, *The Religion of Ancient Greece* (Religions A. & M. Series).)

POSITIVISM. The philosophical doctrine originated by Auguste Comte (1798–1857). Comte held that man can have no knowledge of anything but phenomena and that the knowledge of phenomena is not absolute but relative. He advocated a Religion of Humanity. (See Frederick Harrison, *The Philosophy of Common Sense* (1907).)

POSSESSION, DEMONIACAL. The possession of a man's consciousness by an evil spirit. See *Demonology*; *Spiritualism*.

POSTIL. (1) A marginal note by early Biblical commentators. (2) A homily read after the gospel (Cath.).

POSTILLA. A sermon explaining the gospel read during Mass (Cath.).

POSTILLER. A preacher.

POSTULANT. A candidate for holy orders or monastic life.

PRAEMUNIRE (PREMUNIRE). The offence in English law of appealing to papal or other power against the ruling of the king's authority.

PRAGMATIC SANCTION. A special decree issued by a sovereign with regard to some matter of public moment.

PRAGMATISM. The philosophical doctrine that the whole meaning of a conception must express itself in practical consequences. William James is a representative of this school of thought. (See H. H. Bawden, *The Principles of Pragmatism* (1910).)

PRAJAPATI. The Hindu creator of the world. See *Hinduism*.

PRAKRITI. In the Hindu Sankhya philosophy the essence of all material phenomena. Prakriti is thus the manifestation of soul (*purusha*).

PRANA. The life principle in all things (theos.).

PRAPATTI-MARGA. In Hindu religion the method of complete passive surrender to divine grace. It is an intensification of Bhakti-marga, the way of devotion.

PRATYEKKA-BUDDHA. A saint who has attained Nirvana (q.v.) by many lives of solitary effort *unassisted by any other Buddha*. It is not possible for him in this way to attain perfect Buddhahood (i.e. to become a Master). See *initiation*.

PRAYER. The effort to hold intercourse with God, the Gods or Reality is, in its earliest form, the simple petition or request. As the religious sense develops, prayer merges into love and worship. Then two aspects of prayer often commingle. The single petitionary prayer (as found among primitives who pray for rain, fat harvests, etc.) tends to be selfish, frivolous and materialist. As consciousness and reflection deepen, this aspect falls into the background. Prayer merges into meditation (q.v.) and the desire to co-operate with the laws in which Reality manifests. "Give us this day our daily bread" is surpassed by "Thy will be done in earth as it is in heaven" (cf. Dante's "In His Will is our peace"). Probably the noblest prayer ever penned was that which Plato ascribes to Socrates: "O beloved Pan, and all ye gods whose dwelling is in this place, grant me to be beautiful in soul, and all that I possess of outward things to be at peace with those within. Teach me to think wisdom the only riches. And give me so much wealth, and so much only, as one who is good and holy could manage or enjoy." (See J. B. Pratt, *The Religious Consciousness* (1920).)

PRAYER BOOK. See *liturgy, The English.*

PRAYERS FOR THE DEAD. The earliest expression of a desire to help the dead is seen in the food and drink offerings placed in graves as in Egypt. The belief in an intermediate state in which the dead can be helped, common to Judaism, Christianity, Tibetan Lamaism and many other cults, suggests the offering of prayers on their behalf, masses, etc. At Moslem funerals prayers are offered for the dead (the Fatiha); and the Jewish Kaddish appears to have reference to purgatorial experiences of the dead. The Church of England (despite that excellent medieval work, *The Craft to know Well to Die* [Comper's edition], which considers purgatorial conditions) has repudiated prayers for all save those on the earth plane.

PREACHING. The delivery of a divine message at stated times in church is a feature of the Christian and certain other religions (e.g. Mohammedanism and Buddhism).

In the Patristic Age (to A.D. 430) Tertullian, Cyprian and Origen were noted preachers. Augustine of Hippo was a powerful preacher, often profound in his mysticism.

In the Middle Ages the names of Gregory the Great and Leo the Great stand out as preachers and the missionary monks, Patrick, Columba, Wilfrid, etc., gained wide influence by preaching. Bernard of Clairvaulx's homilies still breathe a gentle power and charm. In the 13th C. new life entered the Church through the preaching of St. Francis of Assisi and St. Dominic, and during the Reformation Period (1500–1700) preaching played a vigorous part in Church life, though much of the pulpit oratory of that time was formal, stilted and pretentious. The Wesleys struck a new note in England in their simple earnestness and profound desire for the salvation of men.

In the modern age preaching has largely lost its force owing to the discontinuance of church-going as a moral necessity and a badge of spiritual solvency. The preachers of to-day are the novelists, writers and journalists. Even popular divines can exercise a greater influence by contributing to the press than by occupying the pulpit. (See E. C. Durgan, *A History of Preaching*.)

PRE-ADAMITE. One who believes (contrary to the teaching of Genesis) that man existed on the earth before Adam.

PREBEND. (1) The food monks received at their common table. (2) The share of Cathedral revenues given to a clergyman attached to the Cathedral.

PREBENDARY. A resident clergyman who enjoys a prebend.

PRECENTOR. The leader of a cathedral choir.

PREDESTINATION. The doctrine that God has fixed unalterably whatever is to happen and that each individual's destiny is determined by divine decree. Augustine and Calvin held this doctrine. The modern view of God, no longer regarding Him as an arbitrary sovereign, has undermined this belief.

PRE-EXISTENCE. The belief that the soul existed before its expression in a physical body. This doctrine was taught by the Church Fathers (notably Origen and Justin Martyr), but has been repudiated by orthodox Christianity. It was a part of the Pythagorean and Platonic systems, and is in favour with the Hindus and the Theosophists. Orthodox Christianity is vague and non-committal on the subject, though the difficulties of believing that individual souls are created at birth are considerable. Wordsworth's Ode, "Intimations of Immortality," is a magnificent poetic approach to the subject, in which he wisely keeps aloof from theological dogma. See *reincarnation*.

PRELATE. A bishop or high dignitary in the Church (Cath. and C. of E.).

PREMONSTRATENSIAN CANONS. A French Catholic order of canons regular founded by St. Norbert (1080–1134).

PREMUNIRE. See *praemunire*.

PREPARATION, DAY OF. The day preceding a holy day, Sabbath or the Passover in Judaism.

PRESBYTER. An officer in the early Christian Church. See *Holy Orders*

PRESBYTERIAN CHURCH, REFORMED (CAMERONIANS). A Scotch religious body who remained separate from the Church of Scotland; the greater part joined the Free Church in 1876.

PRESBYTERIAN CHURCH, UNITED. A former Scotch religious body formed by the union of the Secession and Relief churches in 1847. It united with the Free Church in 1900.

PRESBYTERIANISM. The form of church government by presbyters deriving from Reformation times and especially from the system advocated by John Calvin (q.v.).

PRESBYTERY. (1) A clergyman's house (Cath.). (2) A court of the Presbyterian Church consisting of ministers and elders (laymen).

PRESENTATION. The act or right of presenting to a benefice.

PRETA. A ghost or earth-bound spirit (Hindu).

PRIDEAUX, HUMPHREY (1648–1724). English scholar and divine; dean of Norwich.

PRIEST, PRIESTHOOD. The origins of priesthood in all religions and among all nations appear to lie, broadly speaking, in: (1) The primitive medicine-man, shaman or witch-doctor. (2) The heads of families as conductors of ancestral worship. (3) The need for a differentiation of functions owing to the growing complexity of civilized society.

The power and functions of the priesthood depend on the nature of the religion served and the social conditions prevailing. In a low state of general culture (as in ancient Egypt and medieval Europe) the priestly power becomes considerable and may develop into a theocracy, as in the medieval papacy.

Within Christianity two views of the priesthood prevail: (1) The Catholic doctrine which believes that Christ established an apostolate from which the priestly order was transmitted by Apostolic succession. (2) The Protestant view that every Christian is his own priest, with direct access to God—this belief appears to have been held in the first age of Christianity and was insisted on at the Reformation. (See J. A. Montgomery, *Religions of the Past and Present* (1918); Sir James Frazer, *Early History of the Kingship*.)

PRIESTLEY, JOSEPH (1733–1804). English theologian, chemist and politician. He held ministries in various denominations, discovered oxygen, wrote a reply to Burke's *Reflections on the French Revolution* and, as a result, was elected a French citizen and had his chapel, house and papers destroyed by an infuriated English mob. See Thorpe's monograph (1906).

PRIMATE. An archbishop in his capacity as ecclesiastical head of a district or nation.

PRIME. The first service after sunrise. See *Breviary*.

PRIMITIVE METHODISTS. A branch of Methodists (q.v.) which originated in England in 1810; strongly evangelical. They united with the Wesleyan Methodists and United Methodists in 1932.

PRIOR, PRIORESS. The head of a convent or priory.

PRISCILLIANISM. A Spanish heresy (4th C.), originating with Priscillian, bishop of Avila, partly Gnostic and partly Manichean.

PRIVATE JUDGMENT. The decision of an individual as to the meaning of a Scripture passage as distinguished from the decision of a church or party.

PROBABILISM. The doctrine in casuistry that of two probable opinions, both reasonable, one is at liberty to follow one's own. (Opposed to Probabiliorism, which decrees that it is lawful to follow one's own inclination only when there is weightier opinion in its favour (Cath. theol.).)

PROCESSIONAL. (1) A book of the processions of the Catholic Church. (2) A hymn sung during a procession of clergy.

PROCESSION OF THE HOLY GHOST. The emanation of the Holy Spirit from the Father (single procession) or from the Father and Son (double procession) (theol.).

PROPAGANDA, COLLEGE OF. A college at Rome and assembly of Cardinals devoted to the spread of Catholicism among heretics (Protestants). It was founded in 1622 by Gregory XV.

PROPHECY, PROPHETS. Prophecy, in its higher aspect, is religion as promoted by inspiration.

In primitive conditions of society religion tends strongly towards emotionalism unballasted by other forces. Thus the dervish dances until he becomes " possessed " by a power he calls " God."

As religion develops and knowledge and culture deepen, religious ecstasy or prophecy assumes a more decidedly ethical aspect as with the prophets of Israel. Many of these attained to exalted states of mystic ecstasy, but few of them were sufficiently balanced or controlled to give a spiritual interpretation to their experiences. They were for the most part racially narrow and politically unenlightened. They saw truth " through a glass darkly " and frequently misinterpreted it. In the best of the Jewish prophets the ethical note becomes more and more intense until it finds its full beauty in the inspired utterances of Isaiah, with their deep longing for the purification of mankind. Jesus in his lifetime was regarded as a prophet because he spoke from inward illumination " and not as the scribes." In the oracles of ancient Greece we find phenomena similar to those of prophecy in Israel. Cf. *Mystery Religions.* (See J. M. P. Smith, *The Prophet and His Problems* (1914) ; Carlyle, *Hero and Hero Worship*.)

PROPHETS, THE FORMER. Joshua, Judges, Samuel and Kings (as distinguished from the Latter Prophets).

PROPHETS, MINOR. The prophets from Hosea to Malachi (O.T.).

PROPHETS, SCHOOL OF THE. A college among the ancient Israelites for training young men as religious teachers.

PROPITIATION. See *Atonement*.

PROSELYTE. A convert from one religion to another ; originally a pagan who became a Jew.

PROTESTANT EPISCOPAL CHURCH OF AMERICA. The branch of the Church of England organized in U.S.A. after the Revolutionary war. The Church was organized between

1785 and 1789. Its legislative body consists of a general convention composed of a House of Bishops and a House of Deputies consisting of clergy and laity. The bishops of the Church secured consecration from English and Scottish bishops. See also *United States Protestant Episcopal Church*.

PROTESTANTISM. The original Protestants were those who, in 1529, protested against an edict of Charles V and the Diet of Spires denouncing the Reformation. The term came to be used indiscriminately for the Lutherans and other sects. In England it was applied to all who were opposed to the Papacy and the Catholic Church. See *Reformation*.

PROTHESIS. The preliminary oblation of the eucharistic elements (Gr. Ch.).

PROTHONOTARY. (1) A secretary of the papal chancery. (2) Chief secretary to the Patriarch of Constantinople (Gr. Ch.).

PROVERBS, BOOK OF. An O.T. book of wise maxims ascribed to King Solomon, but probably of considerably later date. (See Prof. Toy, *Proverbs*.)

PROVINCIAL. The superintendent of the religious houses in a province (Cath.).

PROVOST. The dignitary in charge of a college or cathedral.

PRUDENTIUS (c. 348–410). Author of some beautiful Latin hymns. (See Jack Lindsay, *Medieval Latin Poets*.)

PRYNNE, WILLIAM (1600–69). English controversialist of Puritan sympathies; author of *Histrio-Mastix*, an attack on the theatre.

PSALMS, THE. A Book of the O.T. Many of the psalms have been ascribed to King David, but their authorship is open to much debate. They appear to have been written for singing as part of the Temple ritual. (See John Sharpe, *The Student's Handbook to the Psalms* (1894).)

PSALTER. A book of Psalms.

PSEUDEPIGRAPHA. Writings put forth with a false claim as to authorship (e.g. Enoch, Daniel, Tobit, etc., in O.T. literature; The Gospel of Peter, The Gospel of Nicodemus, etc., in N.T. literature).

PSEUDO-ISIDORIAN DECRETALS. A collection of decrees of early bishops of Rome, etc., establishing the absolute authority of the Pope over metropolitans and civil rulers. These documents were made into a collection in the 9th C. The Renaissance scholar Laurentius Valla proved them to be forgeries and his conclusions were (later) admitted by the Catholic Church. See *Papacy*.

PSYCHE. In Greek mythology Psyche is the personification of the soul. The story of how she was beloved by Cupid (Eros) is beautifully told by Apuleius in *The Golden Ass* (Bk. iv). Psyche has to undergo many trials before final deliverance comes to her. The myth has been interpreted as shadowing the three states of consciousness: (1) group-consciousness, (2) ego-consciousness and (3) universal consciousness. See *Consciousness, Cosmic.* The same ideas are enshrined in the old stories of Cinderella and the Sleeping Beauty. (See Edward Carpenter, *Christian and Pagan Creeds*, chap. xiv.)

PSYCHICAL RESEARCH. Investigation of psychical and physical phenomena that physics and psychology are unable to explain. The Society for Psychical Research was founded in London in 1882. It gave great impetus to the investigation of the problems of telepathy, clairvoyance, phantasms, etc., and demonstrated the existence of forces which modern science disregards. The evidence collected to prove communication with the dead, though considerable, leaves open a large field for controversy. The repercussions of psychical research in the religious world have been considerable, compelling a closer consideration of certain Christian doctrines. The main difficulty in the way of psychical research appears to be in the fact that few religious teachers or men of science in the west are sufficiently developed morally and psychically to be able to give an authoritative lead in such studies. (See Sir O. Lodge, *Science and Immortality*; F. W. H. Myers, *Phantasms of the Living*; Podmore, *Studies in Psychical Research*; Julian Franklyn, *A Survey of the Occult* (1935).)

PSYCHO-ANALYSIS. Term applied by Dr. Sigmund Freud in 1906 to the theory and practice of his method of treating psychopathic disorders; the unconscious mind being analysed by the method of "free association."

PSYCHOLOGY. The science which analyses consciousness and phenomena of the mind or thought-processes. The chief "schools" of modern psychology are represented by Freud, Adler and Jung. Freud finds the origin of psychic energy (*libido*) in the sex urge. He has called his contribution to psychology Psycho-analysis. Adler designates his system Individual Psychology. Jung has given the ideas associated with his writings the name of Analytical Psychology. As Freud interprets all phenomena in terms of the sexual instinct, Adler interprets them in terms of the power instinct. For Jung the *libido* is simply psychic energy which may become identified with sex, power or any other instinct. He does not interpret the symphony of life in terms of isolated instruments but views it as a whole. While not identifying himself with any school or system, he gives all schools and systems their due.

The study of Psychology is of immense importance since we are never likely to gain a correct view of any problem until we understand a good deal about our own thought processes and the problems connected with the unconscious. Unconscious or instinctive action is compulsory. Consciousness is too weak to interfere. The savage is almost completely dominated by his unconscious. So, to a great extent, is the child. Hence both are more in harmony with nature than is civilized man, who has to learn to understand and control the dragon of the unconscious. Compare art. *Religion*, §§ 3–5. (See Jung, *Psychological Types*; C. S. Myers, *Experimental Psychology*.)

PSYCHOTHERAPY. The method of restoring health by the application of psychological principles (to be distinguished from psychiatry, the treatment of mental diseases). Modern psychotherapy originated with the English physicians who employed hypnosis, Elliotson, Esdaile and Braide (1837). Their work was carried further by certain French scientists, Bernheim (c. 1860), Charcot and others. The Freudian movement began in 1895, Freud having extraordinary success in curing certain nervous diseases by psycho-analysis. Many diseases owe their inception to mental stress of one kind or another. Psychotherapy aims at relieving this tension and so restoring health. (See Bernheim, *Suggestive Therapeutics*; A. A. Brill, *Psychoanalysis*; J. Franklyn, *A Survey of the Occult*.)

PTAH. The creator-god of ancient Egypt.

PUBLICAN. The men to whom the collection of taxes was farmed out in ancient Rome. The N.T. references reflect their unpopularity. (See Matt. xi. 19; xviii. 17.)

PUBLIC-WORSHIP. The meeting together in church or temple for the worship of a god or gods. Public or corporate worship is not to-day observed so widely as it used to be. The Great War, which broke down many customs and conventions, resulted in a diminished church-attendance. It would be unwise to argue therefrom that faith or the soul's desire for a true inner worship of the Good and the Beautiful, have suffered diminution.

PUJA. Hindu term for religious devotion.

PULPIT. The raised platform in a church from which sermons are delivered.

PURANAS. A collection of eighteen Sanscrit Scriptures, dating from c. 3rd C. B.C. They deal with theology, history, cosmogony, etc.

PURGATORY. The Catholic doctrine that a period of retributive discipline follows death. After death satisfaction cannot be made and therefore each must atone by suffering. Nearly all the Greek and Latin Fathers held that Purgatorial fire is figurative. Purgatory was not defined as a dogma until the Council of Florence (1439). The Protestant view (as far as it can be ascertained) appears to be that the dead pass immediately to heaven and in certain rare instances of extreme wickedness, to hell. It is interesting to compare with the Catholic doctrine of Purgatory the Tibetan *Book of the Dead* (edited by Professor W. Y.

Evans-Wentz). Here the esoteric doctrine of Purgatory is vividly presented. In Charles Kingsley's *Water Babies* the profound doctrine of Karmic and Purgatorial retribution is very beautifully indicated.

PURIFICATION OF THE BLESSED VIRGIN MARY. A Catholic feast in commemoration of the purification of the Virgin Mary, in obedience to Jewish ceremonial custom (Lev. xii. 2), after the birth of Christ (2 Feb.).

PURIM. A Jewish feast to celebrate the deliverance of the Persian Jews as recorded in the Book of Esther. Observed on 14 Adar (March).

PURITANS. The religious party which originated in the time of Elizabeth and the Stuarts. They aimed at greater strictness in the religious life and simplicity and purity of worship. See *Reformation*; *Brownists*.

PURUSHA. The Hindu term for soul, whether of the universe or of the individual. The human soul is also called *atman* or *jivatman*.

PURVA-MIMAMSA. See *Mimamsa*.

PUSEY, EDWARD BOUVERIE (1800–82). One of the leaders of the Oxford Movement (q.v.).

PUSHAN. A sun-god of the Vedic religion.

PYRRHONISM. The doctrines of the Greek philosopher Pyrrho of Elis (c. 360–270). He taught a thoroughgoing scepticism. Man, he held, is incapable of attaining truth.

PYTHAGORAS. Greek philosopher of 6th C. B.C. He founded a school of philosophy at Crotona on the coast of Calabria in 529 B.C. His school appears to have been of the nature of a religious brotherhood seeking to reform society by purifying and enlightening the individual consciousness. Like the Orphics and the Buddhists, the Pythagoreans aimed at enabling the purified soul to escape "the wheel of birth." The influence of Pythagoras' teaching on Plato was considerable. (See E. Schuré, *Pythagoras*.)

PYX. The box in which the host is kept after consecration (Cath.).

Q

Q. Letter used to designate the lost document from which the authors of the gospels, Matthew and Luke, are believed to have derived their non-Markan material. (Ger. *Quelle* = source.)

QADARITES. Islamic sect who believe that man has freewill or power (*qadar*) over his actions; and that predestination does not render him the slave of God.

QADI. A Moslem law officer appointed to deal with cases of marriage and probate.

QUADRAGESIMA. The Latin name for Lent (q.v.).

QUADRATUS. The first Christian apologist. He dedicated a Defence of Christianity to Hadrian (A.D. 117–38).

QUAKERS. See *Friends, Society of.*

QUARTODECIMANS. Name given the early Christians who commemorated Good Friday on 14 Nisan (*quartus decimus*), the date of the Jewish Passover. At the Council of Nicea (325) the Quartodeciman system was abandoned and Easter was appointed to be celebrated on the Sunday following 14 Nisan.

QUATREFOIL (QUARTERFOIL). A carving in four segments resembling an open flower (archit.).

QUESNEL, PASQUIER (1634–1719). French theologian and leader of the Jansenists (q.v.).

QUETZALCOATL ("FEATHERED SERPENT"). A pre-Aztec Mexican sun-god. The Mexicans welcomed the predatory Spaniards of the 16th C. believing they heralded the God's second-coming. (See Prescott, *Conquest of Mexico.*)

QUIETISM, QUIETIST. The name given to the mysticism of the 17th C. in France, Italy and Holland. The Quietists aimed at complete passivity even to the neglect of the ordinary activities of life: "One moment's contemplation is worth a thousand years' good works." In this respect they lacked balance. The chief Quietists were: Miguel de Molinos (1627–1696); Jeanne Marie Bouvier de la Mothe Guyon (1648–1717); Antoinette Bourignon (1616–80); François de la Mothe Fénélon (1651–1715). (See W. R. Inge, *Christian Mysticism*; Rufus M. Jones, *Studies in Mystical Religion* (1909); R. A. Vaughan, *Hours with the Mystics*; *Autobiography of Madame Guyon.*)

QUINQUAGESIMA ("FIFTY"). The Sunday before Ash Wednesday and fiftieth day before Easter.

QUIRINALIA. An ancient Roman festival in honour of the god Quirinus (Romulus), held on 17 February.

QURON. See *Koran.*

QUTB. The Moslem term for a saint of extreme holiness.

R

RA, RE. The ancient Egyptian solar god. During the religious reformation of Ikhnaton, Ra became the one god of a purified cult. See *Egypt, Religion of.*

RABBI, RABBIN ("MASTER" or "LORD"). The name for a Jewish spiritual leader, in ancient and modern times. Rabbinism is the doctrine of the rabbis as expounders of Talmudic literature. See *Talmud*; *Scribe.*

RACHEL. Daughter of Laban, wife of Jacob and mother of Joseph and Benjamin (Gen. xxix. 6).

RAGNARÖK. The end of the world in Norse mythology, when the gods shall be overthrown. (See F. Kauffmann, *Northern Mythology* (Temple Primers).)

RAKSHASAS. Demons of Hindu mythology who cause storms and destruction.

RAM MOHAN ROY (1772–1833). Founder of the Brahma Samaj (q.v.).

RAMA. (1) Hero of the Sanscrit poem, the Ramayana. He defeated the demon Rabana. (2) A sect (Ramaites) of Vaishnavism that arose in the 8th C. A.D.

RAMADAN, RAMADHAN. The ninth month of the Mohammedan year—a time of fasting from dawn to sunset for faithful Moslems.

RAMAKRISHNA (1834–86). The greatest saint of modern Hinduism. He was trained in Yoga (q.v.) and became a religious devotee. He came to regard ultimate Reality as knowable only in phenomenal manifestation. His eclecticism led him to the belief that the practice of all the religions brings man into union with God and therefore all religions are " true." Each should approach God by the system, whether Christian, Islamic, or Buddhist, which suits him best. His greatest disciple was Vivekananda. (See Swami Vivekananda, *My Master.*)

RAMANANDA. A leader of the Hindu Ramaite movement (15th C.). He had an extensive following in India.

RAMANUJA. The first of the Vaisnava teachers of medieval India (12th C.). He proclaimed the unity of the god Vishnu (q.v.) and the love of God as the way of salvation.

RAMAYANA. A Hindu religious epic, written 6th to 4th C.s B.C. and transformed (c. 2nd C. B.C.) into a sectarian poem in praise of Rama as an incarnation of Vishnu. (See R. C. Dutt, *The Civilization of India* (Temple Primers).)

RAMMON, RIMMON. A storm-god of ancient Babylonia.

RANTERS. (1) English sectaries under the Commonwealth who rejected all authority (Bible, church, ministers, etc.). (2) An early nickname for the Methodists.

RASHI (1040–1105). An influential Jewish commentator on the Bible and Talmud. Rashi, also known as Solomon Bar Isaac, was a native of France.

RASHNU. The Spirit of Truth who holds the scales in the Last Judgment in the Zoroastrian religion.

RATIONALISM. Exclusive reliance on human reason. In philosophy and theology it is opposed alike to mysticism and supernatural revelation. Rationalism became fashionable in the 18th C., but the development of modern scientific research has seriously undermined it. (See W. E. H. Lecky, *History of the Rise and Influence of Rationalism in Europe.*)

RE. See *Ra* (the usual form).

REAL PRESENCE. The belief that the body and blood of Christ are present in the Eucharist. This doctrine, with modifications, is held by the Catholic, Anglican, Greek and Lutheran Churches.

REALISM. The Platonic doctrine that universals (i.e. abstract terms) are more real than concrete objects. Realism is opposed to Nominalism which regards universals as mere dreams and external objects as realities. Much ink was spilt in medieval times by Anselm, Abélard, Occam, and others, over this philosophical controversy.

REBIRTH. See *reincarnation.*

RECOLLECT. A member of a Catholic monastic order which originated in Spain (15th C.). So called from the recollection in God at which the founders aimed.

RECTOR. (1) A clergyman in the C. of E. who has charge of a parish where the tithes are not impropriate. (2) A name for all incumbents in the episcopal churches of the U.S.A. and in Scotland. (3) The head of Lincoln and Exeter Colleges, Oxford. (4) The principal of a Jesuit or other Catholic seminary.

RECUSANT. The 16th- and 17th-C. term for those who incurred penalties by their refusal to attend services of the C. of E.—usually Catholics.

RED CROSS. A society founded at Geneva in 1863 by a Swiss physician, Henri Dunant, with the purpose of tending the sick and wounded in war-time under a neutral flag.

REDEMPTION. See *Atonement.*

REDEMPTORISTINES. A Catholic congregation of women founded at Castellamare in 1750 for education and meditation.

REDEMPTORISTS. A Catholic congregation of missionary priests founded by St. Alfonso Maria de Liguori in 1732. They devote themselves to preaching, visiting and hearing confessions.

REFORMATION, THE. The European religious revolution of the 16th C. which gave rise to the various Protestant denominations. The development of all the great religions is marked by similar features. There is a period of primitive simplicity when the Founder expounds the principles of the inner life. This is followed by a period of growth and extension. The pure stream of religion then becomes muddied with political influences and the original teaching changes into something more external and popular. The result of this is, in the next stage, rebellion from within. The sincere truth-seekers declare war on a more or less corrupt political hierarchy. In Buddhist Tibet, Tsong-Kapa opposes ignorant superstition and seeks to bring religion back to its original purity. In Catholic Europe, Martin Luther (q.v.) nails his 95 Theses to the church door at Wittenberg (1517) and thereby lights the fire which it proved impossible to extinguish. Luther's work was carried further by Zwingli (q.v.), Calvin (q.v.) and many others.

The chief results of the Reformation were:

1. Separation of the nations of northern Europe from the ecclesiastical domination of Rome.

2. The introduction of the principle (slow to develop and not yet grown to maturity) of religious toleration.

3. The fostering of the spirit of democracy and liberty as against despotic forms of government.

4. The furthering of intellectual activity and scientific research. The reformed congregations passed beyond the narrow mental restrictions of the Schoolmen.

5. A gradual purification of morals among clergy and laity due, in large measure, to the abolition of a celibate priesthood in non-Catholic countries.

(See *Cambridge Modern History*, vol. II—*The Reformation*; Fisher, *History of the Reformation*.)

REFORMED EPISCOPAL CHURCH OF AMERICA. A body which seceded from the Protestant Episcopal Church in 1873 as a protest against sacramentalism.

REFORMED JUDAISM. A liberal and cultural movement which arose within the Jewish faith during the 18th C. A wider culture within Judaism had been sought during the Protestant Reformation by Azariah dei Rossi of Ferrara (1511–78) and Léon Modena of Venice (1571–1648). But it was not until the 18th C. that decided development took place. Moses Mendelssohn (1729–86) advocated secular education for Jews, and Israel Jacobson of Cassel (1768–1828) introduced the vernacular into synagogue worship. Other prominent names connected with liberal Judaism of the 18th C. are Samuel Holdheim—who advocated the abandonment of circumcision; Abraham Geiger—who repudiated the dogma of a personal Messiah; and Zechariah Frankel—who demanded greater intellectual freedom. (See David Philipson, *The Reform Movement in Judaism* (1907).)

REGENERATION. See *conversion*.

REGISTERS, PAROCHIAL. The books in which births, deaths and marriages in a parish are recorded. The custom dates from 1538.

REGULARS. Catholic monks living under a monastic rule.

REINCARNATION (REBIRTH; TRANSMIGRATION; METEMPSYCHOSIS). The doctrine taught by Plato, and widely held in the east, that a part of man (his soul or self) lives again and again in a human body. According to Eastern teaching the soul's evolution has caused it to live in all forms of life and to pass through the mineral, vegetable and animal kingdoms. Plato's view of reincarnation is stated as follows: "There is a law of the goddess Retribution . . . the law ordains that this soul shall in the first generation pass, not into that of any other animal, but only of man; and the soul which has seen most of truth shall come to the birth as a philosopher or artist, or musician or lover; that which has seen truth in the second degree shall be a righteous king or warrior or lord; the soul which is of the third class shall be a politician or trader or economist; the fourth shall be a lover of gymnastic toils or a physician; the fifth a prophet or hierophant; to the sixth a poet or imitator will be appropriate; to the seventh the life of an artisan or husbandman; to the eighth that of a sophist or demagogue; to the ninth that of a tyrant; all of these are states of probation, in which he who lives righteously improves, and he who lives unrighteously deteriorates his lot" (Timaeus).

Of reincarnation Professor Evans-Wentz writes: "The Gnostic Christian, like the Buddhist . . . held as fundamental the doctrine of rebirth; so that his highest ideal was to acquire such degree of positive and direct spiritual insight while on earth as, after many pious lifetimes, would ultimately produce in him the Enlightenment of Christhood. And the Gnostic Christian prayed that upon his own attainment of Christhood he might be empowered to assist all mankind to reach the same goal. On the other hand, the Church-Council Christian, being forbidden, by the Second Council of Constantinople (A.D. 553), to believe in the doctrine of rebirth ('Whosoever shall support the mythical doctrine of the pre-existence of the soul, and the consequent wonderful opinion of its return, let him be anathema'), was unable to hold the altruistic ideal of his Gnostic brother, and so came to adopt the lesser ideal of salvation for self alone, by faith in the infallibility of the Church's decrees and teachings. The effect on human society of the Gnostic hermit's altruistic ideal is positive, and creative and unlimited, while that of the Church-Council Christian hermit's is, by contrast, negative, non-creative and selfish" (*Milarepa*, p. 12).

RELATIVITY. (1) The doctrine that the nature of human knowledge is determined not merely by the objects known but also by the conditions of our cognitive powers. (2) The theory of the universe propounded by Albert Einstein, that all motion is relative.

RELICS. Sacred objects associated with saints or martyrs. These are held in deep reverence in the Catholic and Greek churches. Miraculous healing—probably the result of Suggestion (q.v.)—has resulted from the worship of such relics, Christian, Buddhist, Hindu, etc.

RELIGION. Religion has been defined in many ways by many men. Perhaps to-day it is most justly described as the moral and intellectual attitude of the soul to certain abiding problems never far from man's consciousness. What is life? What is being? Why are we born? What is time? What is death? The multitude who are content to have their thinking done for them by paid professors can dismiss such questions and seek satisfaction in the day's work. But even for them times of doubt and bewilderment intrude. And the sensitive religious person, for whom the problem of Reality is unescapable, entering the great cathedral of human aspiration, is moved to a deep humility and wonder before the encircling Unknown. Dim aisles bewilder him, gothic pillars soar to the fretted vault, his own footsteps assume an unreal sound as of something apprehended in Dreams. Great poets and thinkers of the past, Dante and Aquinas and Abélard, flit hither and thither, bearing aloft twinkling tapers. The philosopher's meditations, the mystic's visions, the poet's dreams take form like Aladdin's palace, rising to some unheard incantation :

> How strange the sculptures that adorn these towers !
> This crowd of statues, in whose folded sleeves
> Birds build their nests ; while canopied with leaves
> Parvis and portal bloom like trellised bowers,
> And the vast minster seems a cross of flowers !
> But fiends and dragons on the gargoyled eaves
> Watch the dead Christ between the living thieves,
> And, underneath, the traitor Judas lowers !
> Ah ! from what agonies of heart and brain,
> What exultations trampling on despair,
> What tenderness, what tears, what hate of wrong,
> What passionate outcry of a soul in pain,
> Uprose this poem of the earth and air,
> This medieval miracle of song !

How has religion grown? Whence came it ? Where are its foundations ? Vain questionings. For man is a tiny atom in a darkness that no sun can wholly pierce. He scrapes the sand and finds stones, but the stones give no certain answer to his eager questioning.

Primitive man was more sure and less inquisitive. The universe seemed simple to him but the simplicity was in himself. For the universe is the reflexion of a mind. He made gods in his own image, credited them with the power he craved but could not attain, fell down and worshipped them. Society developed ; priests came—men who undertook to relieve mankind of the duties connected with worship. And the priests flourished ; grew to be men of wealth and power ; forgot their old simplicity and honesty and made religion a thing of utility and commerce until honest men turned from it in dismay or disgust. And so religion after religion was born, grew to maturity and passed away.

That, expressed in the simplest and shortest terms, is the history of every religion.

But to get a better knowledge of religion, what it is and what it stands for, we must take a nearer view of man and his needs. Primitive man prays to his God because he wants something badly ; a house, a sword, rain for his crops, victory over enemies. Is he wrong to pray for such things ? Not in his own time and circumstances. But will he get them by these means ? He may, for thought is a powerful force and when heated by emotion, though it may not move the gods, it will certainly stimulate the worshipper. The invincible soldier (Mohammed, Cromwell) is he who fights with faith.

Always a sense of futility attends man. He feels himself to be incomplete. Vision outflies attainment. He can conquer empires and create time-enduring works of art but cannot conquer the tendency to quarrel with his wife. To keep some measure of peace, laws come into being, taboos, decalogues. The priests elaborate these and give them a ceremonial aspect. Some philosophers have inclined to the belief that the sense of sin was artificially fanned by priests in the interests of their own order. That is probably going too far. For man's own urge towards a better state or higher fulfilment is continually flicking him as with a whip. (But he usually misinterprets the situation and hits his neighbour, mistaking *him* for the aggressor.) He makes confession to a priest, joins his fellows in church or temple and together they worship God and seek forgiveness. In earlier ages such united worship brought satisfaction and relief. John Donne, the most gifted and saintly dean St. Paul's has known, wrote a poem during a period of sickness:

Wilt Thou forgive that sin where I begun,
Which was my sin, though it were done before?
Wilt thou forgive that sin through which I run,
And do run still, though still I do deplore?
When thou hast done, Thou hast not done,
For I have more.

RELIGION

Wilt thou forgive that sin which I have won
Others to sin, and made my sin their door?
Wilt thou forgive that sin which I did shun
A year or two, but wallowed in a score?
When thou hast done, Thou hast not done,
For I have more.

I have a sin of fear, that when I've spun
My last thread, I shall perish on the shore;
But swear by Thyself, that at my death Thy Sun
Shall shine as He shines now, and heretofore;
And having done that, Thou hast done,
I fear no more.

Izaac Walton tells us how, on his recovery, Donne caused the verses to be set "to a most grave and solemn tune, and to be often sung to the organ by the choristers of St. Paul's church, in his own hearing, especially at the evening service; and at his return from his customary devotions in that place, did occasionally say to a friend, 'The words of this hymn have restored to me the same thoughts of joy that possessed my soul in my sickness, when I composed it. And, O the power of church music! that harmony, added to this hymn, has raised the affections of my heart, and quickened my graces of zeal and gratitude; and I observe that I always return from paying this public duty of prayer and praise to God with an unexpressible tranquillity of mind, and willingness to leave the world.'" John Donne, for all the medieval saintliness of his later years, was pre-eminently a modern. He knew religion to be an adventure of the spirit, not a traditional convention to insure a good opinion in this world and the provision of a surpliced parson to attend to such ceremonies as baptism, marriage, etc., as are required.

But from the days of Donne (1573–1631) to the England of to-day is a long journey. Much has happened in the interim. Most of the old landmarks have been swept away; those that remain are fast disappearing as the flood of change rises higher and higher.

§ 2. Victorian England became critical of orthodox revealed religion. The men of thought, whose ideas gradually percolated to the people, Spencer, Huxley, Mill, Morley, Leslie Stephen, were sceptical—as they had need to be. Bishop Colenso in his early Victorian steamship came into violent collision with Noah's Ark. Buckle and Lecky showed no regard for official religious susceptibilities. And the preparation of armaments to insure the world's peace culminated in the Great War.

Even before that event there had been a growing impatience of religious creeds and dogmas. Church attendance—Catholic, Anglican and Dissenting—had dwindled. "Lack of faith!" deplored religious officials. But the layman knew better. Honesty prevented him from standing up and repeating the clauses of a creed in which he no longer whole-heartedly believed. ("And in one Lord Jesus Christ, the only-begotten Son of God, Begotten of his Father before all worlds . . . Begotten, not made . . . incarnate by the Holy Ghost of the Virgin Mary . . . He descended into hell and rose again the third day . . . And he shall come again with glory to judge the quick and the dead . . . One baptism for the remission of sins.") Such statements, once accepted literally, might be true in some esoteric sense suited to the temper of a philosophic dean. But why make religion depend upon assertions about fundamental matters of which you are not sure and which are entirely incapable of proof? It is not done in the Law Courts; it is not done in the scientific laboratory; it is not done in economics or business. Why then this bland make-believe, amounting to ignoble dishonesty, in religion?

Then came the triumph of paganism in the Great War. Millions slaughtered; lies and poison gas disseminated wholesale. Then the peace and the gradual return to things as they were. And the suave assurance of religious leaders that all was well in Zion. Bishops who had acted as recruiting sergeants and deans who had written philosophy while paid to teach the creeds and articles of the Church, returned to their pulpits and preached upon the old dogmas with the old unction. And for the result let the empty churches and the voice of statistics speak. It is calculated on a liberal estimate that of the 37,354,617 people in England, only ten millions go regularly or occasionally to church or chapel. The remaining 27,354,917 stay away.[1]

Does this argue the decay of religion? He would be a rash thinker who brought the charge. Religion, which was not killed by the Inquisition, nor by the Borgia popes, nor by the wars of religion, nor by the fires in Smithfield, nor by the French and Russian revolutions, was certainly not killed by the Great War, nor will it be killed by the tenacity with which official religious leaders cling to worn-out creeds and threadbare doctrines.

Let us turn for illustration of the changed religious atmosphere to the story of St. Francis of Assisi. In the last days of his life, St. Francis retired to the bleak retreat of La Verna. While there the mystical experience of the Stigmata came to him; the five wounds of Jesus, on which he had meditated so long, appeared in his hands, feet and side. They were found by the sorrowing friends who laid the body in the tomb. Victorian Scientific England was troubled by that story of the Stigmata, afraid in its heart that someone had told a lie. But already an obscure Austrian Jew, Sigmund Freud, who had studied medicine in Vienna and Paris, had made experiments in psychology which went far to prove the Franciscan tradition true. Freud studied the phenomena of hypnotism under the French savants, Charcot and Janet. These men had demonstrated that a wide variety of physical symptoms could be induced by hypnotic suggestion — burns, swellings, wounds, paralysis. In the light of these researches the truth of what had happened to St. Francis was apparent. He had meditated so long on the passion of Jesus that the forces of the unconscious had stamped his dreams upon his flesh—for the unconscious mind is an all-powerful agent.

The age of Freud was very different from the age of St. Francis. The spirit of religion had given place to the spirit of inquiry. Theological doctrines were beginning to fade into the background; science was coming more and more to the front. Darwin had propounded a theory long since accepted in the East, and the obscure Austrian physician had discovered, in psychotherapy and psycho-analysis, doctrines known and practised long ago by the Greeks in their Mystery Religions. Science had become so all-pervading that even important people like Mr. Gladstone were beginning to wonder whether the archbishop of Canterbury was *quite* as great an authority as the president of the Royal Society. And then some smart journalist invented the headline: IS SCIENCE OPPOSED TO RELIGION?—which has been doing yeoman service ever since.

That topic, so often debated in the popular Press, depends for its newspaper value on the crudeness with which it is handled. "Religion" and "Science" are terms capable of wide—and narrow—significance. The strife is not, and never has been, between religion and science, but between the men who have been trained

[1] E. B. Powley, *Vicisti, Galilæe*, p. 80.

in religion and the men who have been trained in science. Their own passions and prejudices get in the way and obscure their vision. In the words of Francis Bacon : " We will have it that all things *are* as in our folly we think they should be, not as seems fittest to the Divine Wisdom, or as they are found to be in fact ; and I know not whether we more distort the facts of nature or of our own wits."

§ 3. So far as organized religion is concerned—whether Christian, Buddhist or Mohammedan—one thing is abundantly clear ; it has lost its grip on the minds and hearts of the people. The priest is there to officiate or hear confessions ; the rector Sunday after Sunday mounts his pulpit ; the Salvationist beats his big drum in the street, but the people are listening to the wireless or hurrying over the country-side in their cars. Religion only comes into their thoughts at stray moments, and then it is but a vague dream as of something afar off.

And what is the effect of this apathy so widely induced by the official religions of our time, upon the lives of the people ? The answer has been well given by the greatest psychologist of our time, Professor Jung of Zurich : " During the past thirty years, people from all the civilized countries of the earth have consulted me. I have treated many hundreds of patients, the larger number being Protestants, a smaller number Jews, and not more than five or six believing Catholics. Among all my patients in the second half of life—that is to say over thirty-five—there has not been one whose problem in the last resort was not that of finding a religious outlook on life. It is safe to say that every one of them fell ill because he had lost that which the living religions of every age have given to their followers, and none of them has been really healed who did not regain his religious outlook. This of course has nothing whatever to do with a particular creed or membership of a church." [1]

It must be remembered that Professor Jung is here dealing solely with *pathological* cases ; men and women who had become so ill that desperation drove them to the medical specialist. But for the hundreds who succumb to actual physical breakdown as a result of mental stress, there are thousands who suffer from unrest and the evil results of an unbalanced life in lesser degree, and are usually unaware of the root-cause of this disquietude.

The condition of such people at the present day calls for urgent consideration. But where are they to find help ? The sacraments of the church in earlier ages brought comfort to thousands. To-day the numbers who find ease of heart by these means have dwindled. And the tragedy is intensified by the fact that it is the keenly intellectual, the active-minded and spiritually aware who suffer most. Life is a balance between forces of activity and inertia. The active look towards the future ; the inert are con-

[1] C. J. Jung, *Modern Man in search of a Soul*, p. 264.

RELIGION

tent to rest in the mental and spiritual ruts of the past. Conflict, both within and without, is the result. These considerations have been vididly expressed by Professor Jung: "Those of whom I am thinking are by no means sickly eccentrics, but are most often exceptionally able, courageous and upright persons who have repudiated our traditional truths for honest and decent reasons, and not from wickedness of heart. Every one of them has the feeling that our religious truths have somehow or other grown empty. Either they cannot reconcile the scientific and the religious outlooks, or Christian tenets have lost their authority and their psychological justification. People no longer feel themselves to have been redeemed by the death of Christ; they cannot believe—they cannot compel themselves to believe, however happy they may deem the man who has a belief. Sin has for them become something quite relative: what is evil for the one, is good for the other. After all, why should not Buddha be in the right also?"[1]

§ 4. To-day there are no religious leaders whom sincere seekers after truth can trust. There is a wide variety of paid and trained clergy; men of good education, moved by an honest desire to help their fellows. But a gulf has opened between clergy and laity; a gulf due to the fact that the clergy stand for a dogmatic system which modern man has long since outgrown. H. B. Brewster put his finger on the modern pulse

[1] C. J. Jung, *op. cit.*, p. 268.

when he wrote: "I would proclaim unconditional salvation to man. Others have stood forth and said, Believe this or that and your faith will save you; it will show you the meaning and the reward of life; but without this faith there is neither meaning nor reward. I say that your beliefs and your disbeliefs matter no more than your nationality or the colour of your hair."[1] Feeling like that, how can modern man go even to the most intelligent of padres and say: "Show me the meaning of life; tell me how I may attain a faith which shall sustain me in the tumult and the stress."

Shall he then go to the physician trained in the modern schools of scientific materialism? Will the doctor be able to help him. Let us turn again to Jung: "Is the doctor equal to this task? To begin with, he will probably hand over his patient to the clergyman or the philosopher, or abandon him to that perplexity which is the special note of our day. As a doctor he is not required to have a finished outlook on life, and his professional conscience does not require it of him. But what will he do when he sees only too clearly why his patient is ill; when he sees that it arises from his having no love, but only sexuality; no faith, because he is afraid to grope in the dark; no hope, because he is disillusioned by the world and by life; and no understanding, because he has failed to read the meaning of his own existence? . . .

[1] H. B. Brewster, *The Prison*, p. 130.

And where are the great and wise men who do not merely talk about the meaning of life and of the world, but really possess it? Human thought cannot conceive any system or final truth that could give the patient what he needs in order to live: that is, faith, hope, love and insight."[1]

Were modern man able to be still and meditate, the profoundest truths would be open to him. For there is but one well of living water from which all the sages and the saints of all religions and all vital philosophies have drunk: "We are all full of immortality. But it dwells not in the beauty of our mortal person; it stirs and glitters in us under the crust of self, like a gleam of sirens under the ice, and any blow which breaks this crust brings us into the company of the eternal ones whom to feel is to be they. That blow you will surely strike somehow, you who live and die. The film you have spread you will likewise rend; surely, surely, you must slip into heaven. There is no rule of divine conduct, no text-book of enchantments. Say if you will, that they are always the same, one under many forms. Call them disguises of the emancipator. This you may do, but you cannot prescribe to him the method of your emancipation. He tears the veil as he chooses, with dawn-rose fingers of adoration and fiery fingers of enthusiasm, but also with the scarlet band of passion and the livid hand of death.

"Then in the faint grey morning I heard a sound as of distant surf, I breathed a breath of the ocean, and it seemed to me that I was as a doomed ship whose crew—a motley crew of hopes and thoughts and passions—had suddenly recollected that they could not drown, but would surely reappear and, drenched with the brine of oblivion, man some new craft, putting their pride again in some gallant ship of self till its sails too hang in rotten shreds and pitiful timbers give way once more."[1]

Orthodox religion is being steadily neglected for the interest in psychology: "To me, the crux of the spiritual problem of to-day is to be found in the fascination which psychic life exerts upon modern man. If we are pessimists, we shall call it a sign of decadence; if we are optimistically inclined, we shall see in it the promise of a far-reaching spiritual change in the Western world. At all events, it is a significant manifestation. It is the more noteworthy because it shows itself in broad sections of every people; and it is the more important because it is a matter of those imponderable psychic forces which transform human life in ways that are unforeseen and—as history shows—unforeseeable. These are the forces, still invisible to many persons to-day, which are at the bottom of the present 'psychological' interest. When the attractive power of psychic life is so strong that a man is neither repelled nor dismayed by what he is sure to find, then it has

[1] C. J. Jung, *op. cit.*, p. 260.

[1] H. B. Brewster, *The Prison*, p. 131.

RELIGION

nothing of sickliness or perversion about it."[1]

§ 5. If the truths of religion are anywhere, they must be in man's heart and mind. And psychology is the science that explores the hidden places in the heart and mind of man, the science of self-knowledge, the knowledge of the psyche or soul. With the decrease of interest in orthodox religion we have the increase of interest in the unconscious. The concept of God is largely replaced by the conception of the unconscious.

Up to the present the methods of psychology have been mostly analytical. The contents of the unconscious had to be explored before they could be understood. Observation comes first, then experiment, and finally laws and methods of applying them are discovered. Analysis precedes construction. We must discover and assemble the parts before we can make a synthesis.

Yet it is also true that the part can only be understood in the light of the whole. The methods of psycho-analysis are inadequate. It is comparatively easy to take things to pieces, but it is not so easy to put them together again in a new and better form.

Professor Jung has laid the foundations for the constructive psychology of the future. As psychology becomes constructive the psychologist will more and more take the place once held by the priest in his capacity as a spiritual guide: "As a doctor I can easily admit doubts while it is hard for the clergyman to do so. The patient feels my attitude to be one of understanding, while the pastor's hesitation strikes him as a traditional prejudice, which estranges them from one another. He asks himself: 'What would the pastor say if I began to tell him of the painful details of my sexual disturbances?' He rightly suspects that the pastor's moral prejudice is even stronger than his dogmatic bias." The task of the constructive psychologist is the regeneration of the individual. This task involves the understanding, control and development of man's latent creative forces in the interests of the race; the expansion and intensification of consciousness and the identification of consciousness with supra-personal aims and interests; the liberation of instinctive forces and their transformation into conscious wisdom, inspiration and power. Inward vision and clear thinking will replace the authority of churches and the revelations of scripture. External authority will tend to be held of less value than inward integrity. A man will be judged to be sincere to the degree he follows his inward vision of truth ("This above all, to thine own self be true . . .").

§ 6. For many ages the world has grown so accustomed to the external authority of religion as exemplified in churches, sects and creeds, that it has almost forgotten that religion always originates from *within*. The religious experience of a Moses, a Buddha, a Christ, a St. Paul, a St. Francis is always a psychological experi-

[1] C. J. Jung, *op. cit.*, p. 251.

ence. These prophets and masters did not get their gnosis from tradition or by any process of ratiocination, they drew it from the deep wells of the unconscious; wells which are open to all no matter whether they belong to any church or none. All that is demanded is a disciplined life and an earnest seeking for truth. But the discipline requires that a man shall cease to defend and assert himself and instead confess himself fallible and human. Until he is ready to practise this the way to progress is barred, no matter how learned and how clever he be. "Give up what thou hast," it was said in the Greek Mysteries, "and then thou shalt receive."

But the giving up must be utterly sincere and must include all the little roots of the ego; pride and jealousy and self-will and greed, which cling so closely about the heart.

And what future, it may be asked, if Professor Jung be right in his tentative forecast, is there for the clergy? If psychology is to take the place of religion, will they continue as the paid servants of church or state?

Perhaps that question is outside the scope of an article on religion. And yet it is a problem which demands consideration. The time is rapidly approaching when the empty church will force upon an apathetic nation the economic question: "Why and wherefore are we maintaining at great expense this clerical system and these ancient edifices? Are we justified in supporting these servants for performing duties which do not appear to be required?"

The only way in which the ancient and honourable institution of the Church of England —the State or official religion of the whole British Empire—can be saved from final shipwreck is by courageous reform within her own household. And the needed reforms are clear for all to see.

1. By the study of comparative religion she must awake to the fact that it is useless to-day to insist upon the acceptance of dogmas, most—if not all—of which are outworn and therefore to-day untrue. Dogmatic instruction apart, the Church would still have an ample fund from which to teach. The greatest sages and the greatest saints have not insisted upon theological dogma; their stress has been upon ethics and the universal compulsion of the moral law. What is all the dogmatic teaching of St. Paul worth compared with his noble exhortation to the Corinthians (1 Cor. xiii.)? Of what value are any doctrines St. Francis may have taught compared with the quickening inspiration of his life, his faith, his idealism and his joyous Song to the Sun?

2. She must see to it that the clergy are educated in such a way that, free from the bias which the acceptance of traditional dogma has thrust upon them, they are capable of playing the part of leaders, moral and intellectual. The laity are longing for guidance and for light. But they refuse to be guided by an ancient lamp long since blown out. In other

words, the Church must so educate her sons and so train and test them that their inward power, selfless, balanced and inspired by the highest ideals, shall compel respect and win devotion. Otherwise no matter how eloquently they preach or how persuasively they write, their message will fall where there are none to heed.

§ 7. One other question. Will the Christian religion itself pass away?

In a scientific age it should not be necessary to put that question. And yet it is frequently asked. All things, religion included, are and always have been in a state of flux. Every religion in a sense fails. It looks forward to a Millennium, but the Millennium does not come. Just as every tree dies when age overtakes it, so must every religion pass when its work is done. And Christianity is certainly no exception to this wholesome rule. Man is not a complete being. He has risen out of lower forms and will rise to higher. And development lies for him in the cleansing of his heart and the quickening of his higher faculties. Is perfection possible for man? All we can say is that he has attained greatly and will attain far more. He is still mostly animal, as the present state of the world testifies, but there are stirrings of the higher nature within. And, whether attainable or not, the pursuit of the Ideal is entirely justified in its results: "I do not say that people whose interest is in the knowledge and attainment of the perfect life are pursuing a shadow. Though their effort can never—and they are the first to recognize it—be completely achieved, yet it embodies a strong and beautiful passion; it is one of the human crafts and those who join the guild have a fellowship in it and a function by it. They do not pretend to achieve absolute success, yet they can succeed even as an artist whose ideal is greater than his works, and yet his works are great. But as they can be said to succeed, so too from the same standpoint must others be said to fail who have never sought the perfect life, or seeking it have sought in vain. What becomes of these? When we ask this question we are sometimes met with the proud rejoinder that such people do not count, that they have not attained to the human estate, and that having merely vegetated they will merely rot. Surely this is an uncharitable and somewhat flippant reply, reminding one of the axiom laid down by some Austrian nobleman that humanity begins at barons. A view commendable for its drollery but deficient in other respects. No! if we put the religious value of life in the achievement of a certain kind of life, we must offer new and endless chances of success to those who fail in this their first existence and who may fail again an indefinite number of times. We must offer them purgatory or reincarnation."[1]

Always man is hampered by the inner conflict; "for the good that I would I do not, but the evil which I would not,

[1] H. B. Brewster, *op. cit.*, p. 146.

that I do." Only in the perfect Masters such as Buddha and Christ is this conflict transcended. In them the unconscious mind comes under the control of the conscious, bringing a harmony unknown to us, and a power which must seem "miraculous" to those ignorant of the laws of psychology.

Surely in the light cast by such leaders man can go forward confidently into the unknown.

RELIGIOUS EDUCATION. See *Education, Religious.*

RELIGIOUS EXPERIENCE. Religious experience has been well defined as "morality tinged with emotion." Church rituals and the outward observances of religion are of little value except in so far as they deepen the sense of awe and wonder in the Unknown and Unknowable. Religious experience deepens, in certain natures and under certain circumstances, into mystical experience. Religions and creeds, though necessary and useful, are but the leading-strings to teach the child to walk. He must not cling to them too tenaciously. If he does, the greater experiences will not come. Cf. *Initiation.* (See William James, *Varieties of Religious Experience*; Ames, *Psychology of Religious Experience*; Rudolf Steiner, *The Way of Initiation.*)

RELIGIOUS ORDERS. See *Orders, Holy.*

RELIQUARY. A box in which relics are kept.

REMONSTRANTS. A sect of Dutch Protestants who gained their name from presenting a "Remonstrance" in 1610 to the States of Friesland and Holland.

RENAISSANCE (RENASCENCE). The European movement of the 14th and 15th C.s which turned from Scholasticism to the study of the Greek and Latin classics. The outstanding figures of the Renaissance period are: Petrarch, Boccaccio, Salutato, Chrysoloras, Niccoli, Bracciolini, Cosimo de' Medici, Guicciardini. And, slightly later, in the religious field, Reuchlin, Melanchthon and Erasmus, Colet and Sir Thomas More. The movement was also splendidly reflected in the work of the great painters of Italy (Giotto, Michael Angelo, Da Vinci, etc.) and in the liberalism of some of the Renaissance popes. The influence of the Renaissance on the Protestant Reformation was profound. (See J. H. Symonds, *The Renaissance in Italy* (7 vols.); J. A. Gobineau, *The Renaissance* (1913).)

RENAN, JOSEPH ERNEST (1823–92). French theologian and Orientalist. His study of philosophy led him to renounce his orders in the Catholic Church and devote himself to scholarship. Though rejecting supernatural religion he advocated the religion of inner experience. His *Life of Jesus* caused a sensation in the religious world. Renan takes a higher place as a stylist than as a philosopher or theologian. (See William Barry, *Life of Renan.*)

REPENTANCE. Sorrow for what has been done or omitted. True religious experience always begins with that softening of the entire nature and widening of the sympathies called by theologians a "change of heart," and referred to by psychologists as the release of repressions, or inhibitions. It involves a complete re-orientation to life. Repentance for sin is better expressed in modern phraseology as humiliation at the frequent inability to rise above the animal nature.

REQUIEM. A Mass sung for the souls of the dead. (L. *Requiem aeternam dona eis, Domine* = Give them eternal rest, O Lord.)

REREDOS. A screen behind an altar (eccles. archit.).

RESCRIPT. A written reply from the Pope to a legal or ethical question. (From the *rescripts* of the Roman Emperors which had the force of law.)

RESERVATION, MENTAL. See *mental reservation.*

RESERVATION OF THE SACRAMENT. The practice of keeping a portion of the eucharistic elements for the sick who are unable to attend the church service. The custom appears to have arisen in the 2nd C. A.D. In medieval times portions of the Sacraments were set aside for adoration and out of this custom the Feast of Corpus Christi (q.v.) developed. In Protestant churches the custom is to consecrate the elements each time holy communion is administered to the sick.

RESIDENTIARY CANON. See *Canon.*

RESURRECTION OF THE BODY. The doctrines of resurrection on the one hand and reincarnation on the other constitute the chief differences between the four leading religions—Buddhism, Christianity, Brahmanism, and Mohammedanism. "Christianity in its orthodox form, rejects the most ancient and widespread belief of the *Kuklos geneseon* or *Sangsara*, or 'Reincarnation,' and admits one universe only—this, the first and last—and two lives, one here in the natural body and one hereafter in the body of resurrection. . . . The resurrection doctrine limits man's lives to two in number, of which the first or present determines for ever the character of the second or future. . . . To Brahmanism and Buddhism this present universe is not the first and last. It is but one of an infinite series, without absolute beginning or end, though each universe of the series appears and disappears. They also teach a series of successive existences therein until morality, devotion and knowledge produce that high form of detachment which is the cause of liberation from the cycle of birth and death called 'The Wandering' or *Sangsara*. Freedom is the attainment of the Supreme States called the Void, Nirvana, and by other names" (Professor Evans-Wentz, *The Tibetan Book of the Dead*, p. xxvii).

RESURRECTION OF JESUS CHRIST. See *Christ, Jesus,* § 1 (3).

RETREAT. A time or place for religious meditation. Cf. the Hindu Ashram.

RETRO-CHOIR. A space behind the high altar.

REVELATION. Man, since earliest ages, has desired information concerning matters which transcend human knowledge (e.g. Is there a God? A future life? An intelligent force behind or within life? etc.). He has sought to gain this information by many methods: divination, oracles, dreams, ecstasy, sacred books. The great religions have been regarded (and still are by many) as repositories of non-human or miraculous communications of truth. More philosophic views and a better knowledge of psychology have led to a modification of this belief. Revelation is now generally regarded as due—not to an arbitrary divine violation of the laws of nature—but to the exceptional spiritual insight, or illumination of certain prophets, poets, seers and sages. See also *Initiation.*

REVIVALS, RELIGIOUS. Times of renewed zeal which manifest in all religions under certain conditions. In Christianity the earliest religious revival was that which occurred on the Day of Pentecost (Acts ii.) when 3,000 were converted in one day. The work of St. Francis of Assisi in the 13th C. led to a great revival within the Church. The Protestant Reformation may be regarded as a religious revival due in large measure to the power wielded by Luther. Of modern revivals, that of the Wesleys in the 18th C. is the most famous. It quickened the Church of England from a state of apathy to renewed activity. Many revivals have occurred in the U.S.A. during—and since—the 19th C.

§ 2. The phenomena of religious revivals differ only in detail. Religious emotionalism is common to them all, accompanied by conversion (q.v.) or regeneration. There is no doubt that mass suggestion evoked by a powerful preacher operates at such times, no matter whether the revivalist be a Hindu sadhu, an Arab dervish or an Anglican divine. (See J. Burns, *Revivals: Their Laws and Leaders*; G. A. Coe, *The Psychology of Religion* (1916).)

RIDLEY, NICHOLAS (1500–55). English bishop and martyr. He opposed the accession of Mary to the throne on religious grounds. (See J. A. Froude, *History of England.*)

RIGHTEOUSNESS. A theological and ecclesiastical term for holiness or goodness; now little used except in the pulpit.

RIG-VEDA. A collection of 1,028 hymns composed by the early Vedic Aryans. These hymns give us a faithful picture of the civilization of India forty centuries ago, the earliest civilization of the Aryan race. See *Vedic Religion.*

RIMMON. See *Rammon.*

RING, EPISCOPAL. The ritual ring worn by a bishop. The first mention of such a ring occurs in A.D. 610. It was derived from the ordinary signet ring.

RISHI. A Hindu sage or poet. The term is sometimes applied to the authors of the Vedic hymns.

RITUALISM. The popular name for the zealous attention paid to religious ceremonial, vestments, etc., in the High Church party of the Church of England since about 1860. See *Oxford Movement.*

ROBERTSON, FREDERICK WILLIAM (1816–53). Anglican divine, known as "Robertson of Brighton." For six years he was incumbent of Trinity Chapel, Brighton, where his preaching attracted large congregations.

ROCHET. A close-fitting linen or lawn vestment worn by bishops and abbots.

ROCKITE, EXTREME. "One who takes *The Rock,* a clerical newspaper, as gospel and proceeds to preach on this basis. This rock seems to have been based on sand, for it has disappeared." (Eric Partridge, *Slang,* p. 198.)

ROGATION DAYS. The Monday, Tuesday and Wednesday before Ascension Day, so called from the custom of chanting processional litanies on those days. The Rogation Days are of ancient—probably 5th-C.—origin.

ROLLE, RICHARD (c. 1290–1309). Hermit and poet, born at Thornton Dale, Yorkshire. At the age of 19 he ran away from home to Hampole, near Doncaster, and became a hermit. During the next three years he passed through preliminary stages of purification and illumination. He records that he attained the highest stage of ecstasy four years and three months after his conversion. He belonged to no order and acknowledged no rule. He wrote many poems in Latin and English, the most considerable being the *Pricke of Conscience.* (See C. Horstmann, *Yorkshire Writers* (2 vols. 1896, Library of Early English Writers); monograph by D. Harford (1913).)

ROMAN CATECHISM. The catechism of the Catholic Church drawn up by the Council of Trent (1545–63) and designed to oppose the Protestant Reformation.

ROMAN CATHOLIC CHURCH. See *Church, Christian ; Papacy and Popes.*

ROMAN EMPIRE, HOLY. The German Empire (a loose federation of states and towns) was so called from A.D. 962 to 1806 when Francis II of Hapsburg resigned the imperial title.

ROMAN RELIGION. The religion of ancient Rome underwent many modifications during its history from the time of the foundation of Rome to the official recognition of Christianity in the time of Constantine.

During its earliest period, from the Foundation of the City (753 B.C.) to the Dedication of the Capitoline Temple (509 B.C.), Roman religion was of a precise, formal and primitive nature. The people were occupied entirely with agriculture and war. Their gods—of whom there was a multitude—reflected their activities. Saturnus was the god of sowing and reaping; Ceres, the spirit of growth; Flora, of flowers; Pomona, of fruit; Pales, of pasture; Fons, of springs; Vesta, of the hearth. There were also lesser divine powers—Larës, protectors of the home; Penatës, spirits of the penus or store-room; Manes, spirits of the dead; the Genius, man's spiritual double, and the Juno, whose functions were the same for women. Over all these gods and spirits ruled the divine triad, Jupiter, Mars and Quirinus—Quirinus being a local god of war. Religion during this early period was mainly a matter of elaborate ceremonial. There were numerous festivals which were celebrated according to a strict formula of prayers, processions, sacrifices and ritual. Religion was ritualistic rather than ethical and insisted upon the maintenance of public worship on its time-honoured basis.

§ 2. With the Dedication of the Capitoline Temple in 509 B.C. a second period commenced which may be said roughly to close with the beginning of the Second Punic War (218 B.C.). During this time many foreign influences flowed in—the chief being Greek and Etruscan (the Tarquins were Etruscans). The triad of Jupiter, Mars and Quirinus in the Capitoline Temple gave place to the group of Jupiter, Juno and Minerva. From the Greek colonies of southern Italy came the cults of Apollo, Mercury, Hermes and Demeter. With the extension of political power the spectacular element in the State religion became more prominent. Statues and temples increased in number and magnificence. The State Triumph was introduced to signalize a victory. The great festivals of the Lectisternium and the Supplicatio were instituted. The Lectisternium was a banquet of gods. Food offerings were placed on a long table and the images of the gods were arranged on surrounding couches. It became one of the spectacles of Rome and crowds flocked in to see it. The Supplicatio was a festival of prayer. In times of national danger or rejoicing, the people, garlanded and bearing laurel-branches, passed from temple to temple, praying for aid to the gods or giving thanks for a victory.

§ 3. A third period of Roman religion opened with the beginning of the Second Punic War (218 B.C.) and closed with the end of the Republic (27 B.C.). The number of foreign cults increased rapidly, but the old State religion was in its decline. In 205 B.C., the Senate, wearied with the long Carthaginian War, decreed that the worship of the Phrygian Cybele, Great Mother of the Gods, should be introduced into Rome. The cult of Isis entered the city about the same time. Education had made great progress, primitive simplicity had given way to luxury and the cultured classes were becoming familiar with Greek philosophy. The old State religion fell into neglect; ceremonies were disregarded; temples and shrines remained untended.

§ 4. The fourth period of Roman religion, from the reforms of Augustus to the accession of Constantius, was a time of ferment and gradual decline. Augustus tried to stem the rising tide of religious apathy. He reorganized the priesthoods; appointed himself to the office of High Priest of Jupiter (Flamen Dialis) and rebuilt temples and shrines. He also introduced the worship of the Emperors, himself building a temple to Julius Caesar in the Forum. But the old religion would not fit the new times. Foreign cults alone attracted—Isis, Serapis, Mithras, the Carthaginian Caelestis, the Syrian Christ. Among all these cults, that of Christ made slow but steady progress, and when in A.D. 311 the emperors Galerius, Constantine and Licinius granted Christianity official recognition, its triumph was complete. Within three generations the old Roman religion had passed away. (See Warde Fowler, *The Roman Festivals*; J. B. Carter, *The Religion of Numa*.)

ROMANY RELIGION. See *Gipsies, Religion of.*

ROOD-SCREEN. A partition separating the choir from the nave, so called from the crucifix (rood) surmounting it. (A.S. *rod* = cross.)

ROSARY. A string of beads used by Mohammedans, Tibetan Buddhists and Catholics to assist their devotions.

ROSARY, FESTIVAL OF THE. A Catholic festival (1st Sunday in October) commemorating the victory over the Turks at Lepanto in 1571.

ROSE, GOLDEN. See *Golden Rose.*

ROSICRUCIANISM. The name of a 17th-C. fraternity of mystics in Germany and France. The society was strictly secret and anonymous, but its influence was considerable. Nothing is known of the origin of the Rosy Cross, though it is attributed to a certain Christian Rosenkreutz of whom no records remain. Death was said to be the penalty for disclosure of its secrets and activities. Rosicrucian influence is seen in the ritualism of Freemasonry and in much of the literature of the 17th and 18th C.s—notably in Francis Bacon's *New Atlantis.* (See Heckethorn, *Secret Societies of all Ages and Countries*; A. E. Waite, *The Real History of the Rosicrucians.*)

ROSMINIANISM. The philosophical system of Rosmini-Serbati (1737–1855). Rosmini taught that *Being* is the only true form of intelligence.

ROSSI OF FERRARA, AZARISH DEI. See *Reformed Judaism.*

ROSWITHA (c. 960). A German nun who wrote plays based on the lives of saints. She modelled her style on Terence with great success. (See Jack Lindsay, *Medieval Latin Poets* (1934).)

ROUSSEAU, JEAN JACQUES (1712–78). French philosopher and man of letters. His *Émile* had a wide influence on education.

ROW, JOHN (1568–1646). Scottish ecclesiastical historian. His chief work is his *Historie of the Kirk of Scotland*, 1558–1637.

RUBRIC. The directions in liturgies for the conduct of services, formerly printed in red ink.

RUFINUS, TYRRANIUS (c. 343–410). Presbyter and theologian. He was a great friend of Jerome (q.v.), but their friendship was severed because Rufinus supported Origen, of whom Jerome disapproved.

RULE OF FAITH. (1) A formula of belief drawn up by the Catholic Church in the 2nd C. as a defence against Gnosticism (q.v.). (2) In Polemical theology the sources whence Christian doctrines are derived—the Scriptures, the traditions of the Church and the teaching of the Fathers.

RURAL DEAN. See *Dean, Rural.*

RUSKIN, JOHN (1819–1900). English writer on art, economics and sociology. A man of noble character and exalted aspirations. He wielded a powerful influence on the art and economics of his time. As a stylist he occupies a front pew. For his life, see *Praeterita.*

RUSSELL, BERTRAND (b. 1872). A leading English Freethinker and mathematician. Author of *The Conquest of Happiness* (1930), *Sceptical Essays*, etc.

RUSSIAN CHURCH. See *Church, Christian.*

RUTH, BOOK OF. An O.T. book of late authorship or, according to some authorities, an old narrative re-written in a later age. The book presents a charming picture of Oriental domestic life. (See S. R. Driver, *Literature of the Old Testament.*)

RUTHENIAN CHURCH. The church of the Ruthenians, a branch of the Slav race inhabiting the Carpathians. The Ruthenians have their own liturgy but acknowledge the Pope.

RUTHERFORD, SAMUEL (1600–61). Scottish theologian and controversialist. He upheld the divine right of the Presbytery. His fame rests chiefly upon his *Letters.*

RUYSBROECK, JAN VAN (1293–1381). Dutch priest and mystic. At the age of sixty he withdrew to the monastery of Groenendael, near Waterloo, and devoted his time to meditation and mystical writing. He taught that "the soul finds God in its own depths," advancing through three stages: (1) active life, (2) inward life, (3) contemplative life. (See Rufus M. Jones, *Studies in Mystical Religion.*)

S

SAADIA, BEN JOSEPH (A.D. 892–942). Jewish Arabian philosopher who translated the Bible into Arabic. He introduced Arabic speculation into Jewish theology. Author of the *Sefer*

Emunot We Deot (*Book of Faith and Doctrine*).

SABAISM (**SABIANISM, SABAEISM, SABEISM, SABAEANISM**). The doctrines of a semi-Christian Babylonian sect of star-worshippers. (Heb. *tsaba* = host, army.)

SABAOTH. The word occurs only in the Bible phrase "the Lord of Sabaoth," where it is confused with sabbath. (Heb. *tsebaoth*, pl. of *tsaba*=an army.)

SABATIER, LOUIS AUGUSTE (1839–1901). French Protestant theologian. Author of *Outlines of a Philosophy of Religion.*

SABBATARIANISM. (1) A fanatically strict observance of Sunday or the Sabbath. (2) The doctrine of the Seventh Day Baptists that the Jewish Sabbath, or seventh day, should be observed as the Christian day of rest.

SABBATH and **SUNDAY** (or **LORD'S DAY**). The Jews set apart the seventh day of the week for rest; the Christians appoint the first day of the week in memory of Christ's resurrection. The first legal recognition of Sunday ("the venerable day of the sun") occurs in a decree of Constantine in 321. There is no connection between the Jewish Sabbath and the Christian Sunday; the idea of connecting the two arose with the English Puritans of the 17th C.

SABBATICAL YEAR. Every seventh year in which the ancient Israelites left their fields and vineyards fallow.

SABELLIANISM. The doctrine held by Sabellius (3rd C.) that the three Persons of the Trinity are not distinct persons but the same person under three aspects. Callistus banished him from Rome.

SABIANISM. See *Sabaism.*

SACAEA. An ancient Babylonian festival during which a prisoner, condemned to death, was clad in the king's robes, seated on the royal throne, allowed to issue whatever commands he pleased, to eat, drink and enjoy himself. But at the end of five days he was stripped, scourged and hanged. (See Sir J. G. Frazer, *Golden Bough*, "The Dying God.")

SACERDOTALISM. Excessive devotion to priestly authority.

SACRAMENTALISM (**SACRAMENTARIANISM**). The attachment of excessive importance to the Christian Sacraments.

SACRAMENTS. See *Eucharist.*

SACRARIUM. The sanctuary of a church, containing the altar.

SACRED HEART OF JESUS. A Catholic observance (Feast of the Sacred Heart) appointed by Pius IX in 1856 to be kept on the Friday following the octave of Corpus Christi.

SACRED THREAD. The distinguishing mark of the three higher Hindu castes. It is worn on the left shoulder.

SACRIFICE. An offering made to a god. Among all primitive peoples religion has begun with ritual sacrifices—the slaying of a man or an animal to appease angry gods. With the development of civilization the old ideas take new and more refined shape. Blood is no longer spilt, although reference is made to it in the liturgies used. In the festival of the Bouphonia, at Athens, a sacrificial bull was slain. "The hide was stuffed with straw and sewed up, and next the stuffed animal was set on its feet and yoked to a plough as though it were ploughing. The Death is followed by a Resurrection. Now this is all-important. We are so accustomed to think of sacrifice as the death, the giving-up, the renouncing of something. But *sacrifice* does not mean 'death' at all. It means *making holy*, sanctifying: and holiness was to primitive man just special strength and life. What they wanted from the Bull was just that special life and strength which all the year long they had put into him. . . . That life was in his blood. They could not eat that flesh nor drink that blood unless they killed him. So he must die. But it was not to give him up to the gods that they killed him, not to 'sacrifice' him in our sense, but to have him, keep him, eat him, live *by* him and through him, by his grace" (Jane Harrison, *Ancient Art and Ritual*).

SACRILEGE. Profanation of a thing or place regarded as holy. See *Taboo*.

SACRING-BELL. In Catholic worship a hand-bell rung to call attention to the more sacred parts of the Mass.

SACRIST (SACRISTAN, SEXTON). A church officer who rings the bell, digs graves, etc.

SACRISTY (VESTRY). A room in a church where the vestments, robes, etc., are kept.

SADDHARMA-PUNDARIKA ("THE LOTUS OF THE TRUE LAW"). One of the most important documents (2nd C. A.D.) of Mahayana Buddhism (q.v.), highly venerated in China and Japan. The Lotus of the True Law insists that sainthood is the result of seeking to live in harmony with the laws of Reality—and is not due simply to ascetic practices, meditations, etc.

SADDUCEES. A Jewish sceptical and aristocratic party in N.T. times.

SADHANA. Realization of unity, the yogi's aim in the practice of meditation. See *Yoga*.

SADHU. A Hindu hermit who has renounced the world. (Feminine, sadhuni).

SADISM. Sexual perversion inspired by love of cruelty. From the infamous de Sade (1740–1814).

SAHAGUN. Spanish missionary who accompanied the Spaniards in their conquest of Mexico. An honest and courageous man who ventured to point out resemblances to Christian doctrine in the religion of the Aztecs. This infuriated the Catholics, who seized Sahagun's manuscripts, and it was only after an appeal to the Spanish Court that he recovered them. At the age of 80 he sent two big volumes of manuscript back to Spain for safety, but they disappeared immediately on arrival and only turned up two centuries later in a convent at Tolosa (Navarre). Lord Kingsborough published them in England in 1830. His experience bears a curious analogy with that of John William Colenso, bishop of Natal (q.v.). The moral would appear to be that a good missionary, though he cannot have too much zeal, may easily have too much honesty.

SAINT. See *initiation*.

SAINTS. The following are the chief Christian Saints with their symbols:

Saints.		*Symbols.*
Agatha	3rd C.	Her severed breasts in a dish.
Agnes	4th C.	A lamb.
Andrew	1st C.	A saltire cross.
Anne (Mother of the B.V.M.)		A book in her hand.
Anthony	4th C.	A tau cross and a pig with a bell round its neck.
Augustine of Hippo	4th C.	A burning heart.
Barnabas	1st C.	A staff in one hand and the gospel in the other.
Bartholomew	1st C.	A butcher's knife.
Bernard of Clairvaux	11th C.	A beehive.
Bridget of Sweden	14th C.	A crozier and book.
Catherine	4th C.	An inverted sword, or large wheel.
Cecilia	3rd C.	A harp or organ.
Christopher	3rd C.	A giant carrying the Christ-child over a river.
Clement	1st C.	A papal crown or an anchor.
Crispin and Crispian	3rd C.	Two shoemakers at work.
David	5th C.	A leek.
Denys (or Dionysius)	3rd C.	Holding his mitred head in his hands.
Dorothy	4th C.	A basket of apples and roses.
Edward the Confessor	11th C.	Crowned with a nimbus.
Elizabeth (mother of John the Baptist)	1st C.	St. John and the lamb at her feet.
Francis of Assisi	12th C.	A seraph inflicting the five wounds of Christ.
George	4th C.	On horseback, transfixing a dragon.
Giles	8th C.	A hind with its head in the saint's lap.
Hubert	7th C.	A stag bearing the crucifix between its horns.
Ignatius	15th C.	The monogram I.H.S. on his breast.
John the Divine (the disciple whom Jesus loved)	1st C.	An eagle and a chalice from which issues a dragon.
Jerome	4th C.	A cardinal's hat and a large folio. (Jerome was never a cardinal.)
Lawrence	3rd C.	A book and a gridiron.
Lucy	4th C.	A burning lamp and two eyes on a dish.
Luke the Evangelist	1st C.	With an ox, or painting the Virgin Mary.
Mark the Evangelist	1st C.	A couched lion.
Mary the Virgin	1st C.	A lily.

Saints.		Symbols.
Matthew the Evangelist . .	1st C.	An angel.
Michael	5th C.	Holding scales to weigh souls.
Nicholas (of Bari)	4th C.	A tub with naked infants in it.
Paul the Apostle	1st C.	A sword and a book.
Peter the Apostle	1st C.	Keys and a triple cross.
Roche (of Montpellier) . .	14th C.	A dog with a loaf in its mouth.
Sebastian	4th C.	Bound to a tree, and transfixed with arrows.
Stephen (the first martyr) .	1st C.	A book and a stone in his hand.
Thomas (the Apostle who doubted)	1st C.	A builder's rule in his hand.
Ursula	5th C.	A book and arrows.

SAINTS, CANONIZATION OF. Enrolment on the canon of Catholic saints. The process consists of an investigation by two officers — "God's advocate" and "the Devil's advocate"— to determine whether or no the prospective saint has received sufficient popular veneration to merit canonization.

SAINTS, VENERATION OF. During early centuries the Christian Church transformed pagan festivals into Saints' days. Distinction had to be made between worship of God and devotion to the Saints. The Second Council of Nicea (787) defined worship of God as *latreia* and veneration of Saints as *proskunesis*.

SAIVISM. The Hindu worship of Shiva. Shiva is a god of creation as well as of destruction. His symbol is the linga. He is worshipped by multitudes, including the learned and the ignorant in India. See *Shiva*.

SAKTI. Wife of Shiva (q.v.). The Hindus regard the supreme God as passive and contemplative. They therefore ascribe the creative functions manifesting in evolution as due to his wife. Sakti is the energizing force in the world.

SAKYAMUNI. See *Buddha*.

SALVATION. In Christian theology the saving of man from the penalty—or results of sin. All religions, from the earliest times, have been regarded as a bridge to safety from the perils of wrongdoing. The two ways of salvation have been, broadly speaking, (1) Ascetic practice and (2) The observance of ritual. The result has been frequent disputes between the advocates of these two methods. It is seen in the conflict between Christ and the Pharisees; between Luther and the medieval church; and in later times, between philosophy that seeks a way and orthodox religion which claims to have a way founded on traditional dogma and ceremonial. See art. *Religion*, § 4.

SALVATION ARMY. An organization for the spread of evangelical religion mainly among the poor and ignorant, founded by William Booth (q.v.) (1878). (See Railton's, *Life of General Booth* (1912), and St. John Ervine's *God's Soldier* (1934).)

SAMADHI. The condition of non-thought-formation which is the object of Yoga meditation. In samadhi the mind becomes one with that which it contemplates and all sense of separateness (individuality) disappears.

SAMARITAN. An inhabitant of Samaria, in ancient Palestine. The Samaritans were despised by the Jews (Luke x. 30–7).

SAMARITAN PENTATEUCH. A Samaritan version of the Hebrew Pentateuch written in Samaritan characters. It was known to the Fathers but lost and discovered in 1616 by Pietro della Valle.

SAMHAIN. The Celtic November festival of the dead. Bonfires were lighted and divination practised. The Christian Church incorporated some of the old practices and beliefs in All Souls' Day (2 Nov.) (q.v.). Hallowe'en represents, in many aspects, the pagan Samhain.

SAMSARA (also **SANGSARA**). The Hindu belief in the round of births and deaths. Man is driven on by the force of Karma (q.v.) until, by gaining enlightenment, he frees himself from the revolving wheel.

SAMUEL. An important figure in O.T. history. He enabled the Israelites to defeat the Philistines and thereafter became a theocratic judge (1 Sam. vii.).

SAMUEL, BOOKS OF. Two books of the O.T. ranked in the Jewish canon among the Former Prophets (Joshua–Kings). The Books narrate the history of the kingdoms of Saul and David. Their date is uncertain but they incorporate traditions ascribed to the 11th and 10th C.s B.C. (See S. R. Driver, *Introduction to Literature of the Old Testament.*)

SANCTIFICATION. The Christian doctrine of Perfection, attained by regeneration (q.v.) and salvation (q.v.). For its occult and psychological equivalents, see *illumination*.

SANCTUARY. The part of the church containing the altar (archit.).

SANCTUS. In the Catholic liturgy the musical setting of the song, "Holy, holy, holy, Lord God of Hosts" (from Isa. vi.). The sanctus-bell is the bell rung to call attention to the singing of the Sanctus during Mass.

SANDEMANIANS. See *Glassites*.

SANDERSON, ROBERT (1587–1663). English theologian who became bishop of Lincoln. His *Nine Cases of Conscience Resolved* put him at the head of British casuists.

SANGSARA. See *samsara*.

SANHEDRIM (or **SANHEDRIN**). The supreme tribunal of the Jews in ancient Jerusalem. It was composed of scribes, elders and members of wealthy priestly families. It could not pass a death sentence without the sanction of the Roman procurator.

SANKARA (ACHARYA) (A.D. 788–820). The greatest commentator on the Vedanta philosophy of India. Sankara, continuing the work of Kumarila (7th C.), tried to restore the old Vedic rites, which were being neglected for Buddhism. He taught that the only Reality is Brahma. The individual soul, in the toils of mâya (illusion), is bound to suffering until it finds illumination, which brings the knowledge that it is identical with Brahma and has never had a separate existence. The belief in separateness, here and hereafter, persists until illumination is reached.

SANKHYA. A Hindu philosophy —among the oldest and most profound in the world. It is said to have originated with the sage, Kapila. It does not teach that there is a supreme Soul or God, but postulates two ultimate realities, *prakriti* (matter) and *purusha* (spirit). *Prakriti* consists of three constituents or qualities (gunas) of lightness, heaviness and movement in a balanced state. Evolution is due to a disturbance of this balance. The psychical part of man is as material as his body and moves from life to life (reincarnation) until it realizes its entire detachment from the phenomenal world. At death the soul is freed from the body and its psychical counterpart and passes into the deep sleep state of unconsciousness. Only by enlightenment or illumination can this deep sleep condition become conscious. (See Max Muller, *Six Systems of Indian Philosophy*.)

SANNYASI (SANNYASIN). A Hindu ascetic. He usually passes through the four *ashramas* (stages) of student, householder, hermit and ascetic.

SAOSHYANT. The expected prophet or Messiah of the Zoroastrians who will establish the Kingdom of God on earth.

SARDIS, COUNCIL OF. A Church Council, attended by 370 bishops. It condemned Arius (q.v.) (A.D. 347).

SARUM RITE. See *liturgy, The English.*

SATAN. The evil principle of the ancient Israelites, probably derived from the Babylonians. The belief in Satan entered Christianity by way of the gospels. (See Matt. xxi. 26; John xiv. 30; Luke xiii. 16; 1 Cor. v. 5.) (Heb. *satan* = enemy.)

SATYR. A sylvan spirit, half-man, half-beast (Class. myth.). Luther translates the word *feldgeister* = field spirit. Cf. the English Puck.

SAUL. Son of Kish (O.T.) and first king of Israel. He went mad, but David's sweet playing on the harp restored him to sanity (1 Sam. xviii.–xxxi.).

SAVIOUR. The doctrine of a Saviour is world-wide and infinitely old. Research has proved conclusively that belief in a divine Saviour as peculiar to Christianity is erroneous. Christianity merely appropriated the idea and gave it a suitable interpretation. The number of pagan Saviour-gods is enormous. Krishna in India and Indra in Tibet and Nepaul spilt their blood for the salvation of men; Buddha said: "Let all the sins that were in the world fall on me, that the world may be delivered" (Max Muller, *Hist. Sansk. Lit.*, p. 80); the Chinese Tien, "one with God and existing with him from all eternity," died to save the world; the Egyptian Osiris and Horus were called Saviours; the same term was applied by the Persians to Mithras. The Phrygian Attis and the Syrian Tammuz (Adonis) were called Saviours—each rose again from the dead. Bacchus or Dionysus was born of the Virgin Semele to be the Saviour (*Eleutherios*) of mankind. The Mexican Quetzalcoatl, the Saviour, was born of a virgin, was tempted, fasted forty days, was put to death and his Second Coming expected so eagerly that when stout Cortez and his men appeared the Mexicans fell on their knees believing their God had returned. Sahagun (q.v.), the Spanish missionary, was much puzzled by the Mexicans having a Saviour and a Virgin Birth of their own. The universality of this doctrine serves to show that spiritual evolution follows similar lines among all nations and emphasizes the need for toleration and a seeking to *understand* rather than a too eager *readiness to teach*. (See Doane, *Bible Myths*; Sir J. G. Frazer, *Golden Bough*.)

SAVITRI. The sun-god of Hindu Vedic religion.

SAVONAROLA, GEROLAMO (1452–98). Italian monk; a powerful Florentine preacher and reformer. He was burnt on the charge of heresy—his "heresy" being to denounce the proved corruption of the papal court. (See P. Villari, *Life and Times of Savonarola*, trans. by L. Villari.)

SCALA SANTA. A staircase in Rome venerated as being the steps of Pontius Pilate's palace at Jerusalem on which Jesus trod during his trial.

SCAPEGOAT. The goat on which the Jewish high-priest every year symbolically laid the sins of the people. It was then driven into the wilderness (Lev. xvi.). Somewhat similar practices have been used in many parts of the world. Ritual cleansing from sin is so much easier than the fearless seeking for inward and spiritual cleanness. Hence its wide popularity.

SCAPULAR. The working dress of certain monastic orders. It consists of a hood and cloak.

SCEPTICISM. A state of doubt or unbelief. Scepticism is a necessary safeguard against credulity. Balance between these two extremes will lead to a true understanding of most problems.

SCHISM. Separation in, or from, a church owing to diversity of belief.

SCHISM, THE GREAT (or **GREEK**). The separation of the Greek Church from the Latin which took place in 1054.

SCHISM, WESTERN. The division in the Western Church on the appointment of Urban VI by the Romans to the papal chair in 1378 when the French cardinals elected Clement VII who resided at Avignon. The Schism was healed on the election of Martin V by the Council of Constance in 1417. See *Papacy*.

SCHLEIERMACHER, FREDERICK DANIEL ERNST (1768–1834). German preacher and theologian of strongly modernist views.

SCHMALKALD ARTICLES. Articles of faith drawn up by Luther and the German reformers at Schmalkald in 1537.

SCHOLASTICISM. The aims and methods of the intellectual life of the Middle Ages, from the 9th to the 15th c. Scholasticism was marked by unquestioning acceptance of religious dogma and a speculation mainly restricted to the rationalization of theology. Thomas Aquinas (q.v.) was the greatest of the Schoolmen. He was the most advanced "modernist" of his time, and sought to force theological dogma to fit the teaching of Aristotle. Scholasticism broke down in the 15th c. owing to the broader outlook introduced by the Renaissance and the Reformation. (See W. J. Townsend, *The Great Schoolmen of the Middle Ages*.)

SCHOPENHAUER, ARTHUR (1788–1860). German idealist philosopher. Man's greatest need, he taught, is the redemption of the soul from its sensual bonds by the path of renunciation and an ascetic life. (See T. Whittaker, *Schopenhauer*).

SCHWEITZER, ALBERT. A German theologian (b. 1875) noted for the profundity of his thought, the penetration of his criticism, and the width of his sympathy: *Quest of the Historical Jesus; Paul and His Interpreters*. A subtly sane philosopher: *The Philosophy of Civilization*. A doctor-explorer: *On the Edge of the Primeval Forest*. And a famed musical critic: Bach. He is "the very glass" and "the fine flower" of modern Christianity. (See C. T. Campion, *Albert Schweitzer. Some Biographical Notes*.)

SCIENCE, CHRISTIAN. See *Christian Science*.

SCOT, JOHN THE. See *Erigena, John Scotus*.

SCOTLAND, CHURCH OF. See *Church of Scotland*.

SCOTUS, DUNS. See *Duns Scotus*.

SCRIBE. A teacher of the Mosaic law among the ancient Israelites. The Scribes were also known as Rabbis (q.v.). See *Talmud*.

SCRIPTURES. The holy Scriptures of the Great Religions of the world are as follows:

Buddhism.

(*a*) The Hinayana ("Little Vehicle") Buddhism of Ceylon, Burma and Siam, and the Mahayana ("Great Vehicle") Buddhism of Nepal, Tibet,

China and Japan, both accept as their sacred canon the Tipitaka ("Three Baskets"), the Sutta and the Abidhamma. These are written in Pali.

(*b*) The chief Scriptures of the N. Indian Mahayana Buddhism are the Mahavastu, the Saddharma-pundarika ("Lotus of the True Law") and the philosophic Prajna-paramitas.

§ 2

Christianity.

The Bible, consisting of the Old and New Testament canon. See *Bible*.

§ 3

Confucianism.

There are five Chinese Classics: (*a*) The Yi-king or Book of Changes. (*b*) The Shu-king or Book of History. (*c*) The Shi-king or Book of Poetry. (*d*) The Hi-ki or Book of Ceremonial Usage. (*e*) The Chun-chin, a Book of Annals. There are also four Books: (*a*) Lun Yu, Sayings of Confucius. (*b*) Chung Yung, a Book of Moral Conduct. (*c*) Ta Hsueh ("Great Learning") — Confucius's method for cultivating ideal character. (*d*) The Ethical Writings of Mencius (q.v.).

§ 4

Taoism (China).

There are a number of expositions of Taoist doctrine, the chief being the Tao-Teh-King attributed to Lao-Tsze and the philosophy of Chuang-Tsze (q.v.).

§ 5

Hinduism.

The sacred literature of India is enormous. The chief books are as follows:

(*a*) Early Literature. The Rig-Veda, a collection of 1,017 hymns produced by priestly families during many centuries. The Atharva-Veda, a collection of mantras or texts of religion and magic. The Yagur-Veda, a group of liturgies. The Brahmanas, commentaries on the Vedas. The Aranyakas ("Forest Books") and Upanishads—both regarded as inspirational in origin.

(*b*) Later works are the Sutras or priestly commentaries on the Vedas. The eighteen Puranas which deal with cosmology, history and religious philosophy.

(*c*) The popular Vaisnava (or Vishnu-worshipping) literature of India has gathered around the two great epic poems—the Mahabharata and the Ramayana (q.v.). These poems, which have been given religious (Vaisnavite) interest by the priests, are a storehouse of philosophical and theological teaching. The famous Bhagavadgita is a poem within the Mahabharata.

(*d*) The Sankhya-Karita is the classic poem (A.D. 4th C.) of the Sankhya system (q.v.), its theistic element being supplied by the Yoga-Sutra of Patanjali.

(*e*) The Vaisheshika-sutra and the Nyaya-sutra of Gautama are the chief books of the Vaisheshika (q.v.) and Nyaya (q.v.) systems, respectively.

(*f*) The Angas—forty-five in number—constitute the canonical scriptures of the Jains.

§ 6

Judaism.

See *Bible* (*O.T.*); *Talmud*.

§ 7

Egyptian Religion.

The chief surviving Scriptures are:

(*a*) The Book of the Dead—a collection of ritual and magic.

(*b*) The Pyramid Texts, a collection of prayers, myths and hymns.

§ 8

Mohammedanism.

The Koran—a collection of prayers and inspirational utterances of Mohammed made fifteen years after his death (between A.D. 644 and 656). Mohammedans regard every word of it as inspired.

§ 9

Zoroastrianism.

The Avesta, consisting of hymns, legal enactments and liturgies, constitutes the chief Zoroastrian Scripture. It is supplemented by the Pahlavi books written in Pahlavi or Middle Persian.

SEAMEN, THE MISSIONS TO. An English missionary society for the benefit of seamen established in London in 1780. Headquarters: 11 Buckingham Street, Strand, London, W.C.2.

SECOND ADVENT. See *Millenarianism.*

SECT. A group who separate from a church or party.

SECULAR CLERGY. Priests in holy but not monastic orders.

SECULARIZATION. The taking of Church property by the State for its own use. This was done by Sweden in 1527; by England in 1534–8; by Denmark in 1536; by North Germany between 1521 and 1648; and was begun by France in 1790.

SEDER. The Hebrew Passover ceremonial meal.

SEDILIUM. A seat for the officiating clergyman, near the altar.

SEDULIUS (848–74). An accomplished Irish poet. Many of his Latin poems were addressed to Hartgar, bishop of Liège. (See Jack Lindsay, *Medieval Latin Poets.*)

SEE. The jurisdiction of a bishop.

SEE, THE HOLY. The office of Pope. See *Papacy.*

SEEKERS. A Cromwellian sect who stressed the right of individual religious freedom.

SELDEN, JOHN (1584–1654). English lawyer whose *History of Tithes* (in which he denied their claim to divine institution) gave great offence to King James I. Of his *Table-Talk* Coleridge wrote: "There is more weighty bullion sense in this book than I can find in the same number of pages of any uninspired writer." (See Aiken's *Lives of Selden and Usher.*)

SEMINARIST. A Catholic priest educated in a foreign seminary.

SEMITES. The Hebrews, Arabs, Assyrians and Aramaeans—supposed to be descended from Shem, son of Noah.

SEMPRINGHAM. See *Gilbertines.*

SEPARATIST. See *Dissenter*.

SEPTUAGESIMA. The third Sunday before Lent.

SEPTUAGINT. The version of the O.T. in Hellenistic Greek, said to have been made by seventy-two Palestinian Jews at the request of Ptolemy Philadelphus (284–247 B.C.). Written for short as LXX.

SEPULCHRE, THE HOLY. The tomb at Jerusalem in which Christ's body was laid. The Church of the Holy Sepulchre has been built over the reputed site.

SEQUENCE. In Catholic liturgies a hymn sung after the gradual and before the gospel.

SERAPHIC DOCTOR. See *Bonaventura, Saint*.

SERAPHS (SERAPHIM). Celestial beings seen in prophetic vision by Isaiah on either side of the Jehovah's throne (Isa. vi. 2–6).

SERAPION. Bishop of Thebes in Egypt (4th C.) who sided with Athanasius in the Arian controversy. He is the reputed author of one of the early liturgies.

SERAPIS. Ancient Egyptian god of the Underworld; also worshipped as a god of healing.

SERMON. See *homiletics: preaching*.

SERPENT and **SERPENT-WORSHIP.** From the earliest times the serpent has been used as a religious symbol. It was associated with the cult of Asclepius, god of healing, among the Greeks. Owing to its venomous bite it sometimes signifies the malevolent powers. It is also a symbol of renewed life, initiation, regeneration and immortality owing to its capacity for casting its slough and appearing in renewed beauty. Its glittering eyes have caused it to be regarded as a symbol of wisdom. (See C. F. Oldham, *The Sun and the Serpent*; Deane, *Serpent Worship*.)

SERVETUS, MICHAEL (1511–53). Spanish physician and mystic. He entered into controversy with John Calvin and as a result Calvin (unable to refute him by other means) caused him to be burnt as a heretic.

SERVITES. A Catholic mendicant order, dedicated to the service of the Virgin, established in Florence in 1233.

SET. A sun-god of Upper Egypt. He came, in later times, to be regarded as a symbol of the powers of evil.

SETTLEMENT, ACT OF. The Act passed in 1689 to exclude Catholics from the British Throne.

SEXAGESIMA. The second Sunday before Lent.

SEXT (SEXTE). The Catholic midday office. See *Breviary*.

SEXTON. A church officer who digs graves, etc. See also *sacrist*.

SHABBATHAI ZEBI BEN MORDECAI (1626–76). A Jewish youth of

Smyrna who in 1648 declared himself to be the Messiah, causing great excitement among the Jews—for he was of extremely ascetic life and highly developed spiritually. He was arrested by the Sultan and saved his life by embracing Mohammedanism.

SHAIKH. Term for a trained and officially recognized Islamic mystic.

SHAITAN. The Arabic evil spirit or devil.

SHAKERS. (1) An English religious sect founded in Manchester (18th C.). (2) A Quaker sect founded in U.S.A. by Ann Lee. Their religion, as the name implies, is as emotional as it is narrow and fanatical.

SHAKESPEARE, WILLIAM. The greatest of European dramatic poets. From the religious point of view the Shakespeare Plays are of very great importance. Though the writer, or writers, were not moralist in any narrow sense, their influence was consistently on the side of the idealist virtues—courage, magnanimity, gentleness, truth and goodwill to all. In the words of Charles Lamb, the Plays of Shakespeare are " enrichers of the fancy, strengtheners of virtue, a withdrawing from all selfish and mercenary thoughts, a lesson of all sweet and honourable thoughts and actions, to teach courtesy, benignity, generosity, humanity; for of examples, teaching these virtues, his pages are full."

Concerning Shakespeare of Stratford's life, very little is known, and such knowledge of him as we have does not square with the character as self-revealed in the Plays and Sonnets. Hence some have inclined to the view that they were written by Francis Bacon —the greatest and most learned man of the age. The literature gathered around the name of Shakespeare is enormous. An excellent introductory work to Shakespeare study is Logan Pearsal Smith's *Shakespeare*. For serious students, Sir E. K. Chambers's works are of great assistance; and for the Baconian thesis the best and most convincing book is Sir George Greenwood's *Shakespeare Problem Restated*.

SHAKINAH (SHECHINAH). The light, symbolizing the Divine Presence, said to have rested over " the mercy-seat " in the Temple of Solomon at Jerusalem.

SHAMANISM. The religious beliefs and practices of the Turanian races of Siberia. Shamanism is directed by the " shaman " or medicine-man, a priest, doctor and magician combined.

SHAMASH. The Babylonian sun-god.

SHARP, WILLIAM (" FIONA MACLEOD ") (1856–1905). Writer of Celtic tales, poems and novels of fine literary and mystic quality (*The Sin Eater*, *The Washer of the Food*, etc.).

SHEENY. A mainly E. London term for a Jew. (See Eric Partridge, *Slang*.)

SHEN. The good spirits of Chinese folk-lore.

SHEOL. The Hebrew place of departed spirits.

SHIITES. The Mohammedan sect which maintains that Ali, first cousin of Mohammed and husband of his daughter Fatima, was the first legal successor of the Prophet and holder of the Khalifate. They are opposed to the Sunnites, who believe that the Koran and the Sunna (a collection of Islamic traditions) are the true and only sources of authority.

SHI-KING. A collection of Chinese hymns, dating from the 12th to the 6th C. B.C. They laud family worship and the powers of nature.

SHINGON. A mystical Buddhist pantheism taught by the Japanese Kukai (774–835 A.D.).

SHINTO. See *Japan, Religions of.*

SHIVA (SIVA). The Hindu god of Reproduction and Dissolution. His symbol is the *linga* representing the universal creative force. With Brahma and Vishnu he forms the third of the great triad of Hinduism. (Sans. *çiva* = happy).

SHOFAR. The ram's horn sounded at New Moon by the Israelites. It is still blown in the synagogue on New Year's Day.

SHOHET. The Jewish butcher who kills according to ritually prescribed formula.

SHOOL. Jewish term for church or chapel.

SHRADDHAS (SRADDHAS). Hindu family offerings to the souls of dead relatives. They are offered annually on the anniversary of the death.

SHROVE-TIDE. The days preceding Ash-Wednesday. A time for shriving or confession.

SHRINE. A sacred place or altar.

SHRUTI. The inspired scriptures of Hinduism (Vedas, Brahmanas and Upanishads).

SHU-KING. One of the five Chinese classics, probably edited by Confucius. It is a collection of historical and legendary writings. (See *Scriptures,* § 3 (*b*).

SIBYL. A prophetess or sorceress.

SIBYLLINE ORACLES. A collection of Jewish and Christian prophecies in Greek hexameters, the earliest written in the 2nd C. B.C., the latest in the 3rd C. A.D. They were produced to replace the lost Sibylline Books purchased by Tarquin from the Sibyl.

SIDDHIS ("ACCOMPLISHMENT, FRUITION"). Occult powers and supernormal knowledge gained by advanced yogis. See *Yoga.*

SIDDUR. The Jewish prayer-book.

SIDNEY, SIR PHILIP (1554–86). One of the greatest figures of Tudor England, poet, man of letters and soldier. Though outwardly Sidney may not seem to have accomplished much, the profound respect in which he was held by his contemporaries serves to show the brightness of the light that was in him. His friend, Sir Fulke Greville, wrote of him : " But the truth is : his end was not writing, even while he wrote ; nor his knowledge moulded for tables, or schools ; but both his wit, and understanding bent upon his heart, to make himself and others, not in words or opinion, but in life and action, good and great."

SIGEBERT (c. 1030–1112). Latin poet, educated at the monastery of Gembloux, near Liège, to which he returned in later life. A moderate ascetic and fine poet. (See H. Waddell, *Medieval Latin Lyrics.*)

SIGN OF THE CROSS. A movement of the hand outlining an imaginary cross made by Catholics as a sign of devotion.

SIKHS, RELIGION OF THE. A Hindu monotheistic sect founded in the Punjab by Baba Nanak (b. 1469), a disciple of Kabir (q.v.). The Sikhs were originally a quietistic community, but under their leader Arjun (17th C.) developed into a highly armed and trained force. They gained control of the Punjab until conquered by the British in 1849. Their religion represents a revolt against ceremonialism. They believe in one formless, unknowable God of whom individual souls are sparks—salvation consisting in the reunion of the individual soul with God. The Sikhs believe in Karma and reincarnation. Their religion teaches a moral code as exalted as the Christian ; it inculcates loyalty, philanthropy, gratitude, justice, truth, honesty, impartiality. (See Cunningham, *History of the Sikhs* ; Macauliffe, *The Sikh Religion* (6 vols., 1909).)

SIMEONITE. A follower of the Cambridge evangelical preacher Charles Simeon (1759–1836) in whose name the Simeon Trust was established for the purchase of advowsons in the interest of low-church principles.

SIMEON STYLITES (A.D. 390–459). Syrian hermit who lived thirty years on a pillar.

SIMON MAGUS. Samaritan sorcerer who wanted to purchase miraculous powers from Peter and John (Acts viii. 9 ff.).

SIMONY. The crime of presenting to a church benefice in return for money. (From Simon Magus.)

SIN. In theology the doing of acts contrary to divine approval. The seven deadly sins are : pride, covetousness, lust, anger, gluttony, envy, sloth ; cf. the five poisons of Buddhism : lust, hatred, stupidity, egoism and jealousy). See also *scapegoat.*

SIN, ORIGINAL. See *original sin.*

SIVA. See *Shiva.*

SIX ARTICLES. The articles drawn up by Henry VIII in 1543 " for the abolishing diversity of opinions in religion." These articles were mainly anti-Lutheran.

SKANDHAS. In Buddhist doctrine, the aggregate of physical and psychical activities which constitute human personality (the ego). They are the result of the Karmic forces. According to Tibetan Yoga, they consist of five aggregates: body-aggregate; sensation-aggregate; emotion-aggregate; volition-aggregate; consciousness-aggregate. (See Prof. Evans-Wentz, *The Tibetan Book of the Dead.*)

SLYPE. A covered passage connecting the chapter-house to the cathedral (archit.).

SMITH, JOSEPH. See *Mormonism.*

SMITH, SYDNEY (1771–1845). Reputed England's wittiest clergyman. He was one of the founders of the *Edinburgh Review* and became dean of St. Paul's. His reply to a lady who asked if he would object to taking the burial service in the case of a deceased dissenter is characteristic: "Object, madam? I should like to be burying them all day."

SMITH, WILLIAM ROBERTSON (1846–94). Scottish Orientalist and Biblical scholar.

SMITRI. Term for the post-Vedic religious literature of India. It includes the great epics, the Tantras and the Puranas.

SOCIALISM, CHRISTIAN. See *Christian socialism.*

SOCIETY OF JESUS. See *Jesus, Society of.*

SOCIETY FOR PROMOTING CHRISTIAN KNOWLEDGE. See *Christian Knowledge, Society for Promoting.*

SOCIETY FOR THE PROPAGATION OF THE GOSPEL IN FOREIGN PARTS. A C. of E. missionary society with extensive missions in foreign countries. Missionaries (ordained), 989; women, 391; doctors, 18 men, 28 women. Headquarters: 15 Tufton Street, Westminster, S.W.1.

SOCINIANISM. The rationalist Christian doctrines of Laelius Socinus (1525–62) and Faustus Socinus (1539–1604). These two, uncle and nephew, were Italians who migrated to Poland and there gained a following. They denied the doctrine of the Trinity, the deity of Christ, etc. (See T. M. Lindsay, *A History of the Reformation,* vol. ii.)

SOCIOLOGY. The science of human society and culture.

SOCRATES (c. 470–399 B.C.). Athenian philosopher and master of wisdom, comparable with Gautama, the Buddha, Jesus Christ and Mohammed.

Socrates taught, without charge, such young men as cared to come to him. His genius for stimulating reflection and moral purpose was unrivalled and his influence on ethical speculation is still at work. Evil, he taught, is due to ignorance of what is good; good conduct follows from rational insight. His teaching (unlike that of his contemporaries, the Sophists) was consistently positive and constructive. Plato (q.v.), his greatest pupil, deduced his doctrine of Ideas from the Socratic teachings. The Government of Athens, afraid of Socrates' power and influence, condemned him to death by drinking hemlock. (See T. Gomperz, *Greek Thinkers*, vol. ii ; E. B. Osborn, *Socrates and His Friends*.)

SOCRATES (c. A.D. 380–444). Church historian. He was a disciple of Origen (q.v.).

SODALITY. Generic term for a Catholic philanthropic brotherhood.

SOLOMON. Son of David and Bathsheba (1 Kings iii. 5–15). He had the reputation for magnificence and phenomenal wisdom (Matt. vi. 29 ; Luke xi. 31).

SOLOMON BAR ISAAC. See *Rashi*.

SOLOMON, ODES OF. A collection of forty-two hymns (Christian and Jewish) dating from 1st C. (See J. Rendel Harris, *The Odes and Psalms of Solomon*.)

SOLOMON, SONG OF. See *Canticles*.

SOLOMON, WISDOM OF (or **BOOK OF WISDOM**). A work of Greco-Egyptian origin of the 1st C. A.D., probably written by an Alexandrian Jew. See *Apocrypha* (*O.T.*).

SOMA. One of the gods of Hindu Vedic worship. He is the Indian Bacchus, his name being derived from the intoxicating drink made from the soma plant.

SON OF GOD. A term used in the O.T. and N.T. In the O.T. it is occasionally applied to angels and supernatural beings. In apocalyptic writers it is applied to the expected Messiah. In the N.T. it is frequently applied to Jesus as Messiah. Owing to the introduction of the Hellenistic Logos doctrine the term Son of God came to assume a definite doctrinal aspect as applied to Christ. In the hands of the Creed-makers logical definition was carried to ridiculous lengths and religion in Western Europe has had to pay the penalty in the turning away of the more thoughtful section of the community from orthodox organized religion.

SON OF MAN. The term is occasionally used in the O.T. for prophet and Messiah (Dan. vii. 13) and is frequently applied to Jesus in the N.T. It is hard to say how closely it is connected with the Gnostic doctrine of the Ideal and Perfect Man. See *Gnosticism*.

SONG OF SONGS (also called **CANTICLES**). A book that holds a unique position in the O.T. owing to its magnificent lyrical rapture and the unusualness of its content. The old view which ascribed its authorship to Solomon has melted under the scrutiny of scholarship. Cheyne dissipated this theory by his statement that : "The book is an anthology of songs used at marriage festivals, in or near Jerusalem, revised and loosely connected by an editor without regard to temporal sequence." It probably dates from the Greek period, i.e. after 332 B.C. Much allegory has been read into the poem by scholars and theologians. They have not improved it thereby. The most reasonable view is that of Herder in his *Solomon's Song of Love, the Oldest and Sweetest of the East* (1778). Herder, with admirable poetic insight, found in the Canticles the natural expression of innocent and tender love. Viewed in that light the book is one of the lyrical masterpieces of the world.

SOPHISM and **SOPHIST**. The Sophists were professional paid teachers of the 6th C. B.C. in Greece. They travelled from place to place and prepared youth for public life, giving instruction in rhetoric and disputation. Their scepticism, conservatism and general lack of ethical convictions, combined with their aggressive and cocksure professionalism, caused them to become highly unpopular until the term "sophistry" came to denote wilful deception. Socrates frequently made fun of the Sophists, whose influence he regarded as undesirable. The best known Sophists were: Gorgias, Hippias, Prodicus and Protagoras. (See A. W. Benn, *The Greek Philosophers*—I, 53–107.)

SOPHROSUNÉ (SOPHROSYNÉ). The Greek word for a virtue the Greeks prized very highly. It has been translated "soundness of mind," but perhaps "freedom from excess" or "the golden mean" come nearer the meaning. It was used to define the opposite of hubris (hybris) which meant extreme pride or an excessive display of personality.

SORCERY. See *witchcraft*.

SOTERIOLOGY. See *salvation*.

SOUL. The chief ideas underlying this word of vague significance are: (1) The principle of life in men and animals; (2) the principle of thought and action in man; (3) the spiritual element in man in contrast with the purely physical; (4) the seat of the emotions, intellect and spiritual power. Plato and Aristotle taught that man has a "higher" soul to be distinguished from the animal and nutritive; by its means he may enter into intuition (or direct perception) of things divine. In the Hindu and Buddhist systems the body is regarded as a nucleus of qualities carried over from one life to another (see *Skandhas*); man's ultimate destiny being reunion with divine Reality or the One Soul.

SOUTH, ROBERT (1634–1716). English divine, chaplain to Lord Chancellor Clarendon and afterwards to King Charles II. He was notorious for his wit and his sermons are regarded as classics. (See W. C. Lake, *Classic Preachers of the English Church*.)

SPENCER, HERBERT (1820–1903). English philosopher. He held that there is an inscrutable Power behind phenomena. This Power, unknowable by reason, should be held in reverence. (See J. A. Thomson, *Life of Herbert Spencer*.)

SPENSER, EDMUND (1552–99). One of the outstanding poets of Elizabethan England. His influence on his time as a Platonic idealist was very great. He was a friend of Sir Philip Sidney, Sir Fulke Greville, and Sir Edward Dyer. His finest works are *The Epithalamion*, *The Faerie Queen*, *The Ruins of Time* and the *Tears of the Muses*. He had a brilliant sense of colour and many of his poems are a succession of verbal pictures, rich in imagery and music. (See Professor Renwick, *Spenser*.)

SPINOZA, BENEDICT (1632–77). Dutch pantheist philosopher and metaphysician. He taught that God is not only the Creator but Himself the original matter of the universe, all phenomena being a development of Himself. (See Sir Frederick Pollock, *Spinoza, His Life and Philosophy*.)

SPIRIT. The following meanings are, or have been, attached to this term: (1) The vital principle in man or animals. (2) Immaterial being, as opposed to matter or body. (3) That part of a person which passes from the body at death. (4) A supernatural or disembodied being, usually imperceptible to the senses.

SPIRITUALISM (SPIRITISM). The abnormal phenomena purporting to be caused by spirits acting upon highly sensitive persons or mediums. Such phenomena are referred to in all ages from the earliest times. In its modern form spiritualism began to attract attention in 1847—when the famous Fox sisters held séances. The Society for Psychical Research was established in 1882, its aim being to introduce scientific methods into the study of psychic phenomena. The great names associated with the movement are F. W. H. Myers and Sir Oliver Lodge. Occultism in the East, especially in Tibet, furnishes evidence of similar phenomena produced by eastern lamas and yogis. The fact that deception has been proved against certain mediums does not resolve the problems involved. For psychic phenomena have undoubtedly arisen in connection with certain of the saints—men and women whose intelligence and probity were beyond suspicion. (See F. W. Barrett, *Psychical Research*; Frank Podmore, *Studies in Psychical Research*; S. H. Soal in Julian Franklyn's *A Survey of the Occult*.)

SPONSOR. A godfather or godmother.

SPURGEON, CHARLES HADDON (1834–92). English Baptist preacher renowned for his eloquent sermons.

SQUINCH. The small stone arches supporting a spire (archit.).

SQUINT. A narrow opening in the wall of a church to enable worshippers in side-chapels to see the elevation of the host during Mass (archit.).

SRADDHAS. See *Shraddhas*.

STABAT MATER. A Latin hymn on the suffering of the Virgin Mary ascribed to Jacopone da Todi, a 13th-C. Minorite. (See E. H. Blakeney, *Hymns of the Western Church* (1930).)

STALLS. A seat in the choir or chancel of a church or cathedral reserved for the choir and clergy.

STAR OF BETHLEHEM. The legendary star of Christ's nativity (Matt. ii. 2, 9, 10).

STARR, MEREDITH (b. 1890). A constructive psychologist who opened a retreat at East Challacombe, Devon, in 1929. Son of a British father and an American mother, Meredith Starr was brought up in diplomatic and military circles in Vienna and educated at Winchester. After some twenty years of travel, study and meditation he opened his secular retreat to which people of every class and creed might come to actualize their ideals under the discipline essential to such work. The discipline is directed to overcoming personal limitations, the practice of constructive thinking, the attainment of balance, the eradication of harmful habits, control and direction of mental and psychic energy into creative channels, adaptation to environment, and particular attention is given to the practice of awareness. His work has grown steadily and many remarkable results have been obtained. V. H. Mottram, Professor of Physiology in the University of London, wrote of it in an article in the *Star* entitled "Men and Women Re-Made" (11 Feb. 1935): "I have watched people, men and women, becoming gentler and kinder in nature, happier in mind and clearer of skin and brighter of eye from day to day. . . . I find a great difficulty in describing Starr's methods to the general public or even to psychologists. There is nothing remotely resembling hypnotism in them—indeed, he considers hypnotism retrograde and immoral, for it saps the character of the subject. Psycho-analysis in the usually understood sense of that term is not practised . . . though results as, or more, striking are obtained."

In April 1935 Meredith Starr found the Devonshire farmhouse inadequate. He therefore moved to a larger retreat at Frogmore Hall, near Knebworth, in Hertfordshire.

His work is known as Constructive Psychology. He is introducing new methods, adapted to the needs of the individual, into modern psychology. He does not belong to any of the existing schools, while recognizing what is valuable in each. He has more in common with Jung, and, in respect of awareness, with Professor C. Daly King, than with others, and gives precedence to synthesis over analysis.

(See Russell Stannard, *With the Dictators of Fleet Street* (1934); Richard Ince, *Shadow-Show* (1932).)

STEINER, RUDOLF (b. 1861). Austrian philosopher and mystic. He studied the great German philosophers Kant, Fichte and Schelling. His inner life developed rapidly under the instruction of an adept (see *Initiation*) whom he met in early youth. He studied in Vienna, took the degree of Doctor of Philosophy and henceforth devoted himself "to bringing back God into Science and Nature into Religion . . . and thus to re-fertilize Science, Art and Life" (Schurê). He lectured extensively in Germany, Switzerland and England and founded the Goetheanum at Basle as a centre for his teaching. Out of his work grew the Anthropological Society with branches in all countries of Europe. Many of his books are of great value to the occultist and the seeker for enlightenment, especially *The Way of Initiation* and *Initiation and Its Results*, of which there are good English translations.

STEPHEN. The first Christian martyr (Acts vi. 5).

STEPHEN, SIR LESLIE (1832–1904). Man-of-letters and editor of the *Dictionary of National Biography*. He was ordained in the Church of England but changed his views and relinquished his orders under the Clergy Disabilities Act of 1870. (See F. W. Maitland, *Life and Letters of Leslie Stephen*.)

STERLING, JOHN (1806–44). Poet and essayist. He was ordained in the Church of England but gave up ministerial work to devote himself to literature. He was an intimate friend of Thomas Carlyle. (See Carlyle, *Life of John Sterling*; Richard Ince, *Calverley and some Cambridge Wits* (1929).)

STERNE, LAURENCE (1713–68). Rector of Sutton, Yorkshire, and prebendary of York. Famous as a novelist. His wit and delicate style have raised *Tristram Shandy* and *The Sentimental Journey* to the position of classics, and his indecency has given him notoriety. (See H. B. Traill, *Laurence Sterne* (English Men of Letters); L. P. Curtis, *Letters of Laurence Sterne* (1935).)

STEVENSON, ROBERT LOUIS (1850–94). English novelist and essayist of great distinction. His psychological novel, *Dr. Jekyll and Mr. Hyde*, created a sensation in the religious world owing to the vividness with which he portrayed the spiritual and animal forces at warfare in man.

STIGMATA. The marks of wounds similar to those of the crucified Christ found on the body of St. Francis of Assisi at his death in 1224. Similar phenomena are recorded in the case of certain other saints. Modern experiments in hypnotism and applied psychology prove that there is nothing fanciful or exaggerated in the records of such phenomena, since blisters can be raised on the flesh of a hypnotized subject by suggestion. See art. *Religion*, §§ 1, 6.

STILLINGFLEET, EDWARD (1635–99). English theologian. Dean of St. Paul's (1678) and bishop of Worcester (1689). He was author of the *Irenicum*, in which he advocated compromise with the Presbyterians.

STOICISM. The philosophy taught by Zeno (340–260 B.C.). He opened his school in a colonnade called the Stoa Poikile or Pointed Porch at Athens. Stoic philosophy taught that all things consist of matter and an active principle likened to breath (pneuma), spirit or fire. This principle pervades all things. Man's soul is a spark of the world-soul; he is a fragment of God. Stoicism was in its nature constructive and practical; a way of living as well as a way of thinking. Since the guiding rational principle in man is part of the universal reason, he must not become the slave of his animal nature but must seek to control the passions by the will. By thus rising above pleasure and pain, likes and dislikes, man can attain a poise and a self-command which will bring him contentment in all circumstances. The fact that the saintly philosopher-emperor Marcus Aurelius was a stoic—the last and perhaps the greatest—and that he found in the system a satisfaction which he could not find in Christianity speaks eloquently in its favour. Primitive Christianity, as Marcus Aurelius clearly saw, appealed too much to the emotions and too little to the reason and the will. It attracted mainly the ignorant and the self-satisfied, with the result that fanaticism and bloodshed resulted. The system of Zeno could never be popular; it demanded a too great effort on the part of the individual. But in the person of Marcus Aurelius it produced a saint of balanced philosophic temper such as Christianity has been unable to rival. (See A. C. Pearson, *The Fragments of Zeno and Cleanthes*; Zeller, *Phil. d. Griech* (English trans. by Reichel) (1879); S. F. Alleyne, *Eclectics* (1883).)

STOLE. A long narrow band or strip, coloured according to season, worn by bishops and priests.

STOUP (STOOP). A basin for holy water.

STRAUSS, DAVID FRIEDRICH (1808–74). German theologian of destructive influence. His *Life of Jesus* (1835) was highly critical of traditional belief and aroused a storm of abuse. Strauss finally abandoned Christianity for a more congenial form of pantheism.

STUDENT CHRISTIAN FEDERATION, THE WORLD'S. An undenominational organization to unite Christian student movements throughout the world. It was established in Sweden, at Wadstena, in 1895 by leaders of student movements in Scandinavia, Germany, Great Britain, U.S.A. and Canada. It is governed by a chairman, two vice-chairmen and other officers. Headquarters: 347 Madison Avenue, New York, U.S.A.

STUDENT CHRISTIAN MOVEMENT OF GREAT BRITAIN AND IRELAND. A Society to assist and further the interests of Christian students. Headquarters: Annandale, North End Road, Golder's Green, London, N.W.11.

STUPA (TOPE, DAGOBA). A Buddhist shrine usually containing sacred relics.

STYLITES. See *Simeon Stylites*.

SUBDEACON. In the Catholic and Greek churches one next below the rank of deacon.

SUBLAPSARIANS. A group of moderate Calvinists who believe that God merely *permitted* Adam's fall without pre-ordaining it. This doctrine is opposed to that of the Supralapsarians who regarded election and predestination as *preceding* the Creation and the Fall.

SUBLIMINAL SELF. The mental activity which takes place beneath the level of consciousness. See *Psychology*.

SUCCENTOR (also **SUBCANTOR**). The bass soloist in a choir.

SUDRA. A member of the fourth and lowest Hindu caste.

SUFFRAGAN. An assistant bishop.

SUFIISM. Islamic mysticism. The early Sufis practised quietism mainly, but the mystical element deepened later on. The Sufi symbols of Love and Wine indicate experience of the inner raptures of the mystical life. In the 9th C. A.D. Sufiism became markedly theological. Abu Sulaiman in Syria developed the doctrine of gnosis through illumination and ecstasy (see *Initiation*) and the great Persian Sufi Abu Yazid (d. 874) introduced the doctrine of fana (akin to Nirvana) or the passing away of the individual consciousness. According to Sufi teaching the seeker after Reality passes through three main stages or states: (1) Ahwal or spiritual feeling; (2) Mushahadat or contemplation, and (3) Yakin or intuition. The Sufis do not constitute a sect nor profess a creed. They are visionaries with fundamental beliefs and methods in common. ("I went from God to God, until they cried from me in me, 'O thou I'"—Bayezid). The name is derived from Arab. *suf* (wool), from the woollen garments worn by Persian ascetics. (See F. Hadland Davis, *Teachings of the Persian Mystics*; Reynold A. Nicholson, *The Idea of Personality in Sufiism*; *The Secret Rose-Garden*, trans. F. Lederer.)

SUGGESTION. Term used in psychology for the tendency of the mind to accept without criticism ideas presented to it from others. Suggestibility varies greatly in different persons. It is most powerful in children and persons under hypnosis. Many beliefs, religious and philosophical, supposed to be founded on logical process, are due to suggestion.

SULPICIANS. A Catholic congregation founded in 1642 in France by Jean Jacques Olier to promote education for the priesthood.

SUNDAY. See *Sabbath*.

SUNDAY SCHOOLS. Schools to which children of the poorer class are sent for an hour or two on Sundays were initiated by Robert Raikes (1736–1811). In England the teachers are voluntary; usually the rector's daughters or young women addicted to parish work. In America, Sunday Schools are a paid institution, carefully organized and well equipped.

SUNNITES. The orthodox Moslems who venerate the Sunna, or traditional teaching of Mohammed, equally with the Koran. (The Shiites (q.v.) do not accept the Sunna.)

SUPEREROGATION. In Catholic theology good works performed in excess of the requirements for Salvation.

SUPPER, THE LAST. The meal which Jesus took with his disciples before the Passion.

SUPPRESSION OF MONASTERIES. All religious houses were suppressed in England by Act of Parliament in 1539. Many abbeys were suppressed in France in 1790, in Spain between 1837 and 1868 and in Italy between 1866 and 1873.

SUPRALAPSARIANISM. See *Sublapsarianism.*

SUPREMACY, ACTS OF. Various Acts passed to place the ecclesiastical organization of England in the power of the Crown. The first Act was passed in 1534. Another followed in Queen Elizabeth's reign in 1559, when many ecclesiastics who refused to conform were disqualified for office.

SURAS. The chapters into which the Koran is divided.

SURPLICE. A white linen garment worn over the cassock by officiating clergy of all degrees.

SUTRAS. The Hindu prose writings consisting of the rules and aphorisms of the Vedic religion. They consist of the Dharma-sutras, concerning social duties; the Grihya-sutras, dealing with the family cult; the Shrauta-sutras, precepts for the use of Brahmanas (q.v.) and mantras of the Vedas in connection with sacrifice; also certain sutras dealing with magic, grammar, philosophy, etc.

SUTTEE. The ancient Indian custom by which the widow sacrificed herself by burning on her husband's funeral pyre. The British forbade the practice in 1829.

SVASTIKA (SWASTIKA). The Hindu term for the gammate cross or fylfot found in all parts of the ancient world. It is regarded as a symbol of prosperity. In origin it may symbolize the wheel of life or the motion of the sun and planets.

SWEDENBORG, EMANUEL (1688–1772). Swedish mystic; by profession an engineer. A mystical experience led him to become a religious teacher. He taught that the foundation of all things is love and he claimed to have made acquaintance with the conditions prevailing in the after-life. A Church (Church of the New Jerusalem) was established on his teachings. (See B. F. Barrett, *Lectures on the New Dispensation.*)

SWIFT, JONATHAN (1667–1745). One of England's most brilliant satirists. He took Holy Orders and became dean of St. Patrick's Cathedral. He was a friend of Addison, Steele and Congreve and a staunch supporter of the Whigs. *The Tale of a Tub* and *Gulliver's Travels* are acclaimed the greatest satires in the English language. (See *Lives* of

Swift, by Churton Collins, and Leslie Stephen.)

SYLLABUS OF ERRORS, PAPAL. A list of eighty heresies, annexed to the Encyclical Quanto Cura addressed to all bishops by Pius IX in 1864. It condemns pantheism, naturalism, rationalism, socialism, Bible societies, liberalism, etc. etc.—practically everything except Catholicism.

SYLPH. A spirit of the air, or fairy.

SYMBOLS, CHRISTIAN. Symbols for Jesus Christ are: the Fish, the Vine, the Lion, the Lamb. St. Mark's symbol is the Lion; St. Matthew's the Man; St. Luke's the Ox; St. John's the Eagle. The symbol of the Holy Spirit is the Dove; Satan's symbol is the Serpent or Dragon; St. Paul's the Sword; St. Peter's the Keys; St. Andrew's the Cross. The Cock (bird of dawn) is a symbol of Resurrection. (See K. L. Jenner, *Christian Symbolism.*)

SYMEON METAPHRASTES. A 10th-C. Byzantine biographer of the saints.

SYNAGOGUE. A Jewish place of worship (Gr. *syn* = together, *agein* = to lead.)

SYNAXARIAN. In the Greek Church a short biography of a saint.

SYNAXIS. An assembly for worship in the early Christian Church.

SYNCRETISM. Attempted reconciliation of opposed principles, as between Catholics and Protestants or Lutherans and Reformed Lutherans.

SYNERGISM. The doctrine ascribed to Melanchthon that the Divine Spirit and the human will are two efficient agents that co-operate in regeneration. (Gr. *syn* = together, *ergein* = to work.)

SYNESIUS OF CYRENE (c. 373–414). A Greek philosopher who became bishop of Ptolemais in Libya. One of the most independent of bishops in the annals of Christianity, Synesius insisted on retaining his wife and refused to accept the Church's dogma of a literal resurrection. So great was his learning and such the respect and devotion that his life inspired that the bishop of Alexandria (Theophilus) accepted him on these terms. He was a friend of Hypatia (q.v.). (See W. S. Crawford, *Synesius the Hellene*; A. FitzGerald, *Letters of Synesius* (1926).)

SYNOD. (1) An ecclesiastical council. (2) A Presbyterian Church Court.

SYNOPTIC GOSPELS. A name (first used by Griesbach) for the gospels of Matthew, Mark and Luke which present such a similarity in matter that they are believed to be founded on a common document now lost. The various theories concerning the origin of this similarity have given rise to what is known as the Synoptic Problem. (See E. D. Burkitt, *The Gospel History and Its Transmission*; A. J. Jolley, *The Synoptic Problem for English Readers.*)

SYRIA. A country of ancient Mesopotamia, of which Damascus was the capital.

T

TABERNACLE. The tent carried by the Israelites through the desert and used for ritual worship (Exod. xxv.–xxvii. and xxxvi.–xxxviii.).

TABERNACLES, FEAST OF. A Jewish autumn festival to celebrate the harvest. It is observed for eight days in October (Lev. xxiii. 43).

TABLE, THE HOLY. See *altar.*

TABU (TABOO, TAPU). A system among the Polynesians by which certain things are held sacred and their use prohibited. (See J. G. Frazer, *The Golden Bough* (vol. iii); F. B. Jevons, *Introduction to the History of Religions.*)

TALBOT HOUSE. See *Toc H.*

TALISMAN. See *amulet.*

TALMUD. The code of Jewish civil and canonical law, composed of the Mishna (text) and the Gemara (commentary). There are two versions of the Talmud: (1) The Jerusalem Talmud which was closed at the end of the 4th C. A.D. and (2) the Babylonian Talmud completed towards the end of the 5th C. A.D. The latter made use of the former. (See M. L. Rodkinson, *History of the Talmud* (New York, 1903).)

TAMMUZ. A Syrian sun-god worshipped by the Chaldeans and by certain unfaithful Jews in Jerusalem (Ezek. viii. 14).

TANTRAS. The religious books of the Saivite sects of India who worship Sakti, the female energy of the supreme God.

TAOISM. See *Lao-Tsze.*

TAPAS. Bodily austerities practised by Hindu devotees with the object of mastering the passions and attaining supernormal powers.

TAPU. See *tabu.*

TARGUMS. Versions and paraphrases of the O.T. in Aramaic. They were probably made during the Babylonian Exile when Hebrew as the popular language fell into disuse.

TATE, NAHUM (1652–1715). Most daring of English poets who re-wrote Shakespeare's *Lear* and *Richard II* in order to improve them. With his friend Brady he wrote a metrical version of the Psalms.

TATIAN. Christian apologist; author of the *Diatessaron.* (2nd C.)

TAULER, JOHANN (c. 1300–61). German mystic and pupil of Meister Eckhart (q.v.).

TAUROBOLIUM. The rite of baptism in the blood of a bull in the Mysteries of Cybele, the Great Mother. See *Mystery Religions.*

TAYLOR, JANE and **ANN.** Authors of some very popular hymns for children and of the famous poem "Twinkle, twinkle, little star." (18th C.)

TAYLOR, JEREMY (1613–67). English clergyman, famous for his devotional books—*Holy Living* and *Holy Dying*.

TAYLOR, RICHARD. Anglican clergyman and author of *The Devil's Pulpit* (1830), in which he argued the view that Jesus Christ is a Sun-God. He was ejected from the ministry and imprisoned.

TEACHING OF THE TWELVE APOSTLES. See *Didache*.

TE DEUM. A Christian hymn of praise traditionally ascribed to Ambrose of Milan, used in the Catholic and Anglican liturgies.

TEL EL-AMARNA TABLETS. A collection of cuneiform documents discovered in Egypt in 1886–7. They give a vivid picture of Canaan at the time of the entry of the Israelites (c. 1400 B.C.).

TELEOLOGY. The doctrine of the final causes of things. The "teleological argument" is that which seeks to prove God's existence from the evidences of design in the universe.

TELEPATHY. Thought transference from mind to mind. See *Spiritualism*.

TEMPLARS, KNIGHTS. A military and religious order founded in 1119 for the protection of the Holy Sepulchre and pilgrims going there. It was abolished by the Council of Vienna in 1312.

TEMPLE, SOLOMON'S. The Jewish place of worship, of great magnificence, built in 966 B.C. at Jerusalem (1 Chron. xxii. 14; xxix. 4–7). The cost of its erection has been estimated at £7,400,000,000.

TENEBRAE ("DARKNESS"). An office observed in the Catholic Church on Good Friday and the preceding two days. The Church is gradually darkened by extinguishing the candles to symbolize the darkness prevailing at the death of Jesus Christ.

TERCE (**TIERCE**). The Catholic office of the third hour. See *Breviary*.

TEREPHIM. Certain images, idols, etc., used for purposes of divination in the popular worship of the early Israelites.

TERESA, SAINT. See *Theresa, Saint*.

TERSANCTUS. See *Trisagion*.

TERTIARIES. A Catholic congregation within certain orders who live in obedience to the Third Rule, i.e. obey certain rules but do not live in a monastery.

TERTULLIAN (c. 155–220). One of the Latin Fathers of the Church (q.v.). A brilliant apologist, but of narrow views and often bitter in his controversial works. He tried to win the Church to Montanism (q.v.), but failed, and so withdrew from the the Church and founded his own Montanist group.

TEST ACTS. Several Acts passed in England directed against Catholics and Dissenters. Their object was to prevent persons disaffected to the established Church from holding office. The chief Test Acts were passed in 1673 and 1685.

TESTAMENT (O.T. and N.T.). See *Bible.*

TETZEL, JOHANN (1465–1519). That seller of Indulgences to raise funds for the building of St. Peter's, Rome, who aroused Luther's indignation. See *Luther, Martin.*

THEATINES (THEATINS). A Catholic religious fraternity, founded in 1524 at Theate (or Chiete), Italy, to induce the clergy to lead stricter lives. There are also two female Theatine orders.

THEISM (DEISM). Belief in the existence of God but not in a divine revelation. Voltaire was a Deist.

THEOCRACY. A state in which God is regarded as Ruler and the priesthood as His officers. The chief theocracies have been: Ancient Israel, Mohammedanism, Calvin's government at Geneva and Cromwell's in England.

THEODORE OF MOPSUESTIA (c. 350–428). Prominent member of the Antiochian school of theologians who advocated the historical method of exegesis rather than the allegorical method of Origen.

THEOLOGICAL COLLEGES. The chief theological colleges in England for training the clergy and ministry are: King's College; Wells College; Cuddesdon; Mirfield; Leeds College (C. of E.); Mansfield College; Hackney College; New College (Congregational); Wesley College (Methodist); Manchester College (Unitarian).

THEOLOGY. The science which treats of God and the study of religion. It is divided into Natural Theology, which considers religious truth as revealed by reason, and Revealed Theology, which is concerned with a divine revelation. Both branches of theology to-day attract very little attention except among ecclesiastics and theologians. In pre-Reformation times, when Europe was united under a single Church, even the most daring and thoughtful minds were compelled to exercise their faculties within the narrow arena of theology. The Reformation and certain iconoclastic spirits (e.g. Erasmus, Rabelais, Voltaire) caused the windows to be opened, with the result that refreshing breezes of speculation, philosophy and scientific inquiry blew in. The more thoughtful minds of to-day turn from theological dogma to the more practical and immediate problems of psychology. Modern man is not interested (save from the historical viewpoint) in what happened in Palestine in the 1st C. A.D., or in India in the 6th C. B.C., but he is keenly interested in the working of his own psyche and the problems of the unconscious. Theology has served its purpose, but to-day it is an outworn garment. (See Jung, *Modern Man in Search of a Soul* (1934).)

THEOPASCHITES. Another term for the Monophysites (q.v.).

THEOPHANY. An appearance of a god to men. Applied to the appearances of the god at Delphi in the Greek religion; to the appearances of God to Moses (O.T.); and to the incarnation of Christ.

THEOSOPHICAL SOCIETY. The Society founded by Madame Blavatsky (q.v.) in 1875 with the following aims: (1) To form a nucleus of the Universal Brotherhood of Humanity; (2) to encourage the study of comparative religion and philosophy; (3) to investigate the unexplained laws of nature and the powers latent in man. Theosophy, as defined by the Society, is "the body of truths which forms the basis of all religions." The Society teaches that man has seven bodies functioning on different planes. The lowest is the physical, next to which is the astral (seat of the emotions) and the etheric, controlling growth. Man's task is to organize and develop his higher bodies. (See J. N. Farquhar, *Modern Religious Movements in India*; Annie Besant, *The Ancient Wisdom*.)

THEOSOPHY. A term used for: (1) A direct knowledge of God gained by inspiration; (2) inspirational mysticism as exemplified by the Greek Mystery Religions and the later Gnostics. In the broad sense Plotinus, Meister Eckhart and Jacob Boehme were theosophists.

THEOTOKOS (THEOTOCOS) ("MOTHER OF GOD"). A title of the Virgin Mary. It was repudiated by Nestorius and his followers. See also *Nestorius*.

THERAPEUTAE. A 1st-3rd-C. sect of ascetics, living near Alexandria and possibly connected with the Essenes.

THERESA, SAINT (1515–82). Spanish nun who founded the Descalzos or Barefoot Carmelites in opposition to the parent body, the Calzados—which had become slack. While in mystic states she experienced vivid visions. She was canonized in 1622. (See G. C. Graham, *Life of St. Theresa* (2 vols.); A. Whyte, *Santa Teresa*.)

THESMOPHORIA. An ancient Greek festival celebrated by married women in honour of Demeter (Ceres) during October. Pigs and snakes (both emblems of fertility) were used in the ceremonies. (See J. E. Harrison, *Prolegomena to the Study of Greek Religion*.)

THIRTY-NINE ARTICLES. The articles of religious belief finally agreed upon by the bishops and clergy of the C. of E. under Queen Elizabeth in 1562.

THOMAS À BECKET. See *Becket, Thomas à*.

THOMAS À KEMPIS. See *Kempis, Thomas à*.

THOMAS, ACTS OF. An apocryphal Gnostic gospel ascribed

to the 2nd C. See *Apocrypha (N.T.)*.

THOMAS AQUINAS. See *Aquinas, Saint Thomas.*

THOMAS, GOSPEL OF. An apocryphal Docetic gospel ascribed to the 2nd C.

THOMAS, SAINT. The doubting apostle of Jesus also called Didymus (twin) (John xi. 16; xiv. 5; xx. 20–9).

THOMASITES. See *Christadelphians.*

THOMISM. The doctrines of Thomas Aquinas (q.v.) as set forth in his *Summa Theologiae*. Thomists were opposed to Scotists (followers of Duns Scotus), the latter being pro-Immaculate-Conceptionists and the former anti. ("Scotists and Thomists now in peace remain." Pope—*Essay on Criticism*, v. 444.)

THOR. The chief god of the Norse pantheon. Akin to the Roman sky-god Jupiter (Gr. Zeus).

THOROUGH-BASS. See *figured-bass.*

THOTH. The ancient Egyptian god of wisdom. He was regarded as the inventor of the arts and sciences. See *Egypt, Religion of.*

THREE HOURS' SERVICE. An Anglican Good Friday service held from 12 to 3 p.m. to commemorate Christ's passion.

THUGS. A fraternity of Hindu assassins extirpated during 1826–35.

THURIBLE. A censer for burning incense.

THURIFER. The server who carries the thurible.

TIAMAT. The monster symbolizing primeval chaos in Babylonian cosmology.

TIARA. The triple crown worn by the Pope.

TIBET, RELIGION OF. See *Lamaism.*

TIERCE. See *terce.*

TIMELESS BEING. " Purely spiritual philosophy accounts for material organism and environment as a phase of consciousness subsisting as transient change. Transience by its inherent nature is doomed to perish. Time is only a generality for transient material change. Hence when incarnation expires the state of being left by vanishing transience is timeless as well as immaterial " (Archibald Weir). (See Archibald Weir, *Light: A Philosophy of Consciousness*, p. 369.)

TIMOTHY. An early Christian convert and a fellow-worker with Paul (Acts xvi. 1–3). The correspondence between Paul and Timothy known as 1 and 2 Timothy is, in the opinion of many scholars, a later fabrication. (See J. M. Moffatt, *Historical New Testament.*)

TINDALE, WILLIAM. See *Tyndale, William.*

TIPITAKA. Pali term for the Buddhist scriptures. See *Scriptures*, § 1 (*a*).

TISCHENDORF, FRIEDRICH (1815–74). German professor, famous for his textual work on the Greek N.T.

TITHE. A tenth part of the product of land and stock allotted for the maintenance of the clergy. It derives from ancient Babylonian, Egyptian, Greek, Roman, and Hebrew custom. The medieval tithe rents are still collected in certain English parishes, but the opposition to them as an unfair imposition is increasing in intensity.

TITLE. Every man ordained into the C. of E. is required to have a " title " appointing him to serve in a certain parish or office.

TITULAR CHURCH. One of certain parishes in Rome held only by cardinal priests.

TITUS. A fellow-worker with Paul mentioned in the Pauline epistles. The Epistle to Titus is believed by many scholars to be of later date. (See W. Lock, *Titus* (Internat. Crit. Comment.).)

TOBIT. An O.T. apocryphal book. An excellent specimen of the early religious romance. (See A. Neubauer, *The Book of Tobit.*)

TOC H (TALBOT HOUSE). Talbot House (" Toc H ") was a canteen in the Ypres Salient during the Great War. The Reverend P. B. Clayton (" Tubby Clayton ") was the padre in charge. After the War P. B. Clayton refounded Talbot House as Toc H (Royal Charter 1922) as a movement " to teach the younger generation class reconciliation and unselfish service." Branches have been established in U.S.A., Canada, New Zealand, Australia, India, etc. " The business of Toc H is not to frame policies but to furnish a steady supply of men of character and wide outlook to the nation's needs in every sphere. All problems at bottom are human problems " (H.R.H. The Prince of Wales : A speech at Leicester, 1934). Headquarters : 47 Francis Street, London, S.W.1.

TOHU BOHU. Chaos, from the Hebrew of Gen. i. 2 (" without form " and " void ").

TOLAND, JOHN (1670–1702). A noted English deist, author of *Christianity Not Mysterious.*

TOLERATION. The cultivating of sympathy with other people's opinions and points of view. The most difficult of all lessons (especially for keenly religious people) to learn. To stress points of agreement is always wiser than to stress points of difference.

TOLERATION, ACT OF. An Act passed in England in 1689 to relieve Dissenters from certain oppressive Acts passed in the interests of the C. of E.

TOLSTOY, LEO (1828–1910). Russian social reformer and novelist. He sought to follow the words of Jesus Christ *literally* : which led to much exaggeration and a lack of balance in his life and teaching. (See A. H. Crawford, *Religion and Ethics of Tolstoy*.)

TOMBSTONES. The custom of erecting stones and structures to commemorate the dead is of great antiquity. The most famous tombs of antiquity are the Egyptian Pyramids, the Mausoleum (in the British Museum), and the Indian Taj Mahal. The modern tombstone is as ugly and tasteless as the Greek *stele* was beautiful.

TONGUES, GIFT OF (Gr. *Glossolalia*). An abnormal condition due to religious excitement found chiefly in primitive religions. In Acts ii. the ecstatic utterances described have been mistakenly regarded as talking in foreign tongues. The condition referred to is probably of the nature described by Plato in the *Timaeus*. Similar phenomena occurred among the Jansenists, the early Quakers and the converts of Wesley. (See Mrs. Oliphant, *Life of Irving*, vol. ii.)

TONSURE. The ritual shaving of the priest's head in the Catholic and Greek churches. The custom probably entered Christianity from the cults of Isis and Serapis.

TOPE. See *Stupa*.

TOPHET. A synonym for Gehenna, the Jewish name for hell.

TOPLADY, AUGUSTUS MONTAGUE (1740–78). English hymnwriter. Author of "Rock of Ages."

TORAH. The Jewish term for the Mosaic Law.

TORQUEMADA, THOMAS (1420–98). Inquisitor-general of Spain. He introduced some of the worst and most cruel methods into the Spanish Inquisition. (During his eighteen years of office he burnt 10,220 persons.)

TOTEMISM. "An intimate relation which is supposed to exist between a group of kindred people on the one side and a species of natural and artificial objects on the other side, which objects are called the totems of the human group." (See J. G. Frazer.) Totemism has existed among primitive peoples in many parts of the world. A clan will have a bear or crocodile as its totem. Many theories have been advanced to account for the system. Although the totem animal is sacred there is evidence that in certain cases the totem was eaten by the tribe at a kind of sacramental meal. It seems probable therefore that Christian and other religious sacramental meals derive from such primitive customs. (See A. Lang, *The Secret of the Totem*; Frazer's *Golden Bough*, vol. iv.) (Algonquin *otem* = family-mark.)

TRACERY. The stonework in Gothic windows (archit.).

TRACTARIANISM. See *Oxford Movement*.

TRACT SOCIETY, THE RELIGIOUS. A Society for the dissemination of "Christian Literature" founded in London in 1799.

Headquarters: 4 Bouverie Street, London, E.C.4.

TRADITORES ("TRAITORS"). Term applied to the early Christians who, under threat of persecution, betrayed their fellow-Christians.

TRADUCIANISM. The doctrine that the soul as well as the body is procreated by the parents; it opposes the doctrines of creationism and re-birth.

TRAHERNE, THOMAS (c. 1636–74). Anglican clergyman of whose life little is known. He occupies a high place in literature for his poems and his mystical *Centuries of Meditations*.

TRANSCENDENCE. In theological doctrine Transcendence regards God as beyond the reach of human experience. It is usually contrasted with Immanence which considers that God is within all things.

TRANSCENDENTALISM. A type of philosophy which emphasizes the importance of intuitive or subjective knowledge. R. W. Emerson (1803–82) is a good representative of this school.

TRANSEPT. A wing or cross-aisle of a church, at right angles to the nave.

TRANSFIGURATION. The exalted change which comes over the appearance of great prophets and masters under certain conditions. The phenomenon is referred to in all the great religions. For Christ's Transfiguration, see Matthew xvii. The Festival of the Transfiguration is on 6 August. For Moses' Transfiguration, see Exodus xxxiv. 30. For Krishna's Transfiguration, see Edwin Arnold's *Song Celestial* (chap. xi).

TRANSMIGRATION. See *reincarnation.*

TRANSOM. The horizontal mullion or crossbar of a window (archit.).

TRANSUBSTANTIATION. In Catholic doctrine the miraculous change of the eucharistic bread and wine into Christ's body and blood—only the *appearance* of bread and wine remaining.

TRAPPISTS. An order of reformed (1664) Cistercians so named from the French abbey of La Trappe. Their rule is extremely austere. For a sympathetic picture of Trappist life, see J. Huysman, *En Route.*

TRENCH, RICHARD CHENEVIX (1807–86). Archbishop of Dublin; a poet and philologist. Best known for his *English Past and Present* and *Notes on the Parables.*

TRENT, COUNCIL OF. A Church Council convoked in Trent (Austrian Tyrol) in 1545 to consider reforms in the Catholic Church. It sat from 1545 to 1547; from 1551 to 1552 and from 1562 to 1563. The Council made provision for better education of the clergy and decreed the chief Catholic doctrines, the Canon of Scripture, the Seven Sacraments, transubstantiation, celibacy of the clergy, etc. See also *Counter Reformation*.

TRIFA (TRIFER). "Defiled—the opposite of *kosher*; 'ritually unclean' (Zangwill)." (See Eric Partridge, *Slang*.)

TRIFORIUM. The arcade over the arches of a church between nave and aisles (archit.).

TRIMURTI. The three manifestations of supreme Reality in Hinduism under the forms of Brahma (Creator), Vishnu (Preserver) and Shiva (Destroyer).

TRINITARIANS. (1) Those who hold the Christian doctrine of the Trinity. (2) A Catholic order established in Rome in 1198 to ransom Christians held captive by the Mohammedans. (Also called Redemptionists and Mathurins.)

TRINITY. The Christian doctrine of one Godhead and three persons. It came into being as a result of various "heresies." The Arians (q.v.) taught that God was supreme and the Logos created or derived. This doctrine was repudiated by the Church, which under Hellenistic influence delighted in splitting theological straws. Many councils dealt with the problem, one party anathematizing another. The Athanasian Creed finally declared the doctrine indispensable to salvation.

TRINITY SUNDAY. Festival to commemorate the Trinity held on the first Sunday after Whitsuntide (Cath. and Anglican).

TRIPITAKA. See *Tipitaka*.

TRIPTYCH. A set of three tablets, each having a painting and joined together by hinges.

TRIRATNA. The Buddhist "three jewels" consisting of Buddha, the Dharma (Word of Truth) and Sangha (the Order of Monks).

TRISAGION. A hymn used in various liturgies, derived from the early Church ("O Holy God, holy and mighty, holy and immortal, have mercy on us"). Not to be confused with the Tersanctus or Sanctus ("Holy, holy, holy, Lord God of Hosts," from Isa. vi.).

TRITON. Son of Neptune (Gr. myth.).

TROLL. A giant goblin or gnome (Norse myth.).

TROLLOPE, ANTHONY (1815–82). Author of the famous Barsetshire novels depicting life in an English cathedral town. He wrote some fifty novels of a light entertaining nature, satirizing the clergy, but so urbanely that even bishops' wives could read them.

TROPARION. A short hymn in the offices of the Greek Church.

TRUCE OF GOD. An arrangement in force between the 11th and 12th C.s to prevent private feuds. It was observed in England, France and Italy from Wednesday evening to Monday morning in each week during Advent and Lent, and also on certain saints' days.

TULLOCH, JOHN (1823–86). Scottish theologian and Professor of Theology at St. Andrews.

TUNICLE (TUNIC). A short-sleeved vestment worn at Mass by the sub-deacon ; rather smaller than the dalmatic.

TUNKERS. See *Dunkers.*

TUPPER, MARTIN (1810–89). A barrister who took to literature and wrote much in verse and prose. His *Proverbial Philosophy* had an enormous vogue owing to its seemingly wise but entirely commonplace observations such as " the plain man " could understand.

TUSCAN ORDER. The simplest of the five classic orders of architecture. It is a Roman modification of the Doric order, with unfluted columns.

TWELFTH-DAY. See *Epiphany.*

TYMPANUM. The triangular space in the corners of an arch (archit.).

TYNDALE (or **TINDALE**), **WILLIAM** (c. 1484–1536). English divine famous for his translation of considerable portions of the Bible. He was subjected to continual persecution ; travelled in Germany and Holland, and was betrayed, strangled and burned at the castle of Vilvonde in Holland. (See R. Demans, *William Tyndale* ; Fox, *Acts and Monuments.*)

TYRE. A city of ancient Phoenicia, famous for its purple dye.

TYRRELL, GEORGE (FATHER) (1861–1909). A Catholic priest and writer who joined the Modernist movement. He was excommunicated. His chief work was *Christianity at the Cross Roads.* See also *Modernism.* (See M. D. Petrie, *Autobiography and Life of Father Tyrrell.*) (" The work will rank amongst the most intimate and merciless confessions of a soul that have ever been written." —*The Times.*)

U

ULAMA (ULEMA). The collective name for the whole body of theologians (secular clergy) in any Moslem country. Opposed to them are the Arifs, " knowers " or " mystics."

ULFILAS (c. 311–83). Christian missionary of the Goths and Visigoths of the Danube. His early life was spent at Constantinople. He appears to have joined the Arian party towards the end of his life. His great work was the translation of the Bible into Gothic. (See C. A. Scott, *Ulfilas, Apostle of the Goths.*)

ULTRAMONTANISM. The Catholic view of papal authority, so called because its extra-Italian advocates look over (*ultra*) the mountains (*montes*) to Rome for guidance. The objectives of the Ultramontanists are: (1) The authority of the Pope, based on the Decree of Infallibility of 1870. (2) The supremacy of the Catholic Church in all religious matters. The loyalty of individuals to the Church to come first and to the State, second. (3) Catholic loyalty in all schools, colleges, etc., to take precedence of all other loyalties. (4) Opposition to Modernism in all its forms.

UMA. Wife of Shiva (q.v.) and goddess of light and beauty (Hindu myth.).

UNAM SANCTAM. A bull promulgated in 1302 by Boniface VIII which announced that submission to the Pope's authority is essential to salvation. The bull was directed against kings and princes in order to bring them under papal subjection.

UNCTION. The Catholic ceremonial anointing with oil. The practice is derived, through Judaism, from primitive cults. See also *Extreme Unction.*

UNDERHILL, EVELYN (b. 1875). The author of many works on mysticism : *The Mystic Way* ; *Ruysbroeck* ; *Practical Mysticism* ; *The Life of the Spirit and the Life of To-day*. Her interest in mysticism is religious and philosophical rather than historical and her standpoint is definitely Christian and transcendentalist. She is strongly in sympathy with Von Hügel.

UNDINE. A water-nymph (Teut. myth.).

UNIAT. A member of any community of Oriental Christians which acknowledges the papal supremacy, in all else (clerical matrimony, rites, liturgy, etc.) remaining Greek. Uniats are also called United Greeks.

UNIFORMITY, ACTS OF. See *Acts of Uniformity.*

UNIGENITUS. A bull issued by Clement XI in 1713, at the instance of the Jesuits, condemning the Jansenist Quesnel's annotations on the N.T.

UNION, CHURCH. Since the beginning of the 19th C. many movements have been made towards unity among Christian churches. Most of these have failed owing to the reluctance to modify dogma. The Catholic Church is the most stubborn in this respect. In 1817 an amalgamation of the Lutheran and Reformed churches took place in Prussia. In 1900 Scotch Presbyterians accomplished the merging of the United and Free Church parties. A number of movements for union among the Christian sects in America were promoted during the 19th C., with varying success. In England the United Methodist Church was formed in 1907 by the union of three Methodist denominations, the Methodist New Connexion, the Bible Christians and the United Methodist Free Churches. In 1932 the Wesleyan Methodist Church, the Primitive Methodist Church and the United Methodist Church united and became "The Methodist Church."

UNITARIANISM. The theology which insists on the unity of God and is opposed to the doctrine of the Trinity (q.v.). Christianity would certainly have been Unitarian in doctrine had it not been for the Alexandrian Logos doctrine introduced in the 3rd C. During the Middle Ages Unitarianism, thus made a heresy, was continually cropping up (see *Socinians, Arminians*). Modern Unitarianism commences with the opening of a Unitarian chapel in London in 1778 by the Reverend Theophilus Lindsey. The British and Foreign Unitarian Association came into being in 1825. The leading English Unitarians have been: Joseph Priestley (18th C.); Thomas Belsham (18th C.); James Martineau (18th C.); J. R. Beard (19th C.) and L. P. Jacks (b. 1860). There is an active Unitarian group in U.S.A. (See J. W. Chadwick, *Old and New Unitarian Belief* (Boston, 1894).)

UNITED FREE CHURCH OF SCOTLAND. A Presbyterian group formed by the fusion in 1900 of the Free Church of Scotland and the United Presbyterian Church. See also *Wee Free Church.*

UNITED LUTHERAN CHURCH IN AMERICA. The organization which resulted from the fusion in 1918 of the Lutheran General Council, the Lutheran General Synod and the Lutheran United Synod.

UNITED METHODIST CHURCH. The English Methodist Church established in 1907 by the fusion of the Methodist New Connexion with the Bible Christians and the United Methodist Free Churches. It has now become "The Methodist Church." See *Union, Church.*

UNITED PRESBYTERIAN CHURCH. A Scottish Presbyterian group formed in 1847 by the amalgamation of the United Secession and Relief churches. See also *United Free Church of Scotland.*

UNITED STATES PROTESTANT EPISCOPAL CHURCH. The origin of this Church derives from "the church planted in Virginia in 1607 by representatives of the ancient Church of England." Other churches were formed and put under the jurisdiction of the bishop of London, there being no bishop in America. After the War of Independence the Reverend Samuel Seabury (1729–96) of Connecticut was consecrated bishop of Connecticut by the Scotch nonjuror bishops in Aberdeen (1784). In 1787 two other bishops were ordained in the chapel at Lambeth Palace. The Church is officered by the three orders of bishops, priests and deacons and its liturgy is almost identical with the Anglican. In constitution it is more democratic than the C. of E., the laity having more power. (See J. S. M. Anderson, *History of the Church of England in the Colonies.*)

UNIVERSALISM and UNIVERSALISTS. The doctrine of universal salvation for all mankind. The Universalists are an American religious sect who believe in God, Jesus Christ and the Bible, and the final harmony of every soul with God.

UNLEAVENED BREAD. Unfermented bread used by the Jews in celebrating the Passover.

UPANISHADS. Metaphysical and speculative treatises (they number about 170) attached to the Brahmanas (q.v.). The earliest date from the 6th C. B.C. (See P. Deussen, *The Philosophy of the Upanishads.*) See Scriptures, § 5 (*a*).

URIM and THUMMIM. Parf of the Israelitish high priests' divination equipment (Ex. xxviii. 30; Lev. viii. 8).

URQUHART, SIR THOMAS (1611–60). Scottish writer and translator. Famous for his English translation of Rabelais (in which he was assisted by the Frenchman, Peter Anthony Motteux); and for the courage with which he traced his descent through his father to Adam and through his mother to Eve. (See John Willcock, *Sir Thomas Urquhart of Cromartie* (1899).)

URSULA, SAINT. Catholic martyr said to have been put to death by the Huns at Cologne. She has been identified by some with the Norse Freyia.

URSULINES. A female teaching order founded by St. Angela Merici of Brescia in 1537, with St. Ursula as patron saint.

USHAS. The Vedic goddess of dawn.

USSHER (or **USHER**), **JAMES** (1581–1656). Anglican archbishop of Armagh. He received preferment from James I, who had a high opinion of his learning and scholarship. (See W. B. Wright, *The Ussher Memoirs* (1889); Carr, *Life of Ussher* (1895).)

UTILITARIANISM. The ethical doctrine which considers moral excellence to consist in usefulness, i.e. fitness to produce happiness. See *Mill, John Stuart.*

UTNAPISHTIM. The Babylonian hero of the Noah legend. Advised of the advancing cyclonic depression by the god Ea, Utnapishtim built a ship and so escaped drowning in the Flood.

UTOPIA (" **NOWHERE** "). Any idealist picture of an imaginary state. Sir Thomas More's *Utopia* described a land of political and religious freedom. Somewhat similar Utopias have been described by Francis Bacon (*New Atlantis*); Cyrano de Bergerac (*A Voyage to the Moon*) and Edward Bellamy (*Looking Backward*).

UTRAQUISM. The eucharistic doctrine of the Utraquists (Hussites or Calixtines) who claim the right to communicate in both kinds.

V

VAE. Goddess of speech and wife of Brahma (Ved. myth.).

VAIROCHANA. Sanscrit name for the Dhyani Buddha of the Central Realm. Vairochana means " in shapes making visible "; he is regarded as the Noumena or Manifester of phenomena.

VAISESHIKA. The Hindu atomic philosophy which traces all things to indestructible atoms.

VAISHNAVISM. The theistic religion of India which worships Vishnu as supreme God. It is a popular cult with a gospel of salvation through devotion to Vishnu manifested in his human incarnations as Krishna and Rama. There are a number of sects of Vaishnavism such as the Ramanuji, the Ramanandi, etc. (See E. W. Hopkins, *The Religions of India*.)

VAISYAS. The third of the higher Hindu castes consisting of the trading and agricultural classes.

VALENTINE, SAINT. A legendary bishop and martyr of the 3rd C.

VALENTINIANS. A Gnostic sect founded by Valentinus (d. c. A.D. 160).

VALDENSES. See *Waldenses*.

VALHALLA. The Norse heaven or abode of bliss for heroes slain in battle.

VALKYR (WALKYR). One of the nine handmaidens who served Odin at the banquet of Valhalla.

VAMPIRE. An evil spirit in the folk-lore of East Europe who quits his grave to suck the blood of sleeping mortals. (See Bram Stoker's romance, *Dracula*, and Gautier's conte, *Clarimonde*.)

VANIR. A group of Teutonic gods who made war on the Aesir gods. The two groups finally united.

VARUNA. The sky-god or god of righteousness of the Hindu Vedic religion. In later times Indra and other gods of sacrifice took his place.

VATICAN. The palace of the Pope, adjoining St. Peter's, Rome. (See George Seldes, *The Vatican, Yesterday, To-day and To-morrow* (1935).)

VATICAN COUNCIL. The Twentieth Ecumenical Council of 1869–70 which proclaimed the Infallibility of the Pope.

VATICANISM. The ecclesiastical polity based on absolute Papal control. Cf. *Ultramontanism*.

VEDANTA. The chief system of Hindu philosophy which represents a reaction of religious orthodoxy against the systems of philosophers. It teaches that Nature is a multiform manifestation of the universal soul. All phenomena and the apparent separateness of souls are illusory. But religious forms, ceremonies and sacrifices are necessary, the world as apprehended by the senses being a lower form of Reality. Not until the soul becomes one with Brahma does it realize that all phenomena are illusion. ("The sea is one and not other than its water: yet waves, foam, spray, drops, froth, and other modifications of it differ from each other"—Brahmasutra). Vivekananda, disciple of Ramakrishna, was a great modern exponent of the system. (See Paul Deussen, *The System of the Vedanta*.)

VEDAS, THE FOUR. Four collections of ancient Hindu

hymns. They are: (1) The Rig-Veda, (2) The Yajur-Veda, (3) The Sama-Veda, (4) The Atharva-Veda. Each of these has its attendant Aranyakas and Brahmanas (commentaries). The Brahmanas are intended for ritual use in towns and households; the Aranyakas are compiled for hermits living in the forest. It is chiefly in the Aranyakas that occur the Upanishads—sublime metaphysical speculations concerning the individual soul and the Universal Soul. (See Maurice Bloomfield, *The Religion of the Veda*; S. Radhakrishnan, *The Philosophy of the Upanishads*; Gough, *The Philosophy of the Upanishads*.)

VEDIC RELIGION. The religion of the early Aryan invaders of India (c. 2000–1400 B.C.). It was mainly a worship of the personified powers of Nature—the storm-god Indra; the fire-god Agni; the sky-god Varuna. These gods required to be flattered by prayer and worship (see *Vedas*). The doctrine of a future life was taught, but the belief in rebirth or reincarnation entered later. (See M. Bloomfield, *The Religion of the Veda*.)

VEIL. The linen used to cover the eucharistic vessels containing the elements during Mass (Cath.).

VENANTIUS, FORTUNATUS (c. 530–610). Scholar and Latin poet who became bishop of Poictiers. Some of his poems have been very happily translated by Jack Lindsay in *Medieval Latin Poets* (1934).

VENDIDAD. A Zoroastrian priestly ceremonial code resembling Leviticus. It deals with civil law, religious ceremony and mythology.

VENIAL SIN. A sin not involving complete alienation from God, in contradistinction from mortal sin involving the penalty of spiritual death.

VENI CREATOR. A hymn of the Roman Breviary used especially at Whitsuntide and ordinations ("Veni Creator Spiritus").

VENITE. The 95th Psalm ("Venite, exultemus").

VENUS. The Roman goddess of love and of spring, identified with the Greek Aphrodite.

VERGER. The attendant of a cathedral or church. He sometimes carries a "verge" or staff of office. (L. *verga* = branch.)

VERONICA, SAINT. A legendary saint said to have lent Jesus her handkerchief to wipe his face on the way to Calvary, his features becoming miraculously printed on the fabric.

VERSICLE. A liturgical verse spoken by the officiating priest to which a response is made by the congregation.

VERSIONS OF THE BIBLE. The chief versions of the O.T. are:

(1) The Septuagint (3rd and 2nd C.s B.C.).

(2) The Syriac (2nd C. A.D.).

(3) The Latin Vulgate (4th C. A.D.).

The chief versions of the N.T. are:

(1) Syriac versions—the earliest dating from c. 200 A.D.

(2) Latin version. (*a*) The Old Itala (3rd C. A.D.). (*b*) The Latin Vulgate (revised by Jerome c. 360–84).

(3) Coptic versions (2nd and 3rd C.s A.D.).

The chief English versions of the Bible are:

(1) John Wycliffe's Bible (1380–84).

(2) William Tyndale's version of the N.T. and most of the O.T. (1525–36).

(3) Myles Coverdale's edition (complete) first printed in 1535.

(4) The Great Bible (1539–41) edited by Coverdale.

(5) The Authorized Version (1611) issued under the patronage of James I. Forty-seven English scholars produced it.

(6) The Revised Version (1881–5) prepared by fifty British Biblical scholars.

See also *Bible*.

VESICA PISCIS. A fish's bladder, painted in the form of an oval aureole surrounding the figure of Christ—an allusion to the Christian symbol of the fish.

VESTA and VESTAL VIRGINS. Vesta was the Roman goddess of fire and guardian of the hearth. The Vestals were patrician virgins dedicated for thirty years to the service of Vesta. They lived under a strict rule in a nunnery in the Roman Forum. (See T. C. Worsfold, *The History of the Vestal Virgins of Rome*.)

VESTMENTS. Articles of dress worn by the clergy during divine service, e.g. the amice, alb, girdle, maniple, stole, chasuble, etc. Vestments arose about the 9th C. in the Catholic Church. Their origin was due to changing lay fashions of dress and the conservative dislike of the clergy for innovations. Vestments were in most cases articles of dress no longer worn by the laity.

VESTRY. (1) A room adjoining the church in which vestments are kept. (2) A meeting of ratepayers in English parishes to manage parish property.

VIATICUM. The Eucharist administered to people believed to be dying (Cath.).

VICAR. (1) In the C. of E. a parish incumbent who receives a fixed stipend, the tithes being impropriate to a layman or chapter. (2) In the Catholic Church a priest who acts for a bishop.

VICAR APOSTOLIC. Formerly an ecclesiastic to whom the Pope delegated certain powers for special purposes. Now a bishop appointed to officiate in a country where no canonical sees have been established.

VICAR OF BRAY. Simon Alleyn, vicar of Bray from 1540 to 1588 during the reigns of Henry VIII, Edward VI, Mary and Elizabeth. He changed his views whenever policy demanded. (Hence, Vicar of Bray = a turncoat.)

VICAR-CHORAL. A paid choirman in an English cathedral.

VICAR FORANE. See *Dean, rural*.

VICAR-GENERAL. (1) In C. of E. an officer (usually the chancellor of the diocese) who assists a bishop. (2) In the Catholic Church a priest representing the bishop.

VICARIOUS SACRIFICE. The sufferings of Christ accepted by God instead of inflicting punishment on all men tainted with sin.

VIDHAR. The "silent god" of the Tuetonic Aesir gods—possibly personified space.

VIENNE, COUNCIL OF. The Catholic Council held at Vienne, France, in 1311–12. It passed decrees to improve discipline in the Mendicant Orders and the Inquisition.

VIGIL. The eve before a feast or fast day.

VINCENT OF LERINS. A 5th-C. monk and theologian of Lerins (France). He is famous for his terse test of orthodoxy: "Quod ubique, quod semper, quod ab omnibus creditum est" ("What everywhere, always, by all has been believed").

VINCENT DE PAUL, SAINT (1576–1660). Catholic divine who founded the Lazarites or Vincentines (1625) to help the sick and poor. He was canonized in 1737 and the Society of St. Vincent de Paul was founded in 1833 for charitable enterprises.

VIRGIN BIRTH. The orthodox Christian doctrine that Jesus Christ was born of Mary while still a virgin. The term "virgin" is hardly accurate in this connection since the Apostles' Creed affirms that Jesus was "conceived *by the Holy Ghost*." (See also Matt. i. 18; Luke i. 35.) A study of comparative religion shows that this Christian belief of virgin or supernatural birth is a derivative from earlier cults. Thus Mithra was born of a virgin; Adonis or Tammuz was born of a virgin; Attis was born of the virgin Nana; Krishna was born of the virgin Devaki in a cave, the event being announced by a miraculous star. The similarity of these earlier birth-stories to the Christian so troubled the Church Fathers that they ascribed it to the guile of the Devil. It used to be thought that the truth or falsehood of Christianity depended on the establishment and maintenance of belief in cardinal doctrines like that of the Virgin Birth. Historical method and a more enlightened philosophy have shown their relative unimportance except to the historian. (See Doane, *Bible Myths*; Inman, *Pagan and Christian Symbolism*.)

VIRGIN MARY. The mother of Jesus Christ. The belief in the Virgin Birth (q.v.) crept into the Church during the 2nd C. From this doctrine was evolved the later doctrine of the Immaculate Conception (q.v.) which taught that the Virgin herself was conceived "without sin." In the Catholic Church worship of the Virgin Mary became part of the system (hyperdulia). This worship was carried further by the doctrine of the Assumption (q.v.) which taught that Mary was received into heaven bodily without having suffered corruption. This doctrine has not yet been promulgated as a dogma.

VISHNU. The second god of the Hindu Trinity or Triad (Brahma, the Creator; Vishnu, the Preserver; Shiva, the Destroyer). He is regarded as a Saviour God who has taken upon him many incarnations for the benefit of mankind.

VISIONS. Mental states in which the subject seems to see objects not present to the senses. These states form an interesting branch of Religious Experience (q.v.). Though the evidence for their occurrence is enormous, little is known concerning their nature. They belong to the domain of psychology rather than religion. See also *Spiritualism*.

VISITATION. Catholic and Greek festival (2nd July) commemorating the visit of the Virgin Mary to Elizabeth (Luke i. 39, 40).

VISITATION, ORDER (or NUNS) OF THE. (SALESIANS). A Catholic order for the education of girls, instituted by St. Francis de Sales in 1610.

VISITATION OF THE SICK. (1) An Anglican office for the benefit of sick persons. (2) A Catholic office of confession and absolution.

VIVEKANANDA. The chief disciple of Ramakrishna (q.v.). He visited Europe and America where he lectured and taught.

VOLTAIRE, FRANÇOIS MARIE AROUET DE (1694–1778). French deistic philosopher and man-of-letters. By his wit, his cleverness and courage he gained enormous power in France and throughout Europe and became the most dangerous antagonist the Catholic Church has ever had. His ridicule of clerical stupidity and ecclesiastical cruelty set all France laughing with him. His war-cry was "Ecrasez l'infâme" ("Crush the infamous thing")—*l'infâme* being religious intolerance, stupidity and obscurantism. (See S. C. Tallentyre, *Life of Voltaire* (1904), and C. E. Vulliamy's *Voltaire*.)

VOLUNTARY. The organ music played while the congregation is leaving church after a service.

VOLUNTARYISM. The system of maintaining a church by voluntary offerings instead of state aid.

VOTIVE OFFERING. A tablet or picture dedicated in fulfilment of a vow (Cath.).

VOTIVE MASS. A Mass provided by a private person for some special purpose.

VOW. A promise made to a god. Among primitive tribes the vow (not to cut the hair, not to eat flesh, not to drink wine, etc.) is a recognized part of religion. It is a form of tabu (q.v.). The vow of the Nazarite (Num. vi. 1–21) bears a strong resemblance to certain religious tabus among the Polynesians. (See Judges xi.; Acts xviii. 18.)

VULGATE. The Latin version of the Scriptures prepared by St. Jerome (4th C.). See *Versions of the Bible*.

W

WAFER. A thin unleavened cake used in the Eucharist. The Catholic wafer is stamped with the cross and the letters I.H.S.

WAHABITES (WAHABEES, WAHABIS). A sect of reformed Moslems established in Arabia by Abd-el-Wahab (1691–1787). They condemned pilgrimages and the worship of saints as idolatry.

WAKAN or **WAKONDA.** Term used by the Sioux Indians for the spiritual influence in all things. See *mana, numen*.

WAKE. (1) Feast of the dedication of a church. (2) Watch kept over a corpse.

WALAFRID STRABO (A.D. 809–49). Scholar and poet who became abbot of Reichenau. For translations of his Latin poems, see Helen Waddell, *Medieval Latin Lyrics* (1929).

WALDENSES (VAUDOIS). A Protestant sect established by Peter Waldo of Lyons in the 12th C. in France and N. Italy. They cultivated an austere morality and were continually persecuted by the Catholic Church. (See Emilio Comba, *History of the Waldenses of Italy*.)

WALHALLA. See *Valhalla*.

WALKYR. See *Valkyr*.

WANDERING JEW, THE. The Jew of medieval legend who insulted Christ on the way to Calvary and was doomed in punishment to wander till Judgment Day. Many names have been given him : Cartaphilus ; Laquedom; Battadeus, etc.

WANG YANG MING (A.D. 1472–1528). Chinese idealist philosopher. The way to truth (Reality), he taught, is by intuition, not by intellection. By spiritual discipline and keeping the heart clean intuitive knowledge is attained.

WARBURTON, WILLIAM (1698–1779). Theologian of proverbial arrogance and dogmatism. Remembered for his voluminous commentaries on Shakespeare "devoid of taste and genius" (Chambers). He became bishop of Gloucester in 1759.

WAR, FUNDAMENTAL CAUSES OF. Modern psychology finds the ultimate origin of war to reside in the unconscious striving for perfection. Because, in the majority, it is *unconscious* of its true nature, by the process of inversion to which unconscious activities are liable, it is transformed into secondary manifestations such as fear, greed, hatred, patriotism and class feeling and these precipitate wars and revolutions. In proportion as this blind evolutionary urge is raised into consciousness, so do mental and spiritual revolutions (in the individual) replace their physical counterparts. The resulting external changes then take place naturally and without violence. See also *Peace Movements*.

WASHING OF FEET. See *Feet-washing*.

WATER, HOLY. See *Holy water.*

WATSON, JOHN ("IAN MACLAREN") (1850–1907). Novelist and theological writer. Author of many successful novels of the "Kailyard" School.

WATTS, ISAAC (1674–1748). Congregationalist minister in Mark Lane. He was one of the most successful of English hymn-writers. ("When I survey the wondrous Cross"; "O God, our help in ages past"; "There is a land of pure delight," etc., etc.).

WEE FREE CHURCH. The popular name for those congregations of the Free Church of Scotland which refused to unite with the United Presbyterians in 1900.

WEIR, ARCHIBALD (b. 1859). Transcendentalist philosopher. Author of *The Dark, The Light, Our Single Life, For To-day, Shallows and Deeps,* etc. The most withdrawn, impersonal and profound of modern European philosophers. He regards man's consciousness as a small lit area, informed by a vast darkness of unconscious life through which the deep monitions of Reality reach it. Hence the interior life as the spring-head of unconscious sources of wisdom and power is of paramount importance. "Man can make this world a better place to live in by solely attending to the organization of the life within." By reason of this fact the influence wielded by those awakened spirits who have tapped their own spiritual resources is a chief means whereby the enlightenment of other souls is achieved. Thus when new life is accepted as a hint, not as a doctrine, the receiving mind experiences a true increase of life, an incentive to action and through this free action enjoys peace in itself. The spirit which thus receives the awakening suggestion of another, itself, as the mystics would say, has contact with Absolutes "in its ground"—and the impulse to explore and make full use of this our spiritual inheritance is the best result to be won from contact with another living mind. Mr. Weir's thoughts on immortality are significant. He points out that as, during the War, those who had lived in close comradeship in a prison camp often failed to recognize each other when they afterwards met as free men; so "the doubt must be allowed that in freedom denizens of the earth will have developed so variously that they will fail to recognize one another." This means that only in so far as relationship between persons has gone below the surface of existence, and touched the "permanent real" of personality, can we hope that it will survive. "We have to learn to disregard the very things amid which our affection abounded, in order to recover acquaintance with the real object of our love."

WELIS. Moslem saints whose tombs are places of pilgrimage.

WEREWOLF, WERWOLF. In European folk-lore a human being who has the power of assuming the form of a wolf,

WESEL, JOHANN RUCHRAT VON (d. 1481). A daring pre-Reformation Protestant theologian who attacked various church doctrines, the authority of the Pope, the Church, etc. His writings were burned and he was imprisoned in the monastery at Mainz, where he died.

WESLEYANISM. See *Methodism.*

WESLEY, CHARLES (1707–88) and **JOHN** (1703–91). Founders of Methodism (q.v.). John Wesley was probably the greatest revivalist preacher Europe has produced ("he is without a peer among revival preachers in any age"—Frederick Loofs). Charles, though an able preacher, is best remembered for the excellent hymns he wrote. (See Luke Tyerman, *John Wesley* (3 vols.); John Telford, *Life of John Wesley.*)

WESSEL, JOHANN (his real name was **WESSEL HARMENS GANSFORT**) (c. 1420–89). Dutch theologian and a mystic of keen metaphysical insight—"a man of rare erudition in the shadow of papal darkness." (See K. Ullmann, *Reformers before the Reformation.*)

WESTCOTT, BROOKE FOSS (1825–1901). Anglican scholar and bishop of Durham. Best known for his critical edition of the Gr. N.T.

WESTMINSTER CONFESSION. A confession of faith drawn up by the Westminster Assembly of Divines (1643–8) in the reign of Charles I. The Confession embodied the five points of Calvinism and was afterwards adopted by the Scotch Presbyterian and other Presbyterian churches in America. It was the last creed formulated by Calvinist theologians.

WHATELEY, RICHARD (1787–1863). English theologian and archbishop of Dublin. He opposed the Oxford Movement and the Dissenters. Best known for his *Historic Doubts relative to Napoleon Buonaparte* written to ridicule Hume's contention that no evidence at all is sufficient to prove a miracle.

WHEWELL, WILLIAM (1794–1866). Professor of Moral Theology and Master of Trinity, Oxford. A man of encyclopedic knowledge and the author of many works on science, theology and philosophy. Described as an overwhelming and arrogant talker.

WHICHCOTE, BENJAMIN (1609–83). English divine numbered among the Cambridge Platonists (q.v.).

WHISTON, WILLIAM (1667–1752). English theologian whose best known work is his translation of *Josephus.*

WHITEFIELD, GEORGE (1417–1770). Calvinist who assisted the Wesleys in founding Methodism (q.v.).

WHITE FRIARS. See *Carmelites.*

WHITE, JOSEPH BLANCO (1775–1841). Catholic priest and poet who lost his faith and became a Unitarian. Remembered for his sonnet on Night—"the finest and most grandly conceived in our language" (Coleridge).

WHITSUNDAY (WHITSUNTIDE). The 7th Sunday after Easter, commemorating Pentecost, when converts to the primitive church wore white robes (Acts ii.).

WILBERFORCE, WILLIAM (1759–1833). English social reformer and leader of the anti-slavery movement.

WILFRID (c. 634–709). English archbishop who helped to replace the Celtic Church discipline by the Roman. (See Bede, *Hist. Eccles.*, v. 19.)

WILLIAM OF OCCAM. See *Occam, William.*

WILLIBRORD (WILBRORD) (c. 657–738). English missionary to Ireland and to the Frisians.

WISDOM LITERATURE. For the Hebrews " wisdom " was used in the sense of so ordering life as to get the best possible good out of living. The " Wisdom Literature " that gathered about this philosophy comprises proverbs, philosophy, moral maxims, etc. It includes the books of *Proverbs, Ecclesiastes, Job* and certain apocryphal books, e.g. *Wisdom of Solomon, Fourth Maccabees* and *Tobit.* (See T. K. Cheyne, *Job and Solomon*; *Jewish Religious Life.*)

WISDOM OF SOLOMON. See *Solomon, Wisdom of.*

WISEMAN, NICHOLAS PATRICK STEPHEN (1802–65). English cardinal of liberal views. A man of real piety and a keen social reformer.

WITCHCRAFT. The supposedly magic powers exercised by women with evil intent. Among primitive people witchcraft is usually exercised for the cause (and sometimes the cure) of disease, or the bringing of misfortune upon enemies. The witch was a prominent character among the Greeks and Romans (see Theocritus, Idyll II). Throughout the Middle Ages witchcraft flourished in Europe despite the efforts of the Church to extirpate it. It was specially prevalent from the 15th to the 17th C.s and the mania for witch-hunting resulted in the torture and death of many thousands of suspected sorceresses. How far a genuine knowledge of psychic power was used for evil purposes it is hard to determine. See also *magic.* (See Thomas Wright, *Narratives of Magic and Sorcery*; W. E. H. Lecky, *A History of the Rise and Influence of Rationalism in Europe.*)

WODEN. See *Odin.*

WOLSEY, THOMAS (c. 1475–1530). Henry VIII's chief minister, cardinal and archbishop of York. He aspired to the Papacy but failed to win the support of the emperor Charles V to his claims. He fell from power through his failure to secure from Rome Henry's divorce from Catherine of Aragon. (See Creighton, *Wolsey* (Twelve English Statesmen Series); A. F. Pollard, *Henry VIII.*)

WOOLMAN, JOHN (1720–72). Quaker and itinerant preacher.

His *Journal* is valuable for its honest self-revelation. "Get the writings of John Woolman by heart" (Charles Lamb).

WORD, THE. (1) The Christian Scriptures. (2) The Logos (q.v.).

WORDSWORTH, CHRISTOPHER (1807–85). English divine; became bishop of Lincoln (1868). Author of several scholarly books.

WORDSWORTH, WILLIAM (1770–1850). English poet of very high attainment. His close intimacy with nature and his mystic intuition render his work of deep religious significance. His *Intimations of Immortality* and *Tintern Abbey* rise to supreme heights of intuitive perception. Some of his sonnets are among the finest in the language. (See C. H. Herford, *The Age of Wordsworth.*)

WORKUS. "A C. of E. pleasantry at the expense of the Methodist chapels" (Eric Partridge, *Slang*, p. 198).

WORMS, CONCORDAT OF. The settlement reached between Pope Calixtus II and the emperor Henry V in 1122, which terminated the War of Investitures. Henceforth the Pope was to invest bishops with ring and crozier (spiritual power) and the emperor was to invest with regalia (political power).

WORMS, DIET OF. The Imperial Diet summoned by the emperor Charles V in 1521. It was before this Diet that the excommunicated Luther was brought to be examined on a charge of heresy. The decree of the Diet declared the ban of the Empire against Luther and commanded his books to be burned. See *Luther, Martin.*

WORSHIP. Adoration paid to a god. Such observance arose among primitive tribes usually with the desire to placate a supposedly angry god. With the development of civilization ritual became more elaborate and the subjective effect of worship on the worshipper came into prominence. To-day corporate worship is regarded chiefly from the latter standpoint, ritual usage, hymn-singing, incense, etc., leading to exalted and beneficial states of consciousness.

WU-WEI. A Taoist doctrine of quietism or resigning the soul to the universal laws of life.

WYCLIFFE (or WYCLIF) JOHN (c. 1320–84). A forerunner of the Reformation in England. Professor of Divinity in the University of Oxford, he gradually adopted anti-papal doctrines and denounced the dogma of transubstantiation as foolish and blasphemous. He was protected by John of Gaunt, violently attacked by the Church and only saved from martyrdom by an attack of paralysis from which he died. His work was carried on by the Lollards (q.v.).

X

XAVIER, FRANCISCO DE (1506–51). Spanish Jesuit missionary to India, Japan and the Malay Archipelago. His great success was due to his winning personality, wide learning and capacity for hard work. (See H. Coleridge, *S.J.*, *The Life and Letters of St. Francis Xavier* (2 vols.).)

XAVIERIAN BROTHERS. A Catholic teaching association organized by the Belgian, Theodor Jakob Rycken, in 1839 for the Catholic education of deaf-mutes and orphans.

XENOPHANES. Reputed founder of the Eleatic School of Greek Philosophy. He taught the unity of all things: "There is one God who abideth ever in the same place . . . yet men imagine gods to be born like themselves." (6th C. B.C.). (Not to be confused with Xenophon, the Greek historian.)

XIMENES, FRANCISCO DE CISNEROS (1436–1517). Spanish theologian, cardinal and archbishop of Toledo. He was confessor of Queen Isabella and grand inquisitor of Castile.

Y

YAHWEH (also **JAHWEH, JAH**). The pronunciation given by scholars to the Hebrew name for God translated in the Authorized version Jehovah. See *Israel, Religion of*.

YAJUR-VEDA. A liturgical book of the Vedic religion (q.v.). It contains hymns and directions for ritual sacrifices.

YAMA. The Hindu god of the dead. He is regarded as the mythical ancestor of the Indo-Aryans and (as Yima) the ancestor of the Iranian-Aryans.

YANG and YIN. In Chinese philosophy the great extremes of the First Cause, the Yang being the active male principle and the Yin the passive female principle. All phenomena are made up of these interacting principles.

YASHTS. Zoroastrian songs of praise in the Zend-Avesta. See *Zoroaster*.

YASNA. A Zoroastrian liturgical book. See *Zoroaster*.

YAZATAS. The angels in the Zoroastrian religion.

YEZEDIS (YEZEDEES). A religious sect of Arabs inhabiting the mountains north of Bagdad on the Kurdish border near Mosul. They worship the Devil (Shaitan) under the name of Melek Taos (Angel Peacock). They consider God is too far away to try and contact Him. Melik Taos (his name Shaitan is never mentioned) is the ruler of the world, God having given it into his keeping for ten thousand years. (See W. B. Seabrook, *Adventures in Arabia* (1928).)

YGGDRASIL. The world-tree of Norse mythology, binding heaven, earth and hell together. It probably symbolizes the life-giving powers of nature.

YIDDISH. The language (a compound of corrupt Hebrew and provincial German) spoken by the Jews of E. London.

YIMA. See *Yama*.

YIN. See *Yang*.

YOGA. A development of the Sankhya Philosophy into which a supreme soul (Isvara) is introduced. Yoga is a practical system of physical, moral and mental training practised by Eastern people. Yogis are said to possess supernormal powers of various kinds. Yoga aims at the control and perfecting of body and mind and results in skill in action. Training in yoga should not be undertaken without the guidance of a proficient teacher and most yoga practices are unsuitable for Europeans. The wisdom of the East needs to be adapted to Western minds and bodies. (See Geraldine Coster, *Yoga and Western Psychology* (1934); Prof. Evans-Wentz, *Tibetan Yoga* (1935).)

YOGI. See *Yoga*.

YOM KIPPUR. See *Atonement, Day of*.

YOUNG, BRIGHAM. See *Mormonism*.

YOUNG MEN'S CHRISTIAN ASSOCIATION. A Christian organization established in London by George Williams, a clerk, in 1844. The purpose of the organization was "the spiritual development of young men." The Society now has centres throughout the provinces and the Empire and in fifty-five foreign countries. The Young Women's Christian Association was established on similar lines by Lady Kinnaird and Miss Emma Robarts in 1855. George Williams was knighted by Queen Victoria. Headquarters: Great Russell Street, W.C.1. (See J. E. H. Williams, *Life of Sir George Williams*; L. L. Doggett, *History of the Y.M.C.A.*)

YULE, YULETIDE. The season of Christmas. Probably derived from A.S. *geola* = December.

Z

ZABIANISM. See *Sabaism*.

ZABULUS. A corruption for *diabolus* (devil) used by the Church Fathers.

ZANGWILL, ISRAEL. See *Jewish writers*.

ZARATHUSHTHRA. See *Zoroaster*.

ZEALOTS. A Jewish national party whose opposition to Roman dominion led to the war with Rome (66–70 A.D.) and the destruction of Jerusalem.

ZEN. A Japanese Buddhist sect or school with two main divisions, Rinzai and Sodo. It maintains the ancient Hindu system of obtaining enlightenment by *dhyana* (meditation), and asserts that the truth is in man's heart if he will deliberately work to find it. (See D. T. Suzuki, *Essays in Zen Buddhism* (First and Second Series).)

ZEND-AVESTA. See *Avesta*.

ZENO OF CITIUM. The Greek founder of Stoicism (q.v.). (3rd C. B.C.)

ZENO OF ELIA. Greek philosopher; reputed founder of the dialectic method. (5th C. B.C.)

ZENO OF VERONA. Theologian and bishop of Verona. (4th C. A.D.)

ZEUS. The chief god of the Hellenic pantheon. The sky and father god of ancient Greece.

ZION. Jerusalem; also used metaphorically for the Christian heaven.

ZIONISM. The 19th-C. movement for securing Palestine for the Jews and thus repatriating them as a nation. The idea of establishing the European Jews in Palestine was advocated by the German Moritz Hess and the Russian Leon Pinsker (1870–80); and the first Jewish agricultural colony, Rishon Lezion, was founded in Palestine in 1882. This was followed by the formation of similar colonies established by the societies known as "Lovers of Zion." The culmination of the movement came when the British minister Balfour in a Note of November 1917 expressed the sympathy of his government with Zionist endeavours which called forth similar expressions of sympathy from France, Italy and U.S.A. Palestine, which was captured by the British from the Turks during the War, is now administered by Great Britain under a Mandate from the League of Nations. Great Britain agreed to "view with favour" a national home for the Jews in Palestine. From 1920 to 1933, 92,000 Polish and Russian Jews and 63,000 Central European Jews have settled there—mostly in the cities. The chief obstacle in the way of the Zionist ideal appears to be the religious question. If the State were orthodox it would revive the whole Levitical polity which would offend the modern political spirit; if it were secular it would not constitute a Jewish State. (See Nordau, *Zionism, its History and its Aims*; J. de Haas, *Zionism*.)

ZOHAR. A Jewish mystical book attributed to Simeon ben Yohai (2nd C.), but now generally attributed to Moses of Leon (d. 1305). In form a commentary on the Pentateuch, it is really a Kabbalistic interpretation of the universe. (See W. W. J. Colville, *The Kabbalah, the Harmony of Opposites* (1916).)

ZOROASTER and **ZOROASTRIANISM.** The Persian religion founded by Zoroaster (Zarathushthra) c. 1000 B.C. Zoroaster's teaching was dualistic. On one side was Ahura Mazda (Ormuzd) ("The Wise"), creator of Good, and on the other Ahriman, Angra Mainyu ("Hostile Spirit"), creator of Evil. Attendant on Ahura Mazda are the six Amesha Spentas or archangels, typifying *Good Thought, Righteousness, Sovereignty, Devotion, Health* and *Immortality*. Allied to Ahriman are the Daevas or Demons (in Hinduism the devas are angels). Fire is held sacred by Zoroastrians as being the source of all things. Zoroastrianism was in early days severely practical. Man was to overcome evil by good in thought, word and deed. It was only in later times that an elaborate ritual under the priests (Magi) grew up. The religion was at its best in the period of the Achaemenian Kings (558–330 B.C.). During the Mohammedan invasions, starting in the 7th C. A.D., Zoroastrianism was completely crushed. Many Zoroastrians fled to India, where they have continued as the Parsees (q.v.). (See J. H. Moulton, *Early Zoroastrianism* (1914) ; *The Treasure of the Magi* (1917).)

ZUCCHETTO. A skull-cap worn by Catholic priests, covering the tonsure.

ZWINGLI and ZWINGLIANS. The Swiss reformer Huldreich Zwingli (1484–1531) differed from Luther on the doctrine of the Eucharist. Zwingli and his followers rejected every form of local or corporeal presence in the eucharistic elements. "This is my body," he interpreted to mean "This represents my body." He denied absolutely that the sacraments convey divine grace. Zwingli was killed at the battle of Kappel in the civil war between the Catholic and Protestant Swiss States. (See S. M. Jackson, *Huldreich Zwingli*.)

WORKS BY THE GENERAL EDITOR

THE FRENCH ROMANTICS' KNOWLEDGE OF ENGLISH LITERATURE. Champion, Paris; 48 francs.

EIGHTEENTH-CENTURY ENGLISH ROMANTIC POETRY. Champion; 30 francs.

A CRITICAL MEDLEY. (English, French, Comparative Literature.) Obelisk Press, 338 Rue St. Honoré, Paris; 25 francs.

THE POETRY OF CUTHBERT SHAW AND THOMAS RUSSELL, with a biographical and critical notice. Dulau; *7s. 6d.*

ROBERT EYRES LANDOR, A BIOGRAPHY (*10s. 6d.*); ROBERT LANDOR, SELECTIONS (*7s. 6d.*) Scholartis Press. (*Both out of print.*)

PERSONAL RECORDS OF THE GREAT WAR, with R. H. Mottram and John Easton. Wm. Glaisher; *3s. 6d.*

SONGS AND SLANG OF THE BRITISH SOLDIER, with John Brophy. Oxford University Press; (3rd edition) *10s. 6d.*

Francis Grose's CLASSICAL DICTIONARY OF THE VULGAR TONGUE, with extensive annotations and biographical notice. Oxford University Press; *42s.*

LITERARY SESSIONS. General; biographical; medico-literary. Scholartis Press; *7s. 6d.*

WORDS, WORDS, WORDS!, studies in word history. Methuen; *6s.*

SLANG TO-DAY AND YESTERDAY, a study and a history, with vocabularies (including American). Routledge; 2nd Edition, *10s. 6d.*

NAME THIS CHILD: a dictionary of Christian names. Methuen; *5s.*

GLIMPSES: a story-sequence. Scholartis Press; *7s. 6d.* (*Out of print.*)

THE SCENE IS CHANGED: a novel. John Heritage; *3s. 6d.*

In Preparation.

A DICTIONARY OF UNCONVENTIONAL ENGLISH, *i.e.* of all save Standard English and Dialect. Routledge; *42s.*

All prices net.

Published by

Facsimile Publisher
Ashok Vihar, Delhi-110052 (India)
Website: www.facsimilepublisher.com

Distributed by

Gyan Books Pvt. Ltd.
5, Ansari Road, Daryaganj, New Delhi-110002 (India)
E-mail: books@gyanbooks.com, Website: www.gyanbooks.com

2 222000 010270